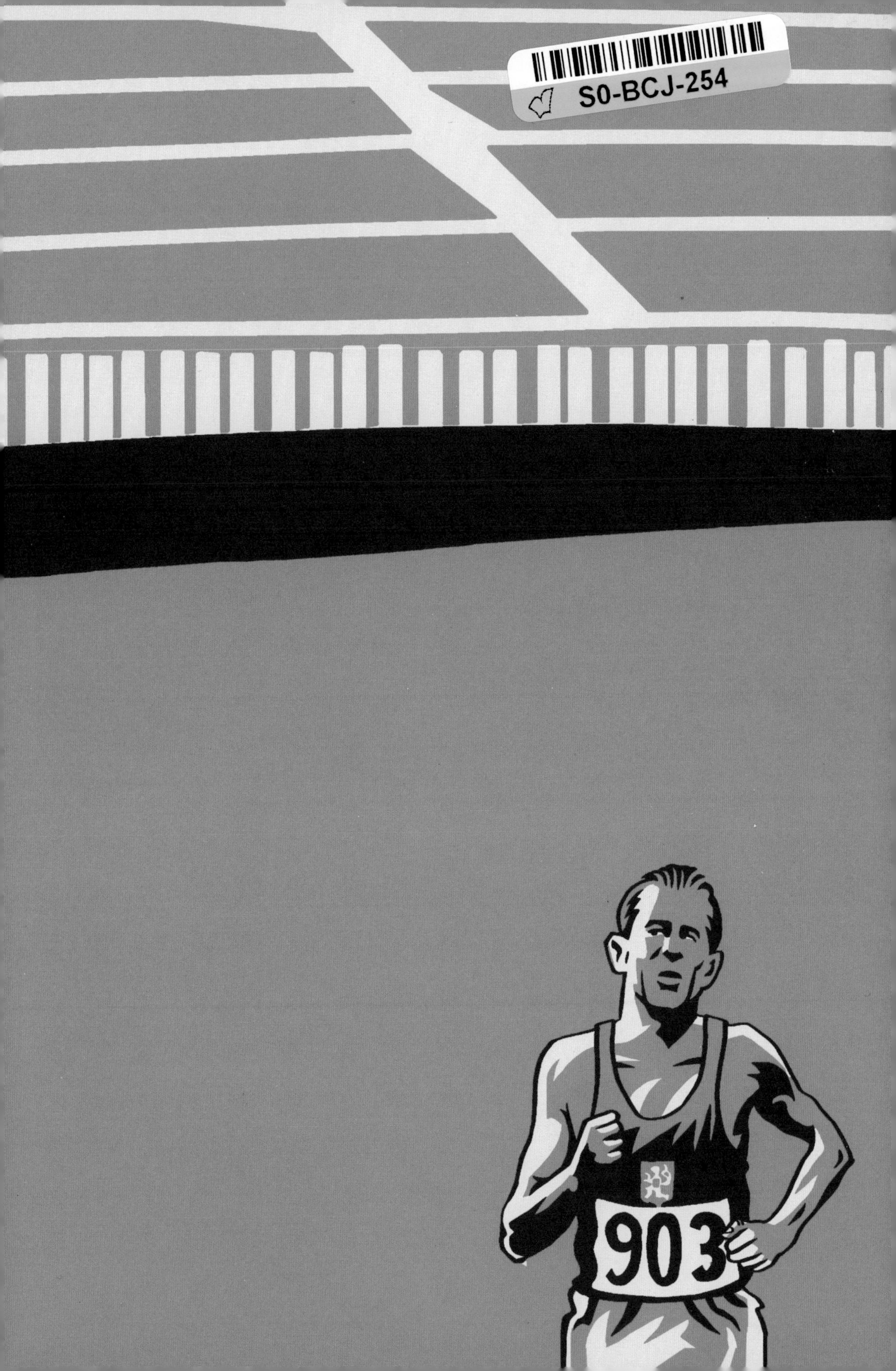
903

Jan Novák
Jaromír 99

ZÁTOPEK

"When you can't
keep going,
go faster!"

SELF
MADE
HERO

First published in English in 2020
by SelfMadeHero
139–141 Pancras Road
London NW1 1UN
www.selfmadehero.com

Written by Jan Novák
Illustrated by Jaromír 99
Translated from the Czech by Jan Novák

Publishing Director: Emma Hayley
Editorial & Production Director: Guillaume Rater
Publishing Assistant: Stefano Mancin
Designer: Txabi Jones
UK Publicist: Paul Smith
US Publicist: Maya Bradford
With thanks to: Paul Kaye, Jan Zikmund and Dan Lockwood

A CIP record for this book is available from the British Library

ISBN: 978-1-910593-88-2

10 9 8 7 6 5 4 3 2 1

Printed and bound in the Czech Republic

MINISTRY OF CULTURE
CZECH REPUBLIC

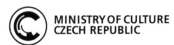

This publication was supported by the Ministry of Culture of the Czech Republic

MIX
Paper from responsible sources
FSC® C014138

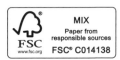

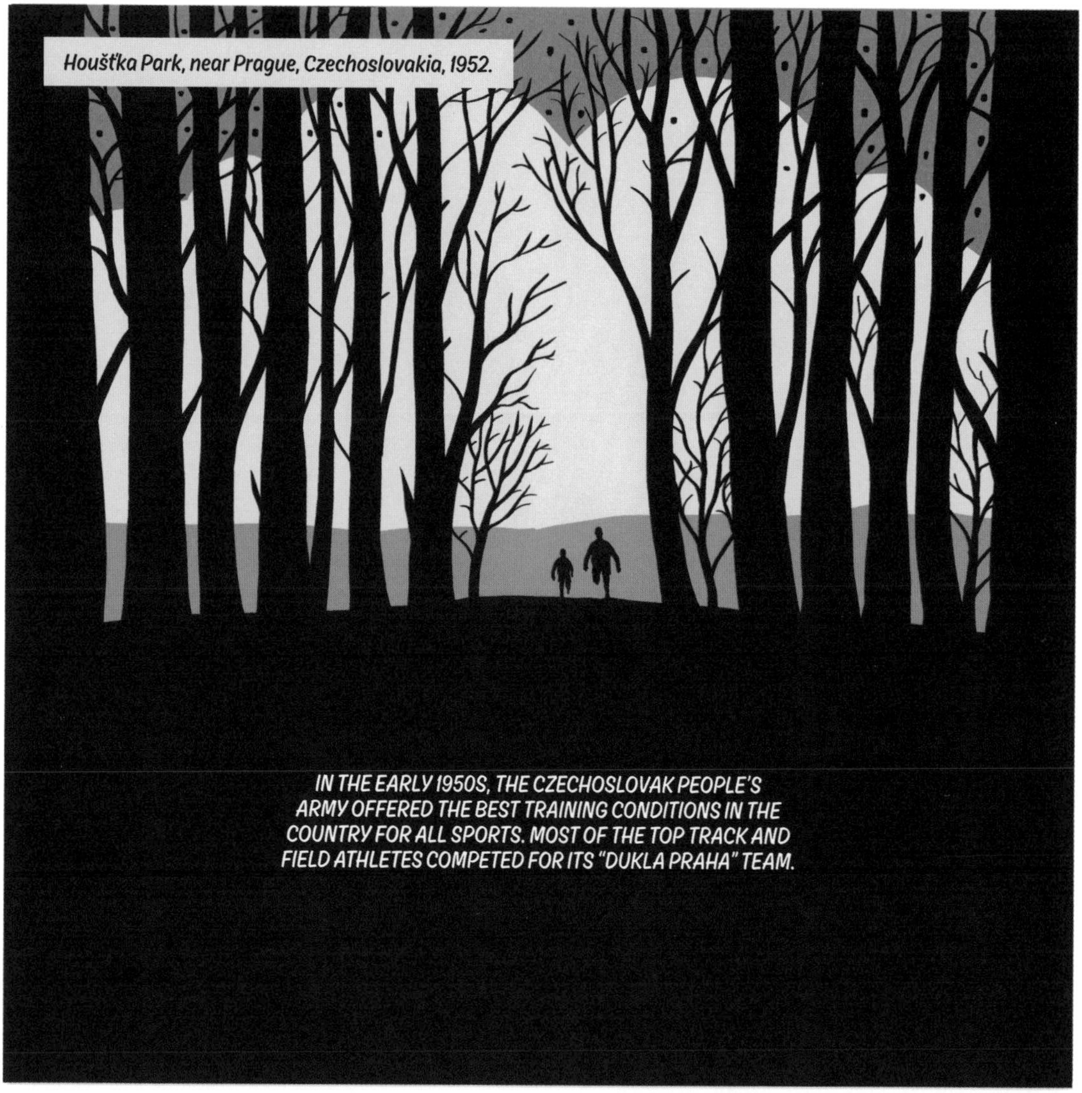
Houšťka Park, near Prague, Czechoslovakia, 1952.
IN THE EARLY 1950S, THE CZECHOSLOVAK PEOPLE'S ARMY OFFERED THE BEST TRAINING CONDITIONS IN THE COUNTRY FOR ALL SPORTS. MOST OF THE TOP TRACK AND FIELD ATHLETES COMPETED FOR ITS "DUKLA PRAHA" TEAM.

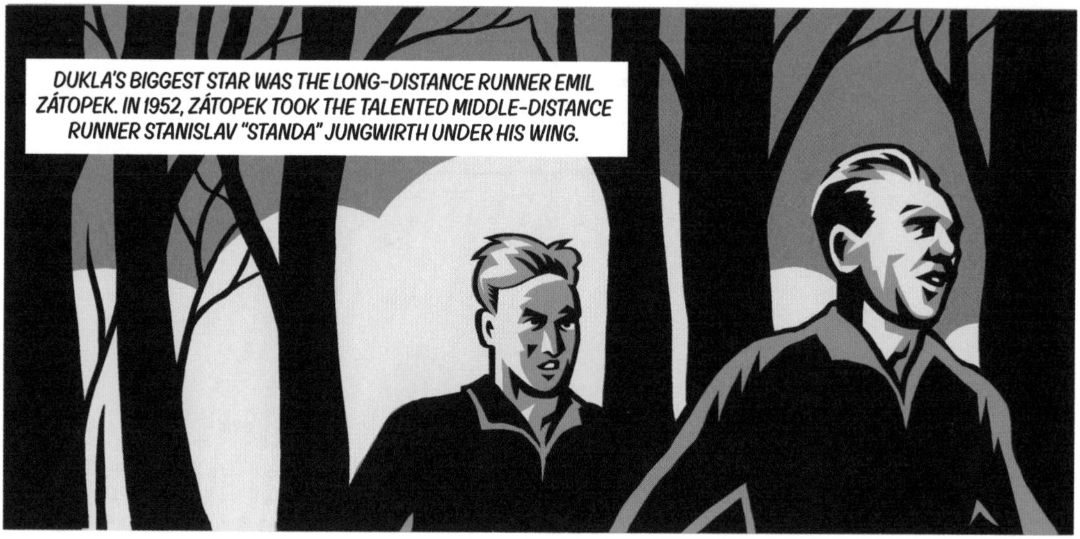
DUKLA'S BIGGEST STAR WAS THE LONG-DISTANCE RUNNER EMIL ZÁTOPEK. IN 1952, ZÁTOPEK TOOK THE TALENTED MIDDLE-DISTANCE RUNNER STANISLAV "STANDA" JUNGWIRTH UNDER HIS WING.

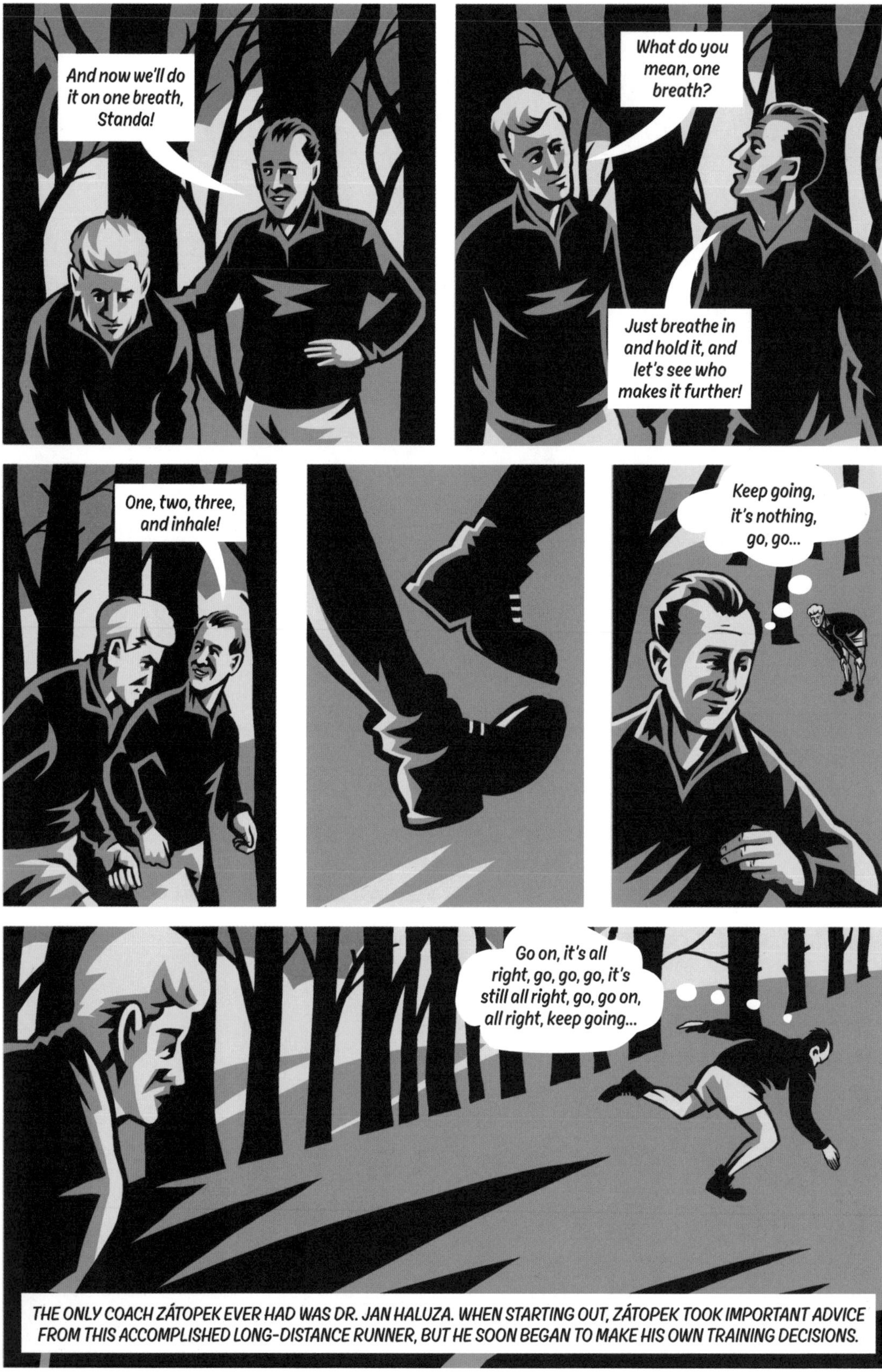
And now we'll do it on one breath, Standa!
What do you mean, one breath?
Just breathe in and hold it, and let's see who makes it further!
One, two, three, and inhale!
Keep going, it's nothing, go, go...
Go on, it's all right, go, go, go, it's still all right, go, go on, all right, keep going...
THE ONLY COACH ZÁTOPEK EVER HAD WAS DR. JAN HALUZA. WHEN STARTING OUT, ZÁTOPEK TOOK IMPORTANT ADVICE FROM THIS ACCOMPLISHED LONG-DISTANCE RUNNER, BUT HE SOON BEGAN TO MAKE HIS OWN TRAINING DECISIONS.

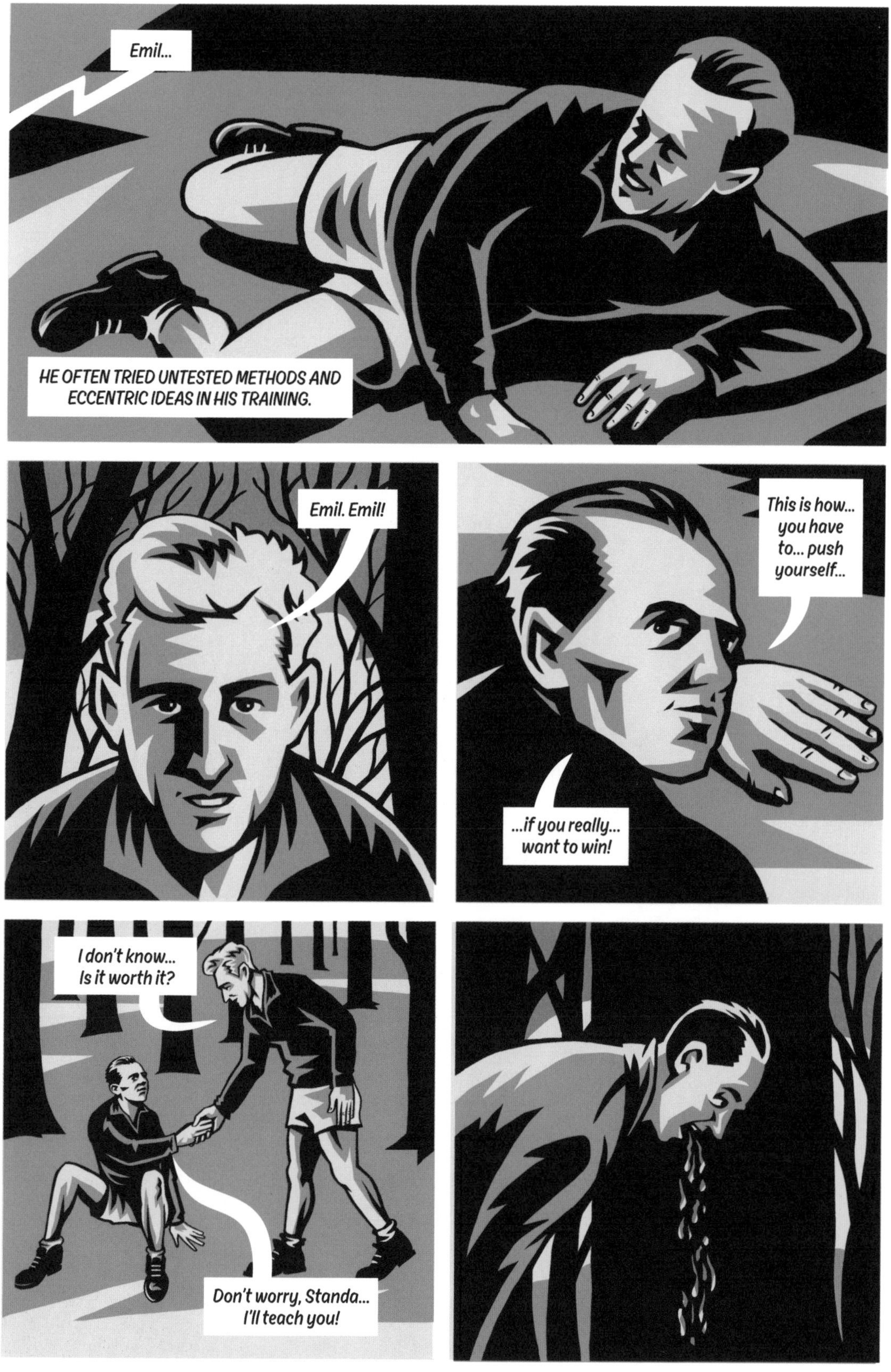
Emil...
HE OFTEN TRIED UNTESTED METHODS AND ECCENTRIC IDEAS IN HIS TRAINING.
Emil. Emil!
This is how... you have to... push yourself...
...if you really... want to win!
I don't know... Is it worth it?
Don't worry, Standa... I'll teach you!

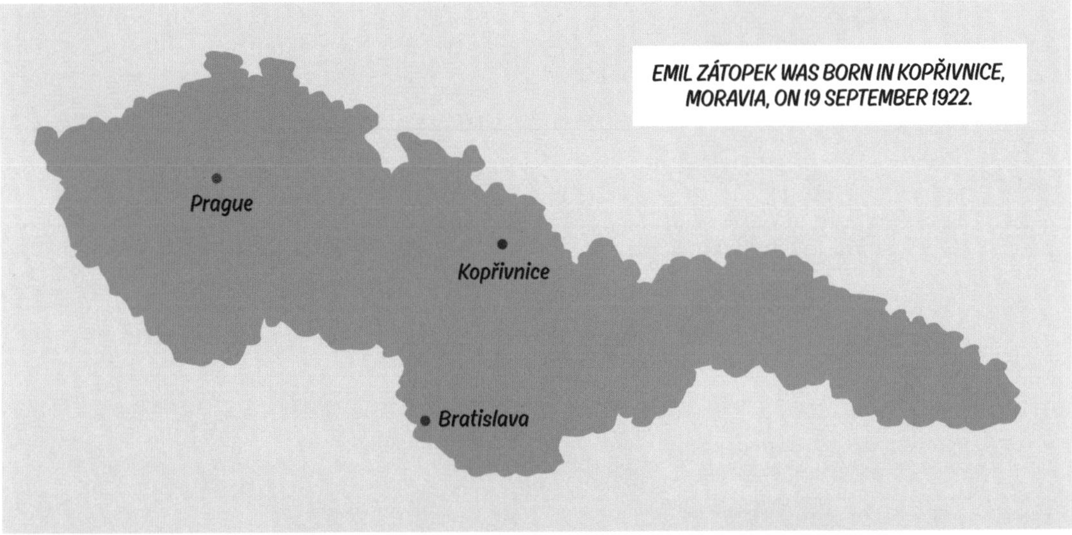
EMIL ZÁTOPEK WAS BORN IN KOPŘIVNICE, MORAVIA, ON 19 SEPTEMBER 1922.
Prague
Kopřivnice
Bratislava

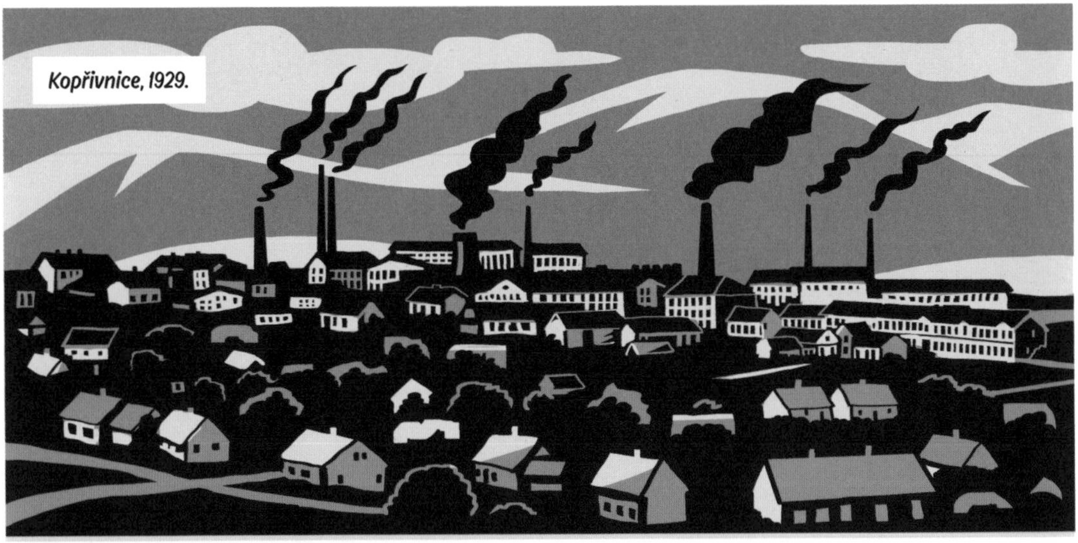
Kopřivnice, 1929.

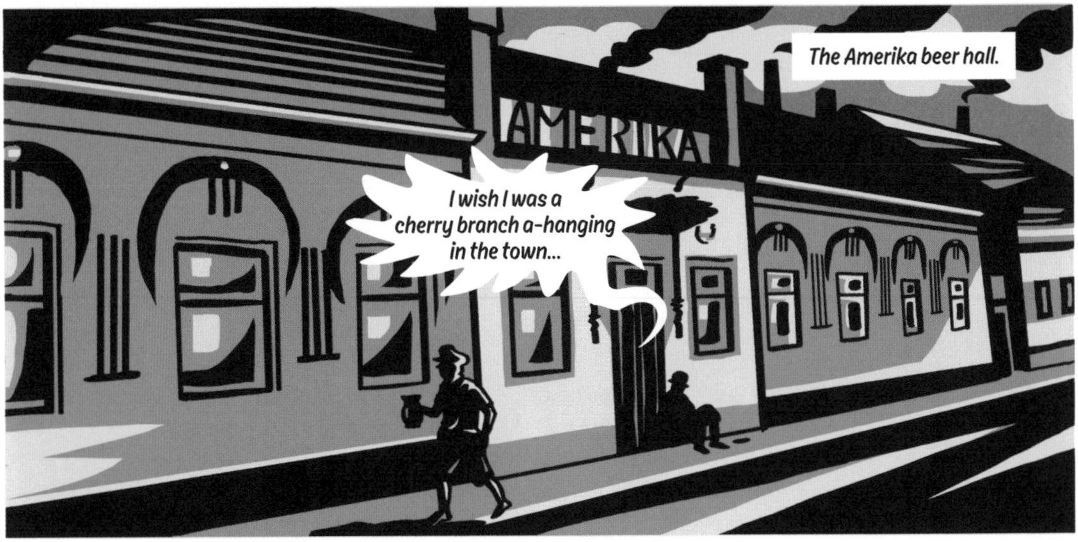
The Amerika beer hall.
AMERIKA
I wish I was a cherry branch a-hanging in the town...

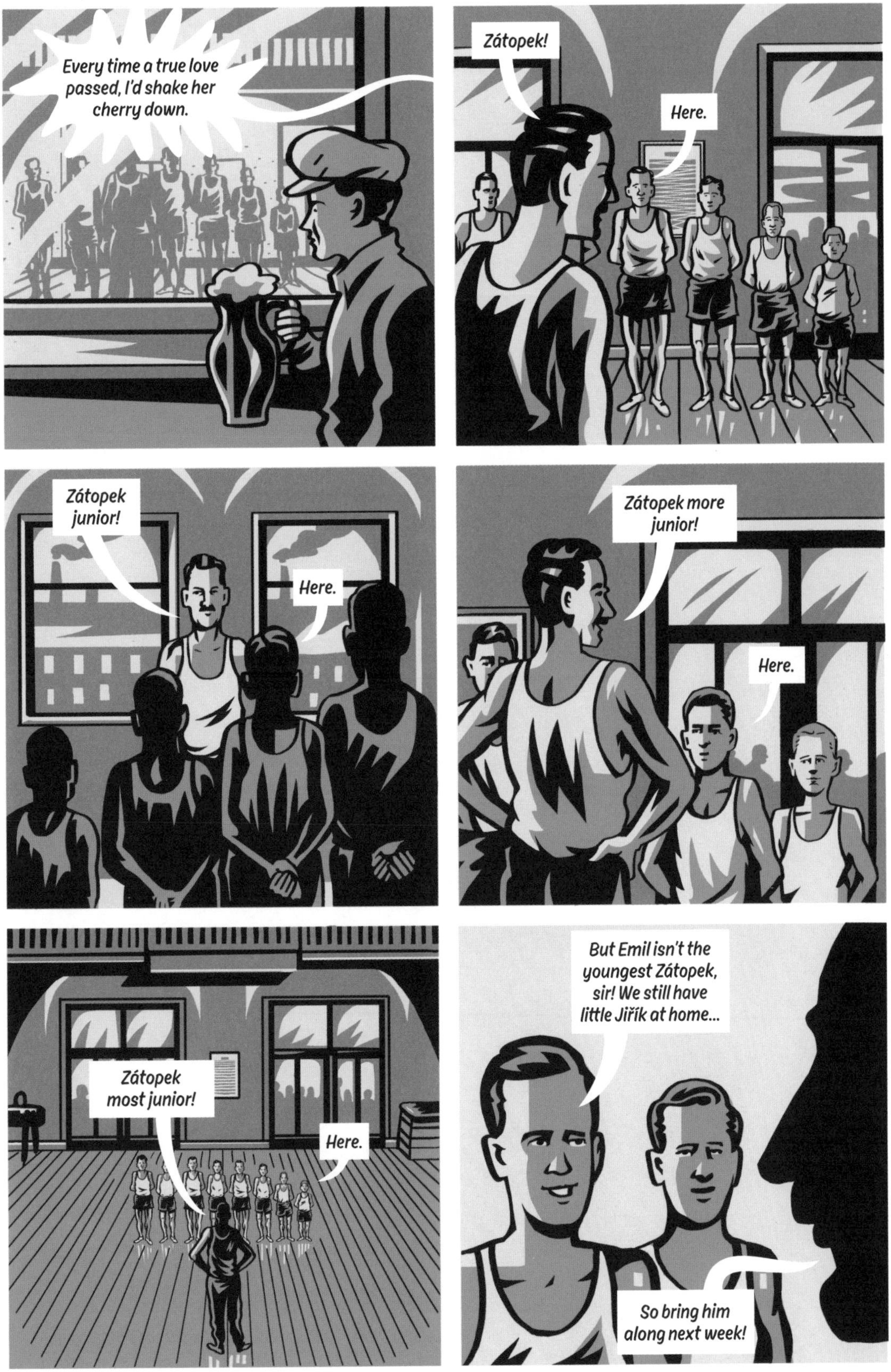
Every time a true love passed, I'd shake her cherry down.
Zátopek!
Here.
Zátopek junior!
Here.
Zátopek more junior!
Here.
Zátopek most junior!
Here.
But Emil isn't the youngest Zátopek, sir! We still have little Jiřík at home...
So bring him along next week!

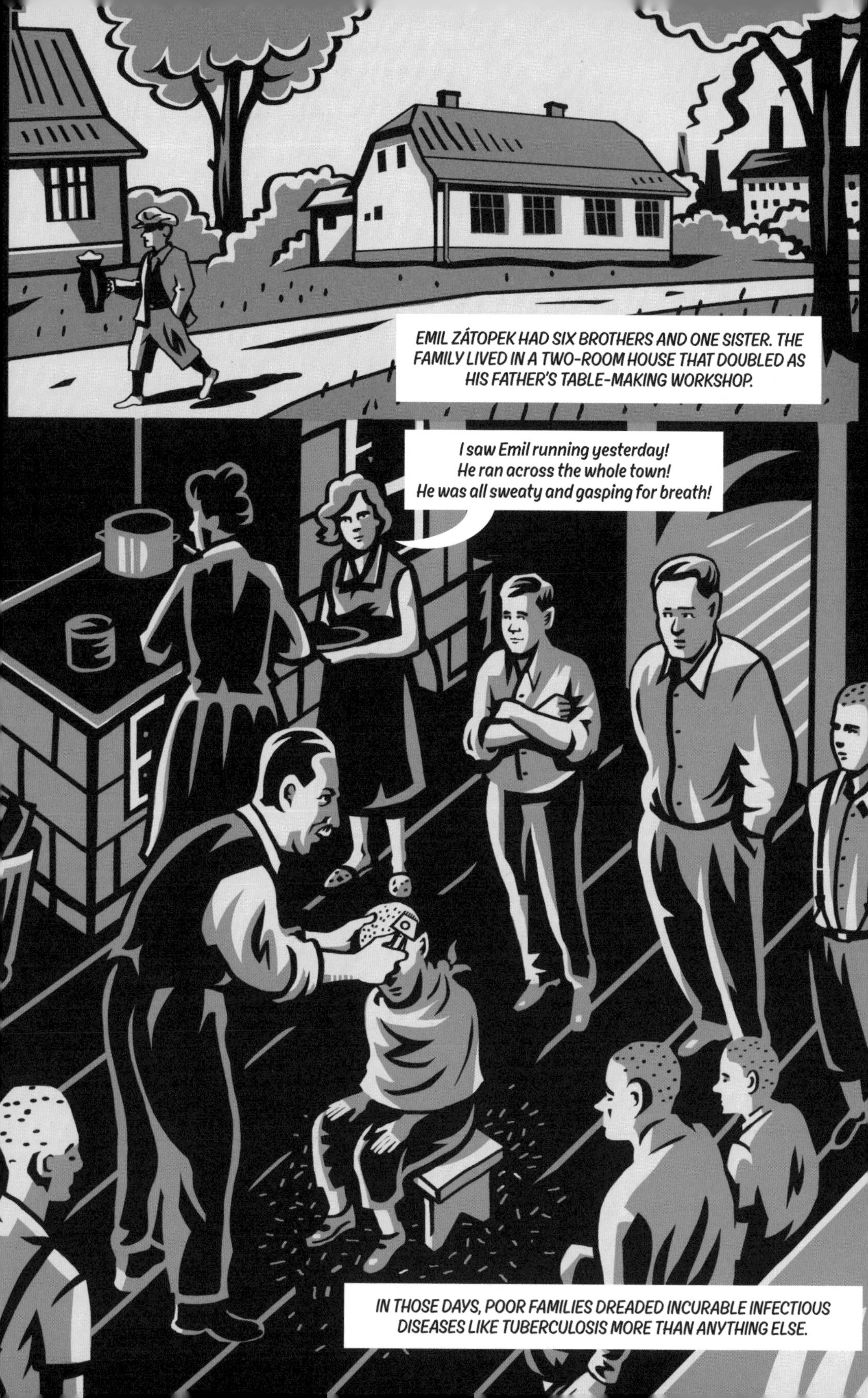
EMIL ZÁTOPEK HAD SIX BROTHERS AND ONE SISTER. THE FAMILY LIVED IN A TWO-ROOM HOUSE THAT DOUBLED AS HIS FATHER'S TABLE-MAKING WORKSHOP.
I saw Emil running yesterday! He ran across the whole town! He was all sweaty and gasping for breath!
IN THOSE DAYS, POOR FAMILIES DREADED INCURABLE INFECTIOUS DISEASES LIKE TUBERCULOSIS MORE THAN ANYTHING ELSE.

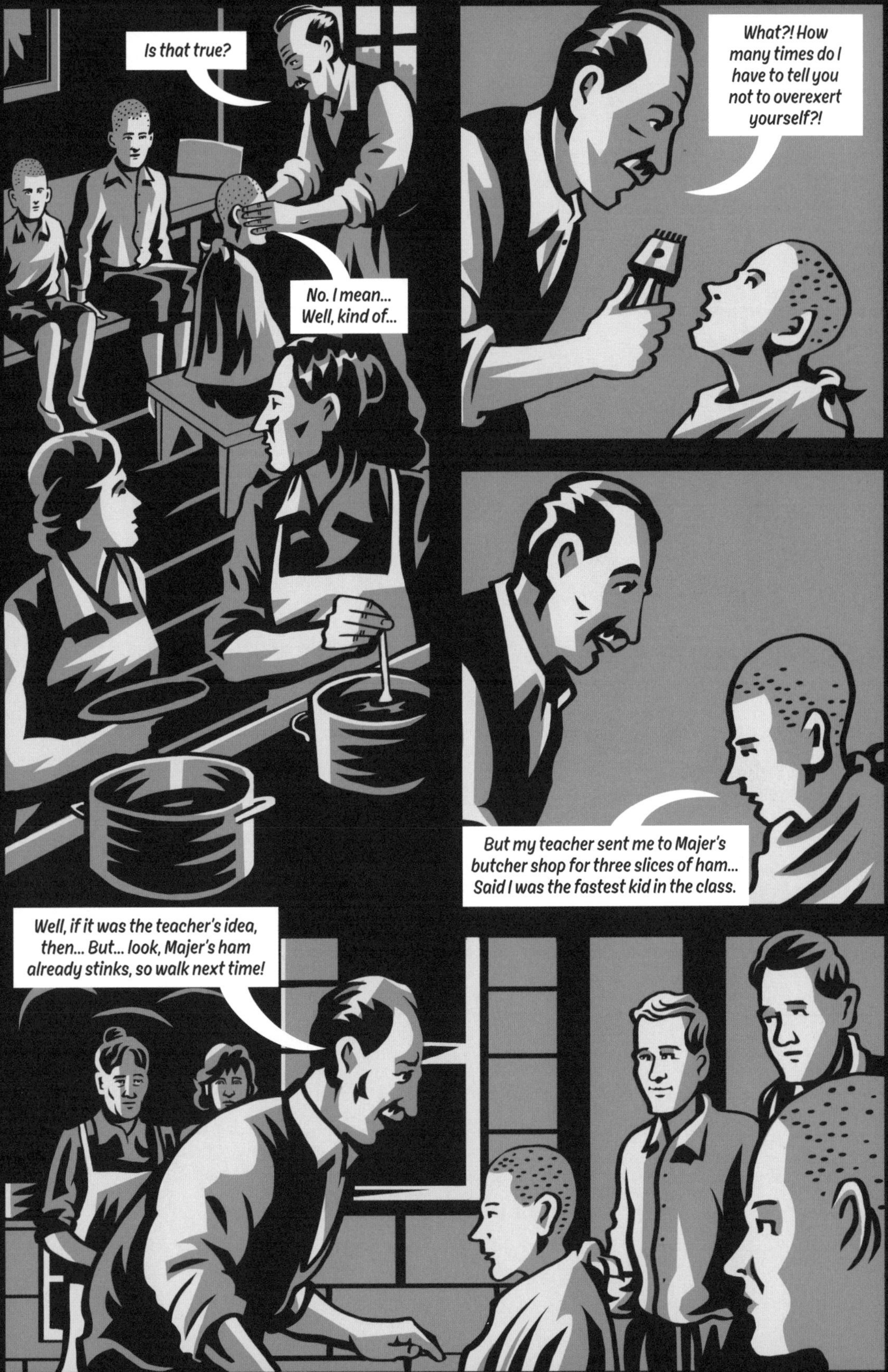
Is that true?
No. I mean... Well, kind of...
What?! How many times do I have to tell you not to overexert yourself?!
But my teacher sent me to Majer's butcher shop for three slices of ham... Said I was the fastest kid in the class.
Well, if it was the teacher's idea, then... But... look, Majer's ham already stinks, so walk next time!

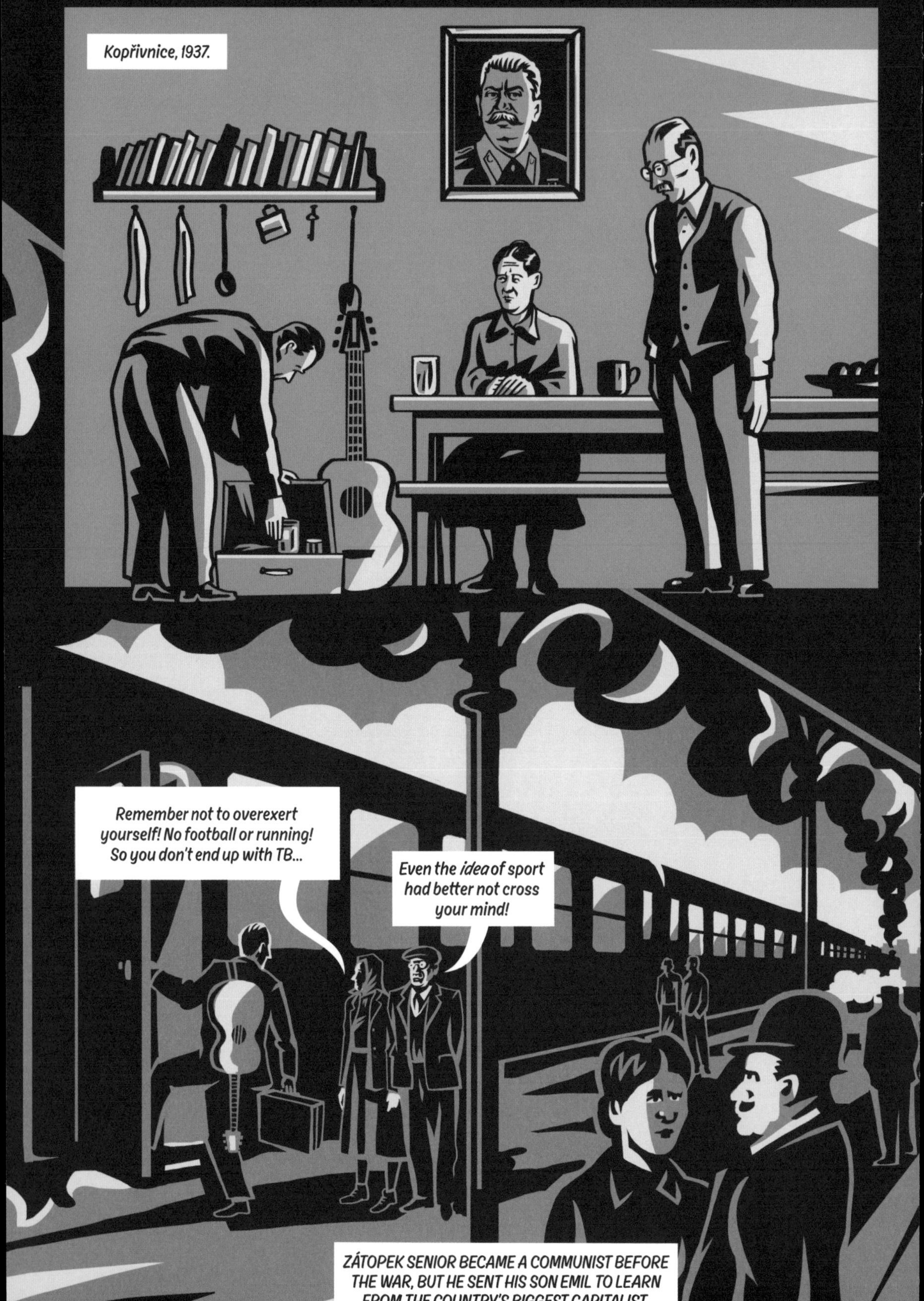

Kopřivnice, 1937.
Remember not to overexert yourself! No football or running! So you don't end up with TB...
Even the *idea* of sport had better not cross your mind!
ZÁTOPEK SENIOR BECAME A COMMUNIST BEFORE THE WAR, BUT HE SENT HIS SON EMIL TO LEARN FROM THE COUNTRY'S BIGGEST CAPITALIST.

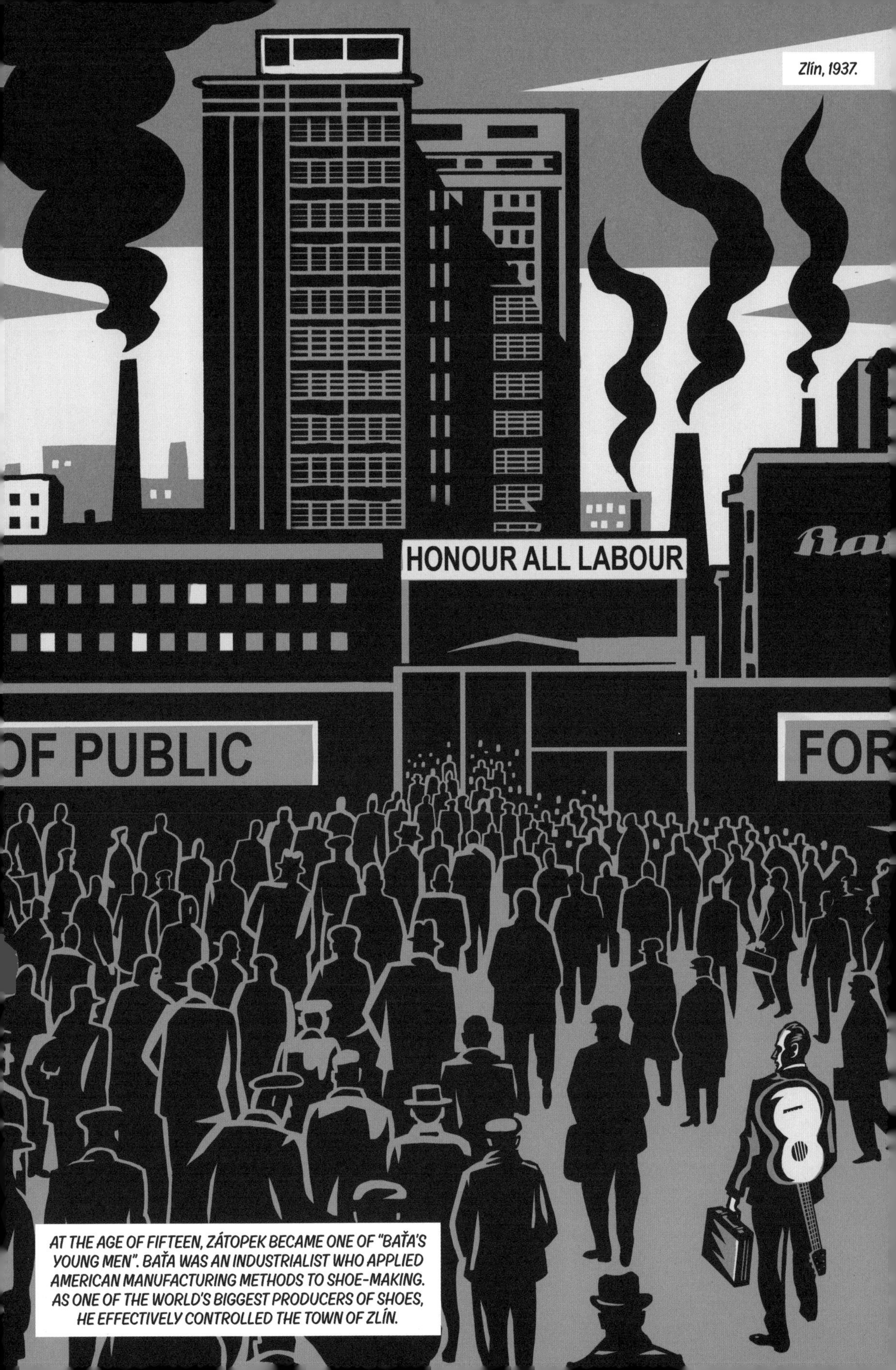

Zlín, 1937.
HONOUR ALL LABOUR
OF PUBLIC
FOR
AT THE AGE OF FIFTEEN, ZÁTOPEK BECAME ONE OF "BAŤA'S YOUNG MEN". BAŤA WAS AN INDUSTRIALIST WHO APPLIED AMERICAN MANUFACTURING METHODS TO SHOE-MAKING. AS ONE OF THE WORLD'S BIGGEST PRODUCERS OF SHOES, HE EFFECTIVELY CONTROLLED THE TOWN OF ZLÍN.

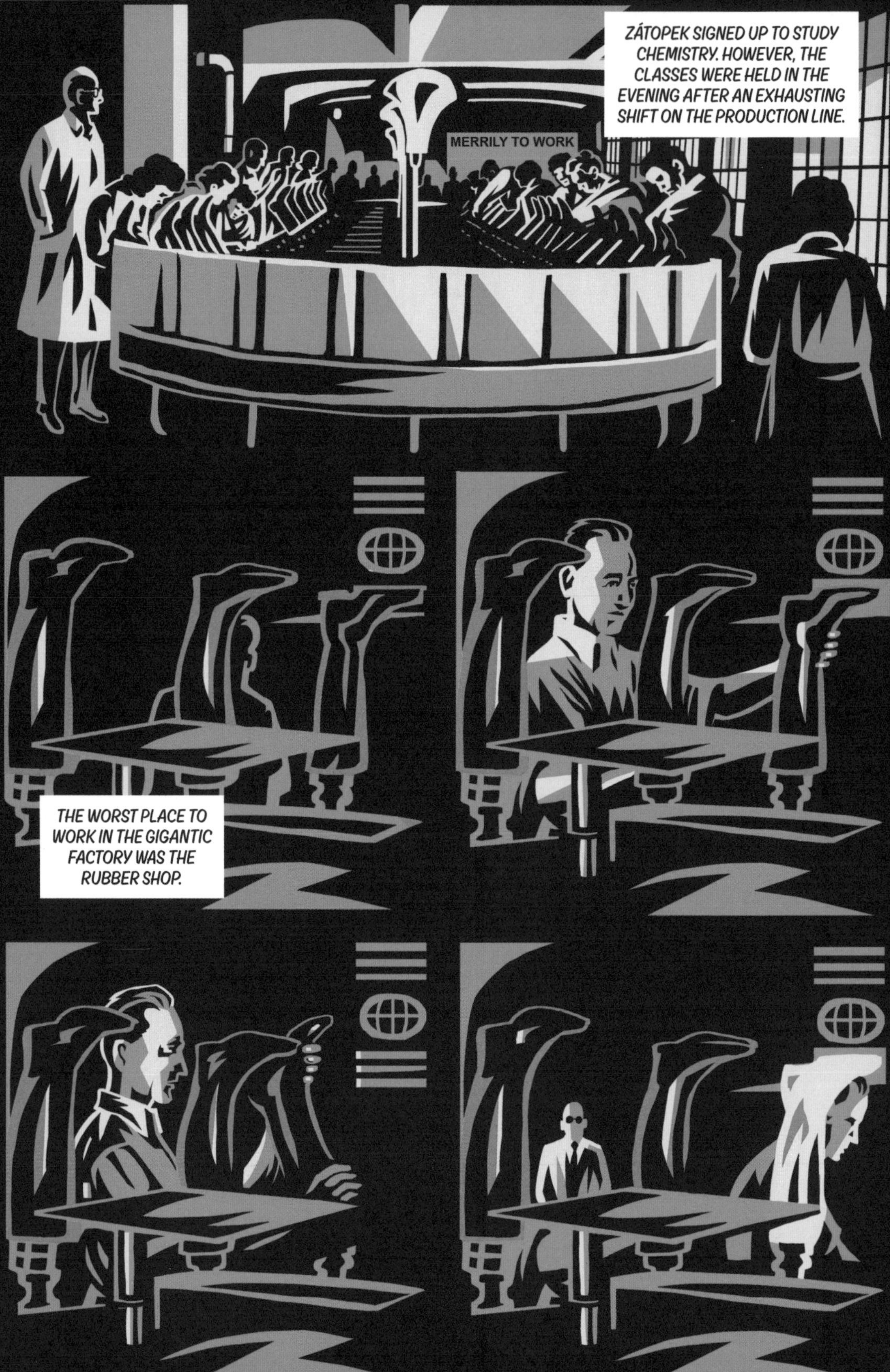
ZÁTOPEK SIGNED UP TO STUDY CHEMISTRY. HOWEVER, THE CLASSES WERE HELD IN THE EVENING AFTER AN EXHAUSTING SHIFT ON THE PRODUCTION LINE.
MERRILY TO WORK
THE WORST PLACE TO WORK IN THE GIGANTIC FACTORY WAS THE RUBBER SHOP.

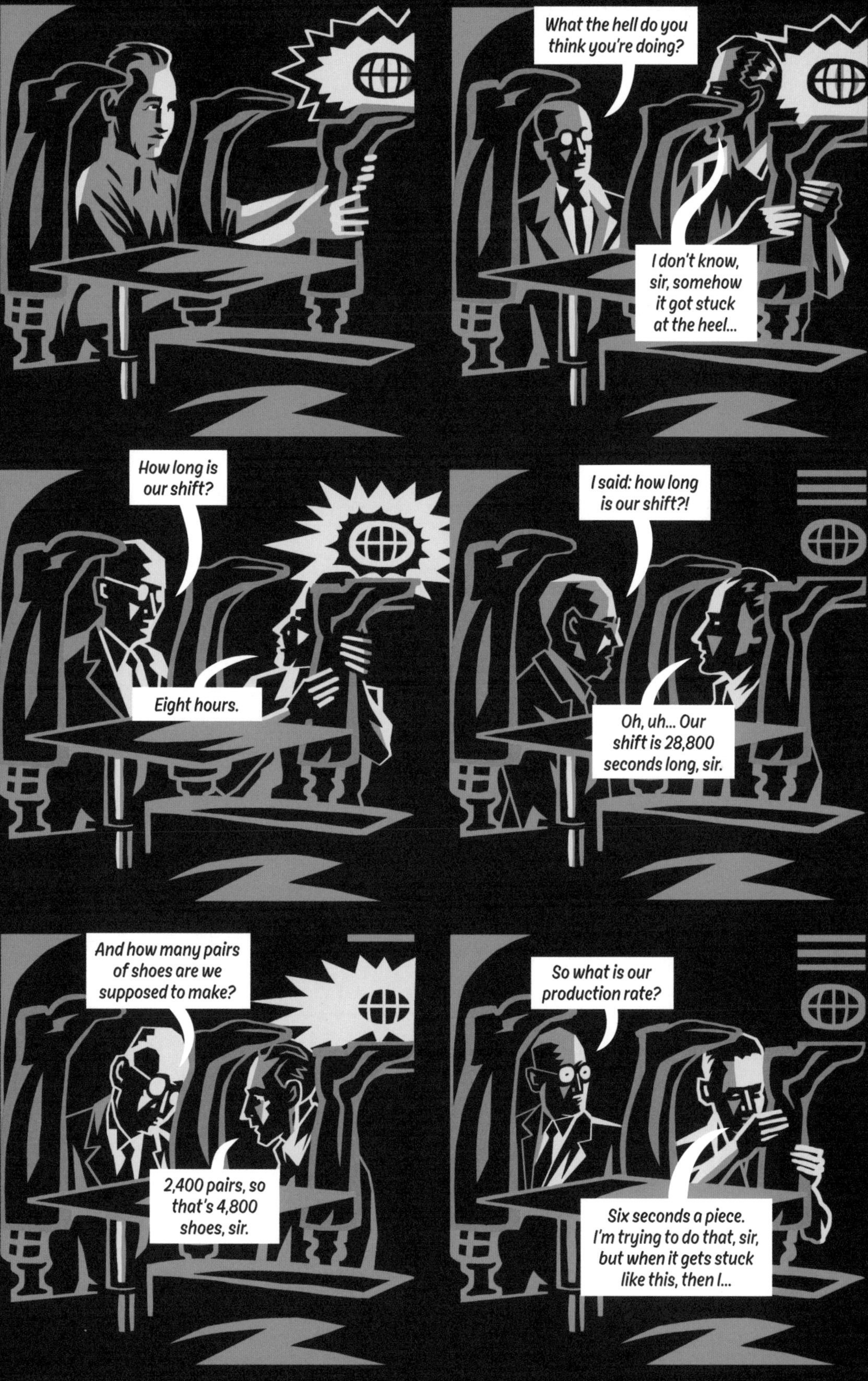
What the hell do you think you're doing?
I don't know, sir, somehow it got stuck at the heel...
How long is our shift?
Eight hours.
I said: how long is our shift?!
Oh, uh... Our shift is 28,800 seconds long, sir.
And how many pairs of shoes are we supposed to make?
2,400 pairs, so that's 4,800 shoes, sir.
So what is our production rate?
Six seconds a piece. I'm trying to do that, sir, but when it gets stuck like this, then I...

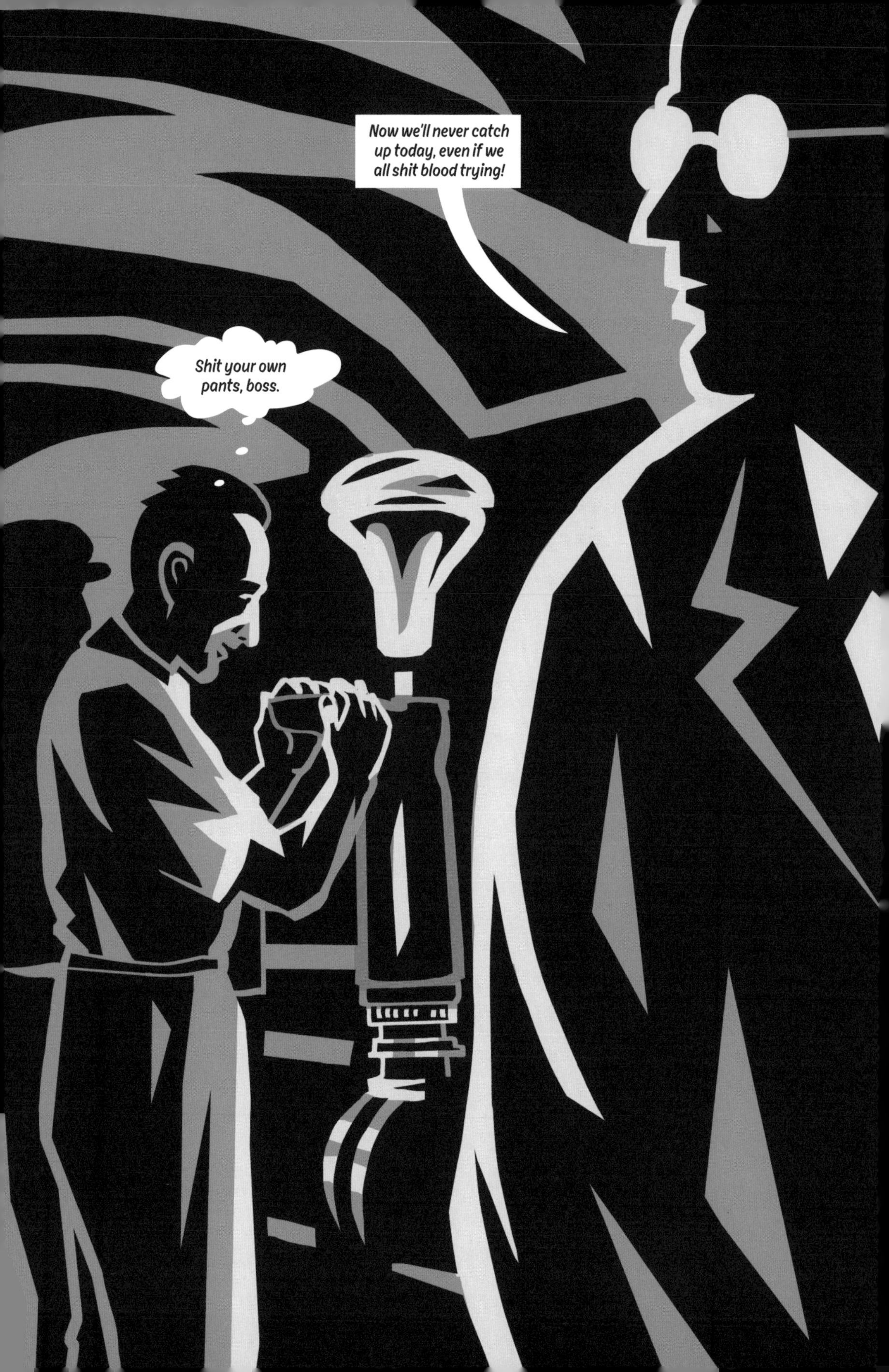
Now we'll never catch up today, even if we all shit blood trying!
Shit your own pants, boss.

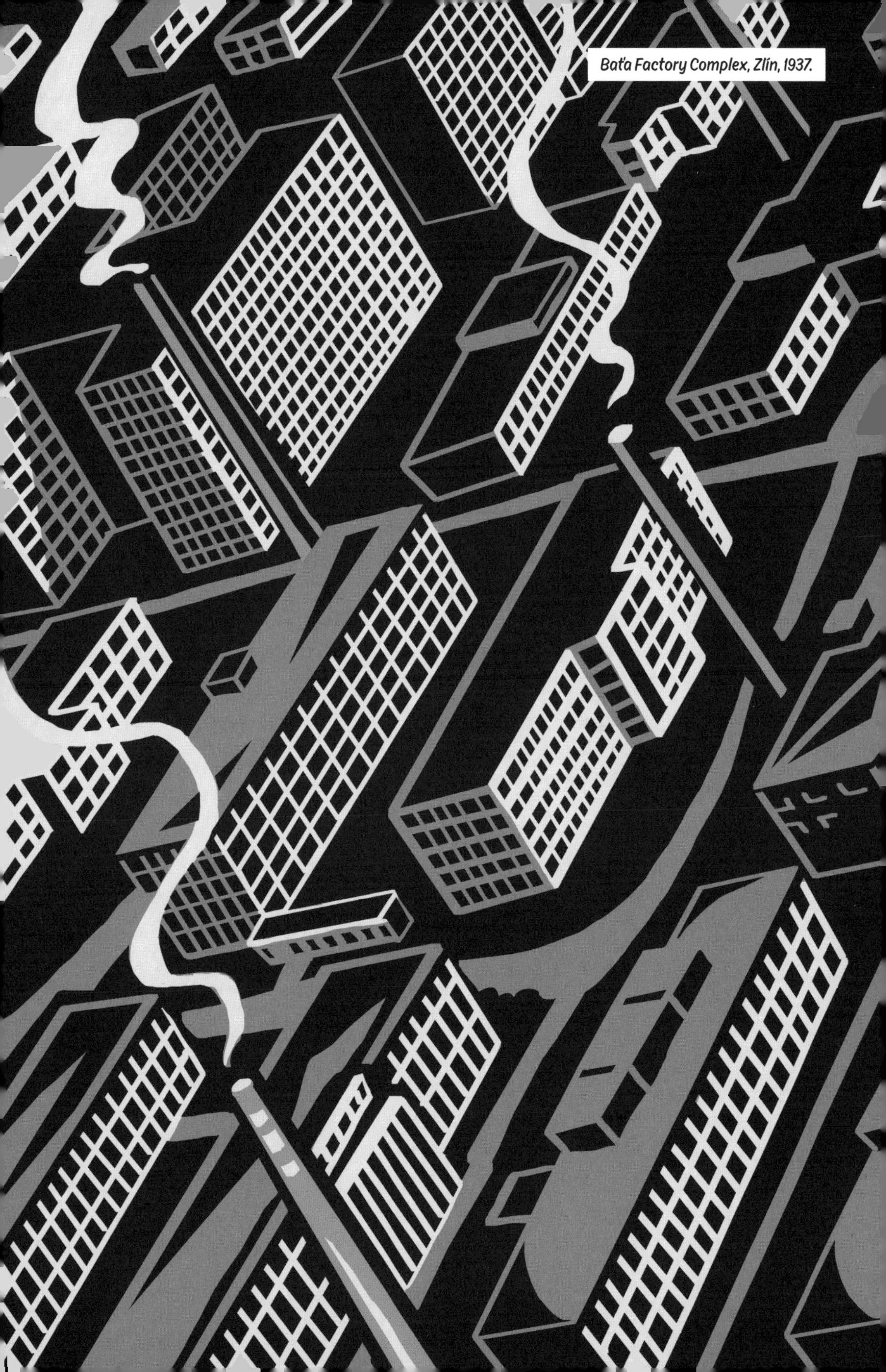

Baťa Factory Complex, Zlín, 1937.

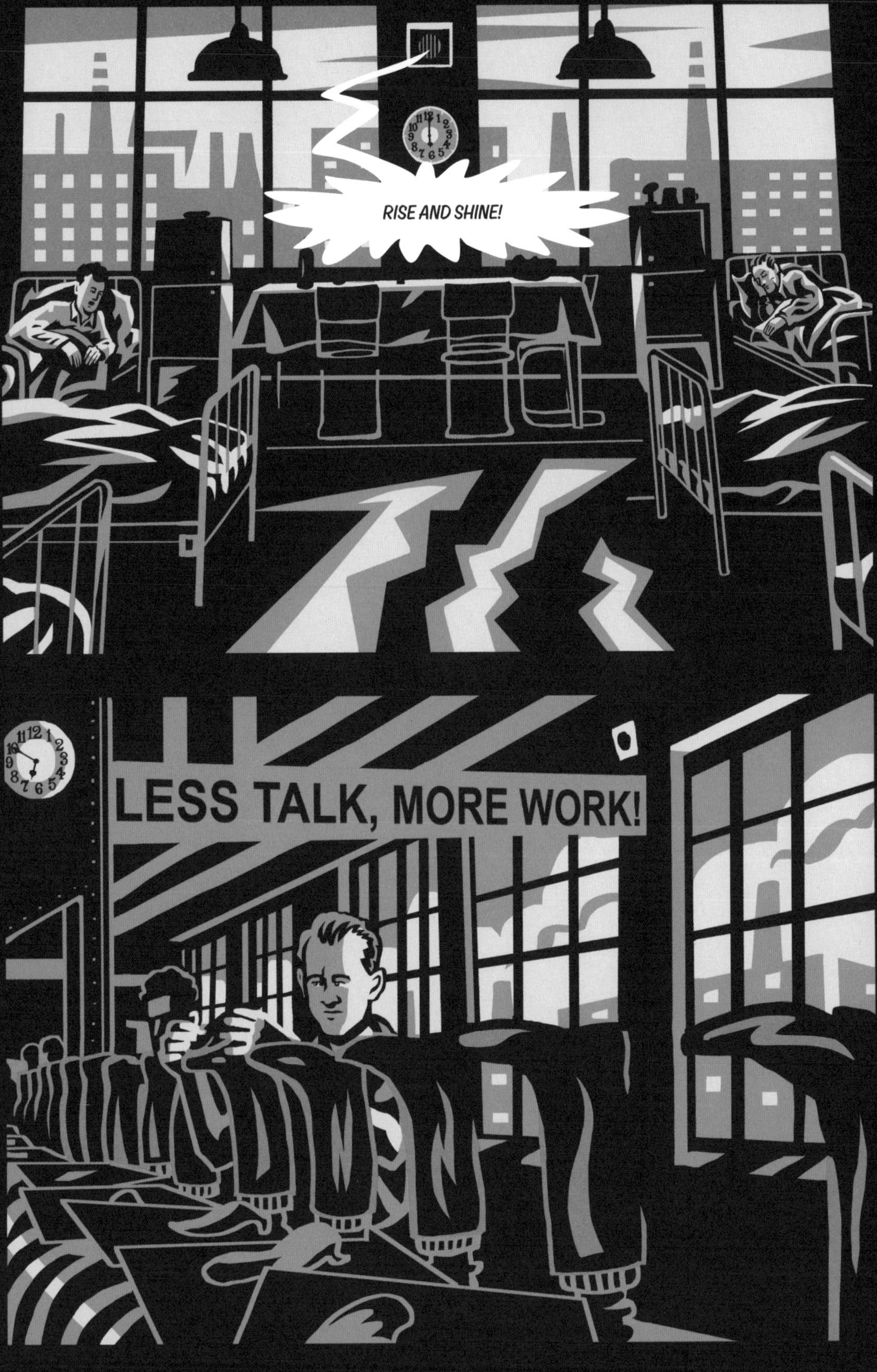
RISE AND SHINE!
LESS TALK, MORE WORK!

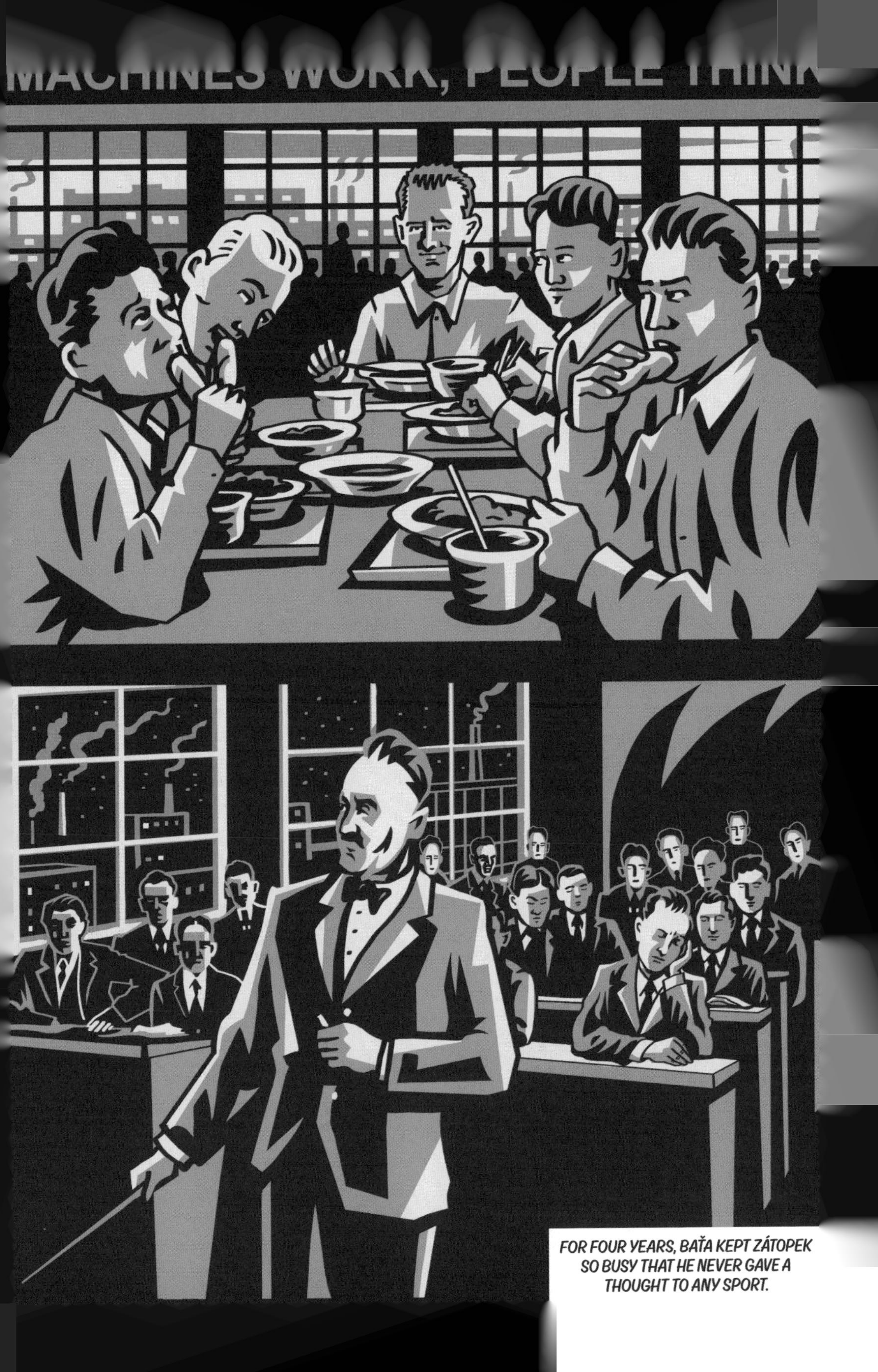
MACHINES WORK, PEOPLE THINK
FOR FOUR YEARS, BAŤA KEPT ZÁTOPEK SO BUSY THAT HE NEVER GAVE A THOUGHT TO ANY SPORT.

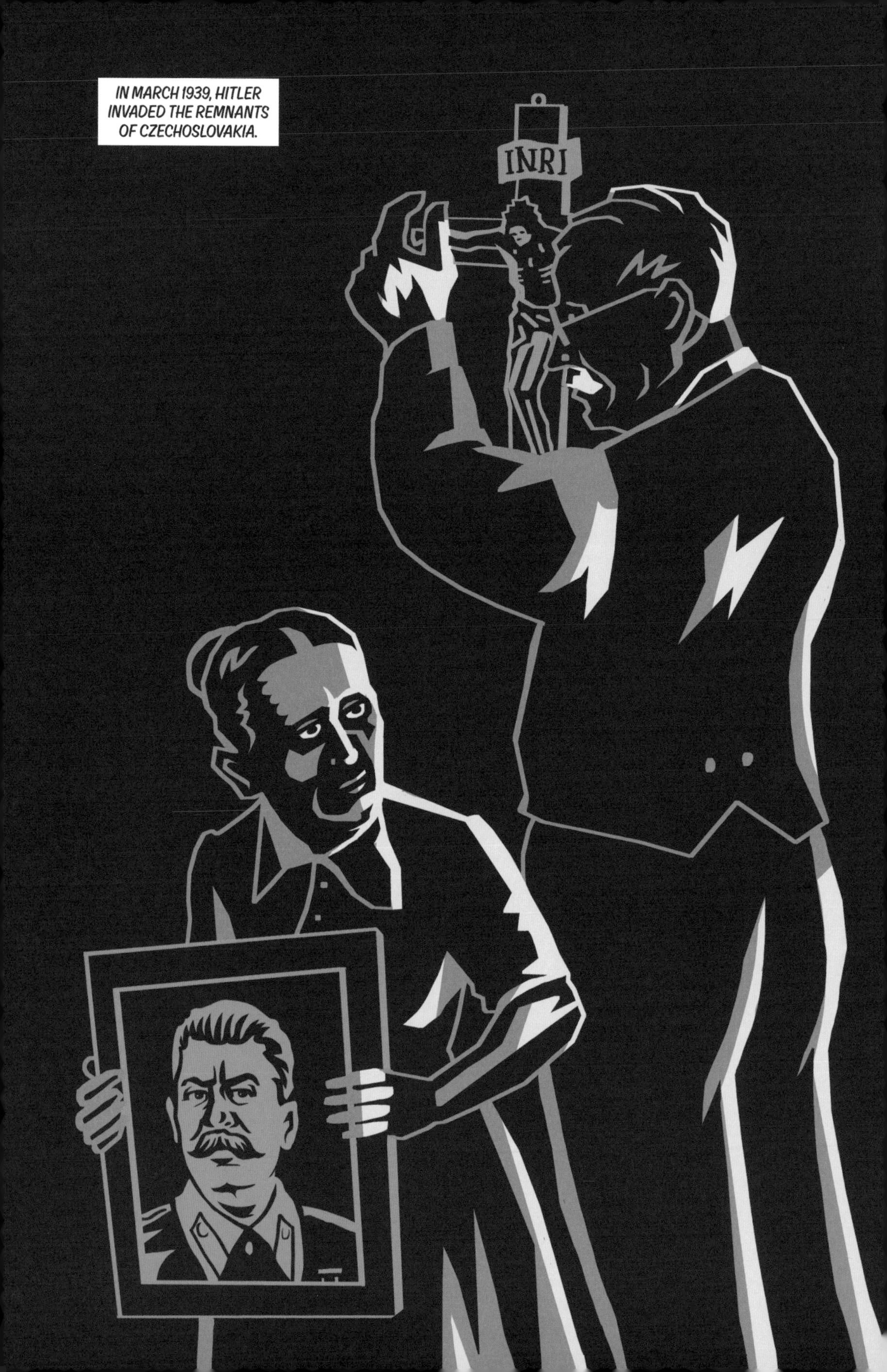
IN MARCH 1939, HITLER INVADED THE REMNANTS OF CZECHOSLOVAKIA.
INRI

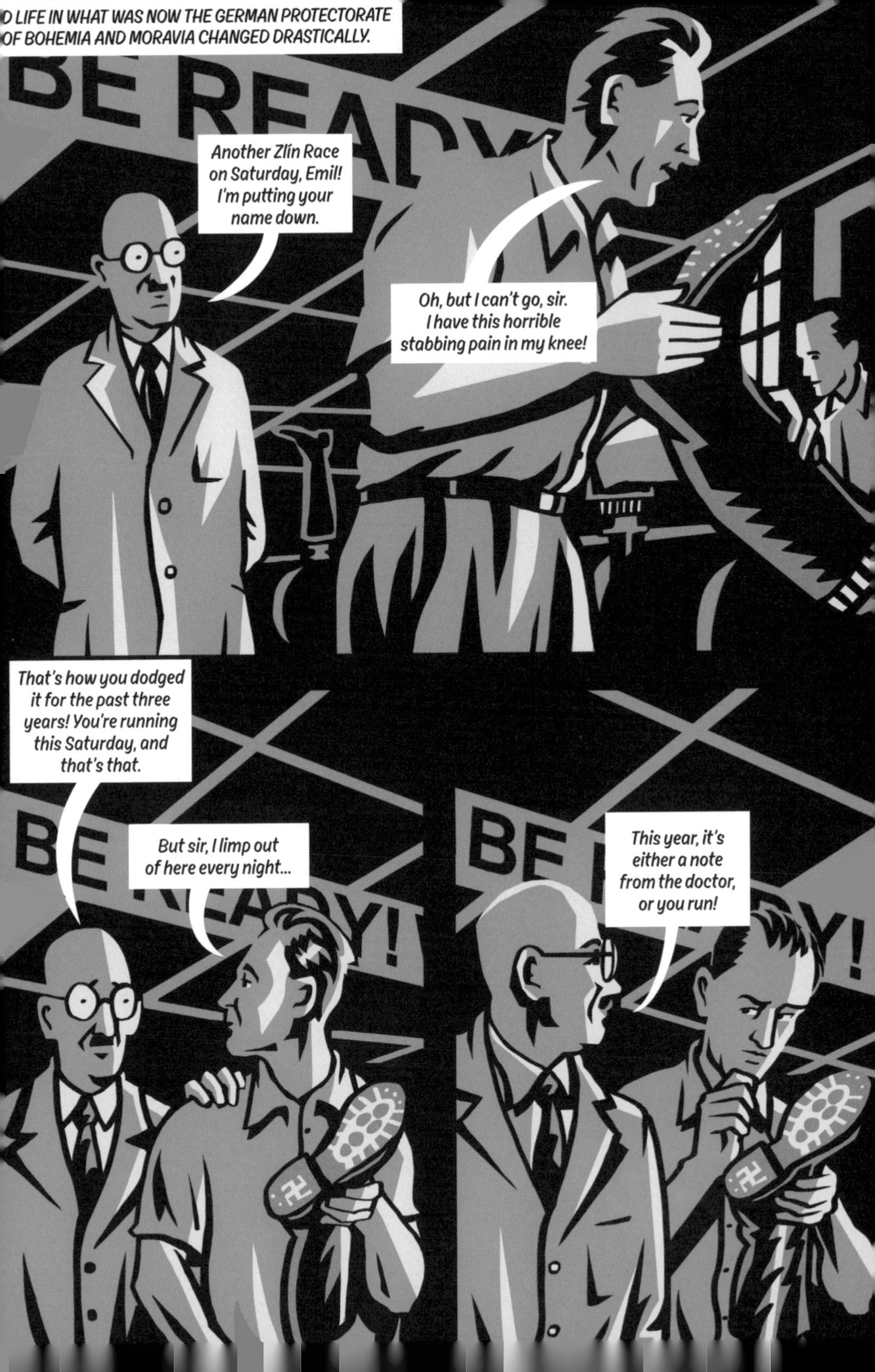
D LIFE IN WHAT WAS NOW THE GERMAN PROTECTORATE OF BOHEMIA AND MORAVIA CHANGED DRASTICALLY.
Another Zlín Race on Saturday, Emil! I'm putting your name down.
Oh, but I can't go, sir. I have this horrible stabbing pain in my knee!
That's how you dodged it for the past three years! You're running this Saturday, and that's that.
But sir, I limp out of here every night...
This year, it's either a note from the doctor, or you run!

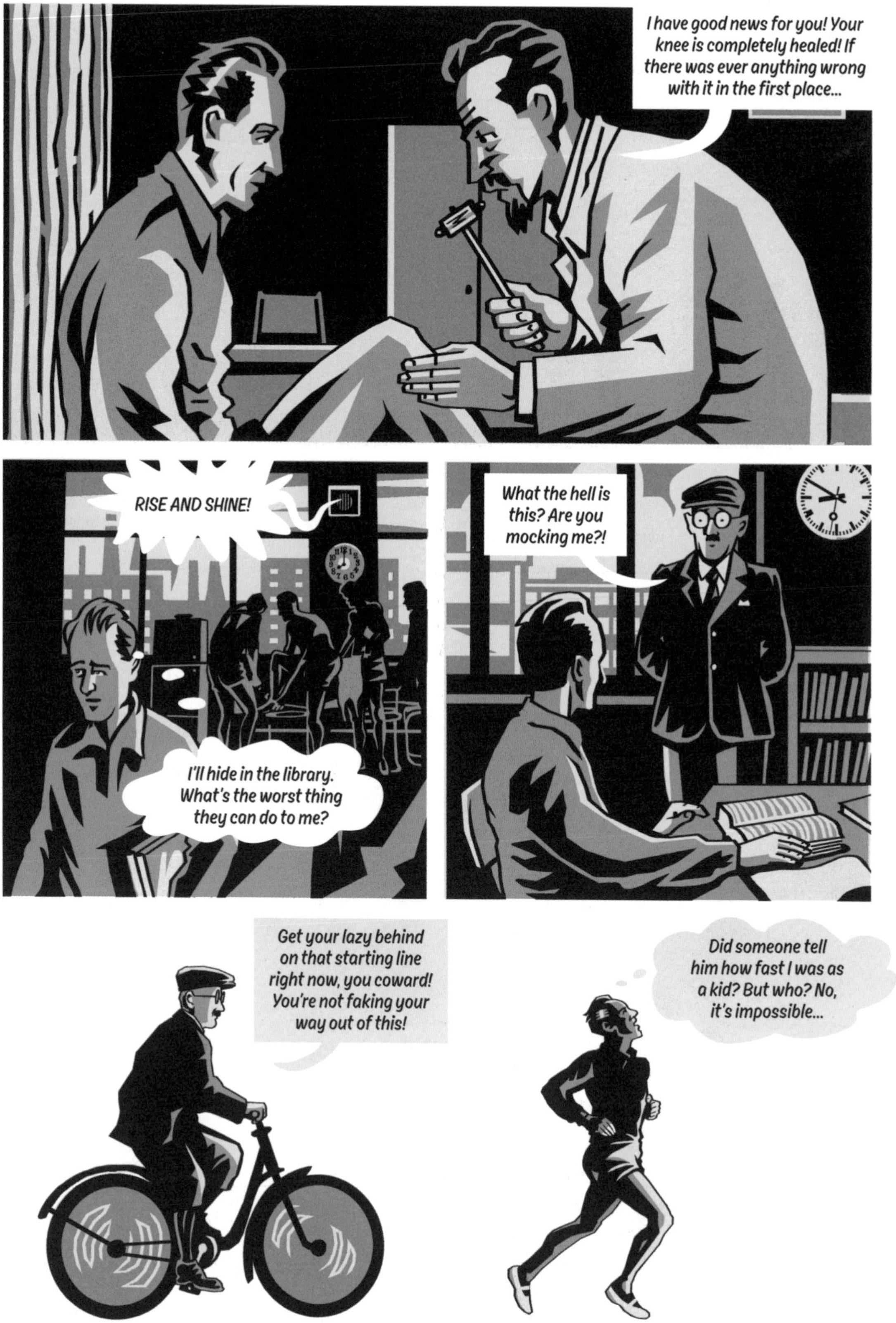
I have good news for you! Your knee is completely healed! If there was ever anything wrong with it in the first place...
RISE AND SHINE!
I'll hide in the library. What's the worst thing they can do to me?
What the hell is this? Are you mocking me?!
Get your lazy behind on that starting line right now, you coward! You're not faking your way out of this!
Did someone tell him how fast I was as a kid? But who? No, it's impossible...

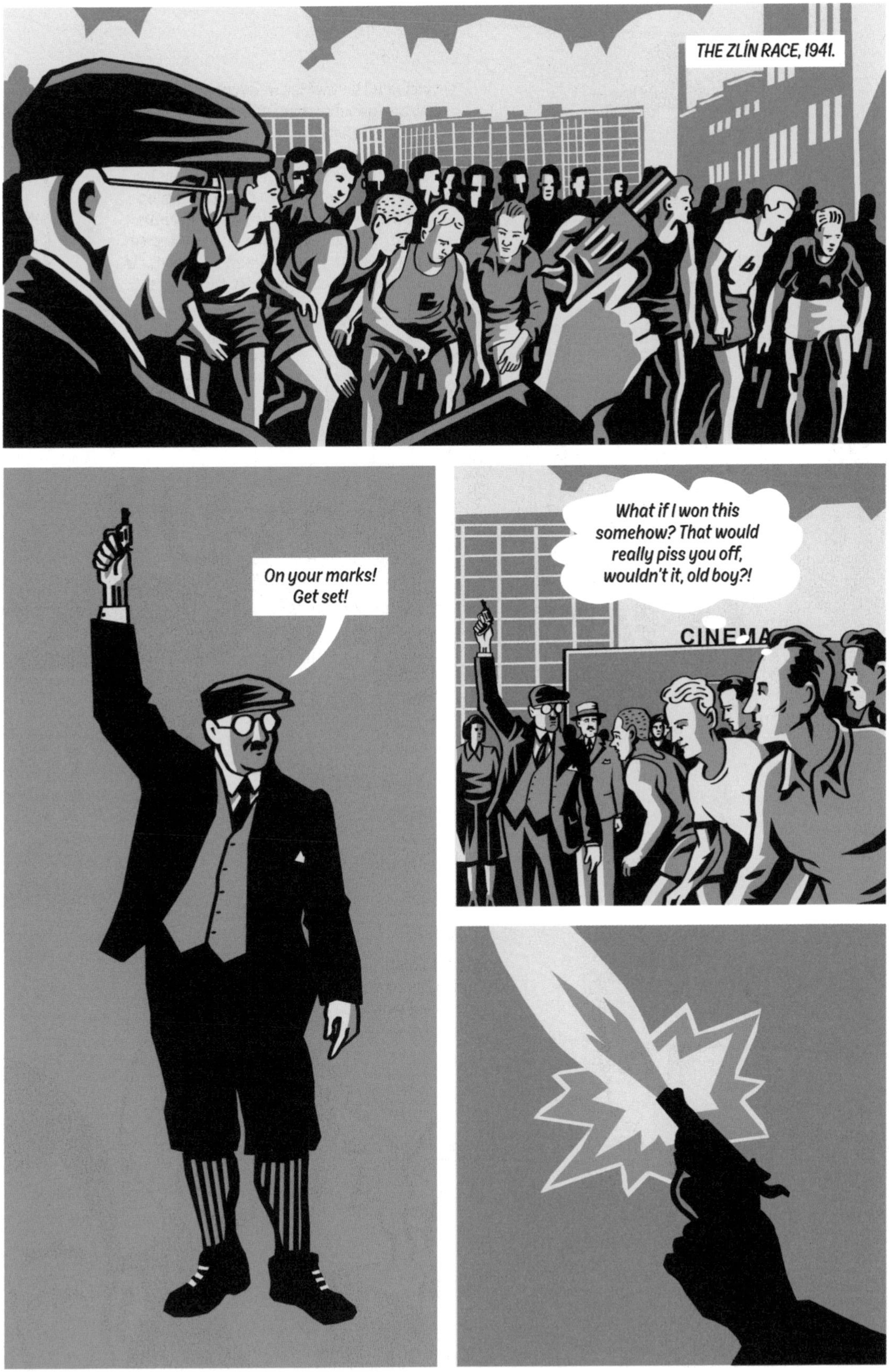
THE ZLÍN RACE, 1941.
On your marks! Get set!
What if I won this somehow? That would really piss you off, wouldn't it, old boy?!
CINEMA

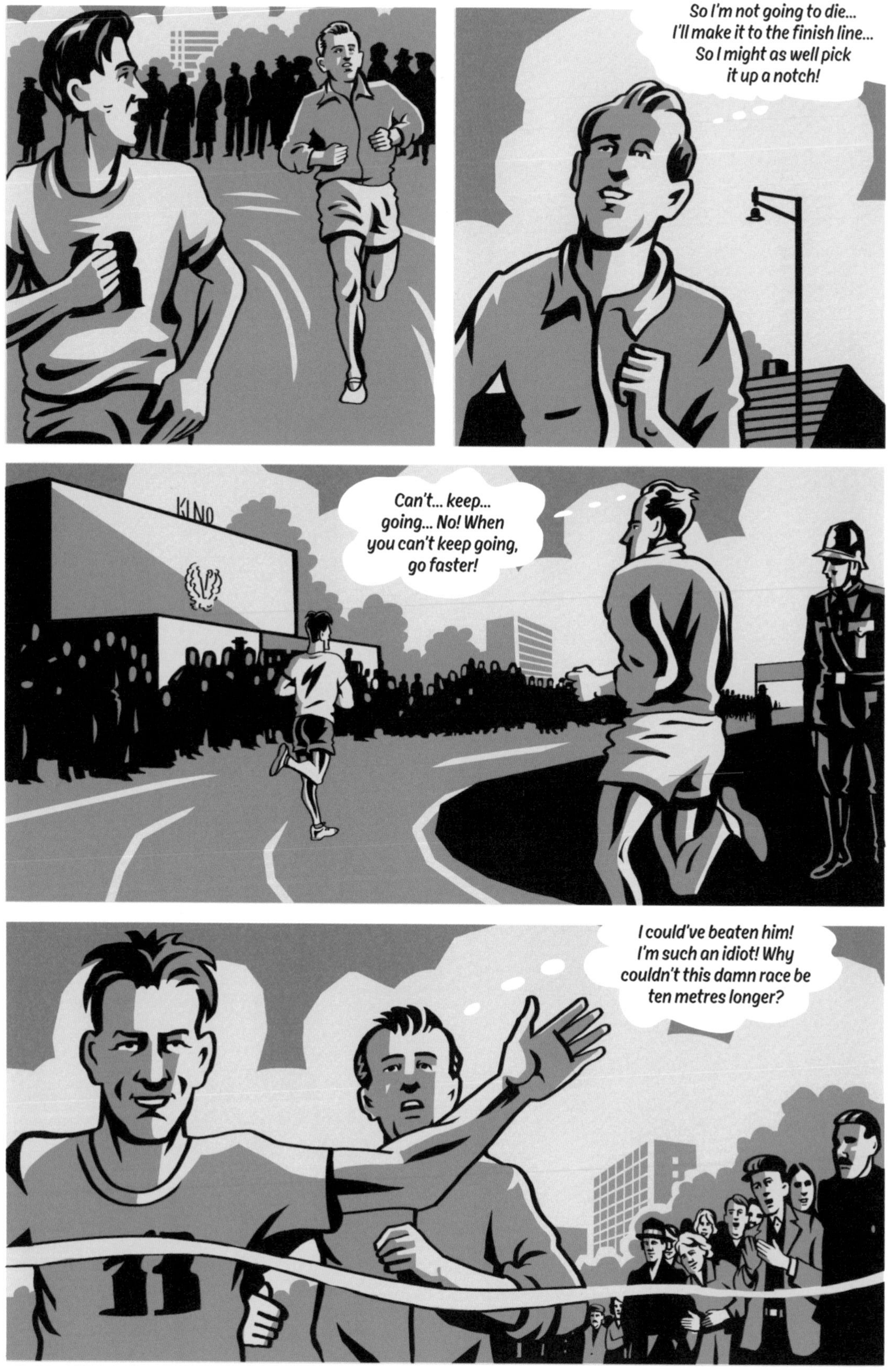
So I'm not going to die... I'll make it to the finish line... So I might as well pick it up a notch!
KINO
Can't... keep... going... No! When you can't keep going, go faster!
I could've beaten him! I'm such an idiot! Why couldn't this damn race be ten metres longer?

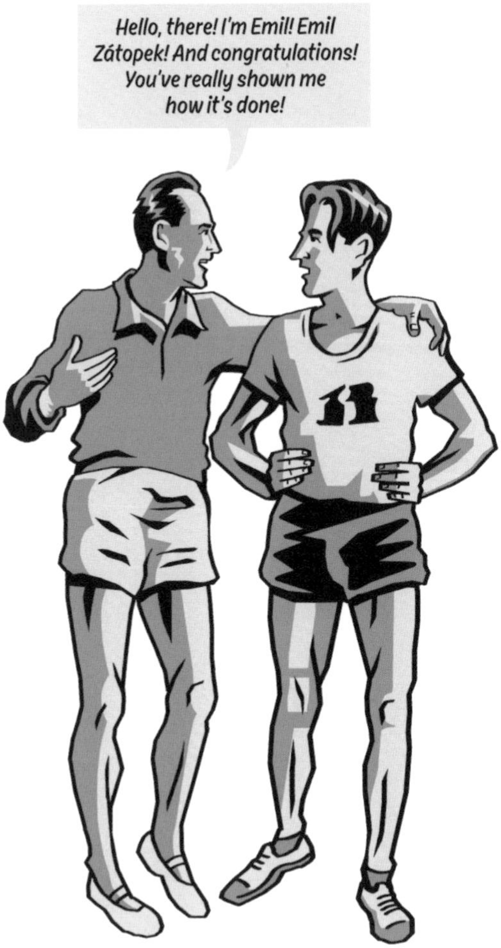
Hello, there! I'm Emil! Emil Zátopek! And congratulations! You've really shown me how it's done!

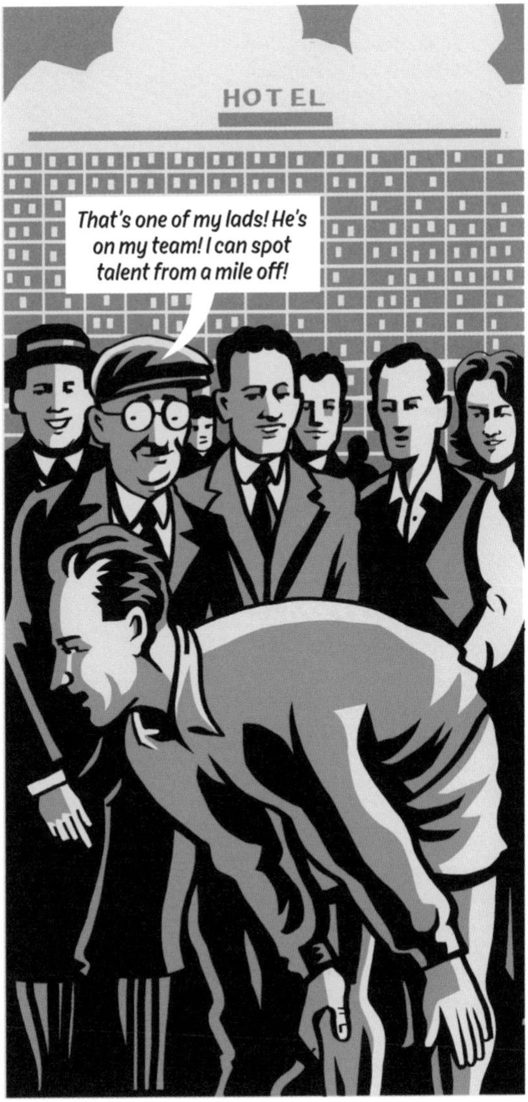
HOTEL
That's one of my lads! He's on my team! I can spot talent from a mile off!

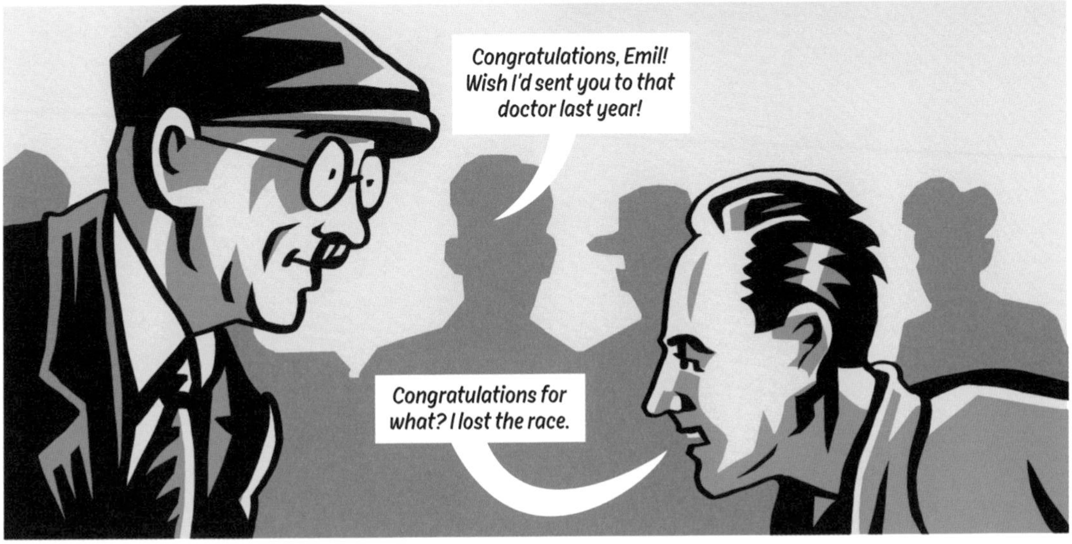
Congratulations, Emil! Wish I'd sent you to that doctor last year!
Congratulations for what? I lost the race.

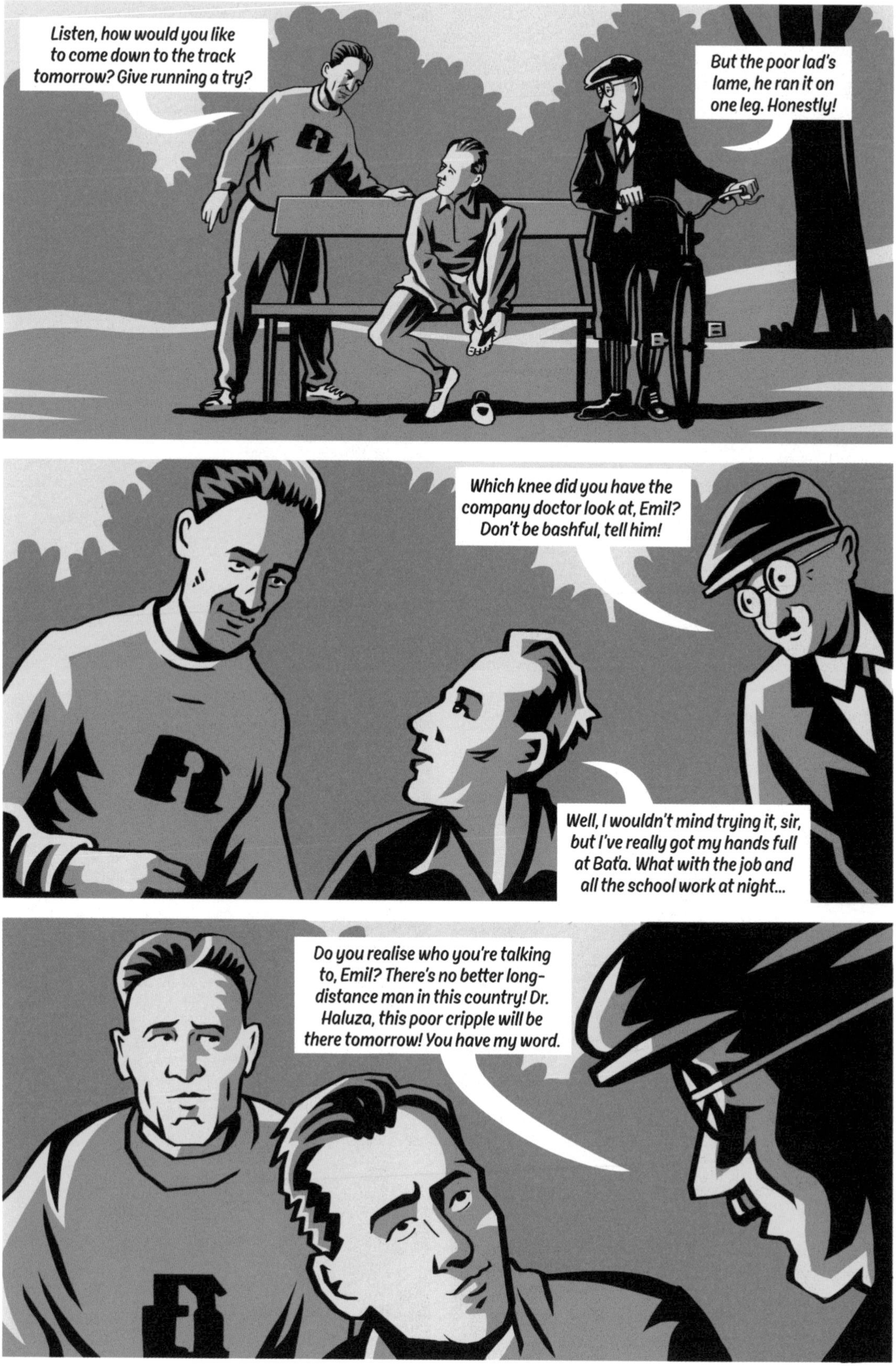
Listen, how would you like to come down to the track tomorrow? Give running a try?
But the poor lad's lame, he ran it on one leg. Honestly!
Which knee did you have the company doctor look at, Emil? Don't be bashful, tell him!
Well, I wouldn't mind trying it, sir, but I've really got my hands full at Baťa. What with the job and all the school work at night...
Do you realise who you're talking to, Emil? There's no better long-distance man in this country! Dr. Haluza, this poor cripple will be there tomorrow! You have my word.

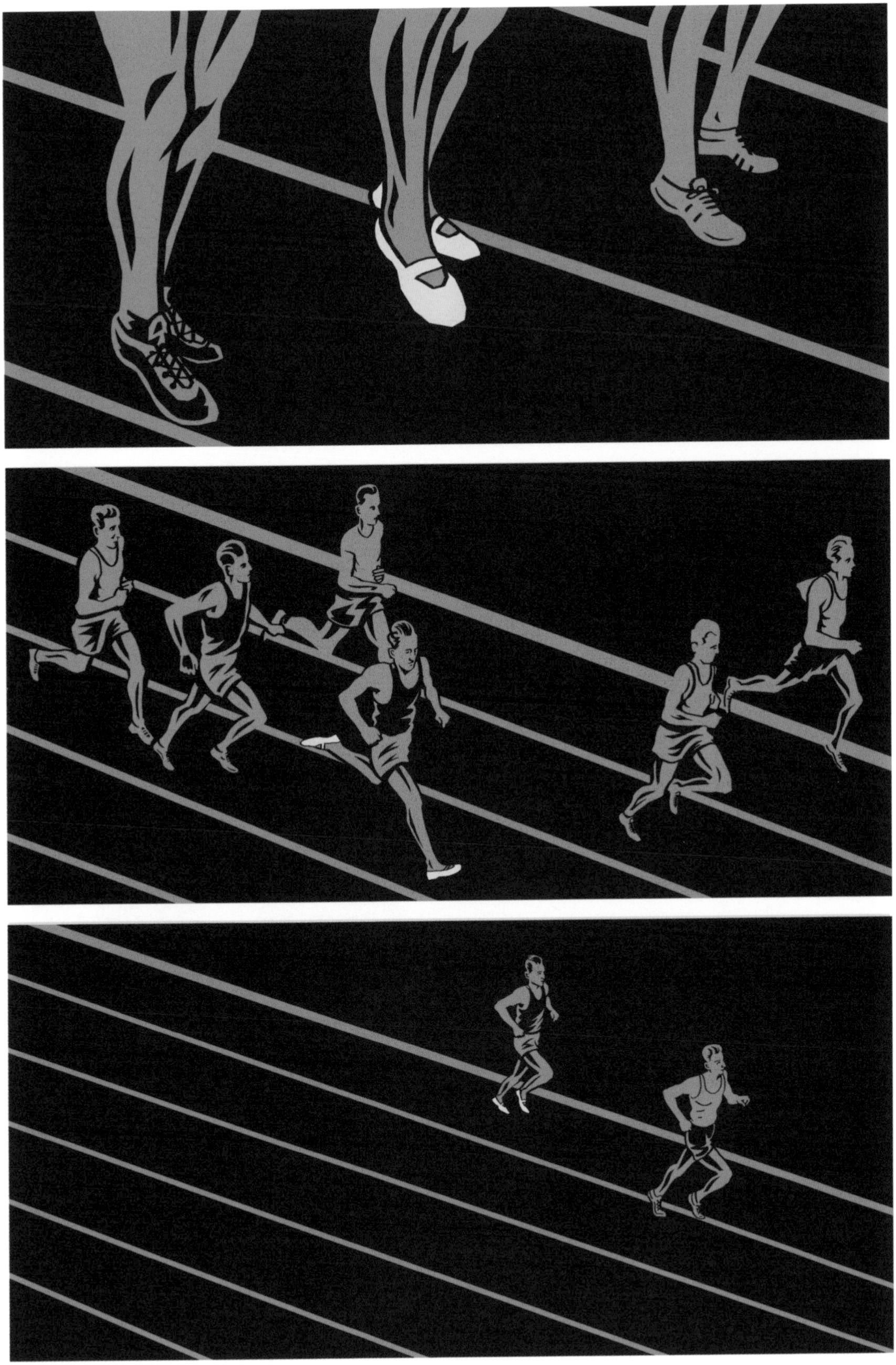

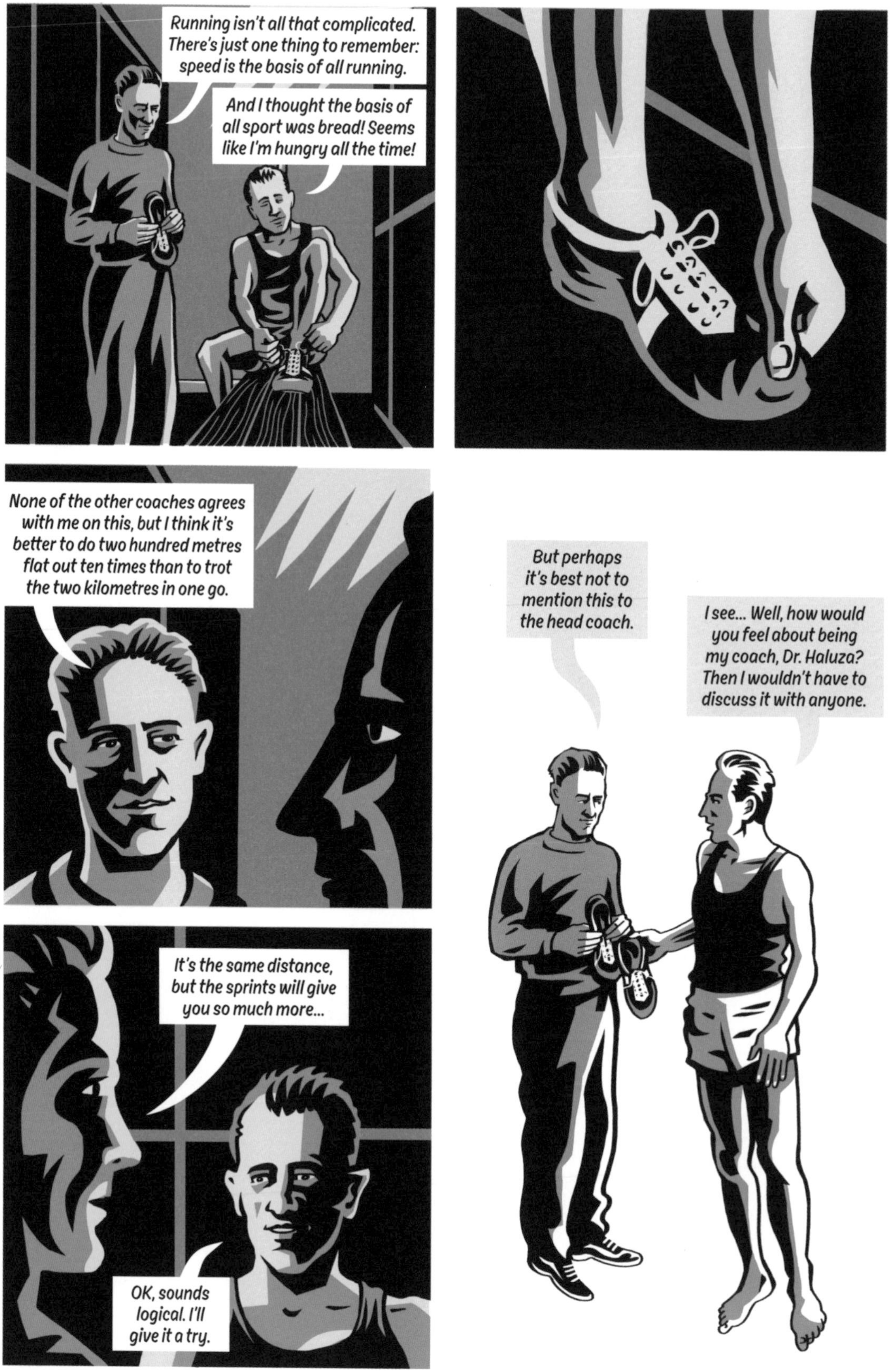

Running isn't all that complicated. There's just one thing to remember: speed is the basis of all running.
And I thought the basis of all sport was bread! Seems like I'm hungry all the time!
None of the other coaches agrees with me on this, but I think it's better to do two hundred metres flat out ten times than to trot the two kilometres in one go.
It's the same distance, but the sprints will give you so much more...
OK, sounds logical. I'll give it a try.
But perhaps it's best not to mention this to the head coach.
I see... Well, how would you feel about being my coach, Dr. Haluza? Then I wouldn't have to discuss it with anyone.

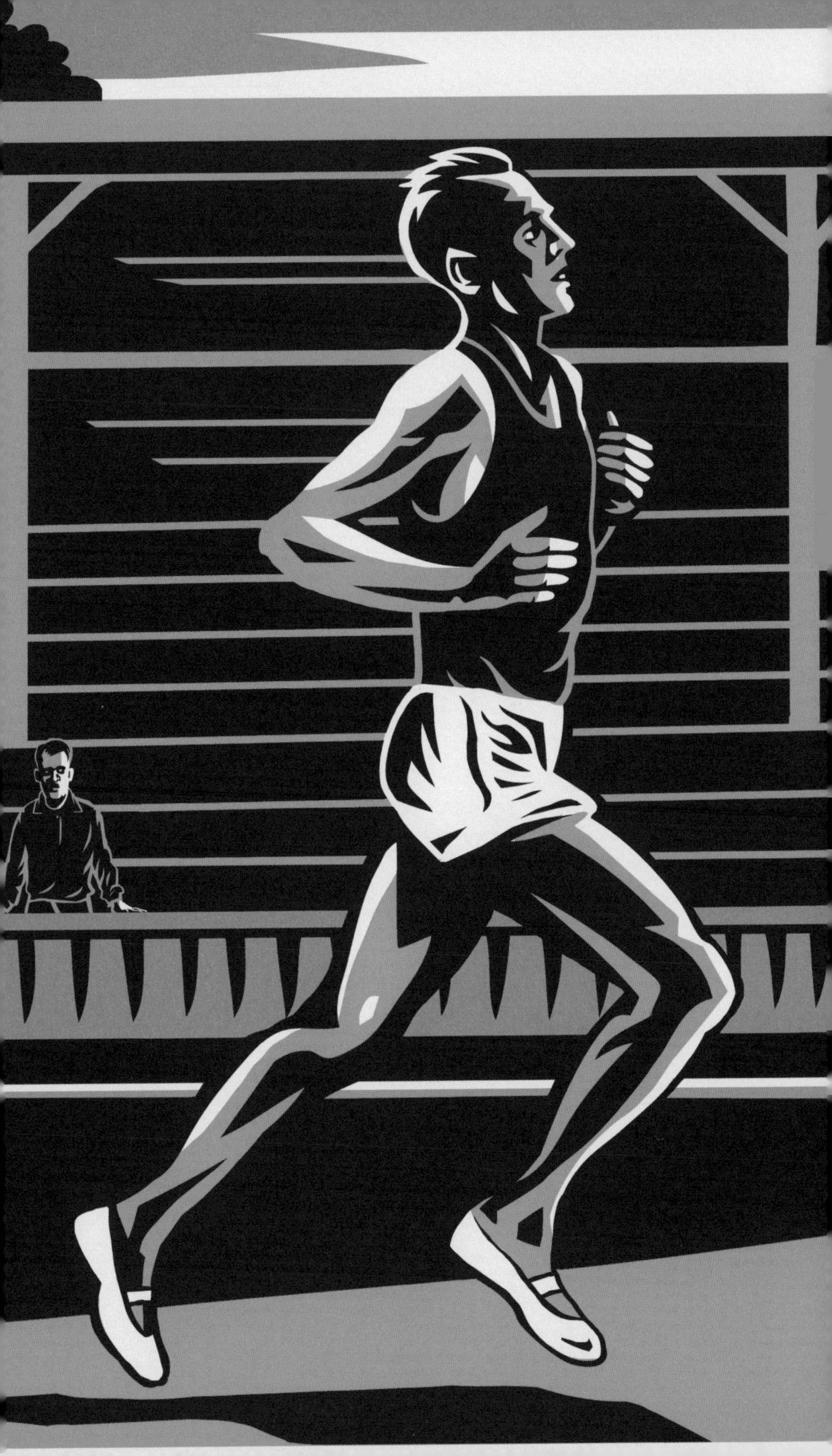

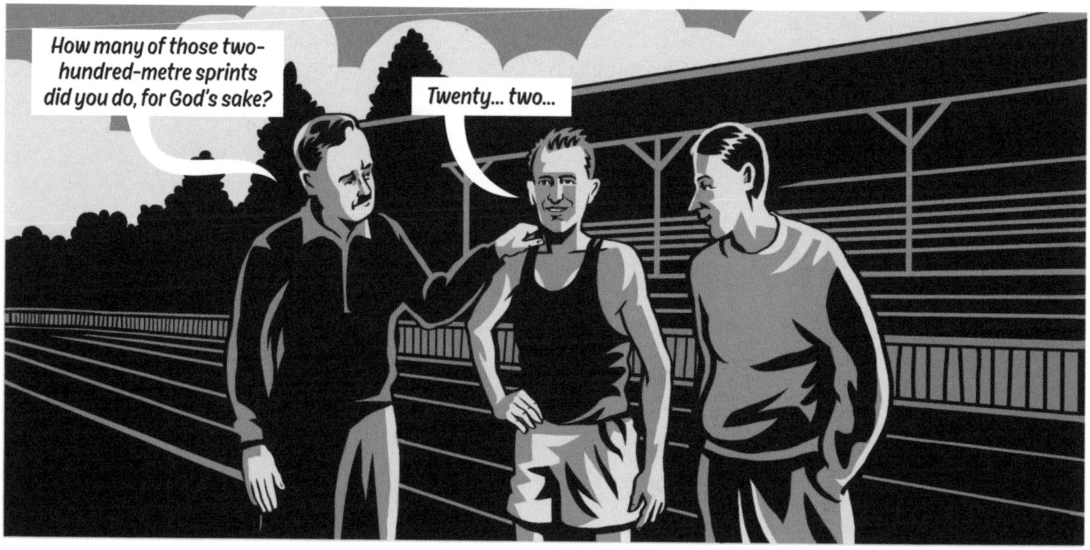
How many of those two-hundred-metre sprints did you do, for God's sake?
Twenty... two...

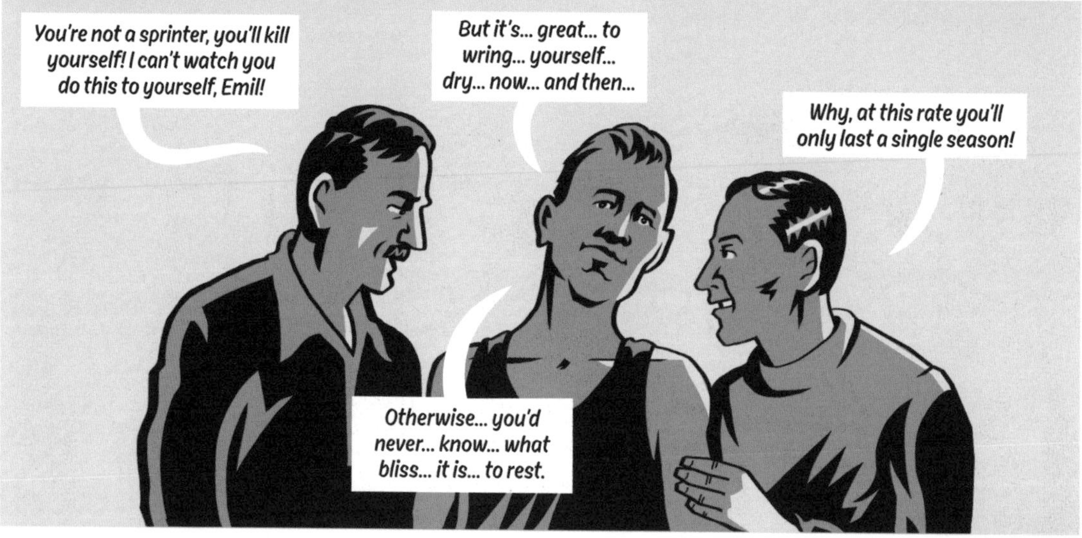
You're not a sprinter, you'll kill yourself! I can't watch you do this to yourself, Emil!
But it's... great... to wring... yourself... dry... now... and then...
Why, at this rate you'll only last a single season!
Otherwise... you'd never... know... what bliss... it is... to rest.

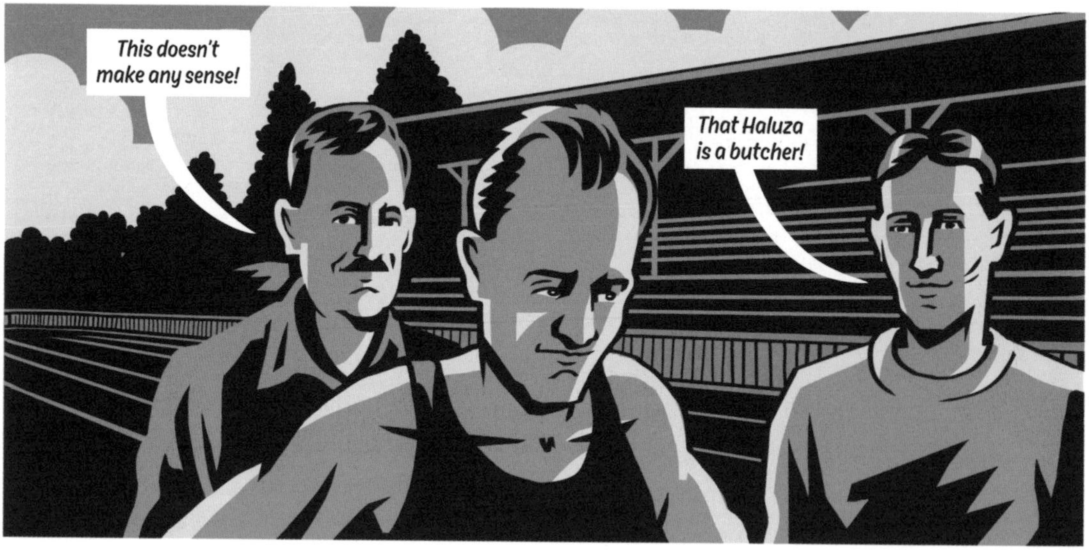
This doesn't make any sense!
That Haluza is a butcher!

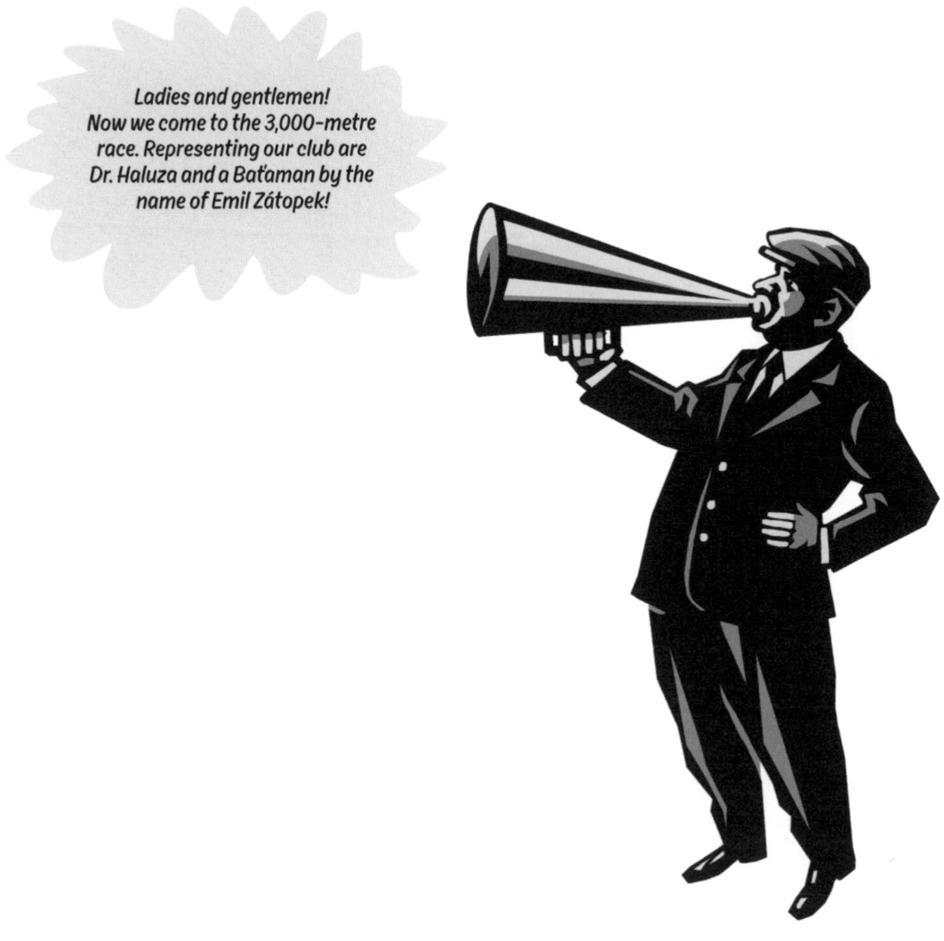
Ladies and gentlemen! Now we come to the 3,000-metre race. Representing our club are Dr. Haluza and a Baťaman by the name of Emil Zátopek!

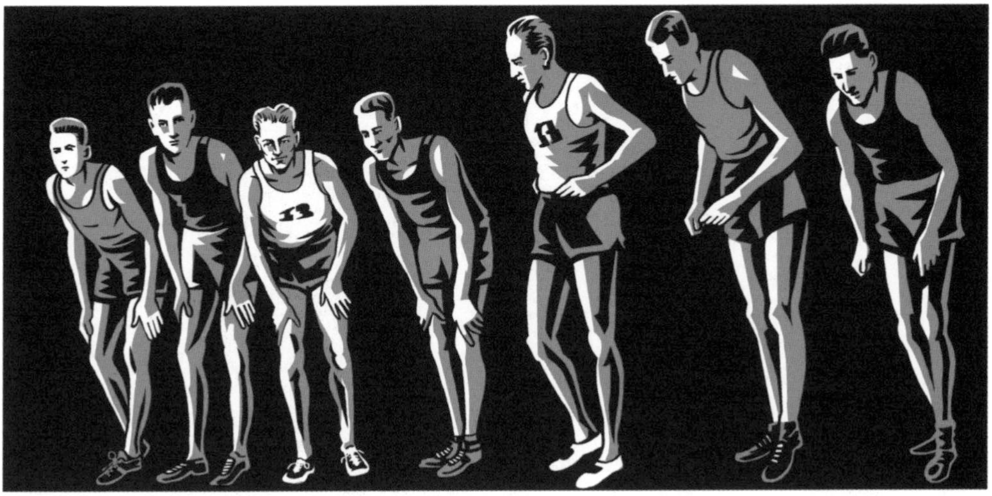

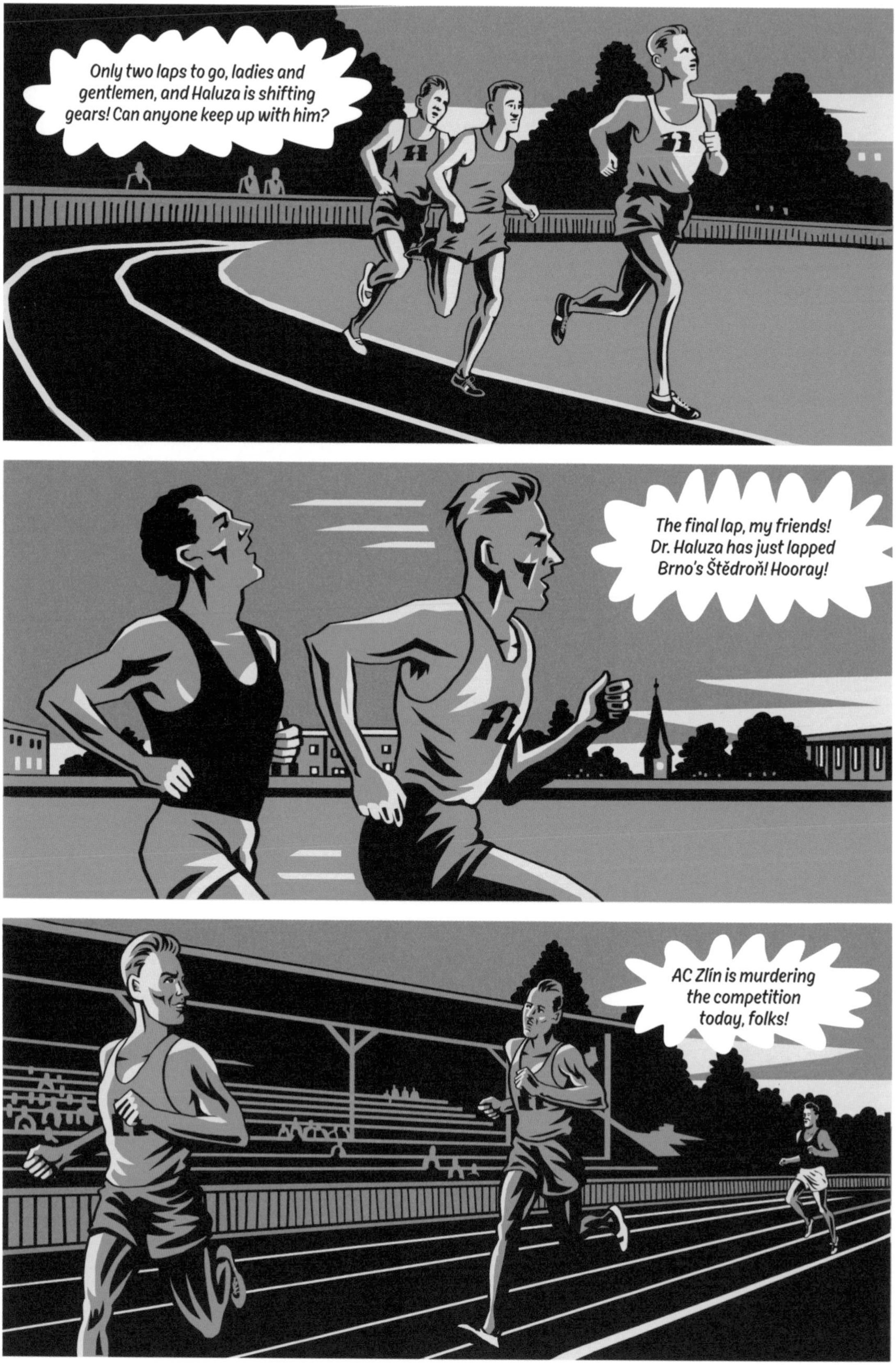
Only two laps to go, ladies and gentlemen, and Haluza is shifting gears! Can anyone keep up with him?
The final lap, my friends! Dr. Haluza has just lapped Brno's Štědroň! Hooray!
AC Zlín is murdering the competition today, folks!

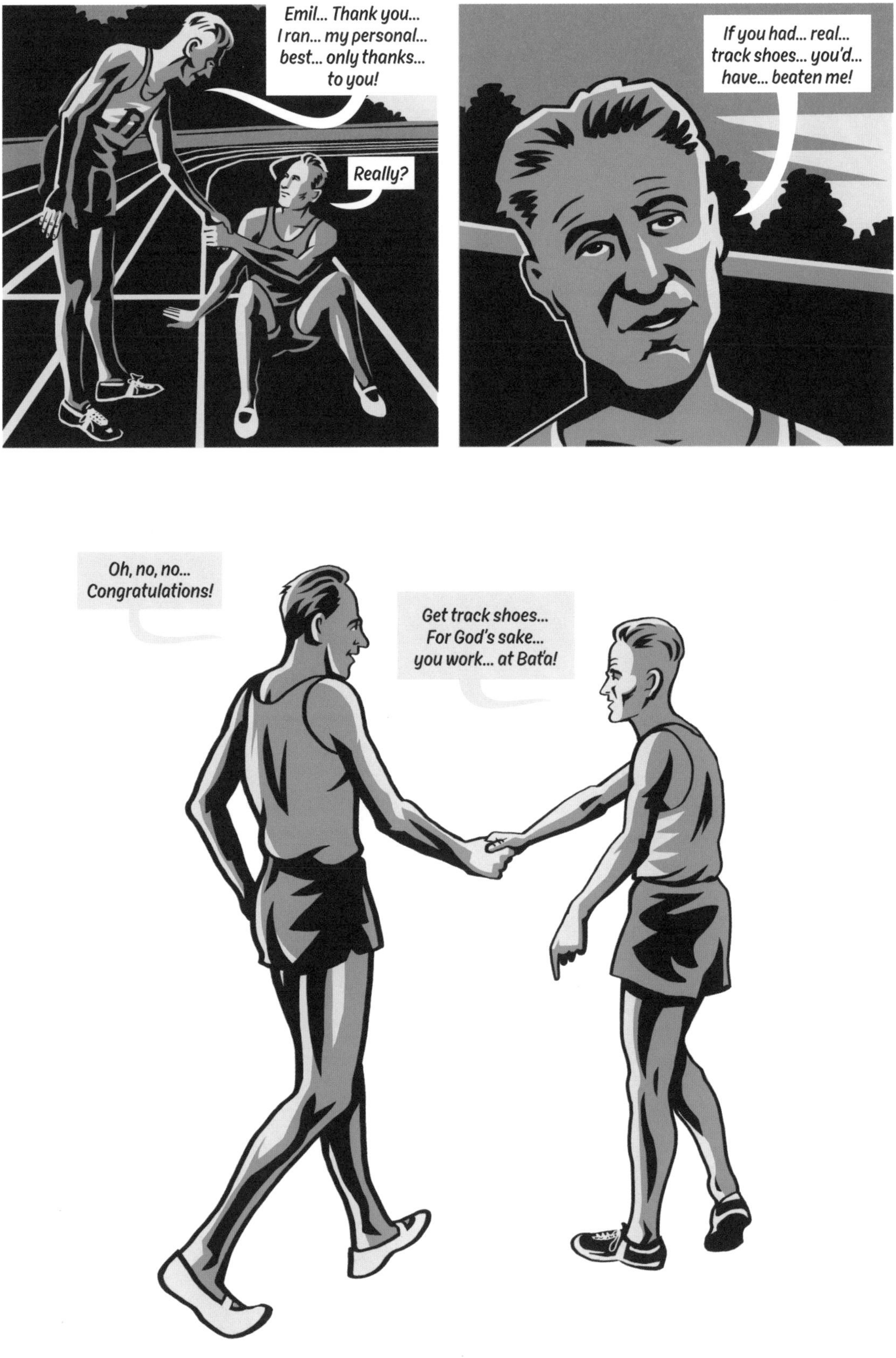
Emil... Thank you... I ran... my personal... best... only thanks... to you!
Really?
If you had... real... track shoes... you'd... have... beaten me!
Oh, no, no... Congratulations!
Get track shoes... For God's sake... you work... at Baťa!

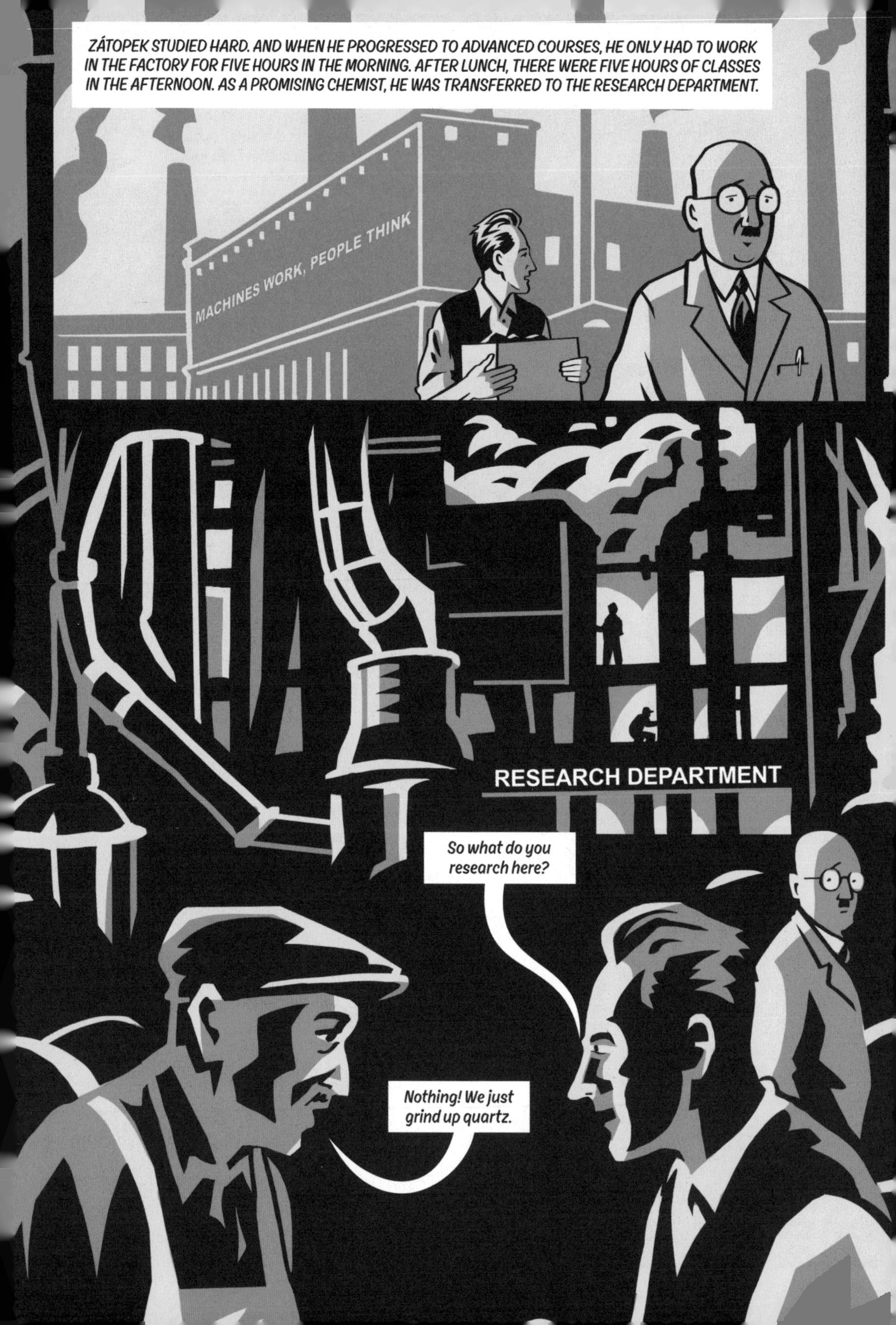
ZÁTOPEK STUDIED HARD. AND WHEN HE PROGRESSED TO ADVANCED COURSES, HE ONLY HAD TO WORK IN THE FACTORY FOR FIVE HOURS IN THE MORNING. AFTER LUNCH, THERE WERE FIVE HOURS OF CLASSES IN THE AFTERNOON. AS A PROMISING CHEMIST, HE WAS TRANSFERRED TO THE RESEARCH DEPARTMENT.
MACHINES WORK, PEOPLE THINK
RESEARCH DEPARTMENT
So what do you research here?
Nothing! We just grind up quartz.

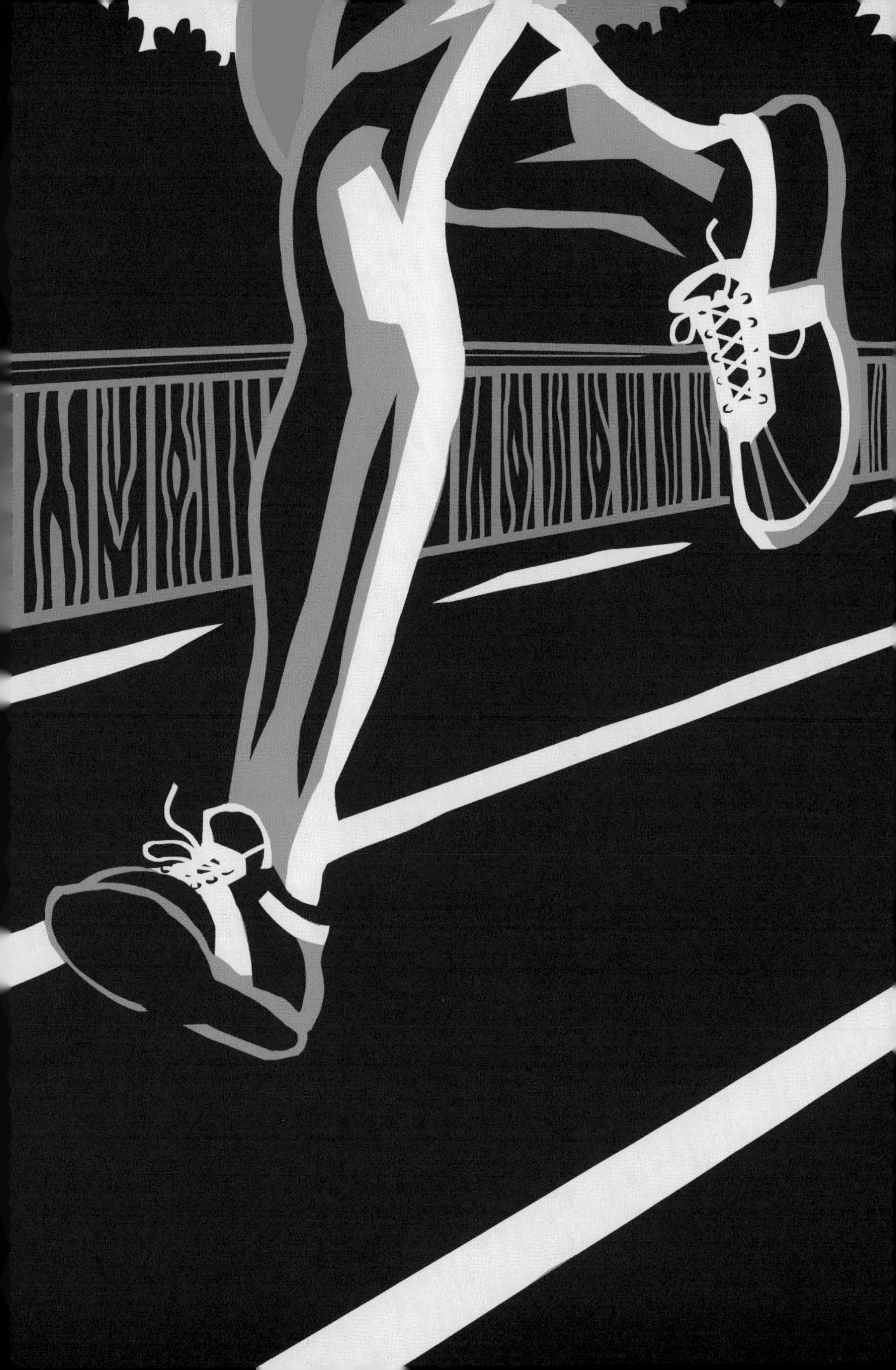

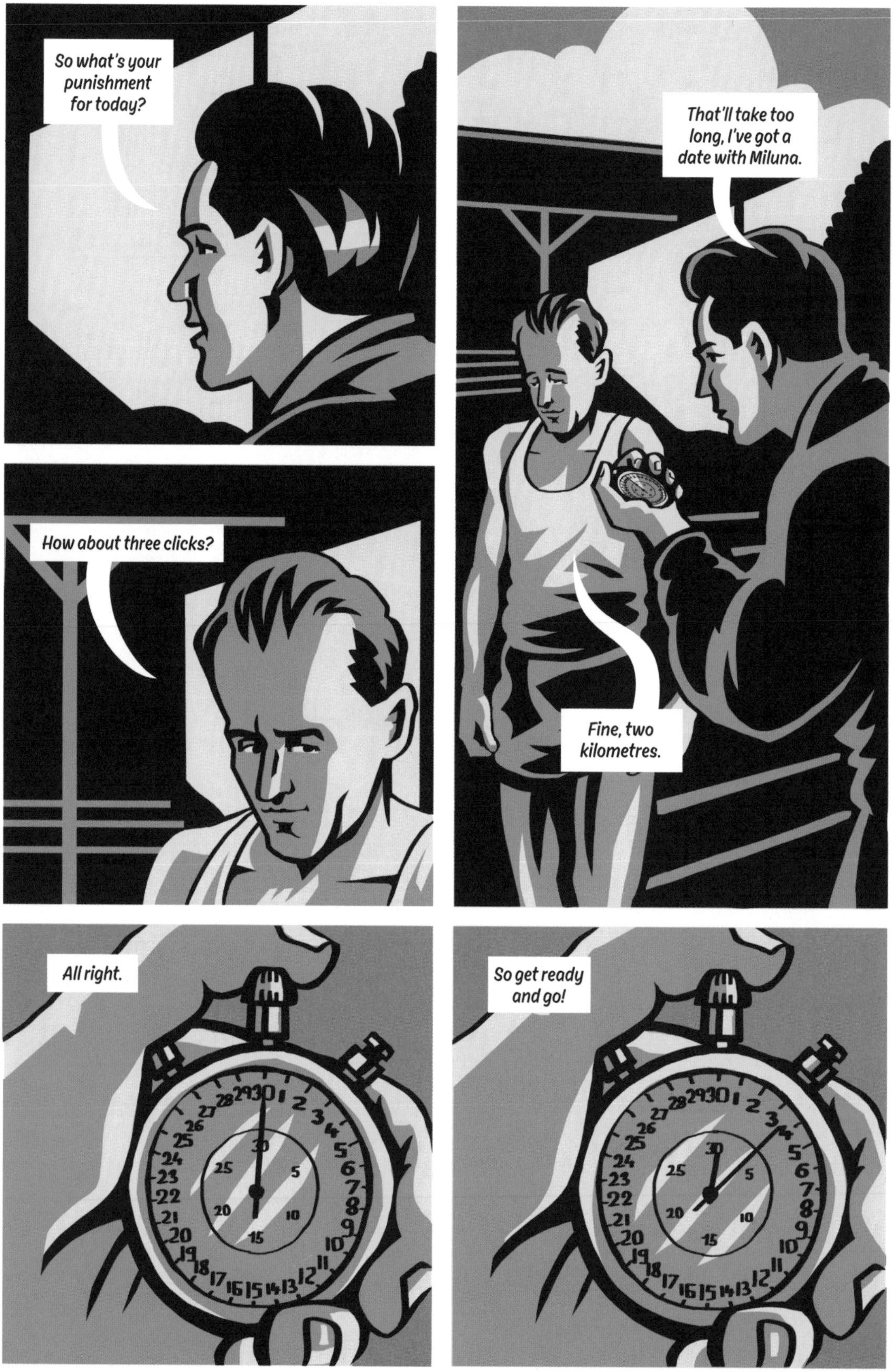
So what's your punishment for today?
That'll take too long, I've got a date with Miluna.
How about three clicks?
Fine, two kilometres.
All right.
So get ready and go!

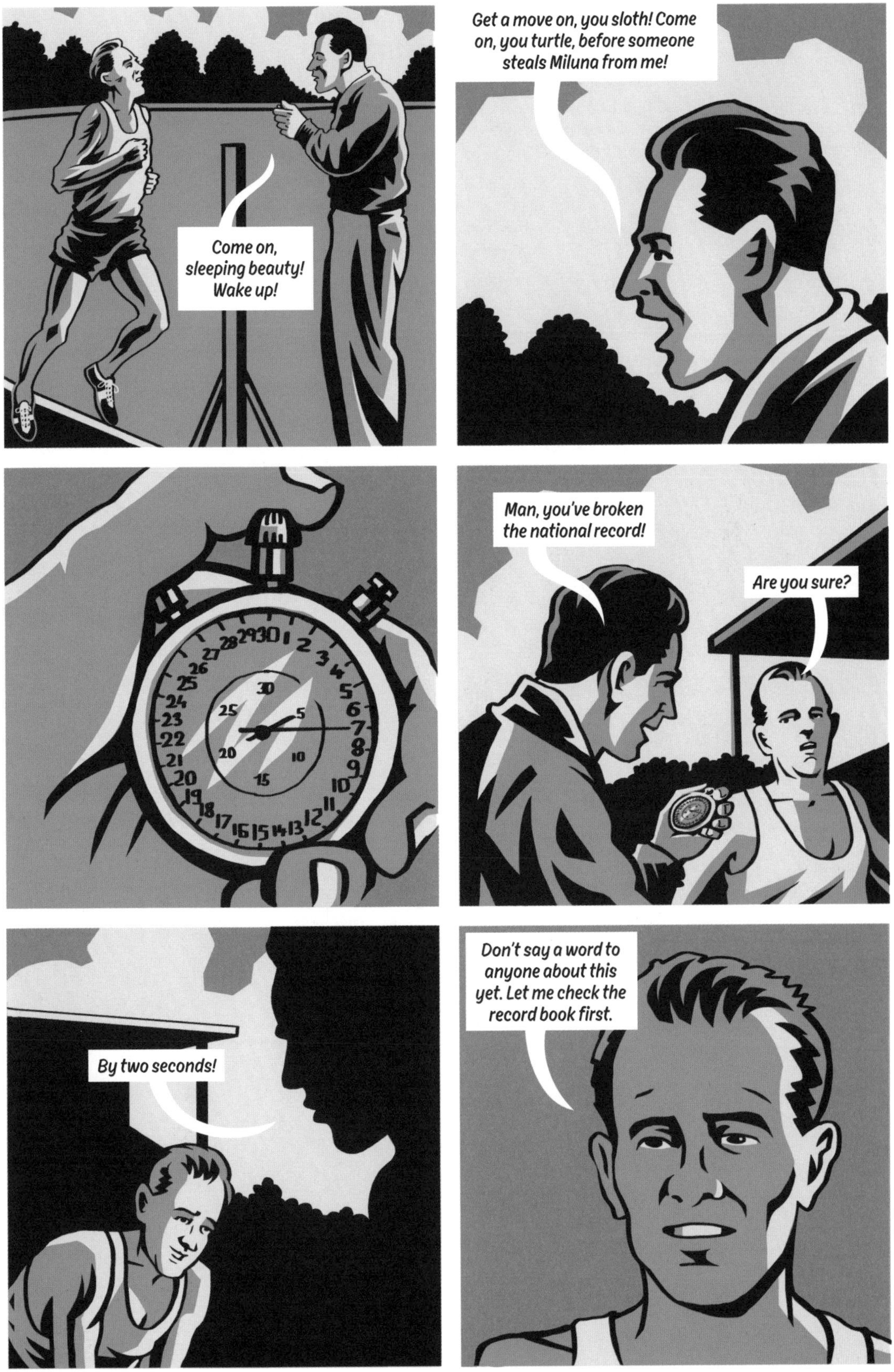
Come on, sleeping beauty! Wake up!
Get a move on, you sloth! Come on, you turtle, before someone steals Miluna from me!
Man, you've broken the national record!
Are you sure?
By two seconds!
Don't say a word to anyone about this yet. Let me check the record book first.

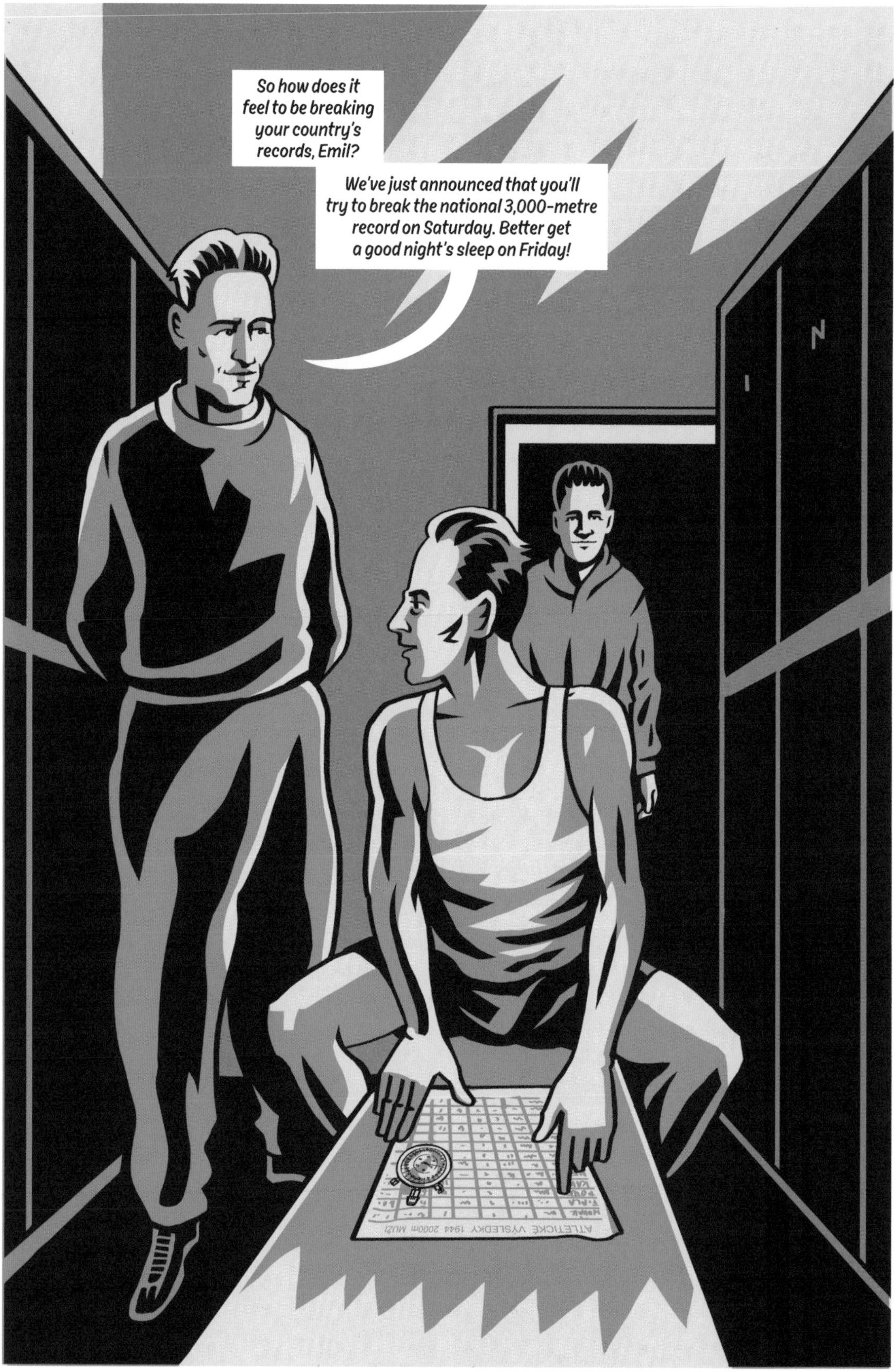
So how does it feel to be breaking your country's records, Emil?
We've just announced that you'll try to break the national 3,000-metre record on Saturday. Better get a good night's sleep on Friday!

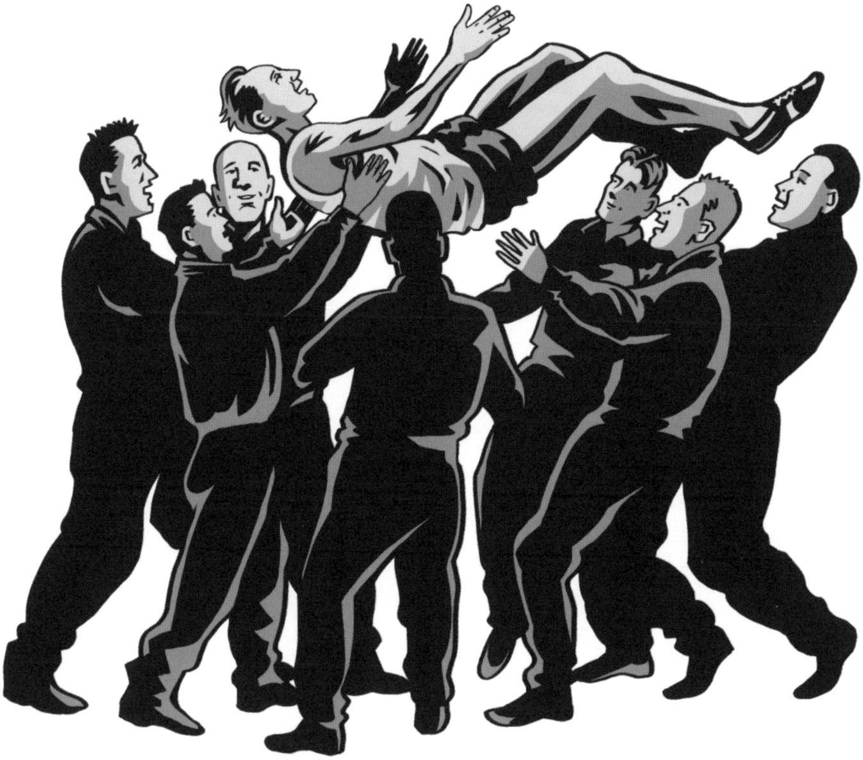

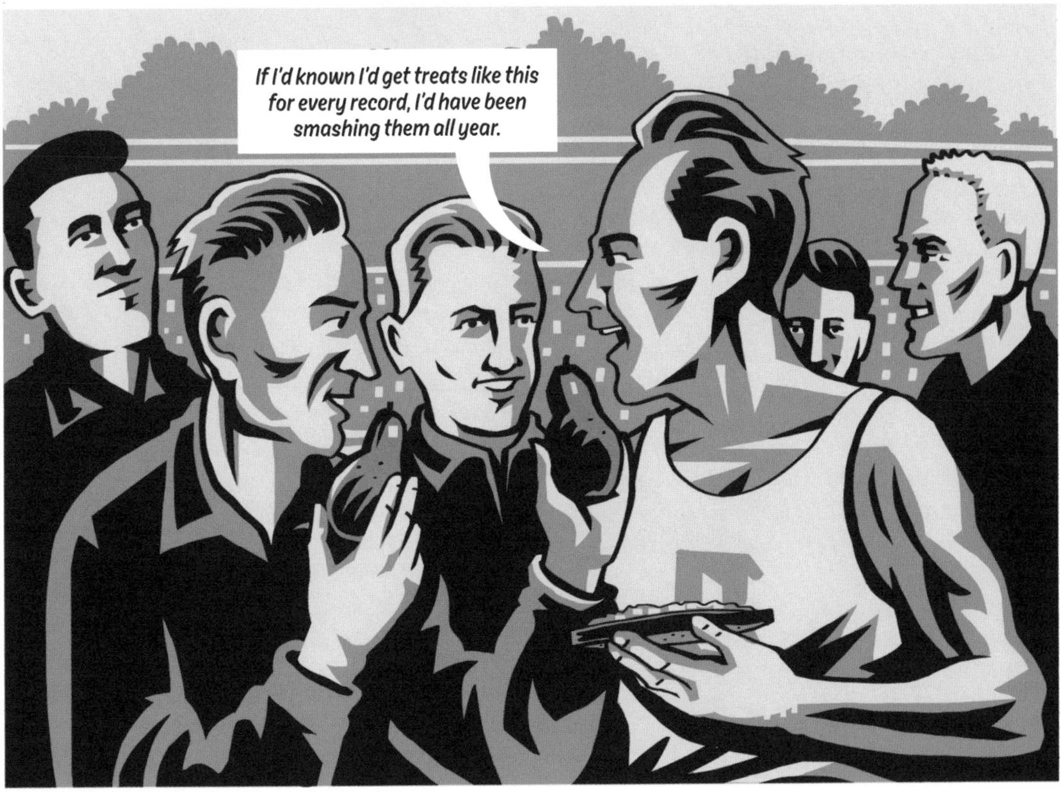
If I'd known I'd get treats like this for every record, I'd have been smashing them all year.

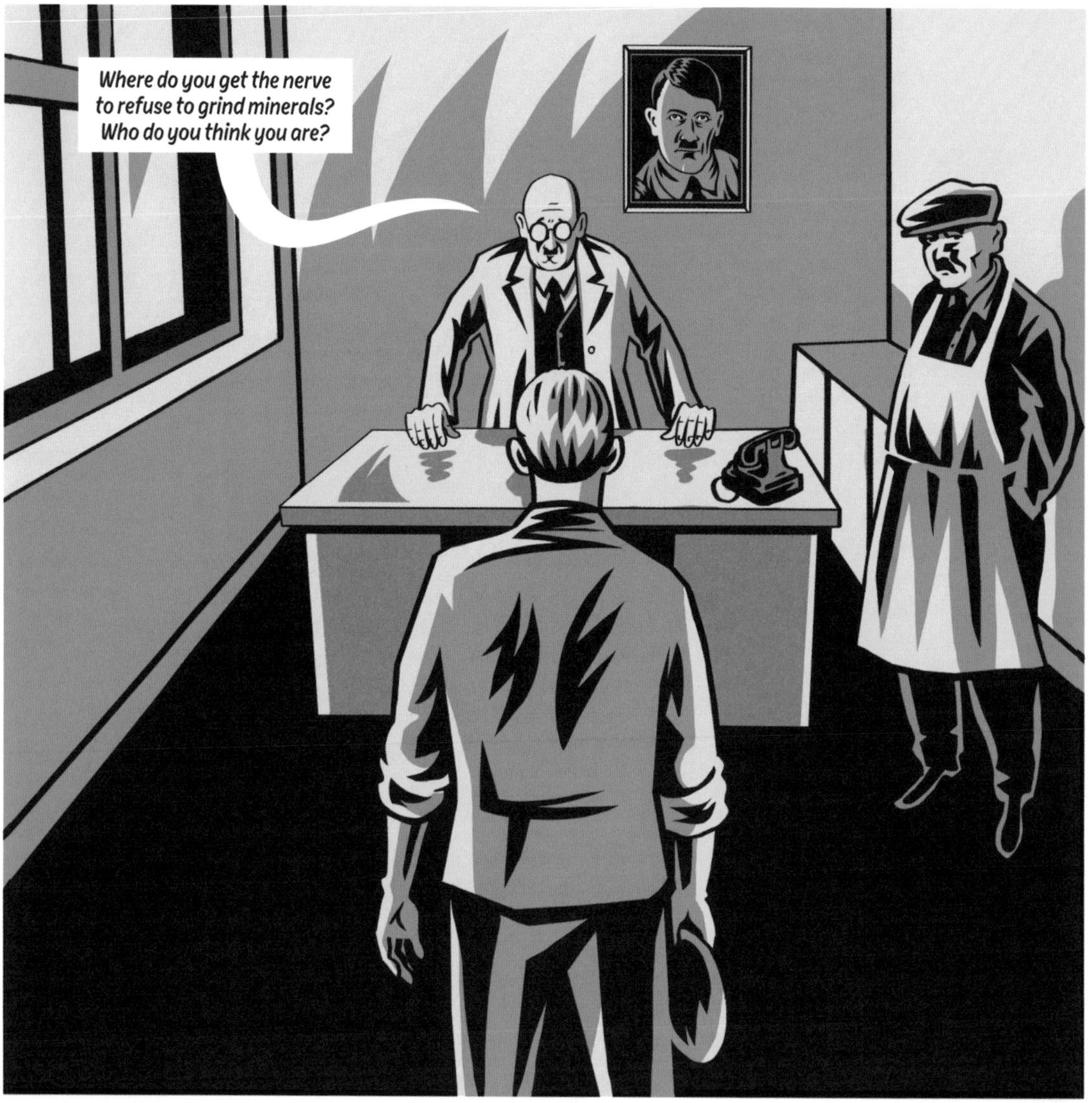
Where do you get the nerve to refuse to grind minerals? Who do you think you are?

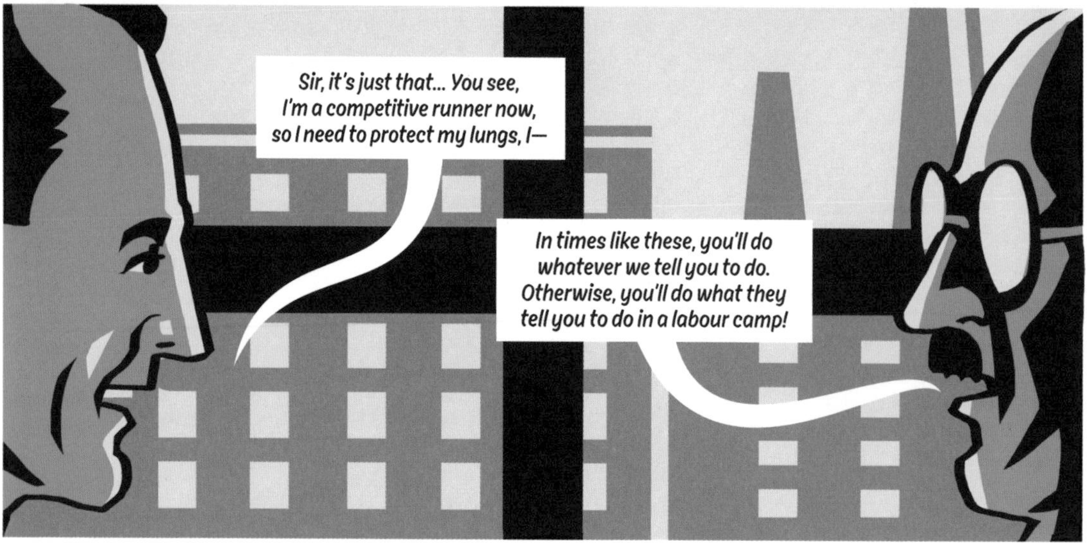
Sir, it's just that... You see, I'm a competitive runner now, so I need to protect my lungs, I—
In times like these, you'll do whatever we tell you to do. Otherwise, you'll do what they tell you to do in a labour camp!

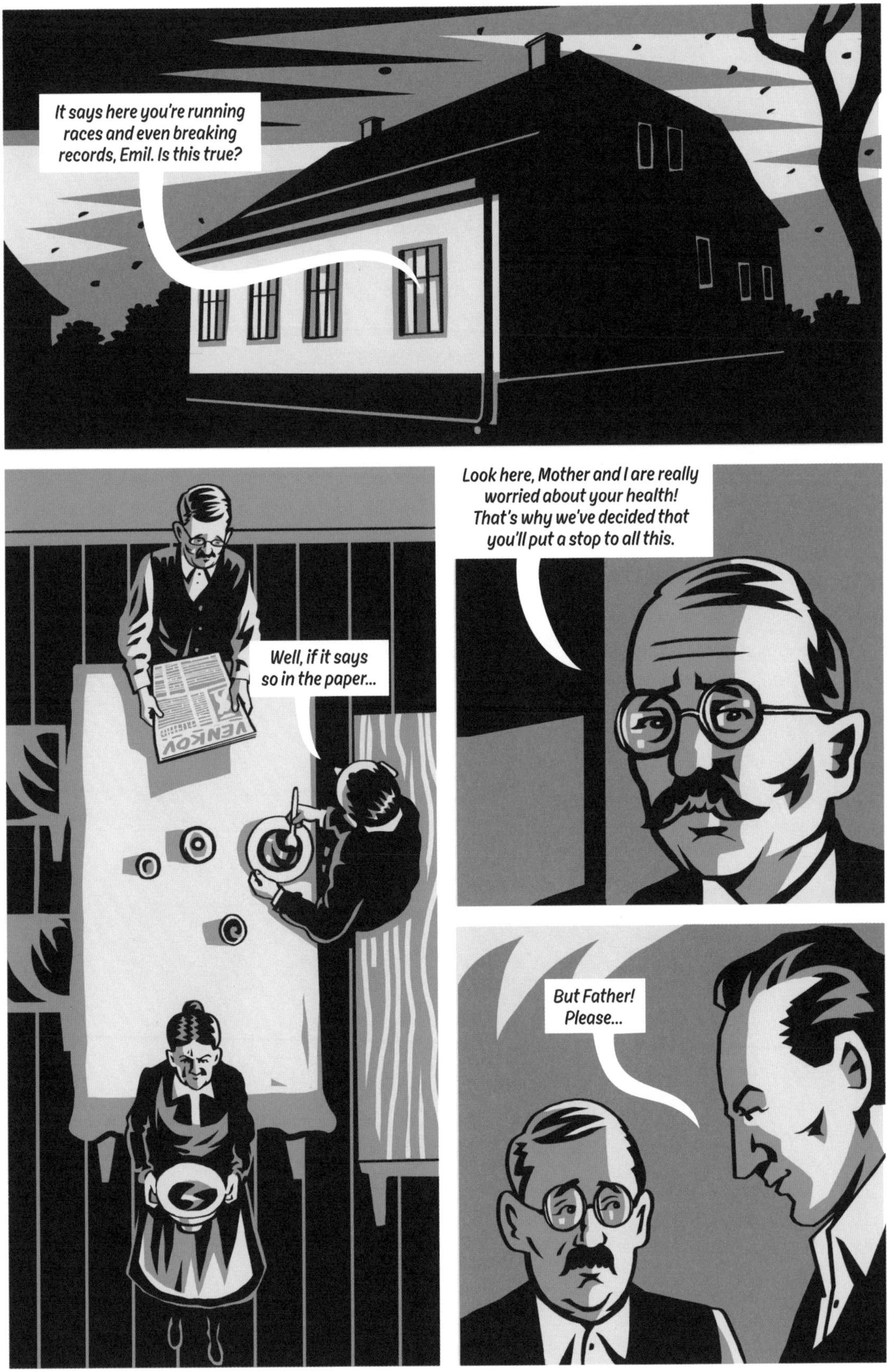
It says here you're running races and even breaking records, Emil. Is this true?
Well, if it says so in the paper...
VENKOV
Look here, Mother and I are really worried about your health! That's why we've decided that you'll put a stop to all this.
But Father! Please...

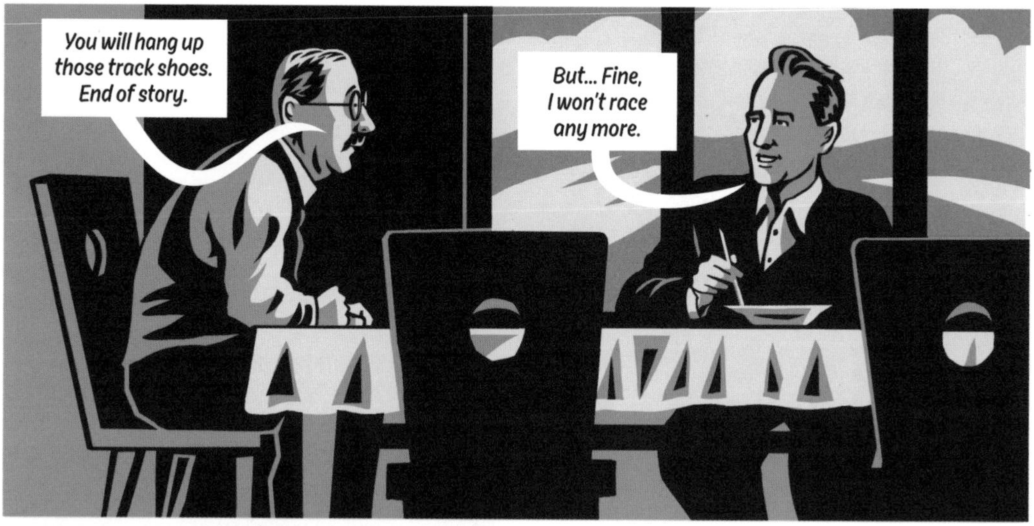
You will hang up those track shoes. End of story.
But... Fine, I won't race any more.

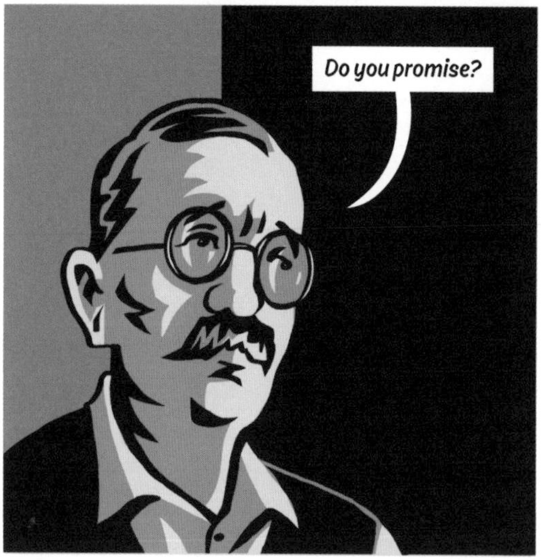
Do you promise?

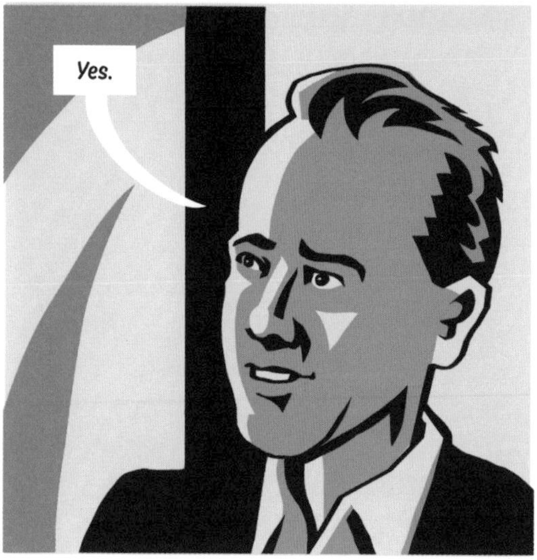
Yes.

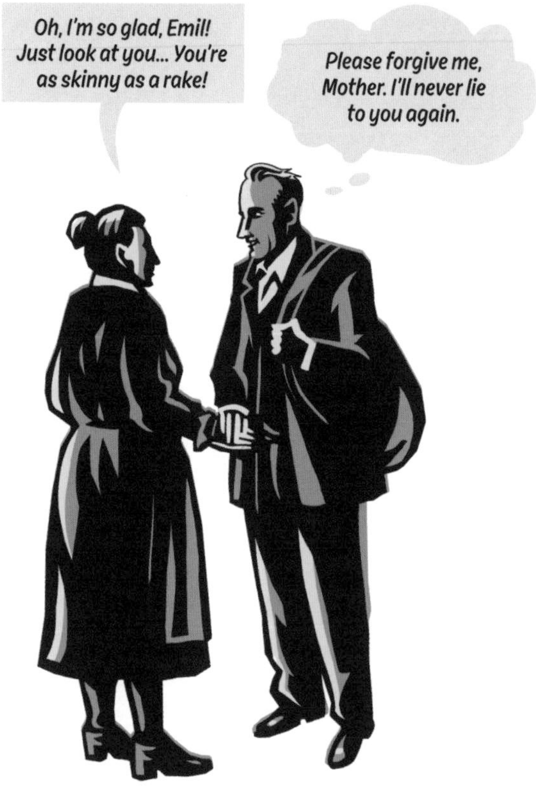
Oh, I'm so glad, Emil! Just look at you... You're as skinny as a rake!
Please forgive me, Mother. I'll never lie to you again.

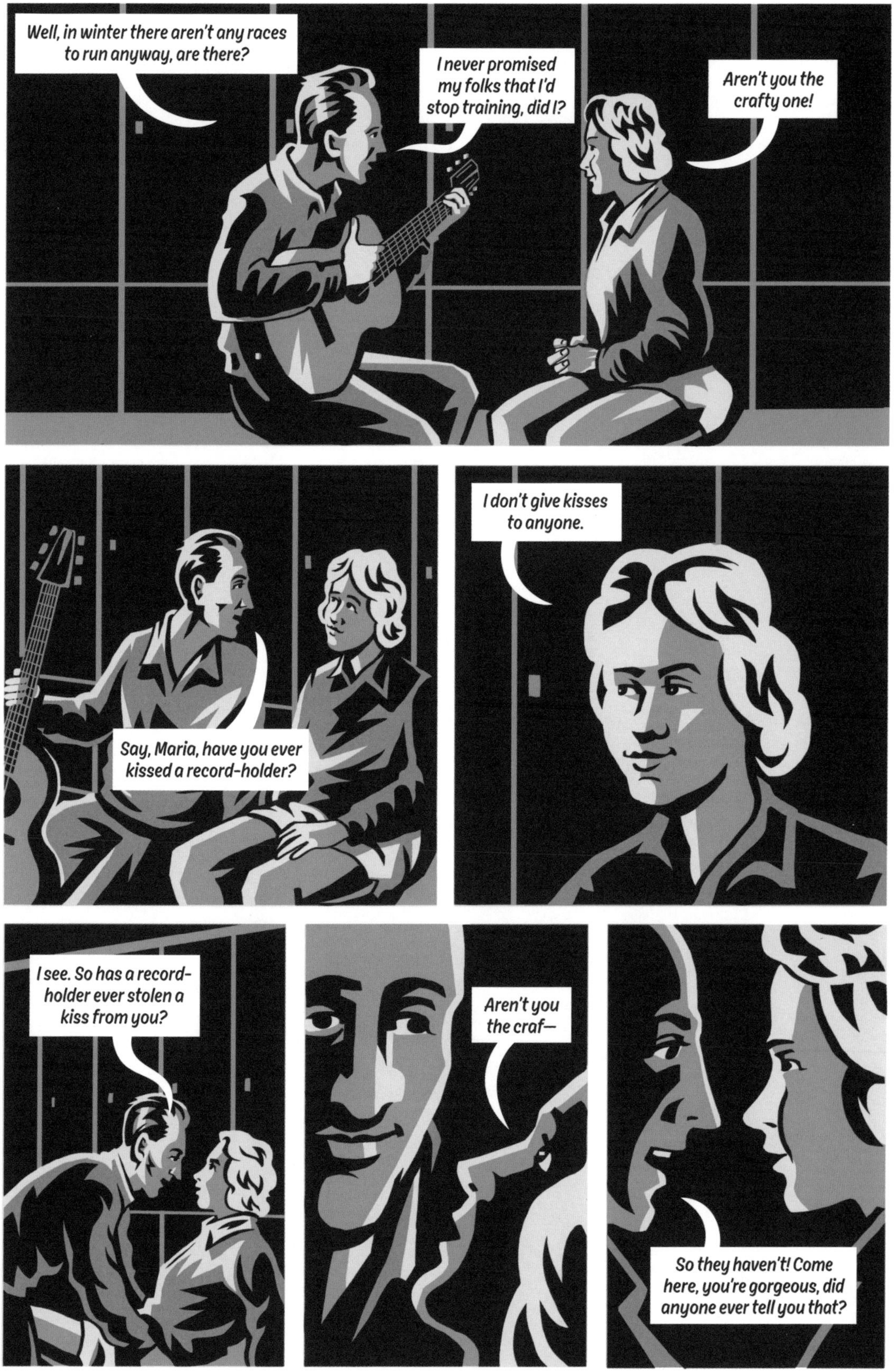
Well, in winter there aren't any races to run anyway, are there?
I never promised my folks that I'd stop training, did I?
Aren't you the crafty one!
Say, Maria, have you ever kissed a record-holder?
I don't give kisses to anyone.
I see. So has a record-holder ever stolen a kiss from you?
Aren't you the craf—
So they haven't! Come here, you're gorgeous, did anyone ever tell you that?

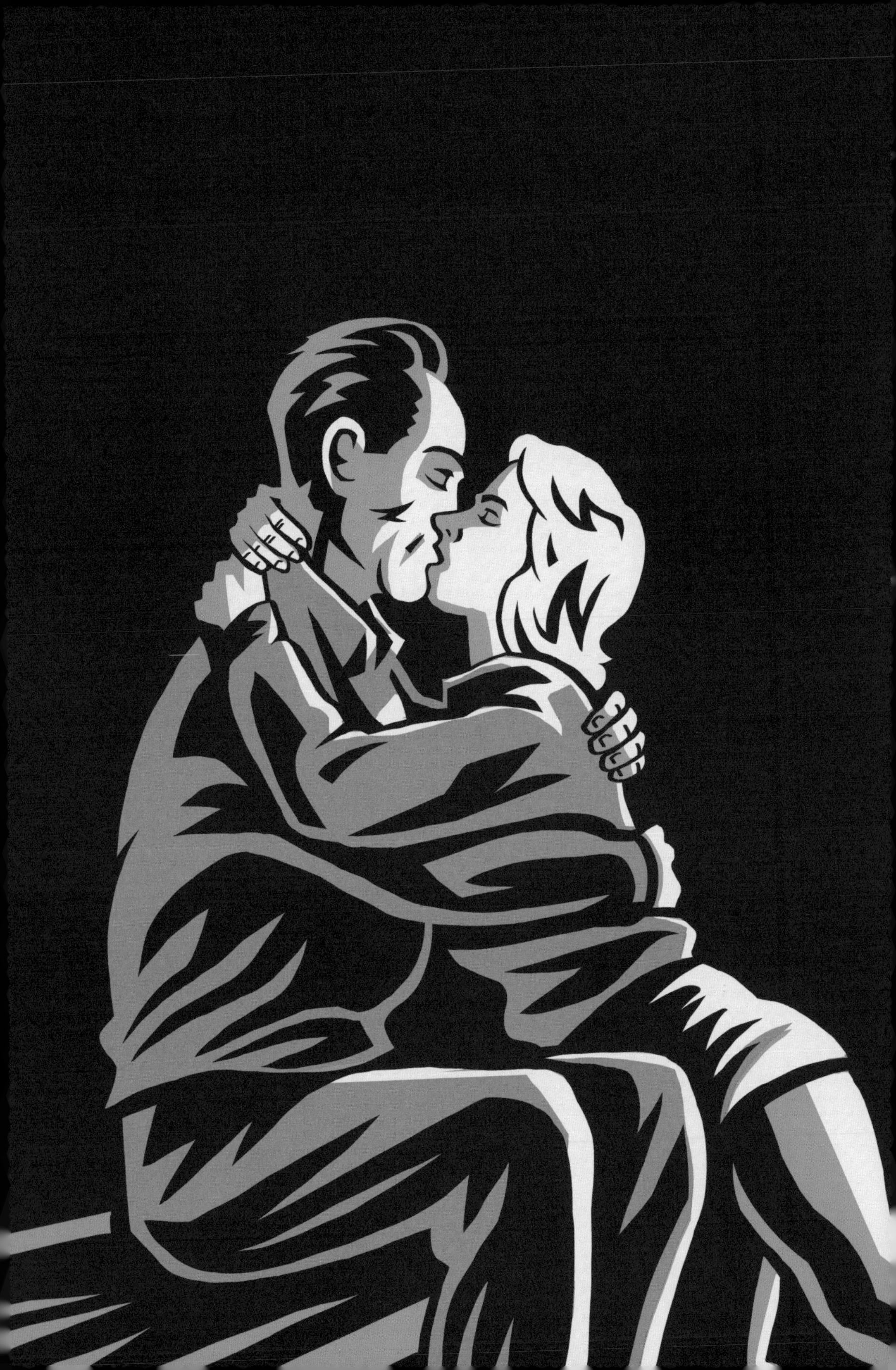

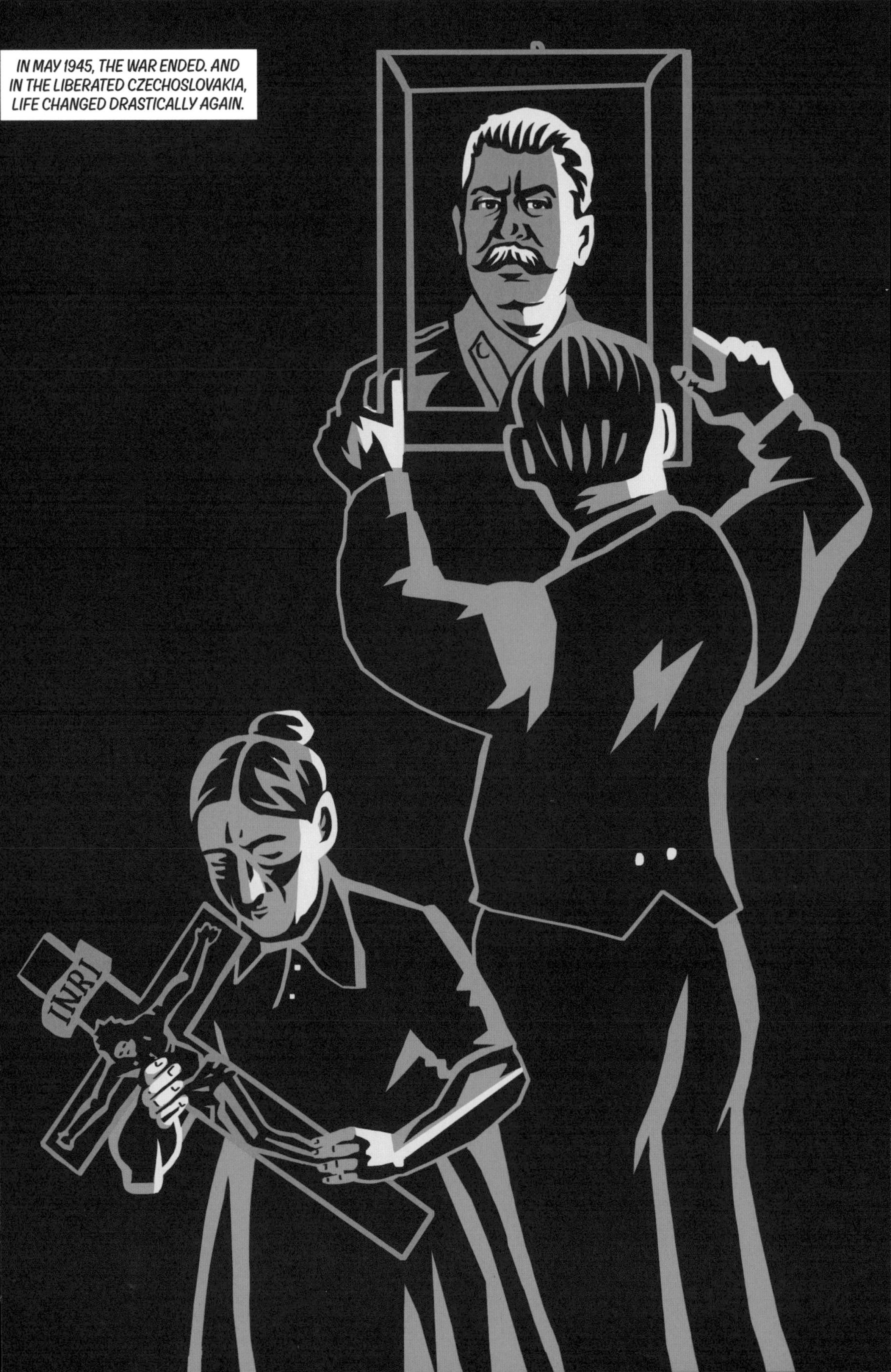
IN MAY 1945, THE WAR ENDED. AND IN THE LIBERATED CZECHOSLOVAKIA, LIFE CHANGED DRASTICALLY AGAIN.
INRI

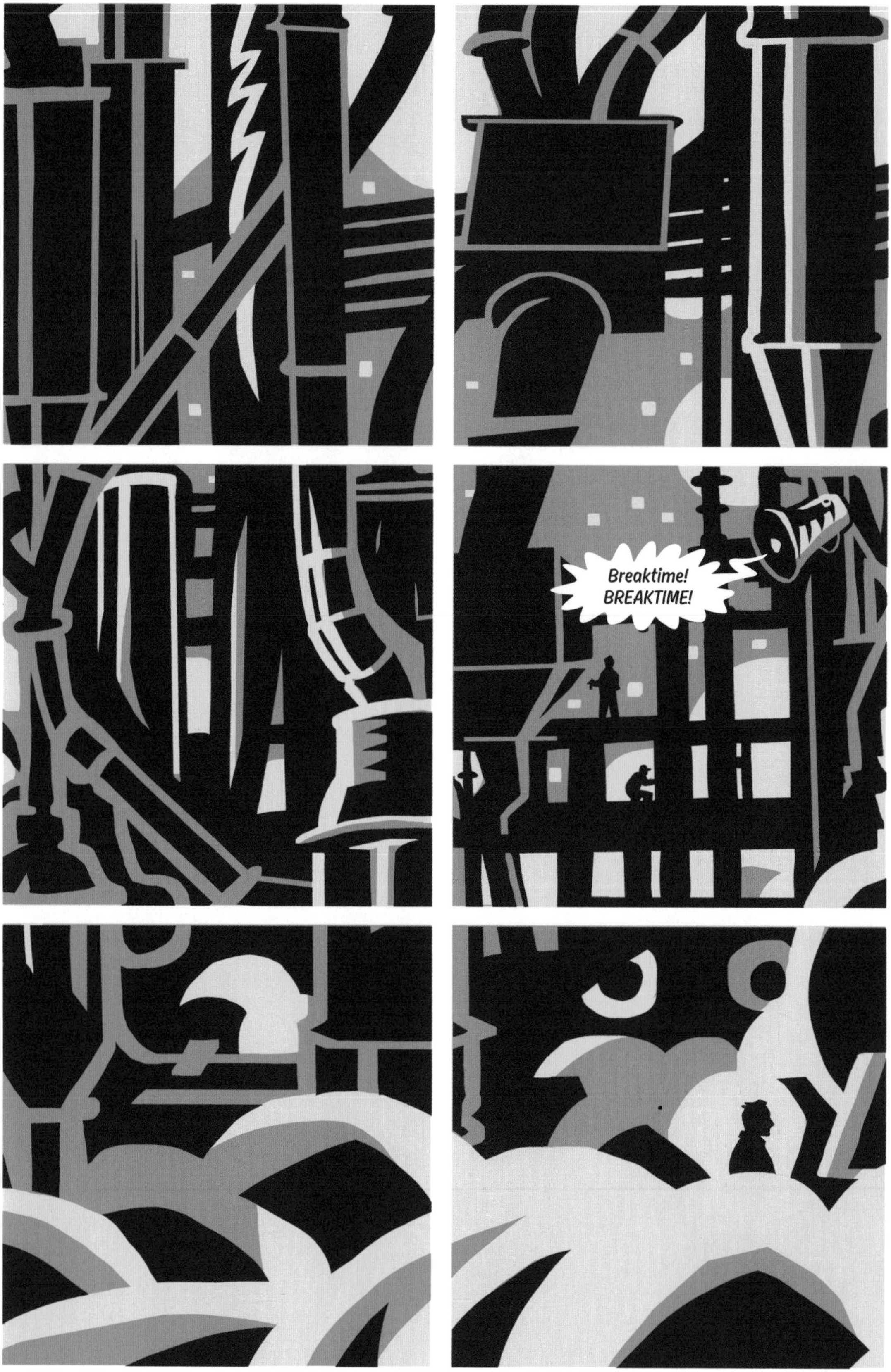
Breaktime! BREAKTIME!

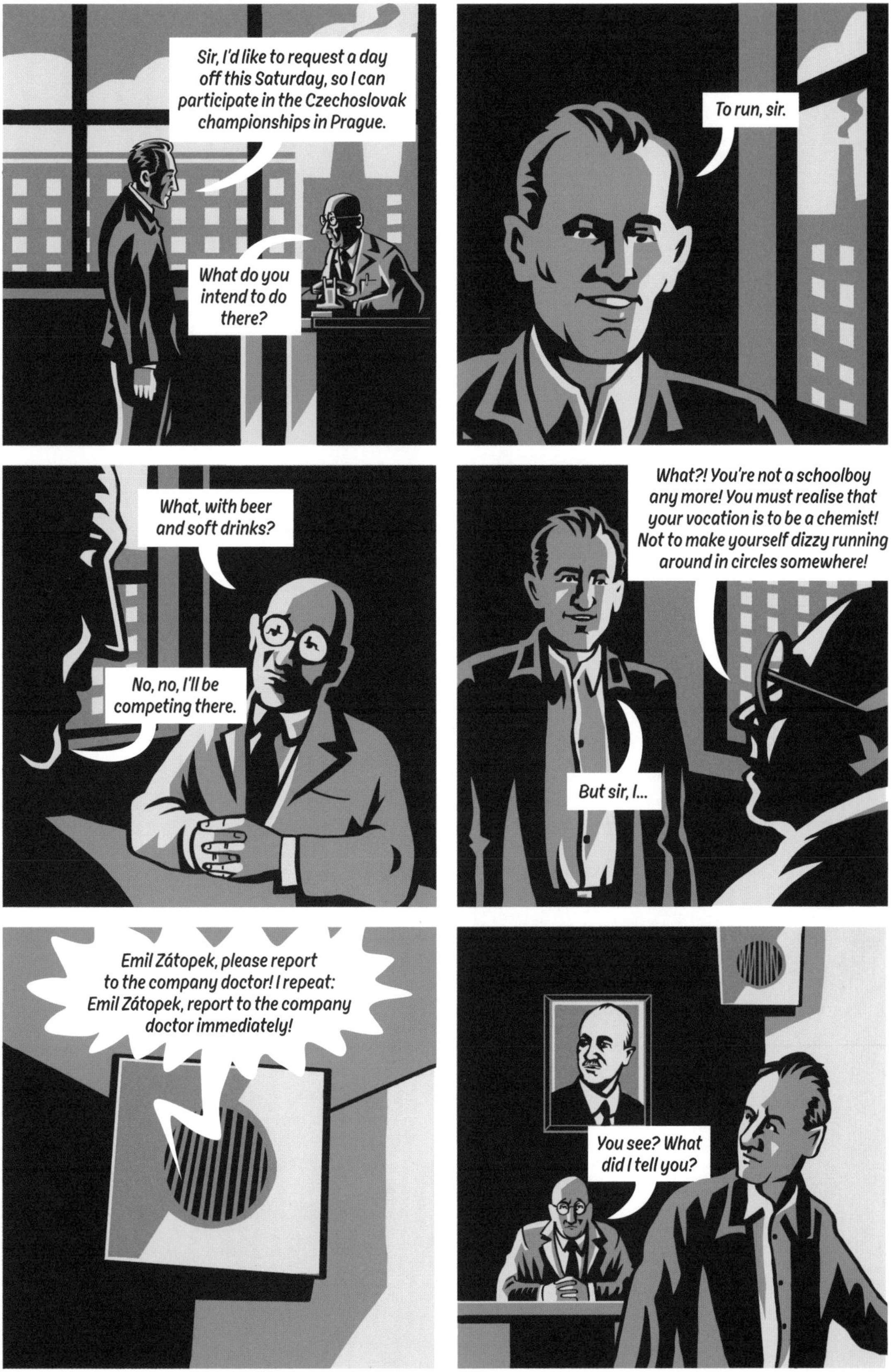

Sir, I'd like to request a day off this Saturday, so I can participate in the Czechoslovak championships in Prague.
What do you intend to do there?
To run, sir.
What, with beer and soft drinks?
No, no, I'll be competing there.
What?! You're not a schoolboy any more! You must realise that your vocation is to be a chemist! Not to make yourself dizzy running around in circles somewhere!
But sir, I...
Emil Zátopek, please report to the company doctor! I repeat: Emil Zátopek, report to the company doctor immediately!
You see? What did I tell you?

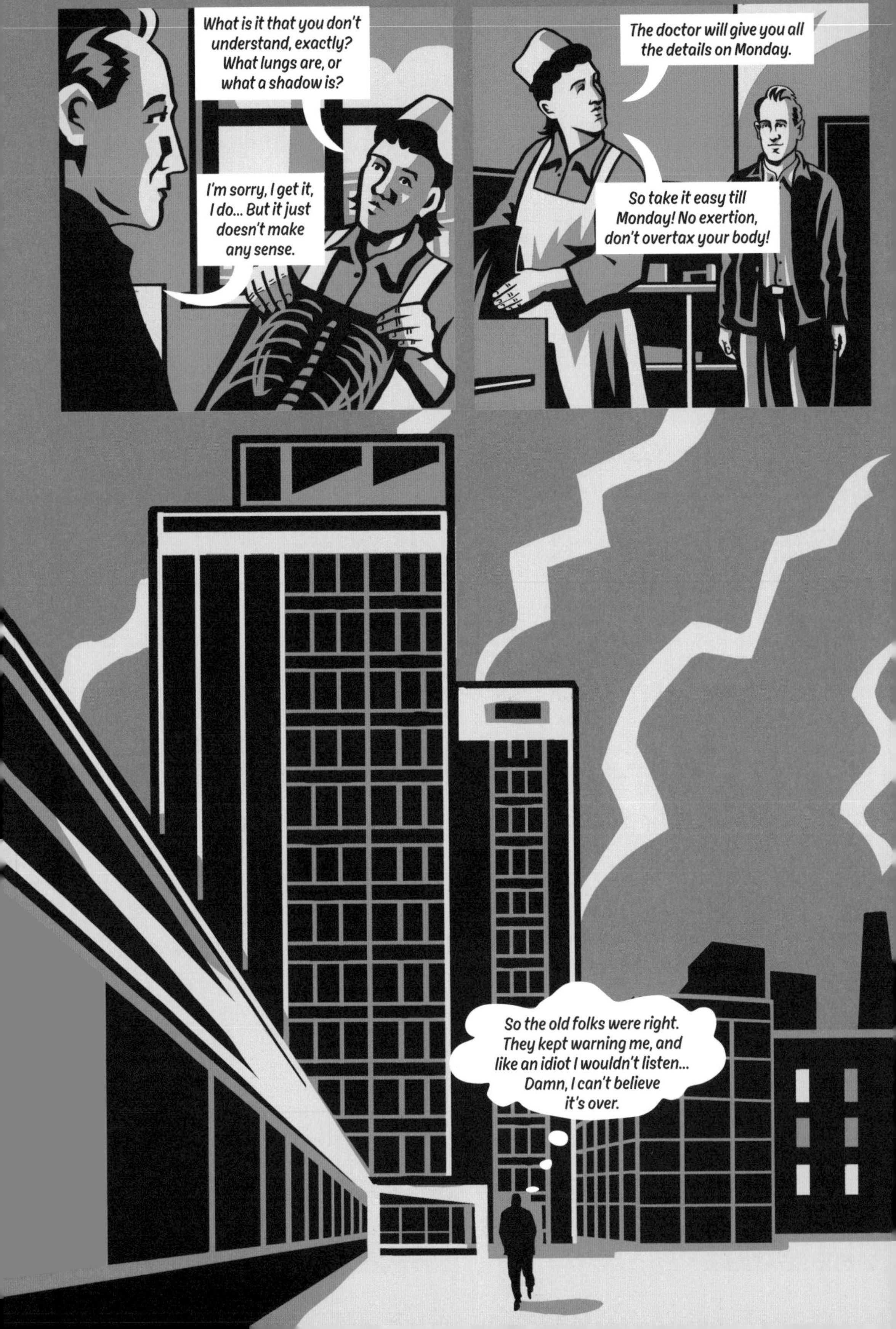
What is it that you don't understand, exactly? What lungs are, or what a shadow is?
I'm sorry, I get it, I do… But it just doesn't make any sense.
The doctor will give you all the details on Monday.
So take it easy till Monday! No exertion, don't overtax your body!
So the old folks were right. They kept warning me, and like an idiot I wouldn't listen… Damn, I can't believe it's over.

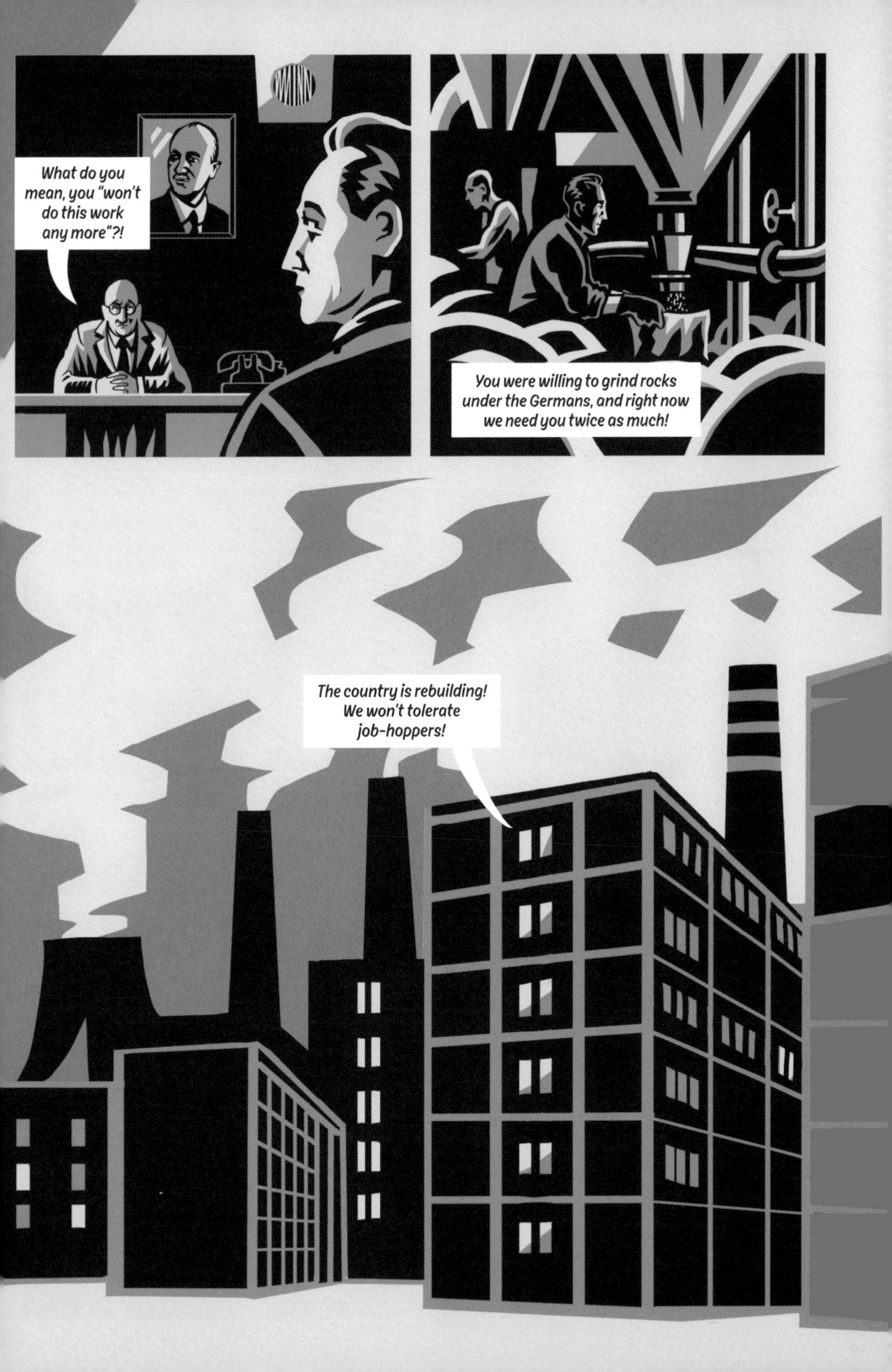
What do you mean, you "won't do this work any more"?!
You were willing to grind rocks under the Germans, and right now we need you twice as much!
The country is rebuilding! We won't tolerate job-hoppers!

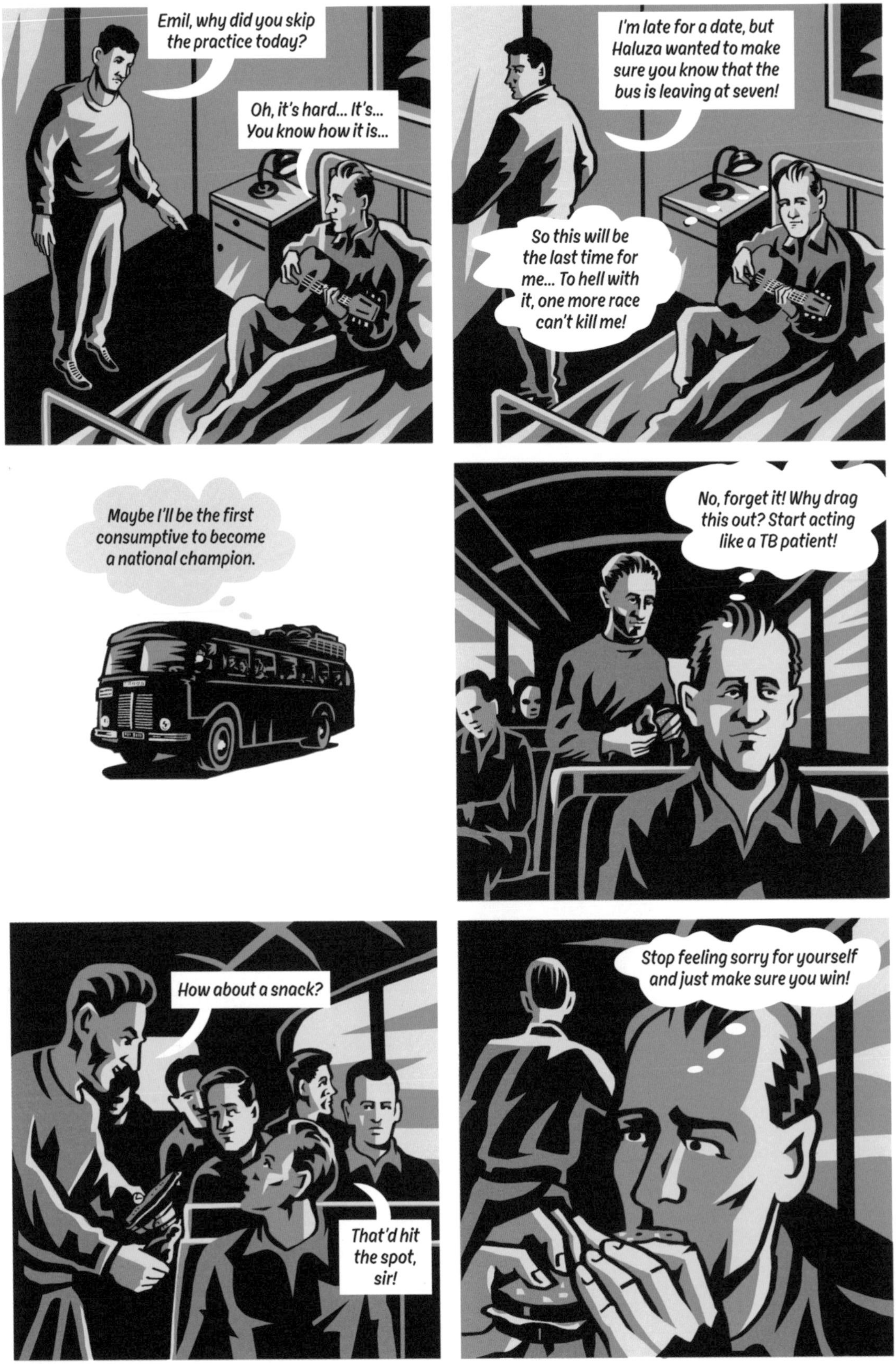
Emil, why did you skip the practice today?
Oh, it's hard... It's... You know how it is...
I'm late for a date, but Haluza wanted to make sure you know that the bus is leaving at seven!
So this will be the last time for me... To hell with it, one more race can't kill me!
Maybe I'll be the first consumptive to become a national champion.
No, forget it! Why drag this out? Start acting like a TB patient!
How about a snack?
That'd hit the spot, sir!
Stop feeling sorry for yourself and just make sure you win!

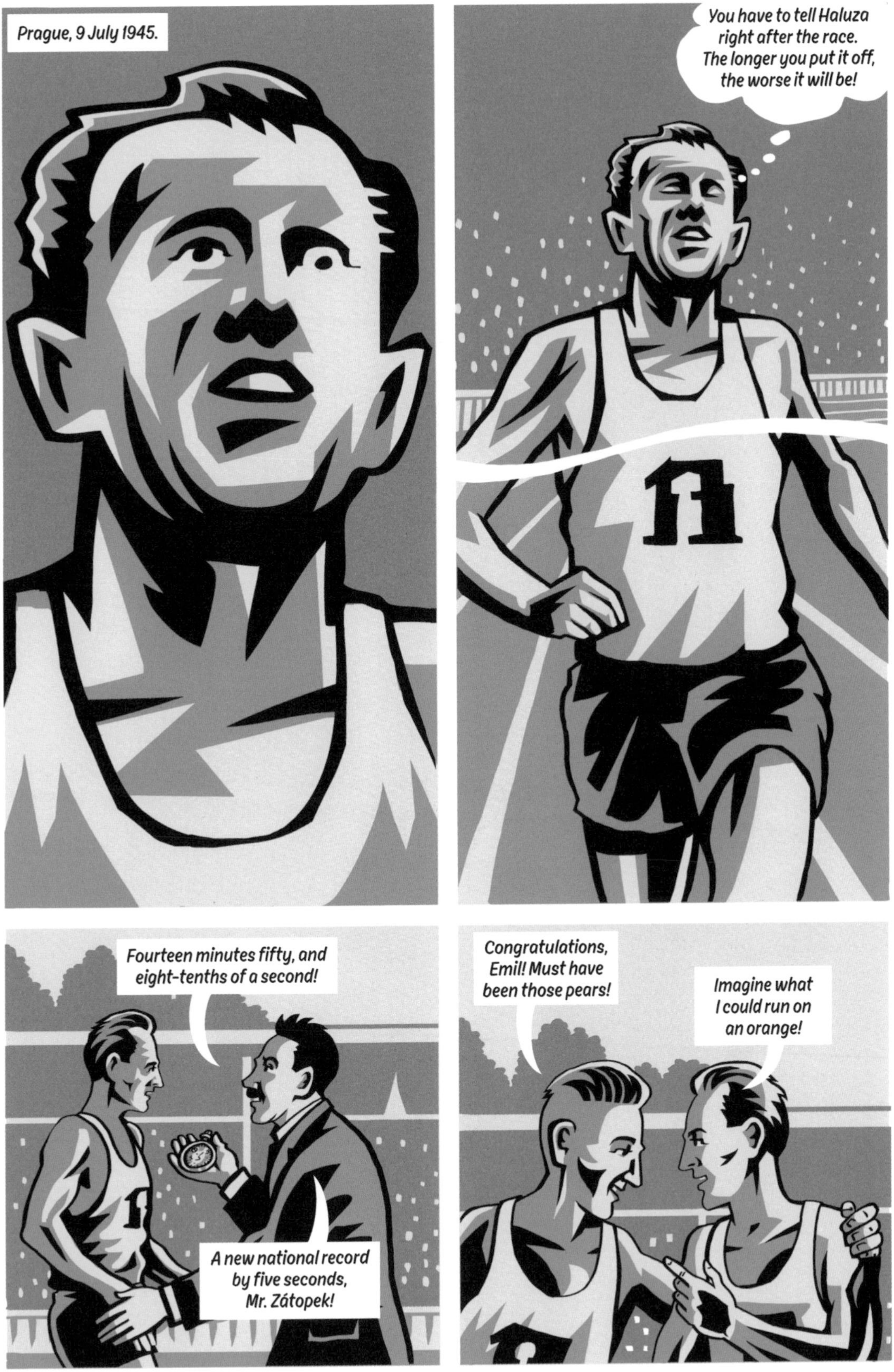

Prague, 9 July 1945.
You have to tell Haluza right after the race. The longer you put it off, the worse it will be!
Fourteen minutes fifty, and eight-tenths of a second!
A new national record by five seconds, Mr. Zátopek!
Congratulations, Emil! Must have been those pears!
Imagine what I could run on an orange!

So who's your coach in Zlín? No one, am I right? With us in the army, you'll get the best coaches, the best doctors, the best masseurs!

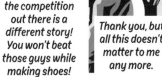

The war's over now, and our members are going abroad to represent our country! And the competition out there is a different story! You won't beat those guys while making shoes!

Thank you, but all this doesn't matter to me any more.

Nowadays, the army is the only way to get ahead!

Next time, I *will* get you that orange from somewhere, Emil!

Fifty-three bottles of beer on the wall...

If one of those bottles should happen to fall...

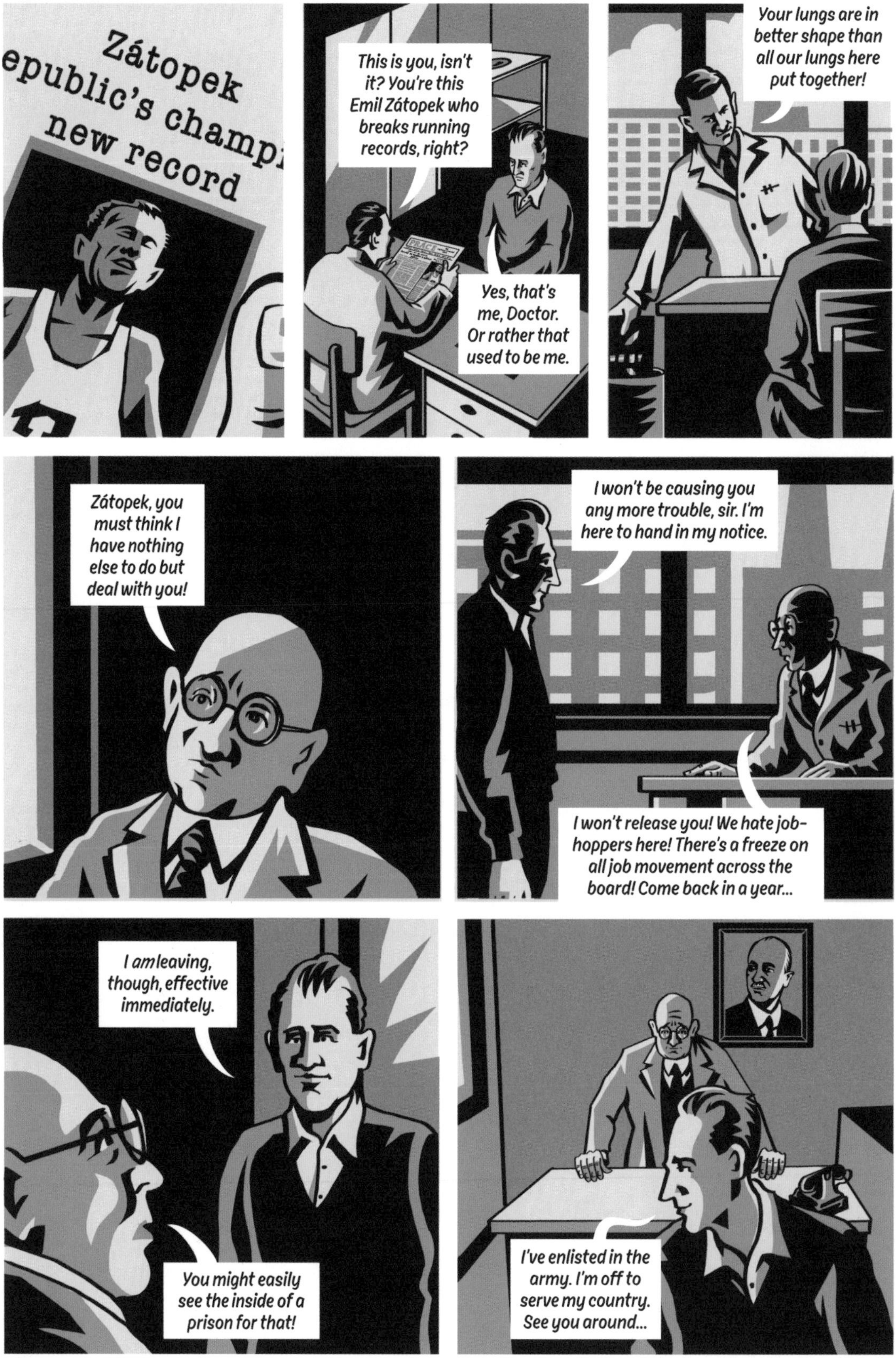
Zátopek
epublic's champi
new record
This is you, isn't it? You're this Emil Zátopek who breaks running records, right?
Yes, that's me, Doctor. Or rather that used to be me.
Your lungs are in better shape than all our lungs here put together!
Zátopek, you must think I have nothing else to do but deal with you!
I won't be causing you any more trouble, sir. I'm here to hand in my notice.
I won't release you! We hate job-hoppers here! There's a freeze on all job movement across the board! Come back in a year...
I *am* leaving, though, effective immediately.
You might easily see the inside of a prison for that!
I've enlisted in the army. I'm off to serve my country. See you around...

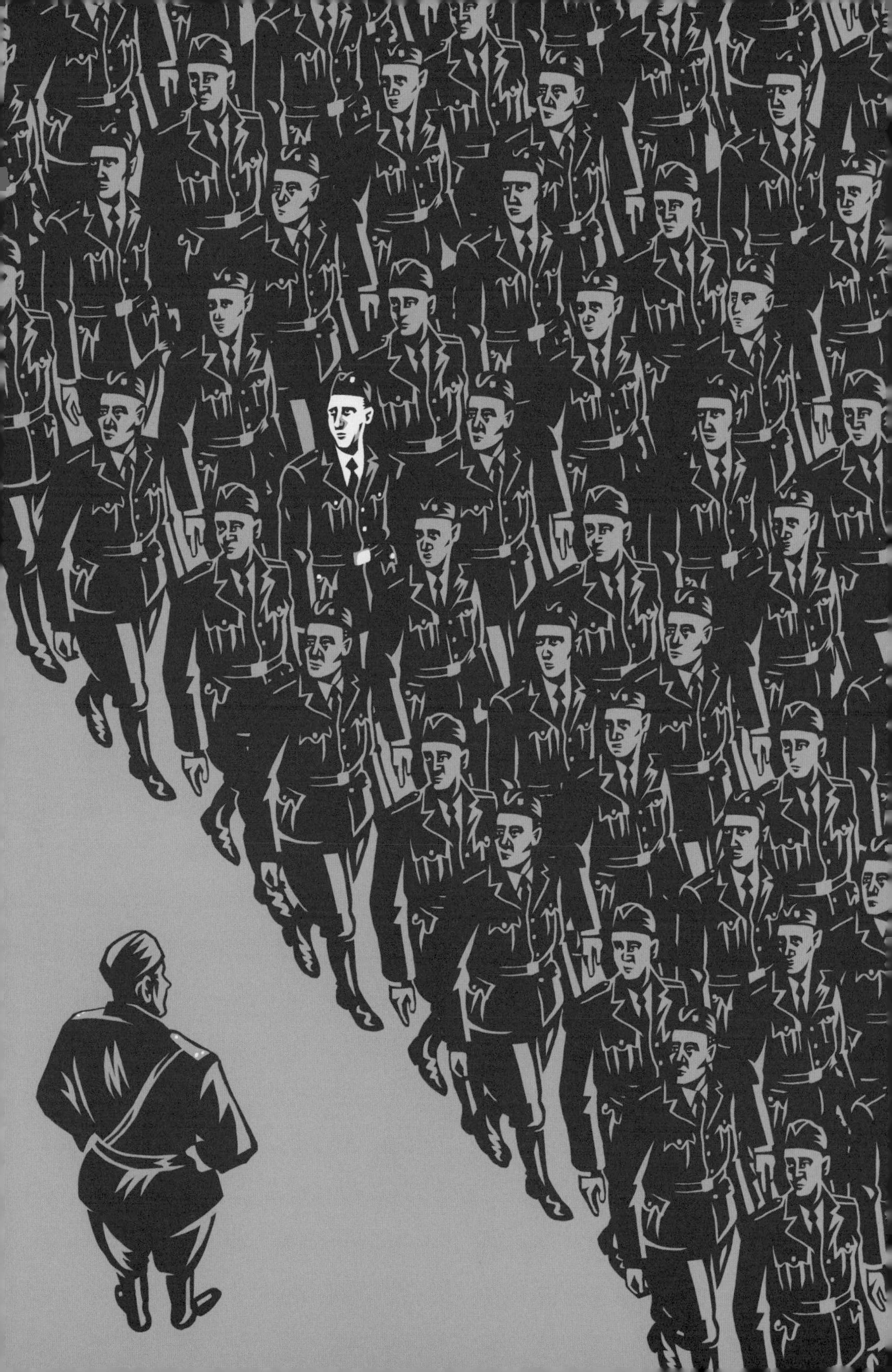

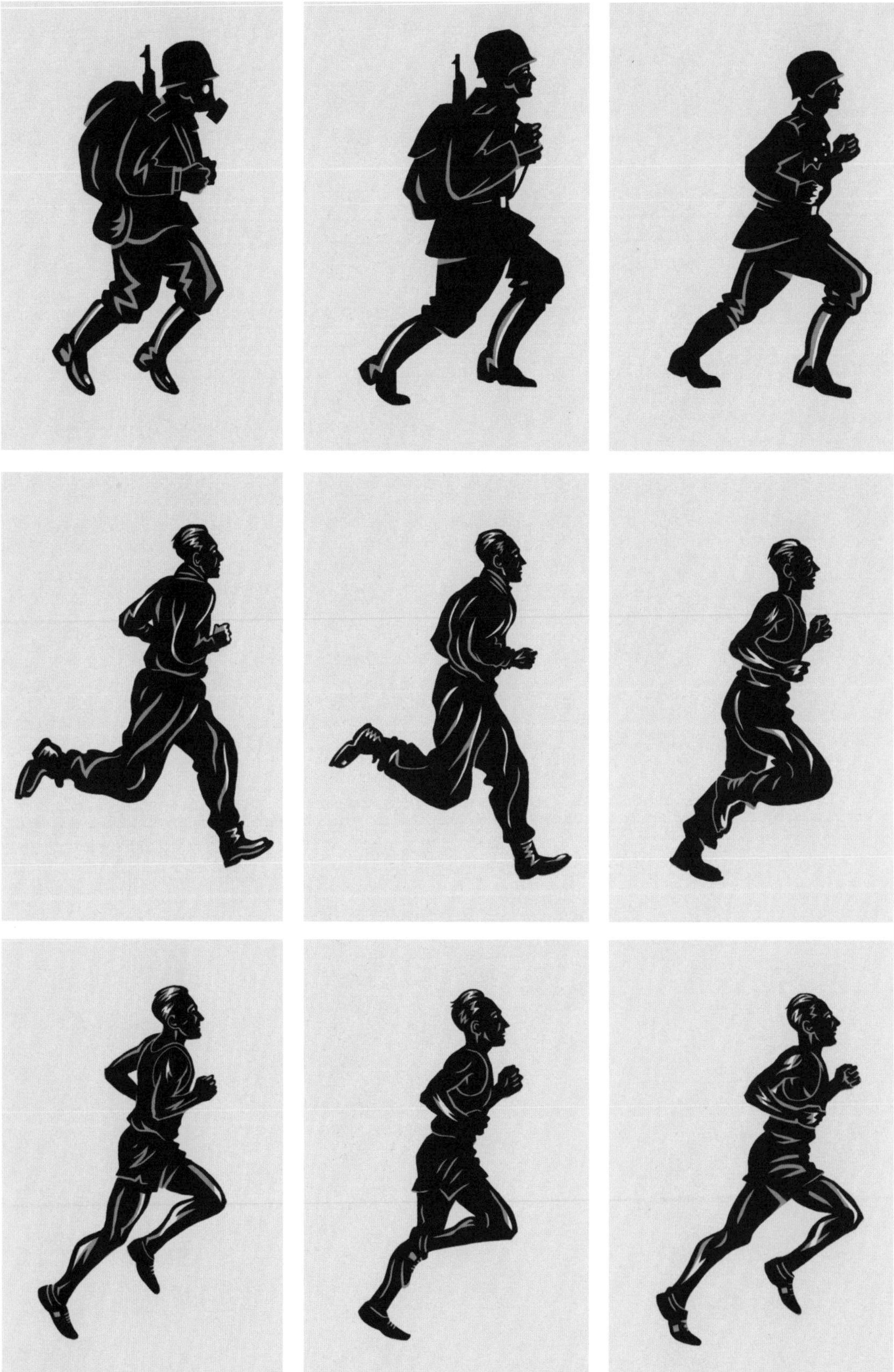

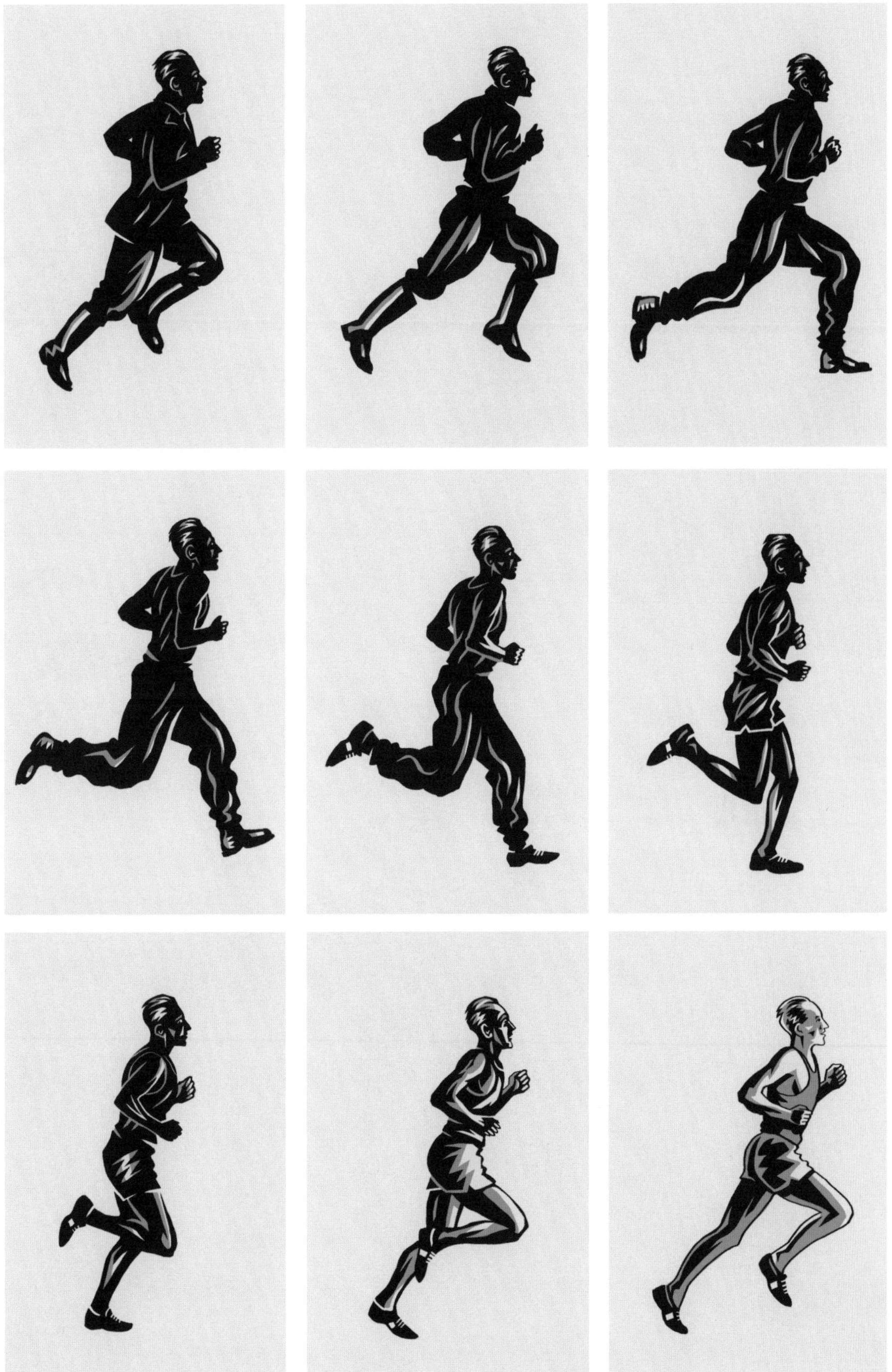

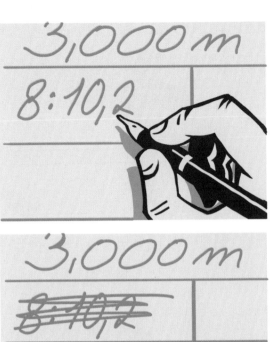

3,000 m

8:10,2

3,000 m

~~8:10,2~~

8:08,8

CZECHOSLOVAK NATIONAL
CHAMPIONSHIPS, 1946.

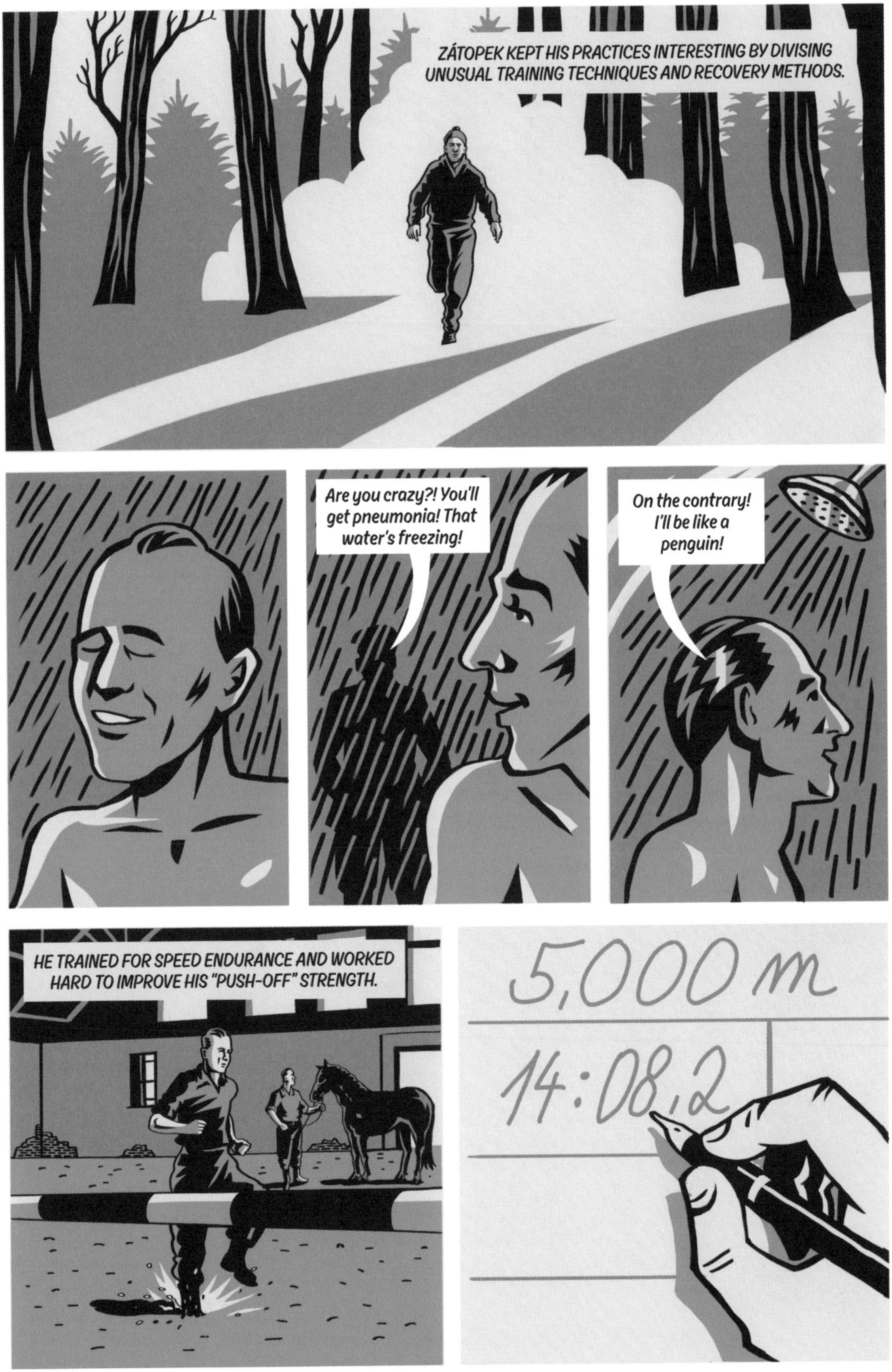
ZÁTOPEK KEPT HIS PRACTICES INTERESTING BY DIVISING UNUSUAL TRAINING TECHNIQUES AND RECOVERY METHODS.
Are you crazy?! You'll get pneumonia! That water's freezing!
On the contrary! I'll be like a penguin!
HE TRAINED FOR SPEED ENDURANCE AND WORKED HARD TO IMPROVE HIS "PUSH-OFF" STRENGTH.
5,000 m
14:08,2

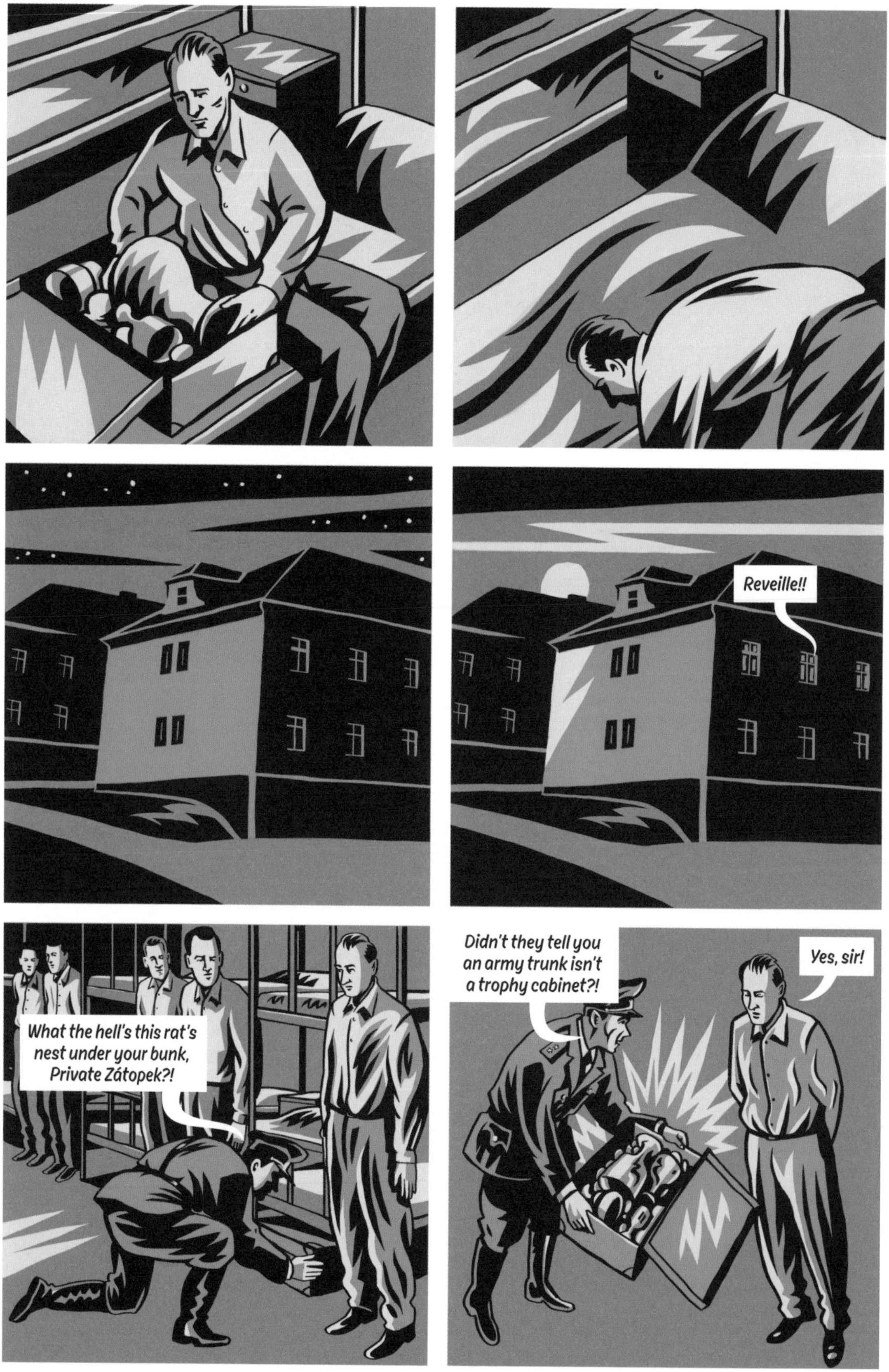
Reveille!!
What the hell's this rat's nest under your bunk, Private Zátopek?!
Didn't they tell you an army trunk isn't a trophy cabinet?!
Yes, sir!

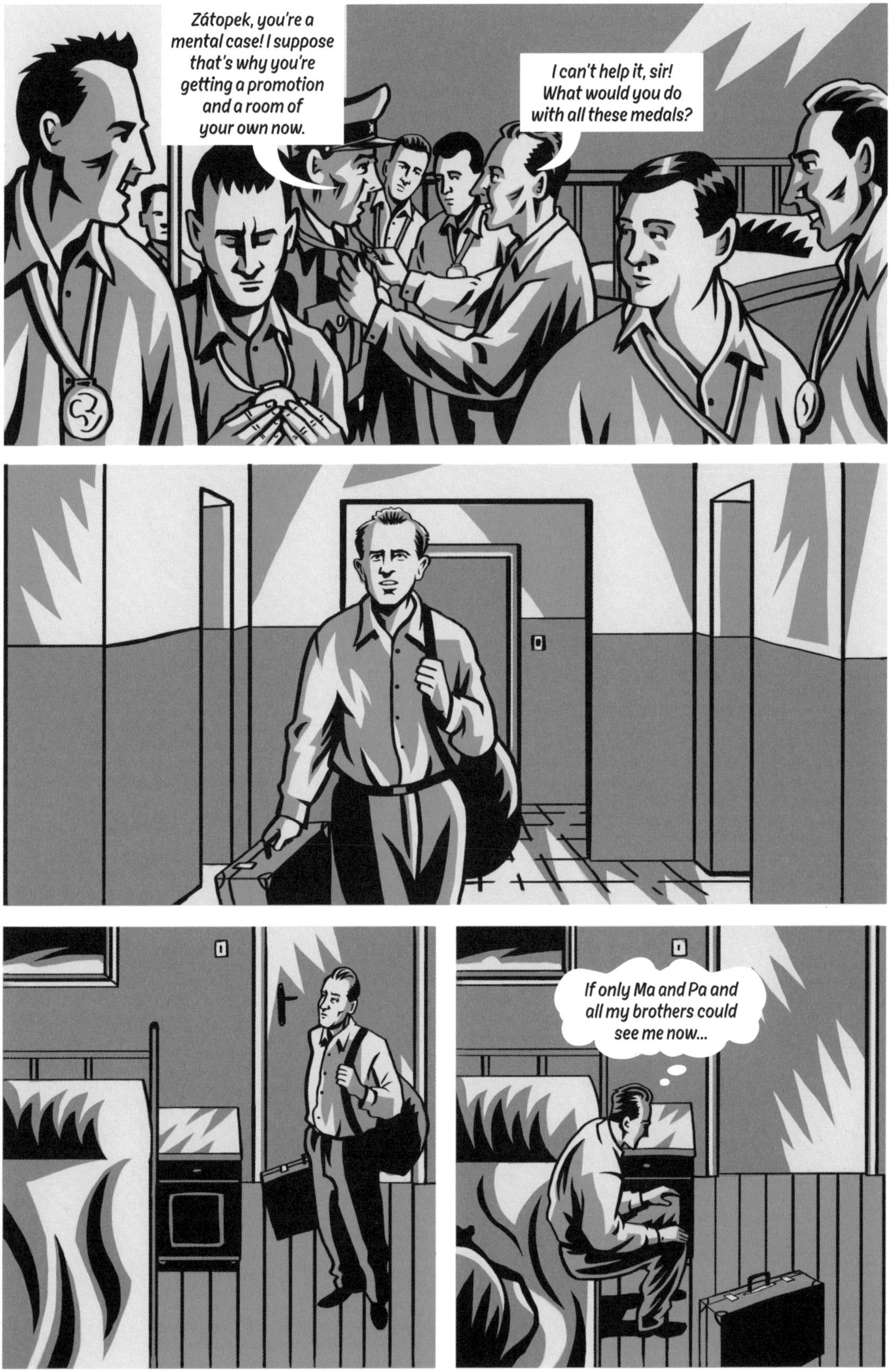
Zátopek, you're a mental case! I suppose that's why you're getting a promotion and a room of your own now.
I can't help it, sir! What would you do with all these medals?
If only Ma and Pa and all my brothers could see me now...

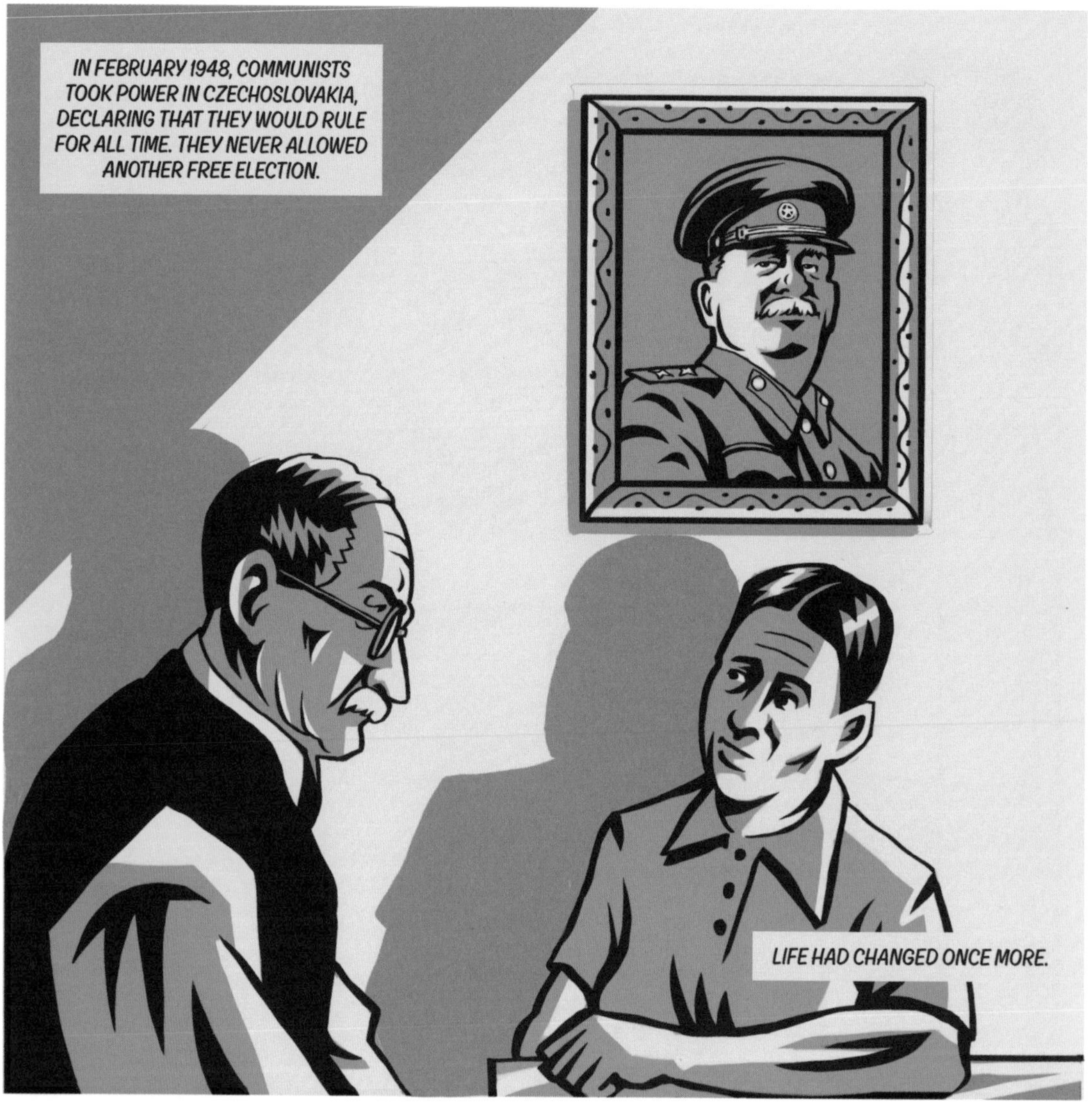
IN FEBRUARY 1948, COMMUNISTS TOOK POWER IN CZECHOSLOVAKIA, DECLARING THAT THEY WOULD RULE FOR ALL TIME. THEY NEVER ALLOWED ANOTHER FREE ELECTION.
LIFE HAD CHANGED ONCE MORE.

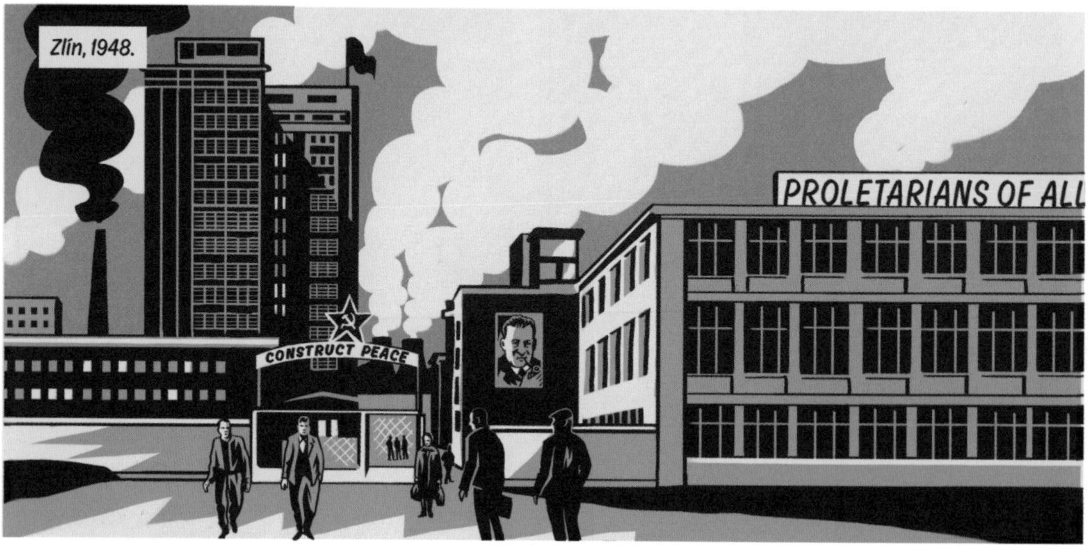
Zlín, 1948.
PROLETARIANS OF ALL
CONSTRUCT PEACE

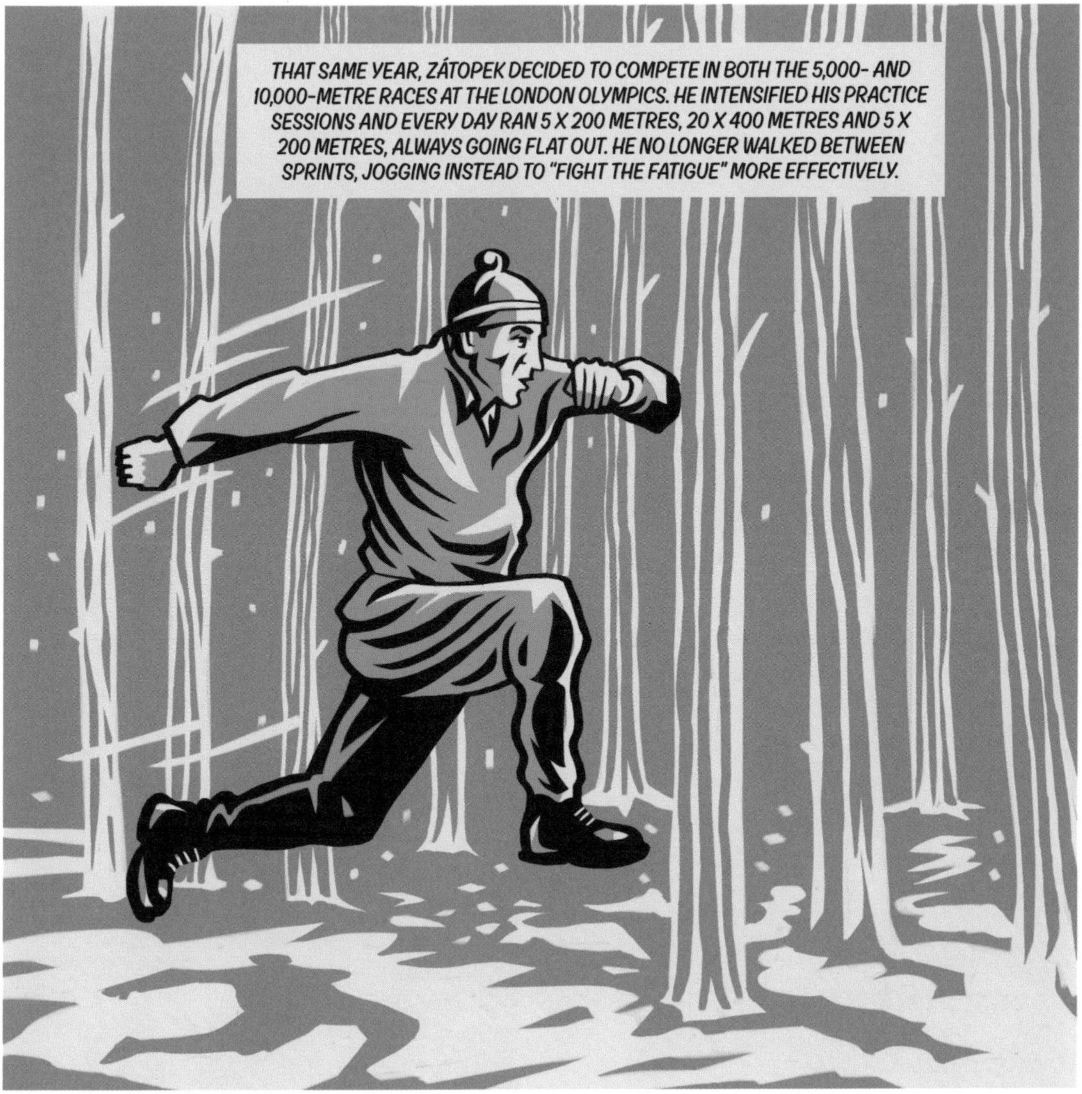
THAT SAME YEAR, ZÁTOPEK DECIDED TO COMPETE IN BOTH THE 5,000- AND 10,000-METRE RACES AT THE LONDON OLYMPICS. HE INTENSIFIED HIS PRACTICE SESSIONS AND EVERY DAY RAN 5 X 200 METRES, 20 X 400 METRES AND 5 X 200 METRES, ALWAYS GOING FLAT OUT. HE NO LONGER WALKED BETWEEN SPRINTS, JOGGING INSTEAD TO "FIGHT THE FATIGUE" MORE EFFECTIVELY.

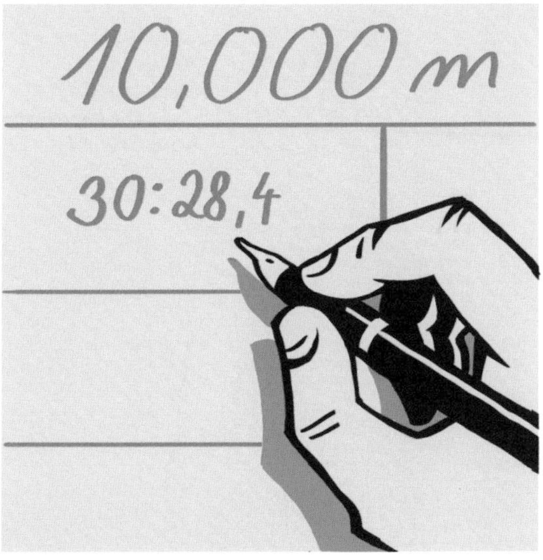
10,000 m
30:28,4

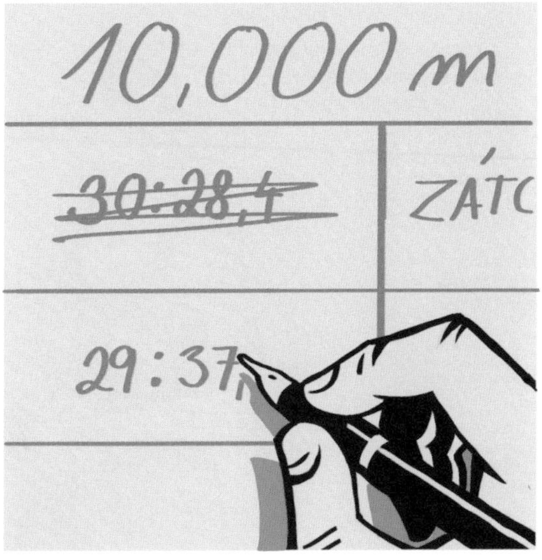
10,000 m
~~30:28,4~~
ZÁTO
29:37,

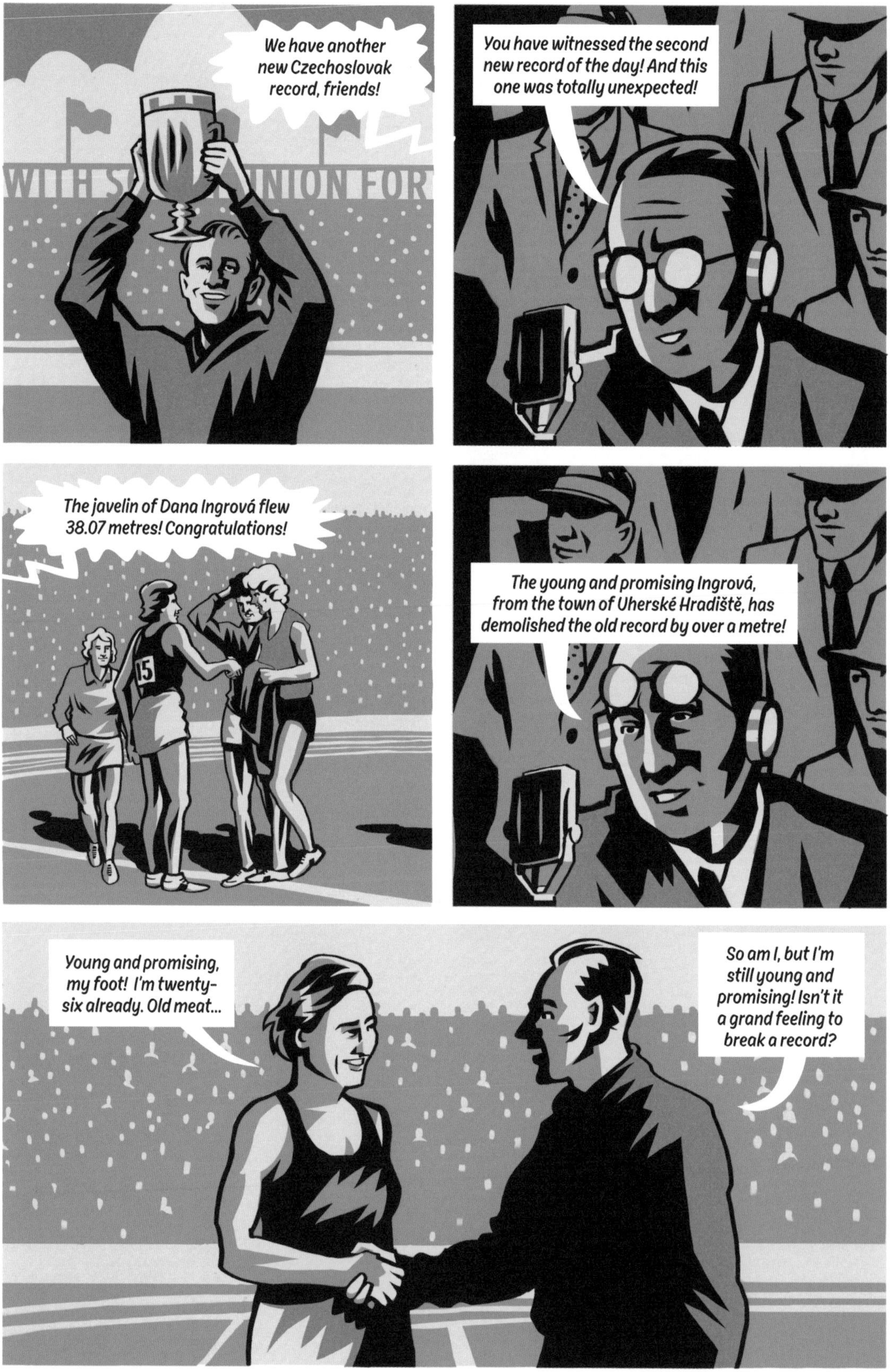

WITH S UNION FOR
We have another new Czechoslovak record, friends!
You have witnessed the second new record of the day! And this one was totally unexpected!
The javelin of Dana Ingrová flew 38.07 metres! Congratulations!
15
The young and promising Ingrová, from the town of Uherské Hradiště, has demolished the old record by over a metre!
Young and promising, my foot! I'm twenty-six already. Old meat...
So am I, but I'm still young and promising! Isn't it a grand feeling to break a record?

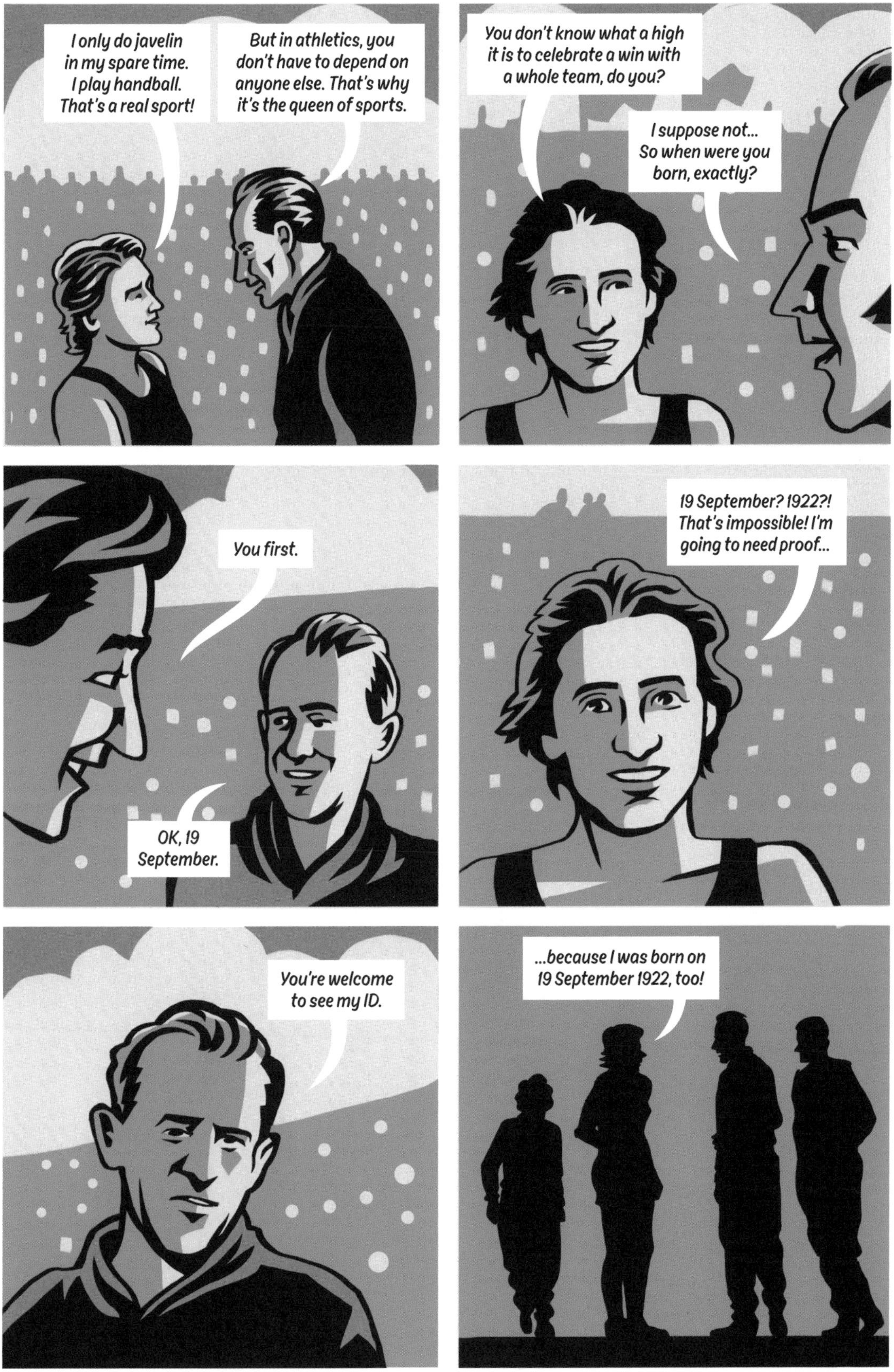
I only do javelin in my spare time. I play handball. That's a real sport!
But in athletics, you don't have to depend on anyone else. That's why it's the queen of sports.
You don't know what a high it is to celebrate a win with a whole team, do you?
I suppose not... So when were you born, exactly?
You first.
OK, 19 September.
19 September? 1922?! That's impossible! I'm going to need proof...
You're welcome to see my ID.
...because I was born on 19 September 1922, too!

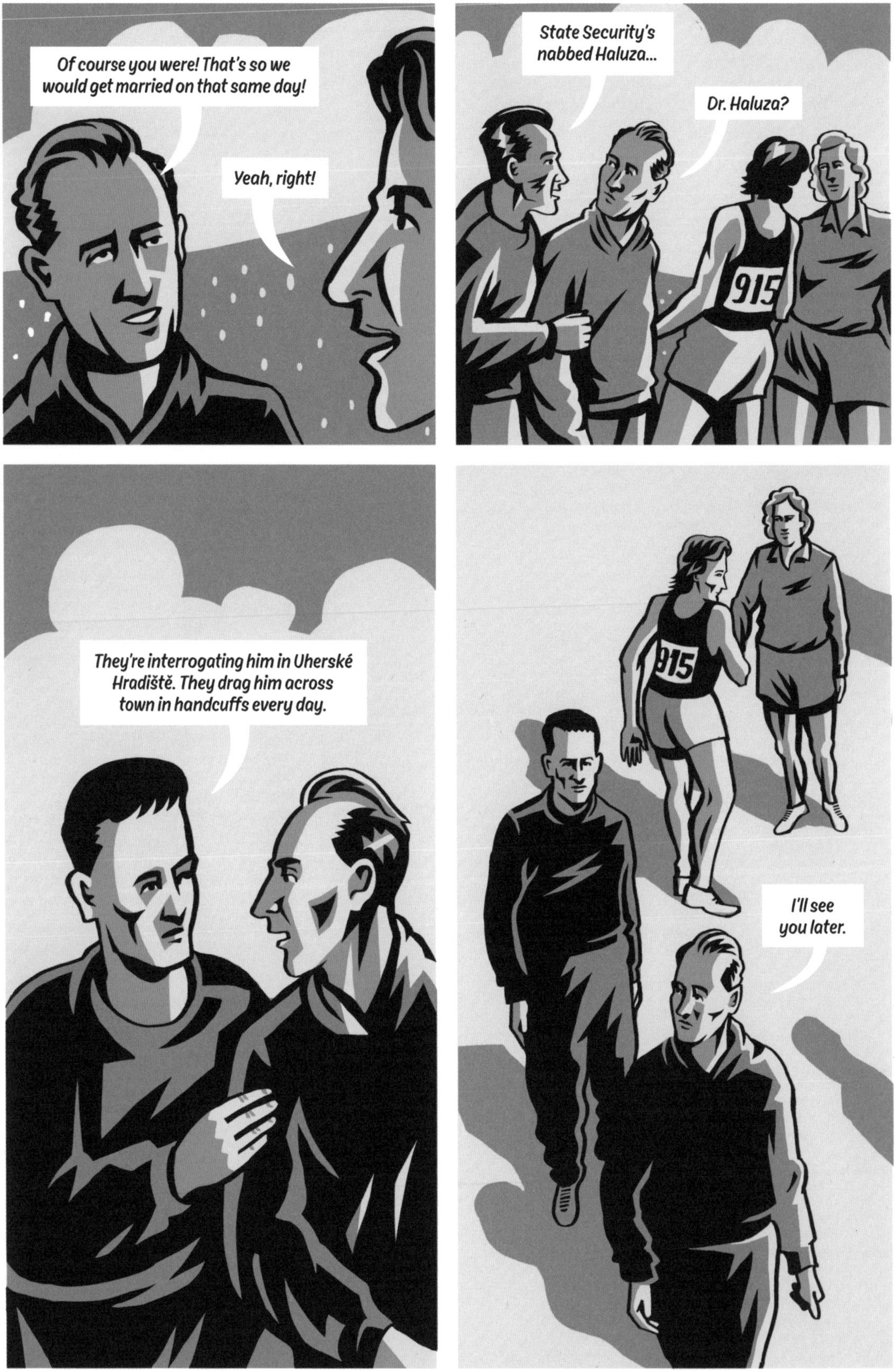
Of course you were! That's so we would get married on that same day!
Yeah, right!
State Security's nabbed Haluza...
Dr. Haluza?
915
They're interrogating him in Uherské Hradiště. They drag him across town in handcuffs every day.
915
I'll see you later.

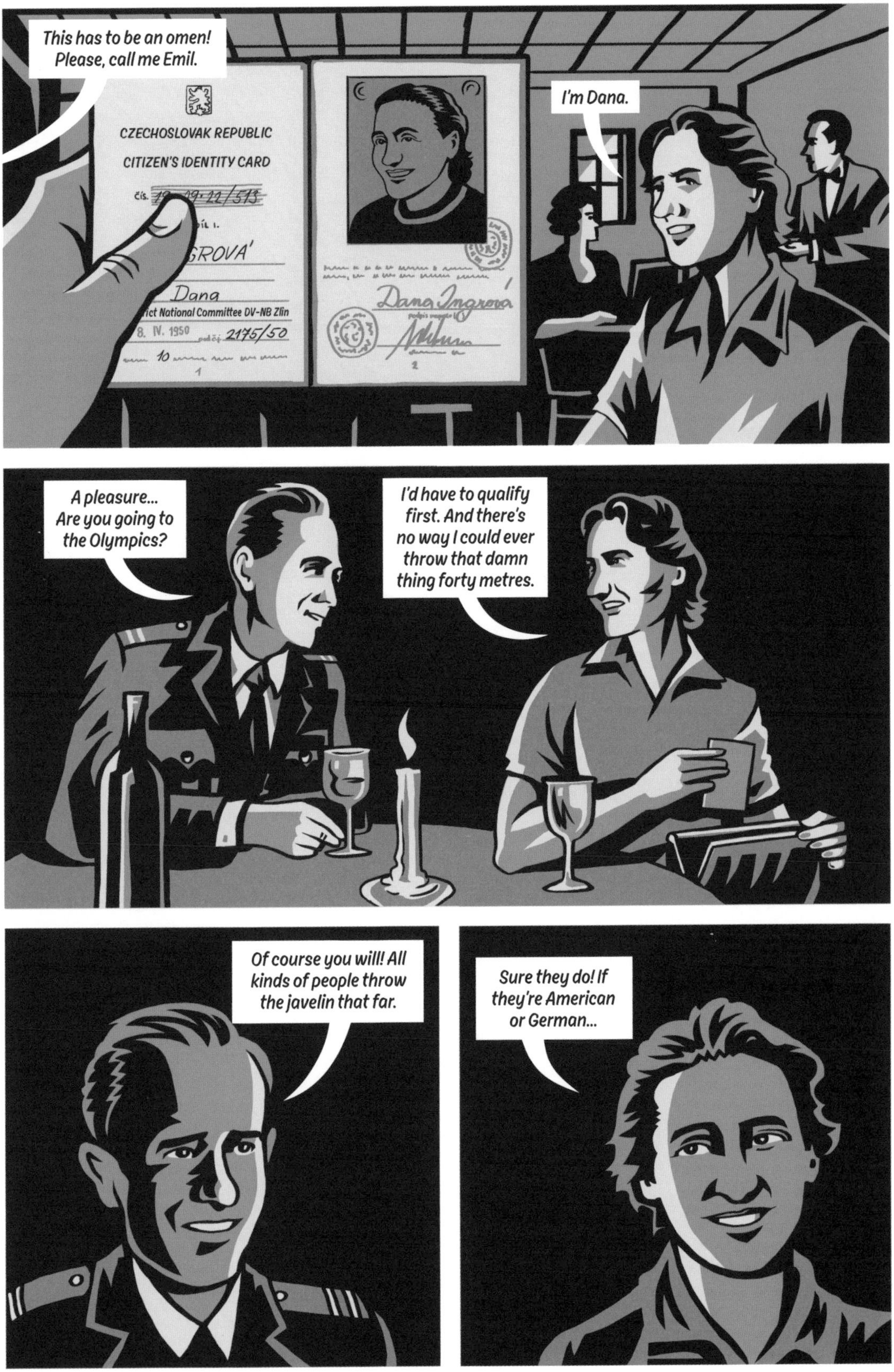
This has to be an omen! Please, call me Emil.
CZECHOSLOVAK REPUBLIC
CITIZEN'S IDENTITY CARD
Dana
8. IV. 1950
2175/50
Dana Ingrová
I'm Dana.
A pleasure... Are you going to the Olympics?
I'd have to qualify first. And there's no way I could ever throw that damn thing forty metres.
Of course you will! All kinds of people throw the javelin that far.
Sure they do! If they're American or German...

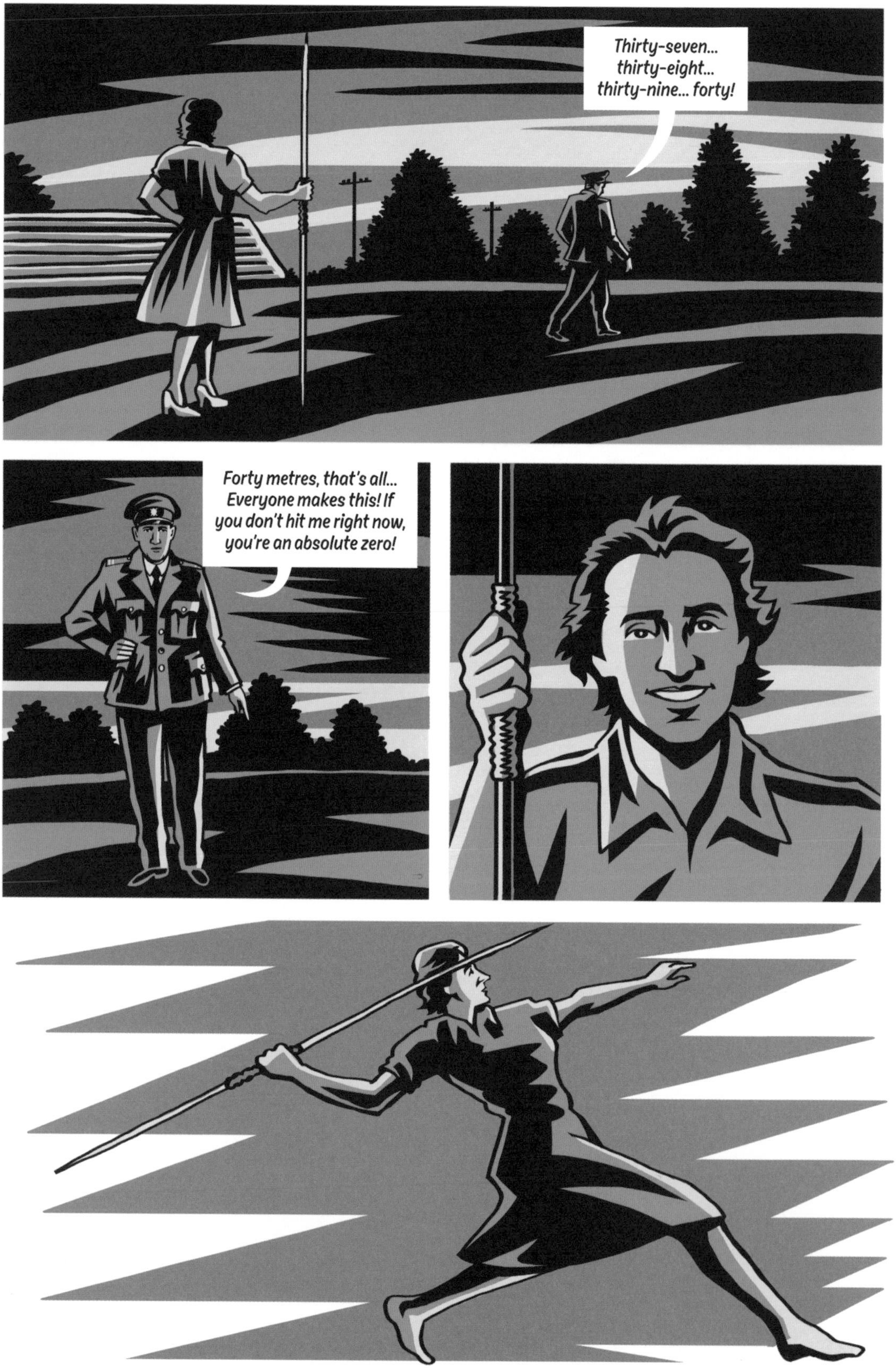

Thirty-seven... thirty-eight... thirty-nine... forty!
Forty metres, that's all... Everyone makes this! If you don't hit me right now, you're an absolute zero!

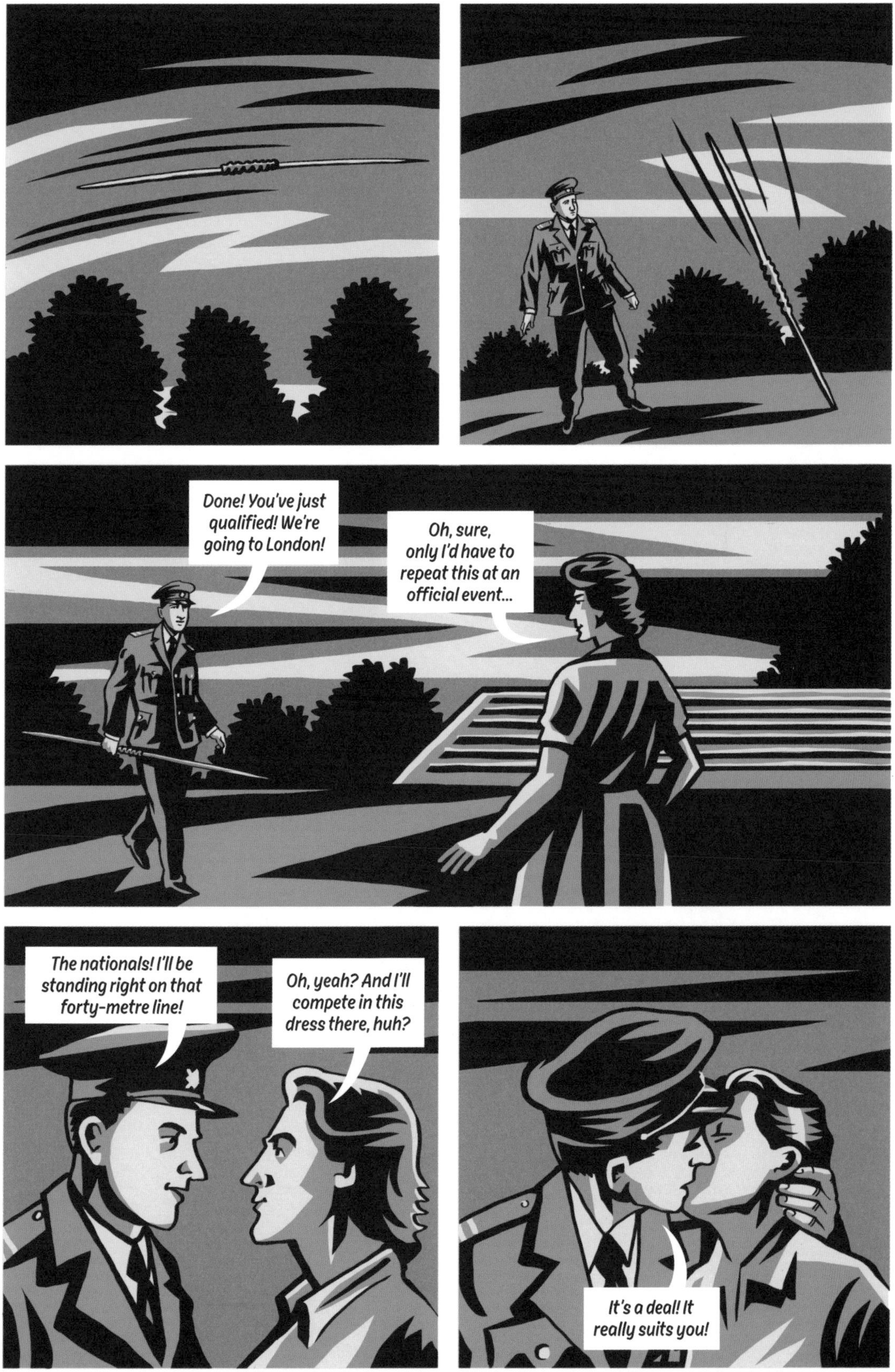
Done! You've just qualified! We're going to London!
Oh, sure, only I'd have to repeat this at an official event...
The nationals! I'll be standing right on that forty-metre line!
Oh, yeah? And I'll compete in this dress there, huh?
It's a deal! It really suits you!

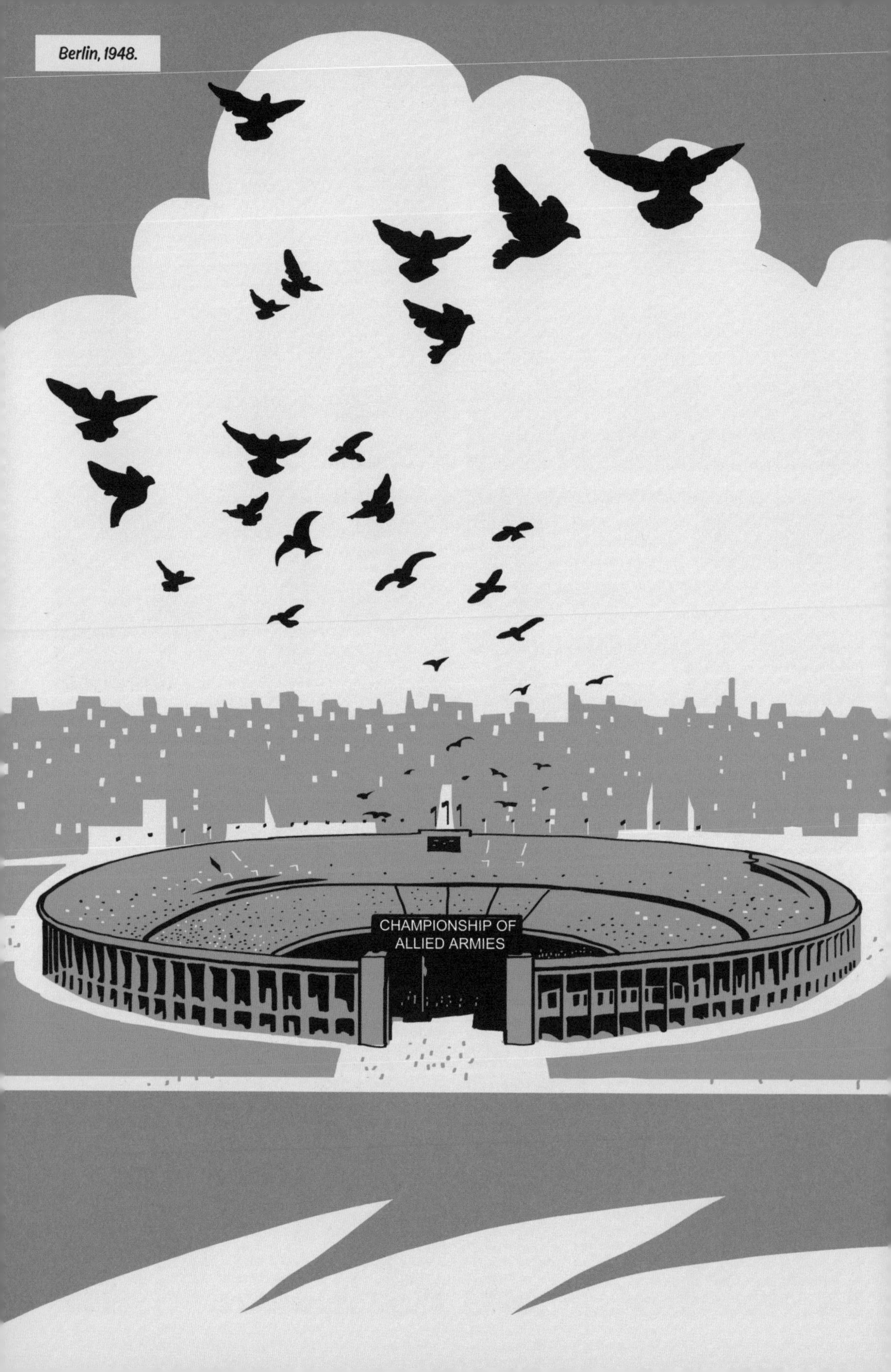
Berlin, 1948.
CHAMPIONSHIP OF
ALLIED ARMIES

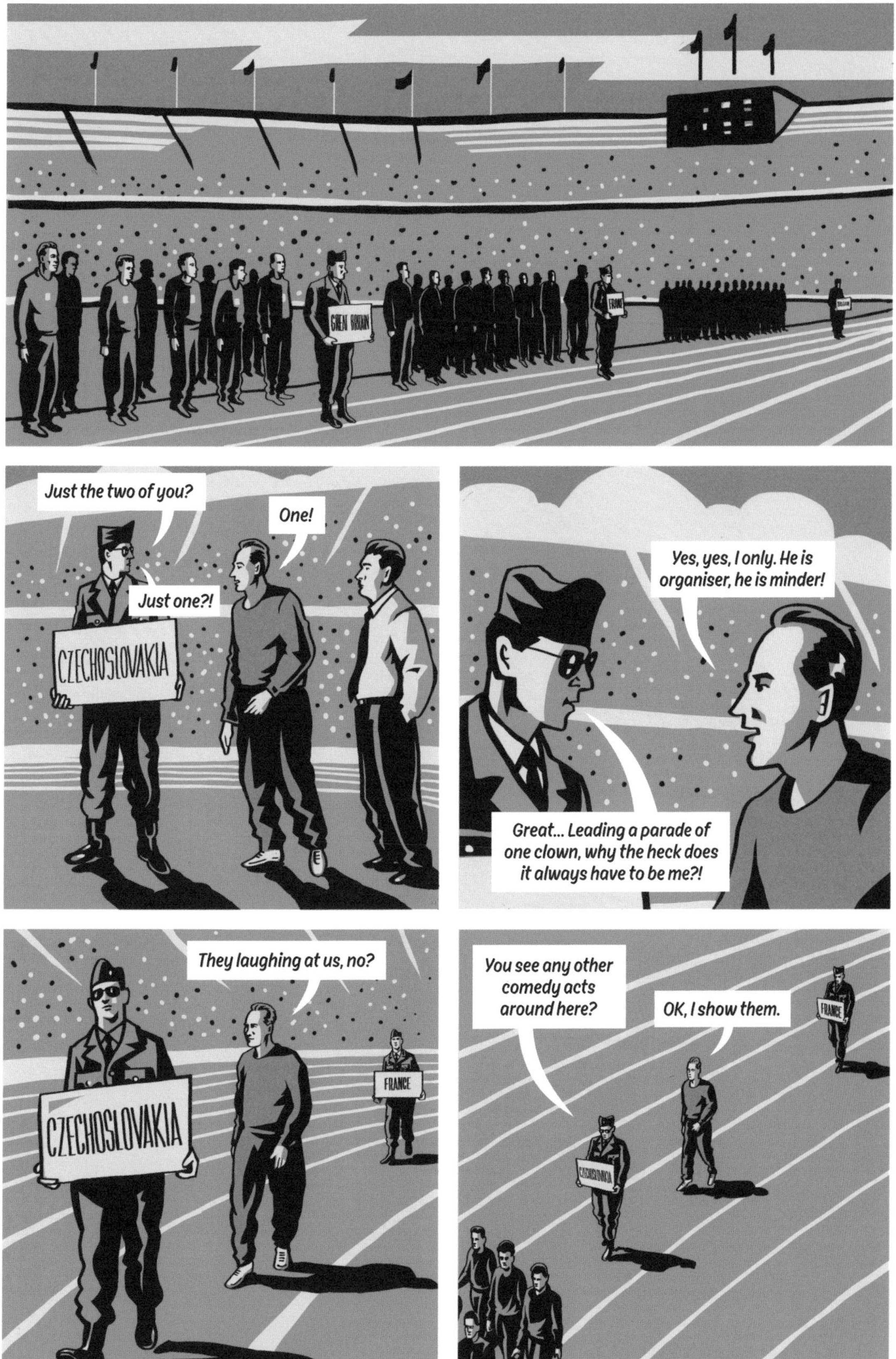
GREAT BRITAIN
Just the two of you?
One!
Just one?!
CZECHOSLOVAKIA
Yes, yes, I only. He is organiser, he is minder!
Great... Leading a parade of one clown, why the heck does it always have to be me?!
They laughing at us, no?
CZECHOSLOVAKIA
FRANCE
You see any other comedy acts around here?
OK, I show them.
FRANCE

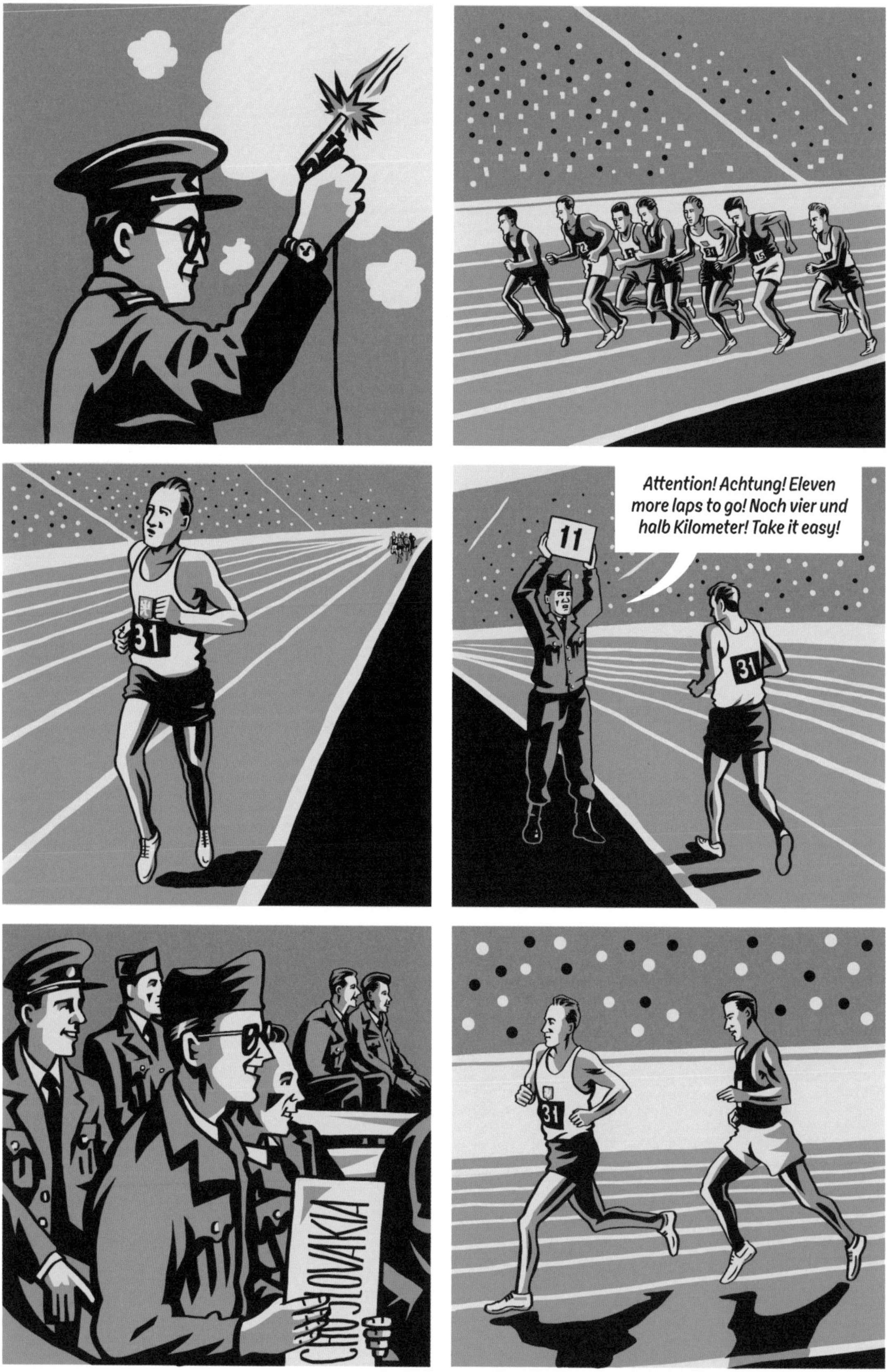
11
Attention! Achtung! Eleven more laps to go! Noch vier und halb Kilometer! Take it easy!

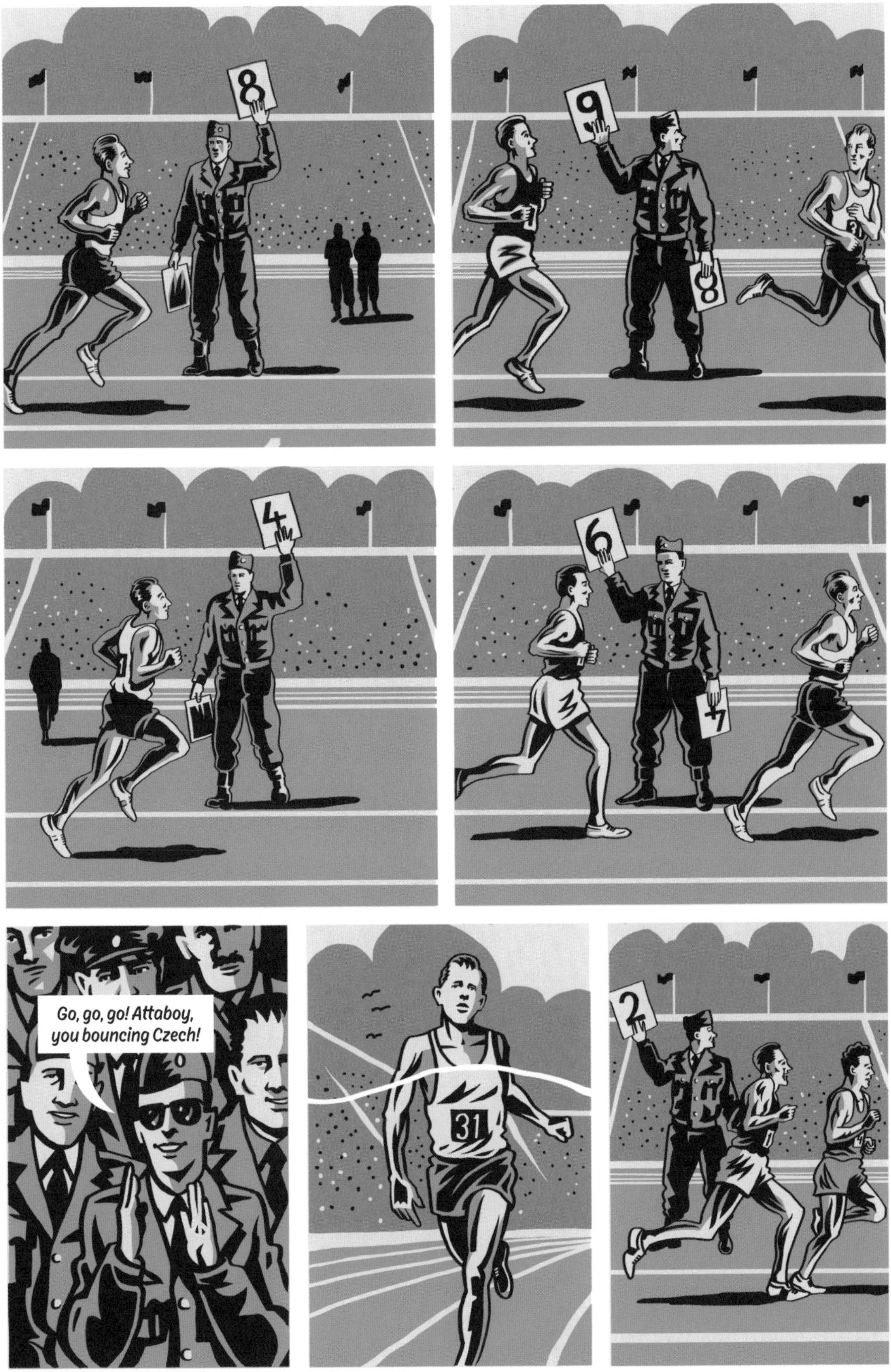
8
9
8
4
6
7
Go, go, go! Attaboy, you bouncing Czech!
31
2

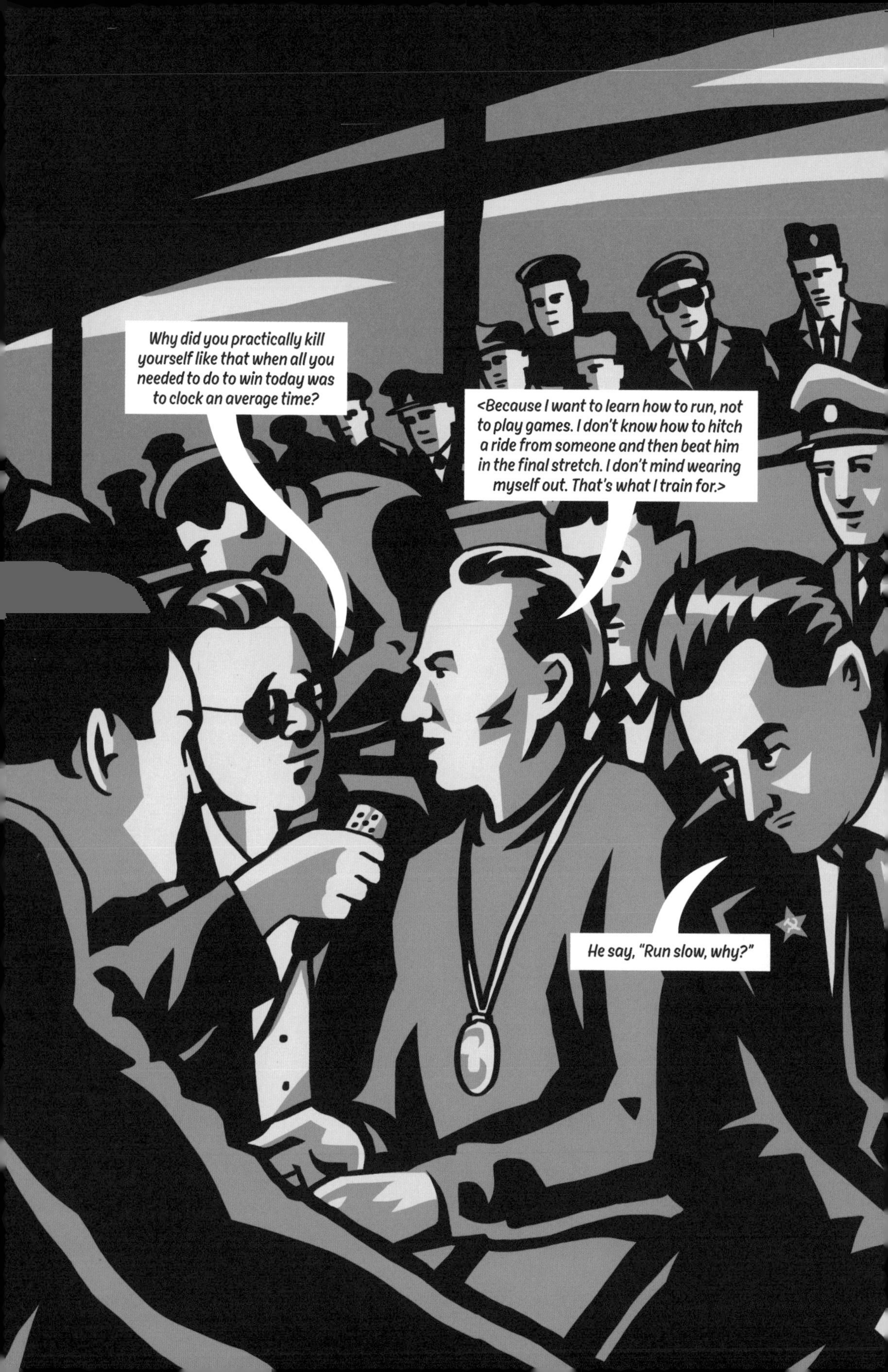
Why did you practically kill yourself like that when all you needed to do to win today was to clock an average time?
<Because I want to learn how to run, not to play games. I don't know how to hitch a ride from someone and then beat him in the final stretch. I don't mind wearing myself out. That's what I train for.>
He say, "Run slow, why?"

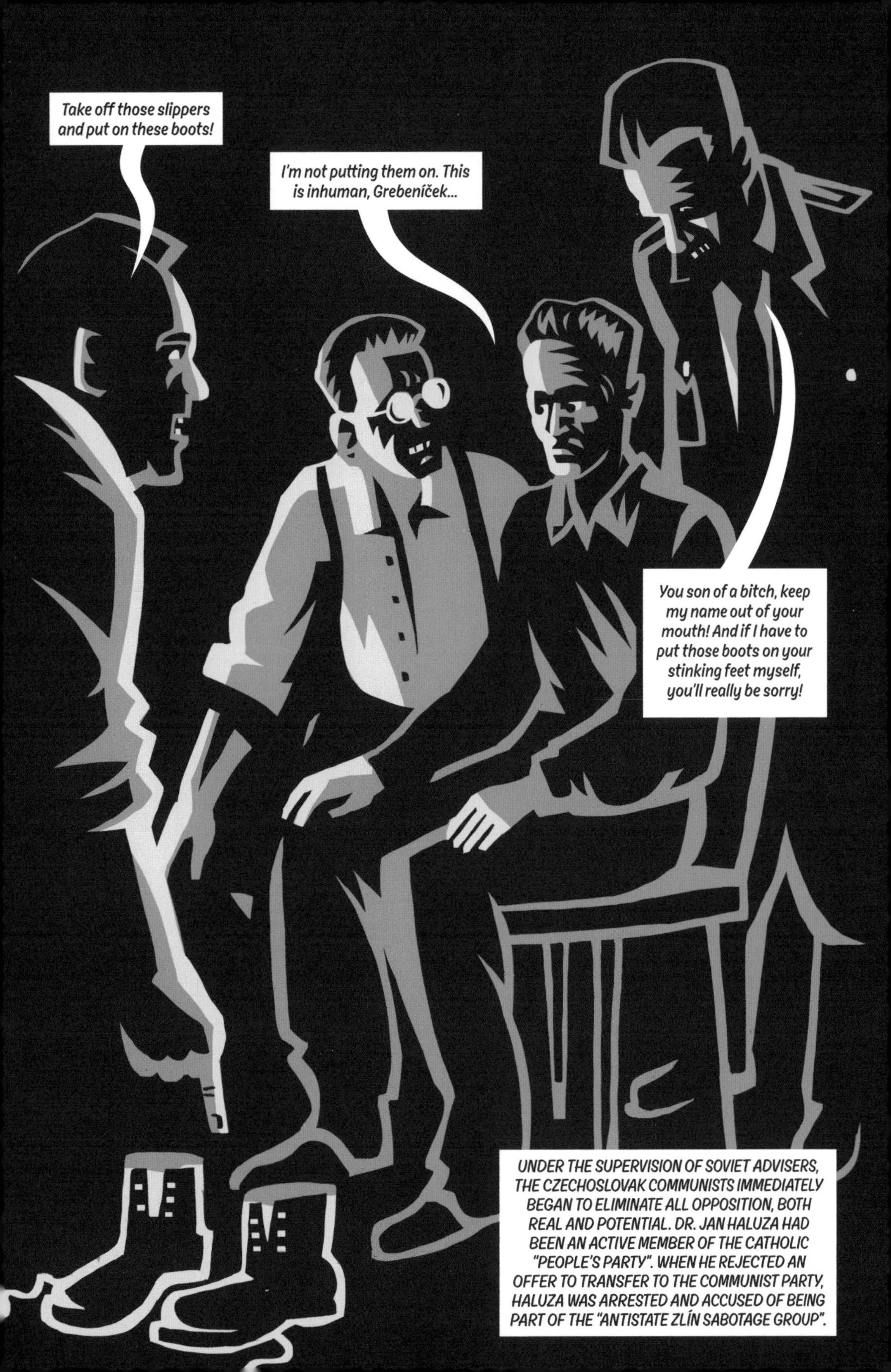
Take off those slippers and put on these boots!
I'm not putting them on. This is inhuman, Grebeníček...
You son of a bitch, keep my name out of your mouth! And if I have to put those boots on your stinking feet myself, you'll really be sorry!
UNDER THE SUPERVISION OF SOVIET ADVISERS, THE CZECHOSLOVAK COMMUNISTS IMMEDIATELY BEGAN TO ELIMINATE ALL OPPOSITION, BOTH REAL AND POTENTIAL. DR. JAN HALUZA HAD BEEN AN ACTIVE MEMBER OF THE CATHOLIC "PEOPLE'S PARTY". WHEN HE REJECTED AN OFFER TO TRANSFER TO THE COMMUNIST PARTY, HALUZA WAS ARRESTED AND ACCUSED OF BEING PART OF THE "ANTISTATE ZLÍN SABOTAGE GROUP".

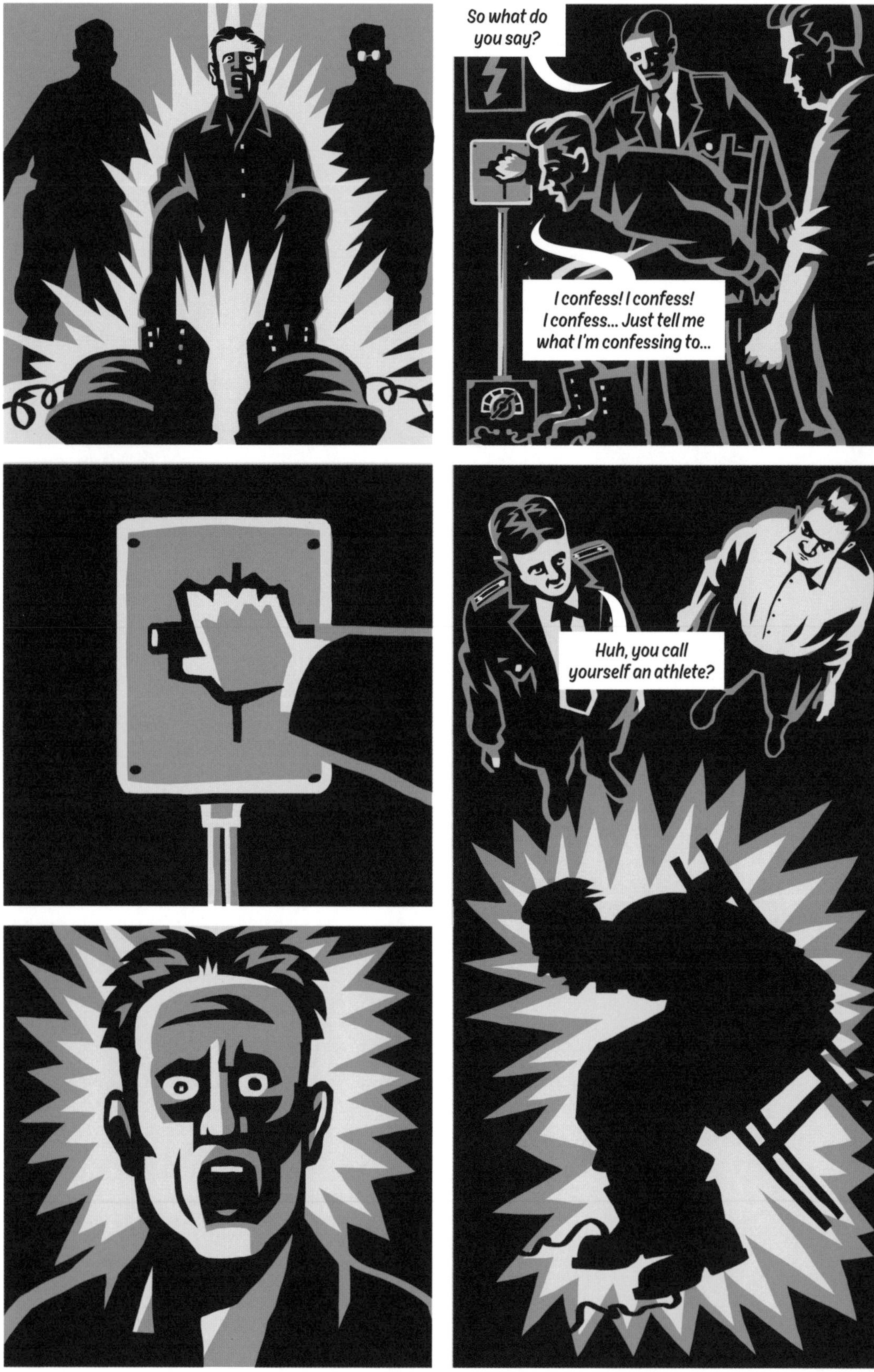
So what do you say?
I confess! I confess! I confess... Just tell me what I'm confessing to...
Huh, you call yourself an athlete?

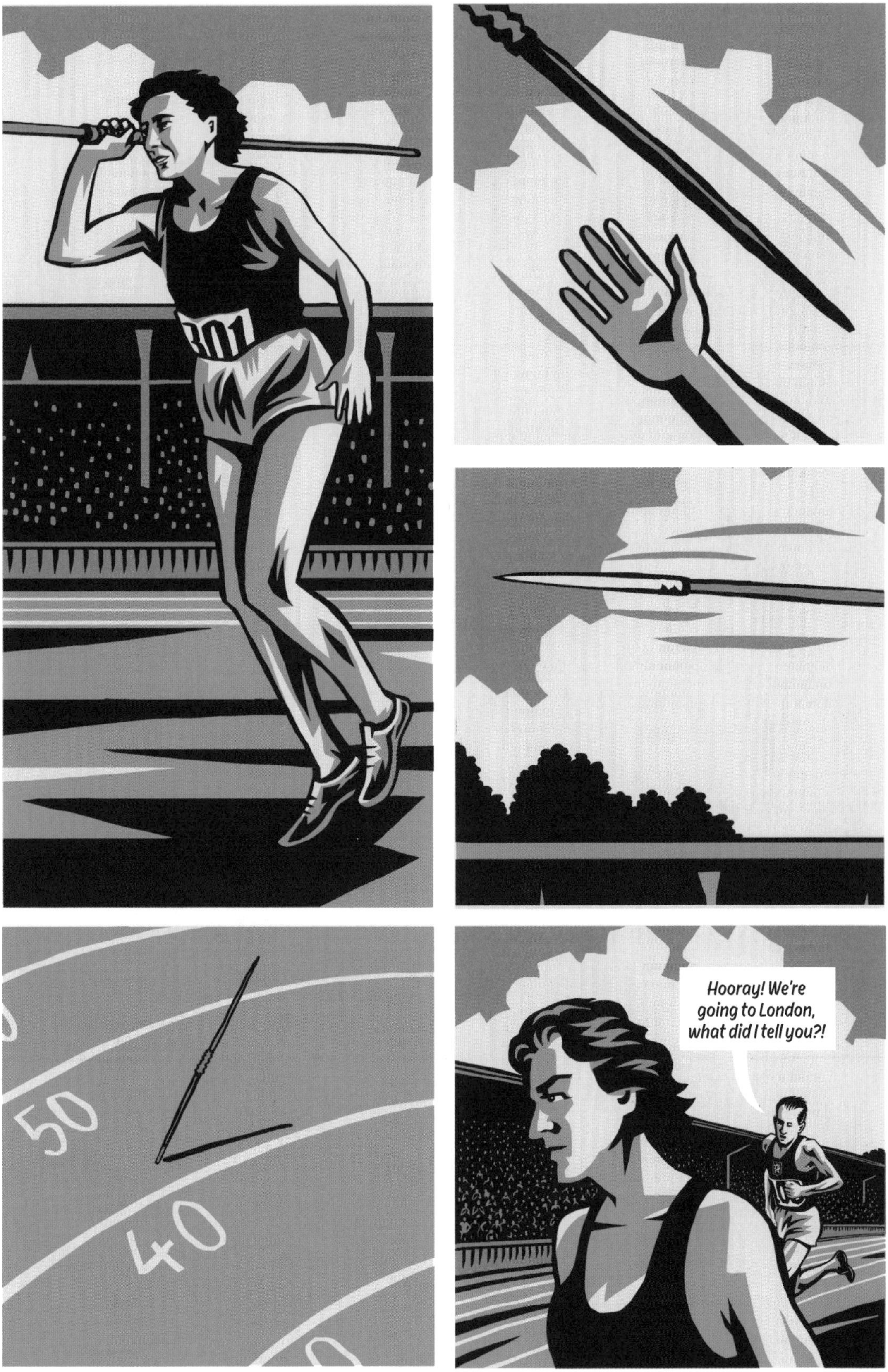
301
50
40
Hooray! We're going to London, what did I tell you?!

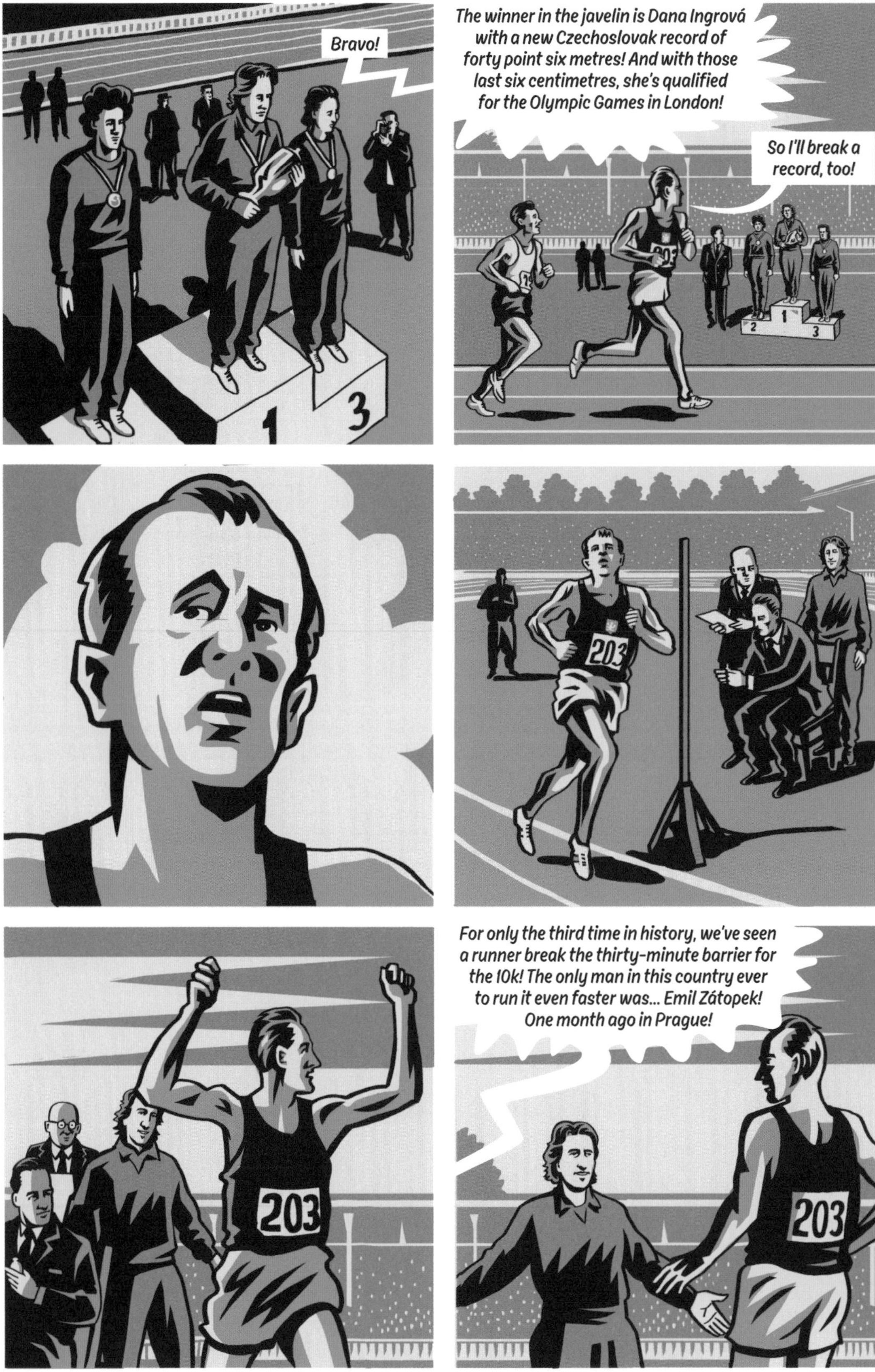
Bravo!
The winner in the javelin is Dana Ingrová with a new Czechoslovak record of forty point six metres! And with those last six centimetres, she's qualified for the Olympic Games in London!
So I'll break a record, too!
1
2
3
203
203
203
For only the third time in history, we've seen a runner break the thirty-minute barrier for the 10k! The only man in this country ever to run it even faster was... Emil Zátopek! One month ago in Prague!
203

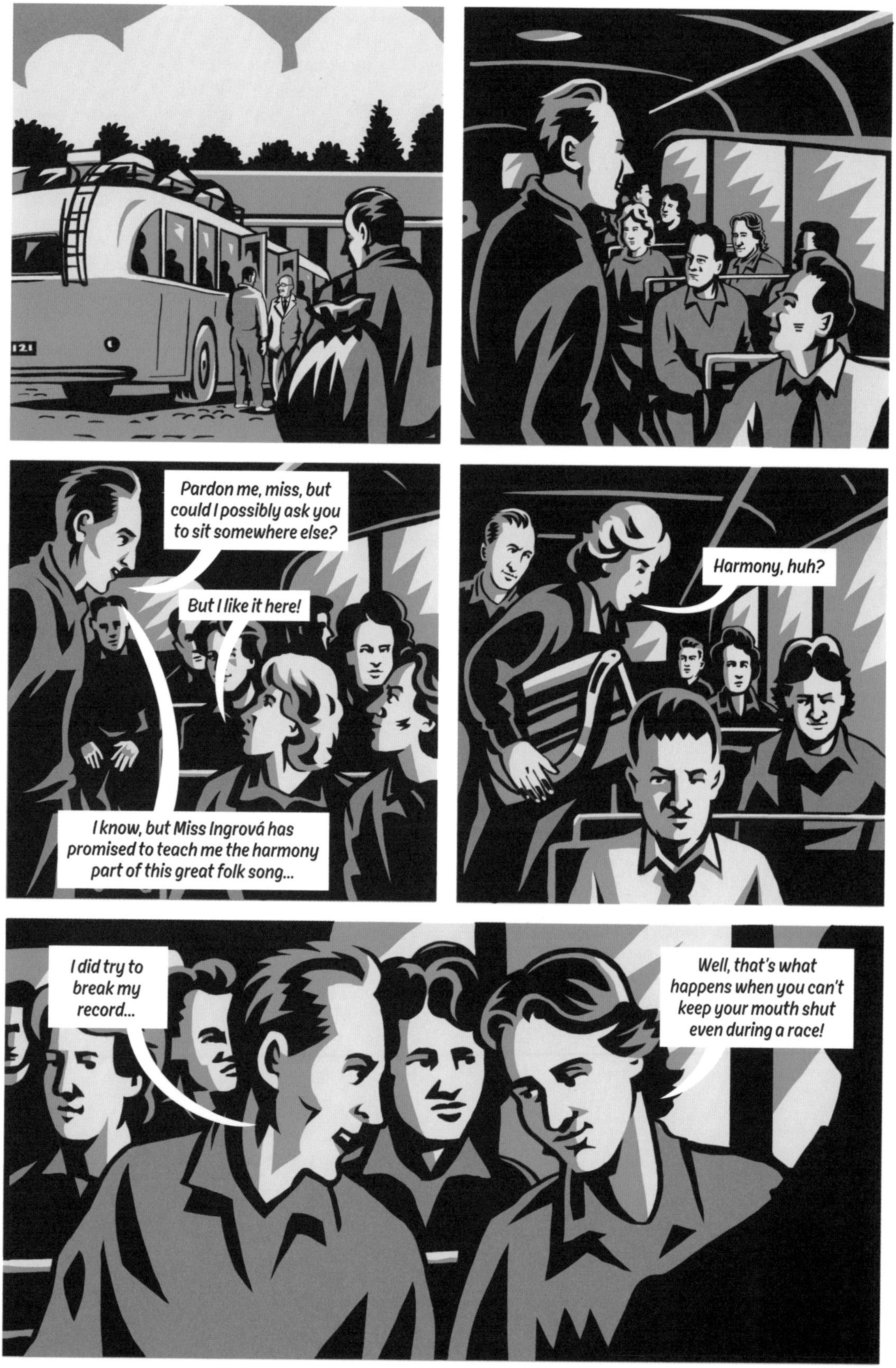
Pardon me, miss, but could I possibly ask you to sit somewhere else?
But I like it here!
I know, but Miss Ingrová has promised to teach me the harmony part of this great folk song...
Harmony, huh?
I did try to break my record...
Well, that's what happens when you can't keep your mouth shut even during a race!

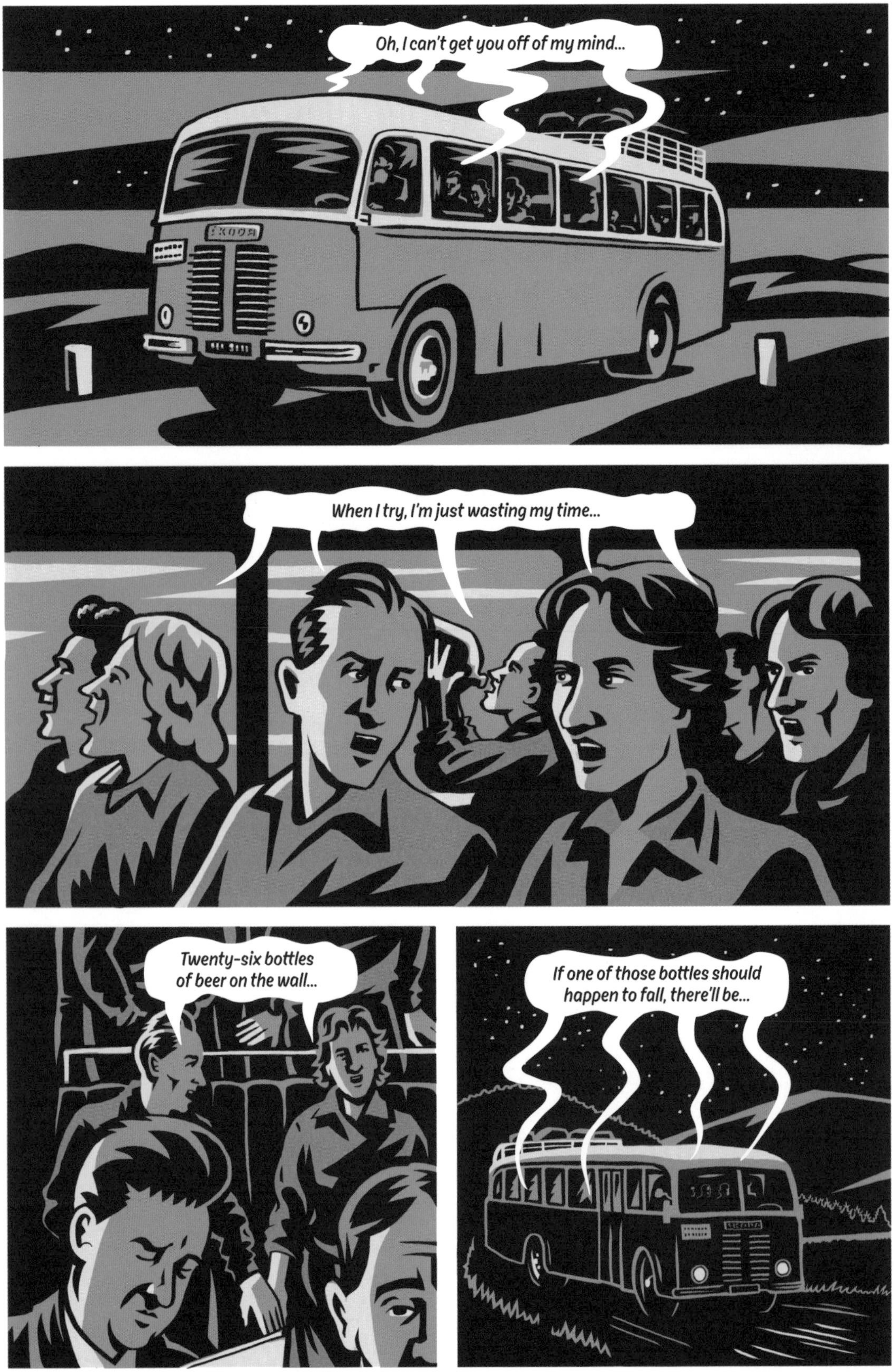
Oh, I can't get you off of my mind...
When I try, I'm just wasting my time...
Twenty-six bottles of beer on the wall...
If one of those bottles should happen to fall, there'll be...

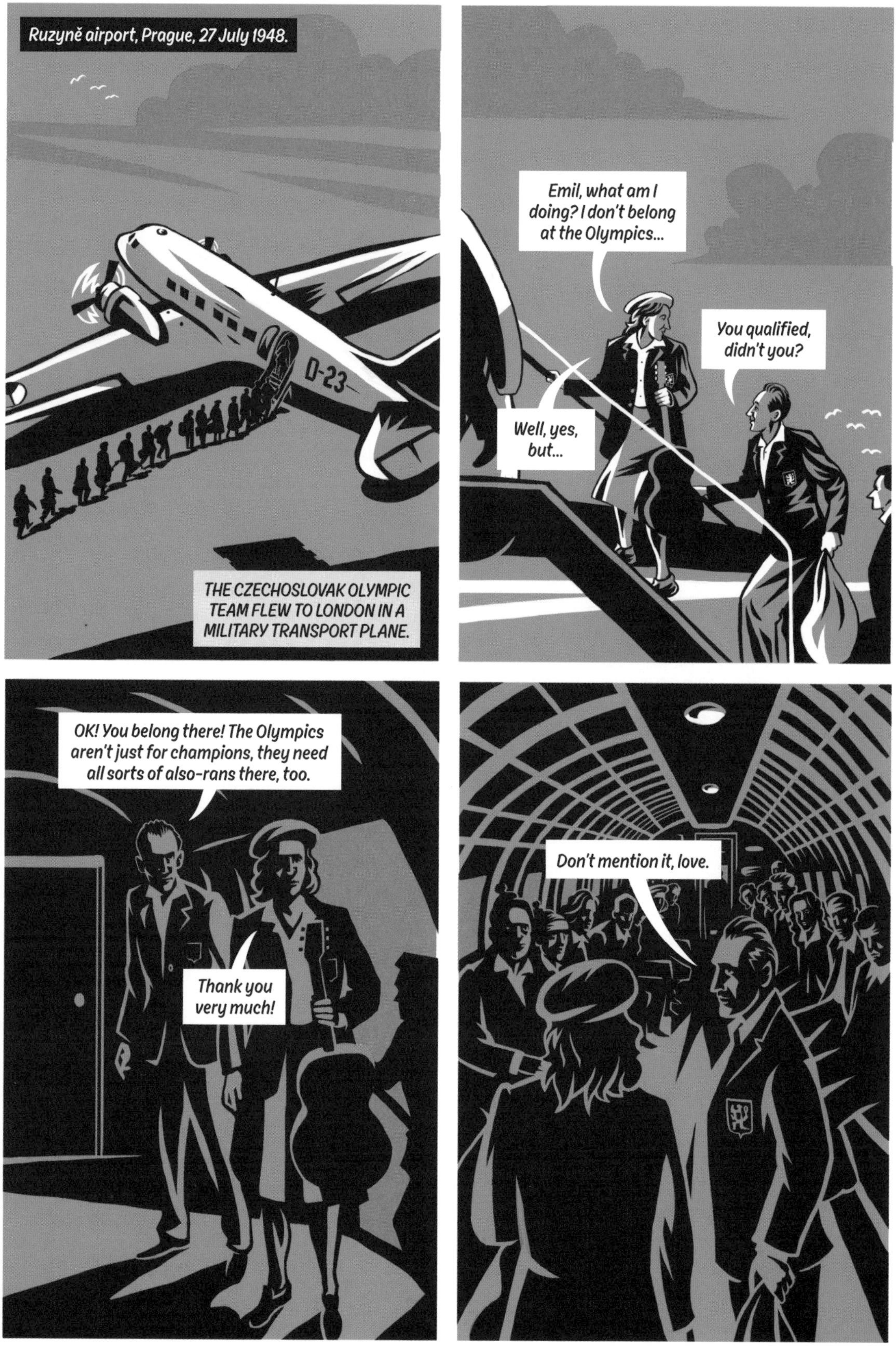
Ruzyně airport, Prague, 27 July 1948.
D-23
THE CZECHOSLOVAK OLYMPIC TEAM FLEW TO LONDON IN A MILITARY TRANSPORT PLANE.
Emil, what am I doing? I don't belong at the Olympics...
You qualified, didn't you?
Well, yes, but...
OK! You belong there! The Olympics aren't just for champions, they need all sorts of also-rans there, too.
Thank you very much!
Don't mention it, love.

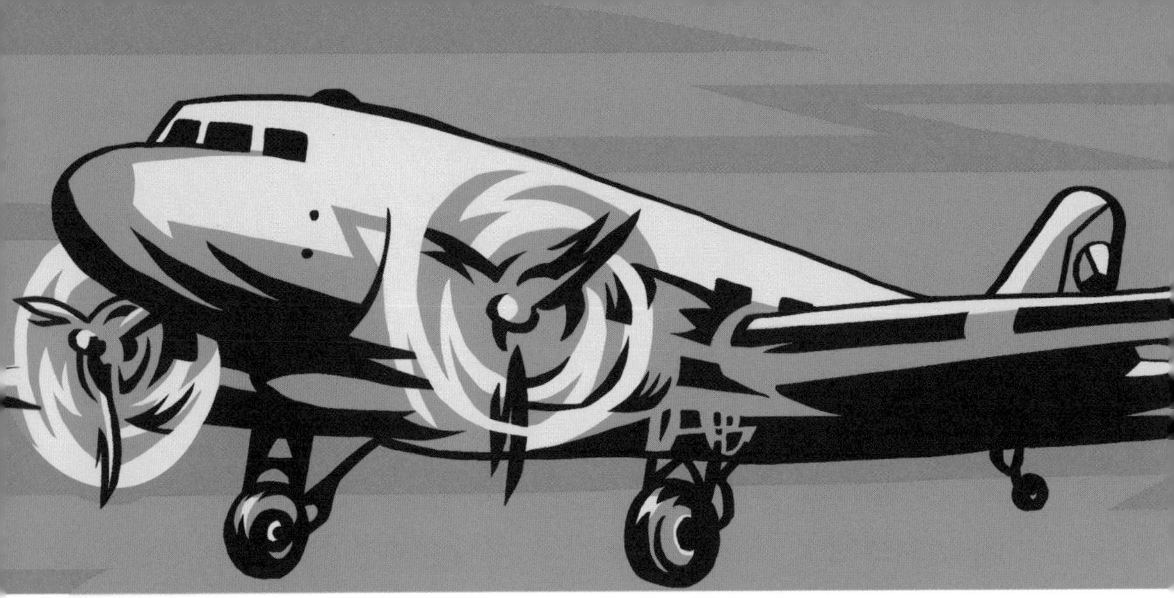

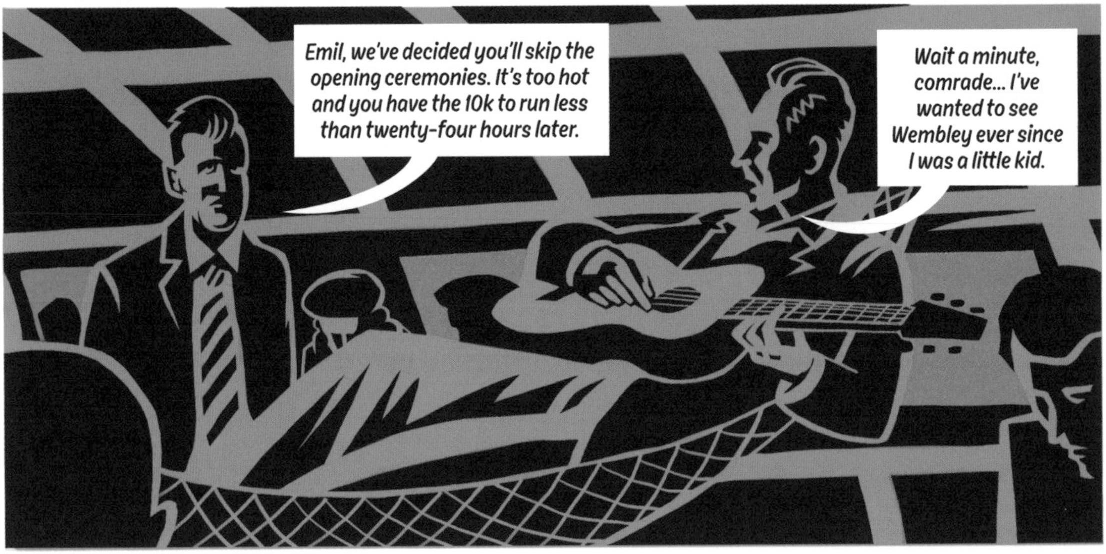
Emil, we've decided you'll skip the opening ceremonies. It's too hot and you have the 10k to run less than twenty-four hours later.
Wait a minute, comrade... I've wanted to see Wembley ever since I was a little kid.

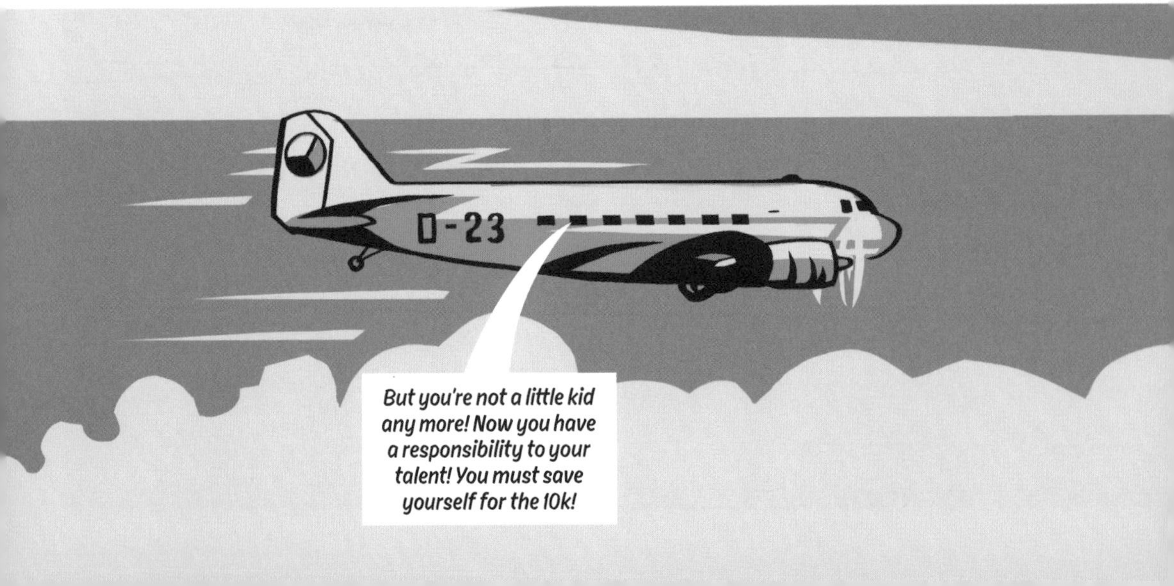
D-23
But you're not a little kid any more! Now you have a responsibility to your talent! You must save yourself for the 10k!

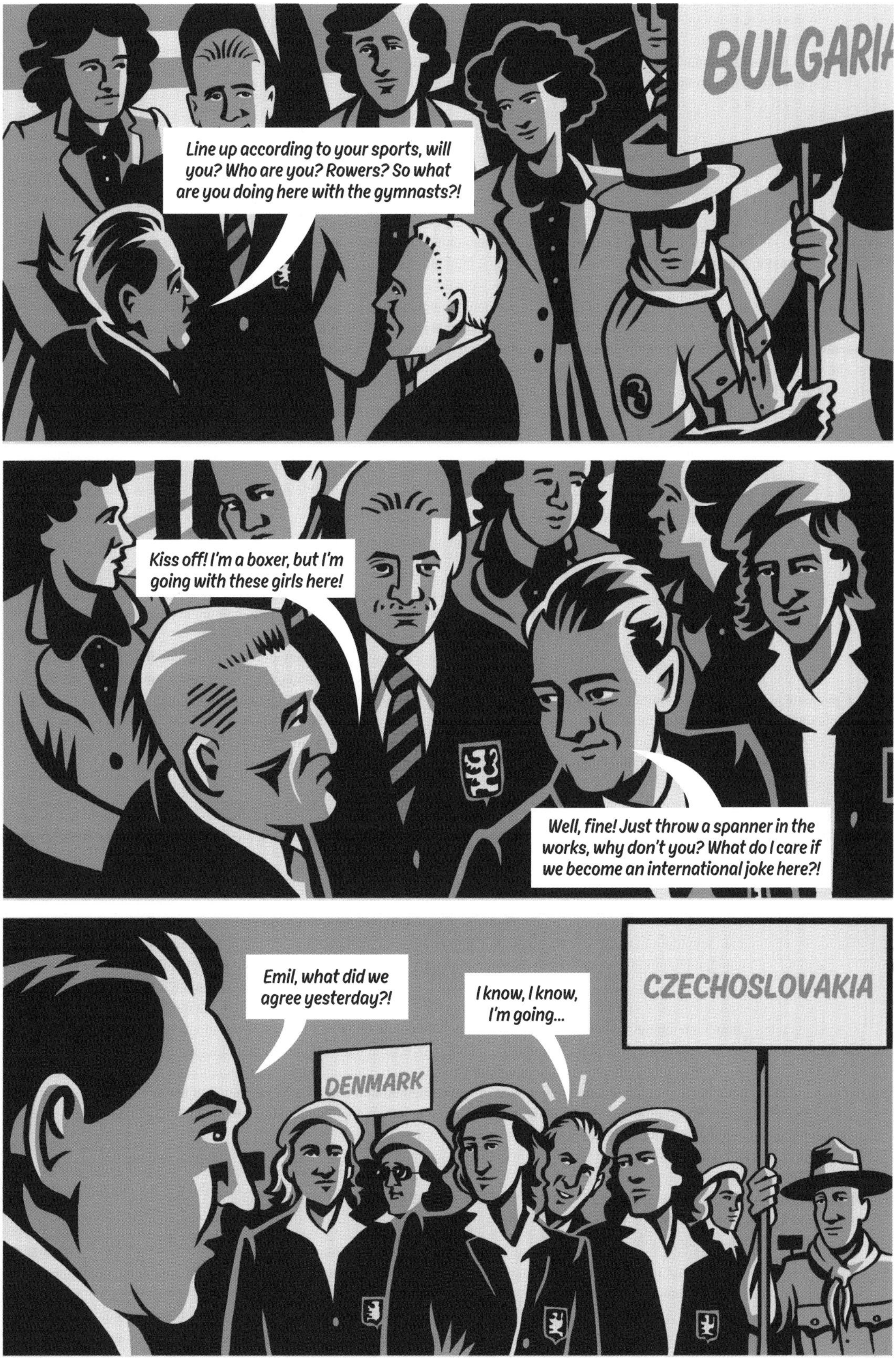
BULGARIA
Line up according to your sports, will you? Who are you? Rowers? So what are you doing here with the gymnasts?!
Kiss off! I'm a boxer, but I'm going with these girls here!
Well, fine! Just throw a spanner in the works, why don't you? What do I care if we become an international joke here?!
CZECHOSLOVAKIA
Emil, what did we agree yesterday?!
I know, I know, I'm going...
DENMARK

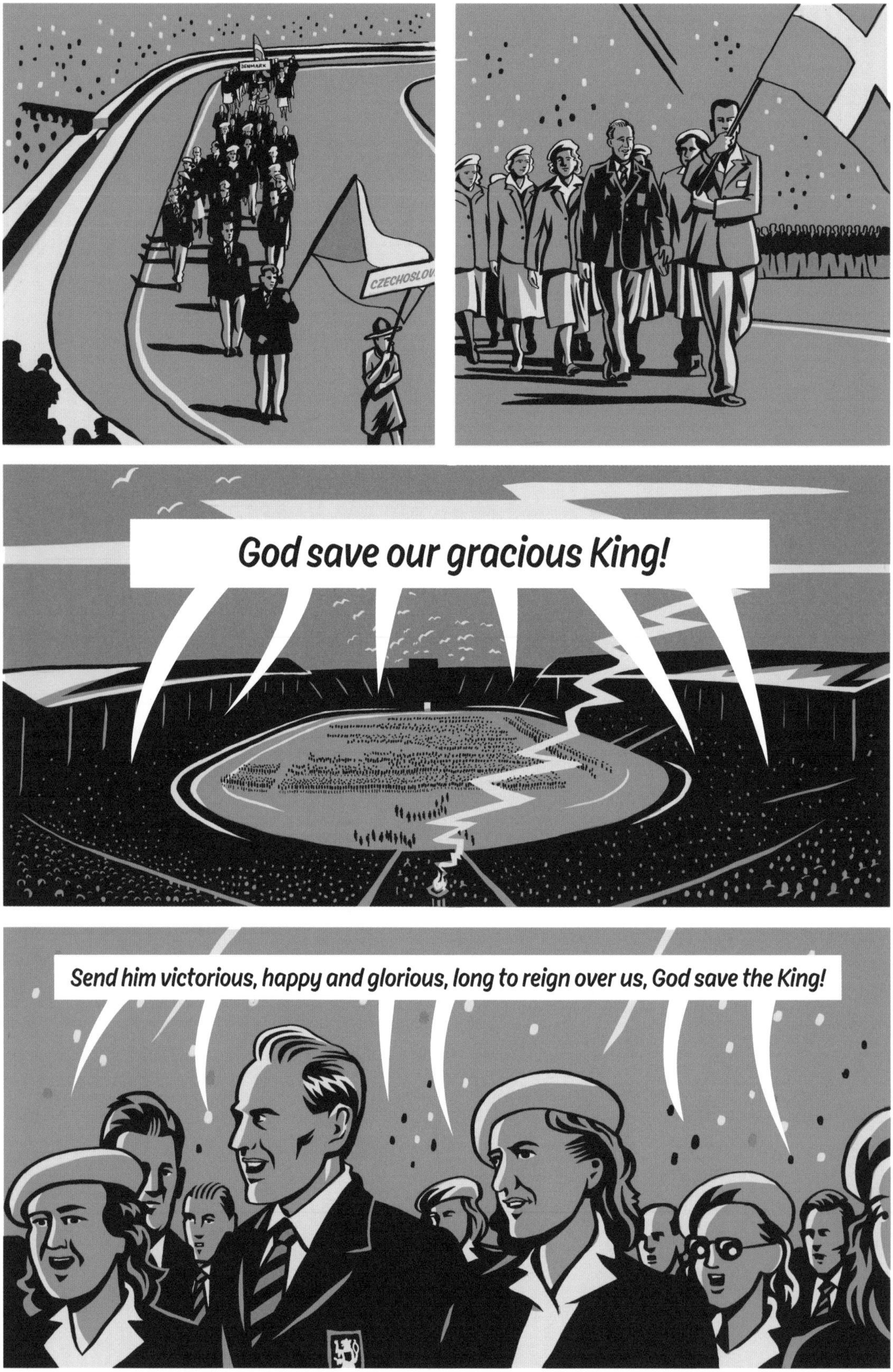
DENMARK
CZECHOSLOV
God save our gracious King!
Send him victorious, happy and glorious, long to reign over us, God save the King!

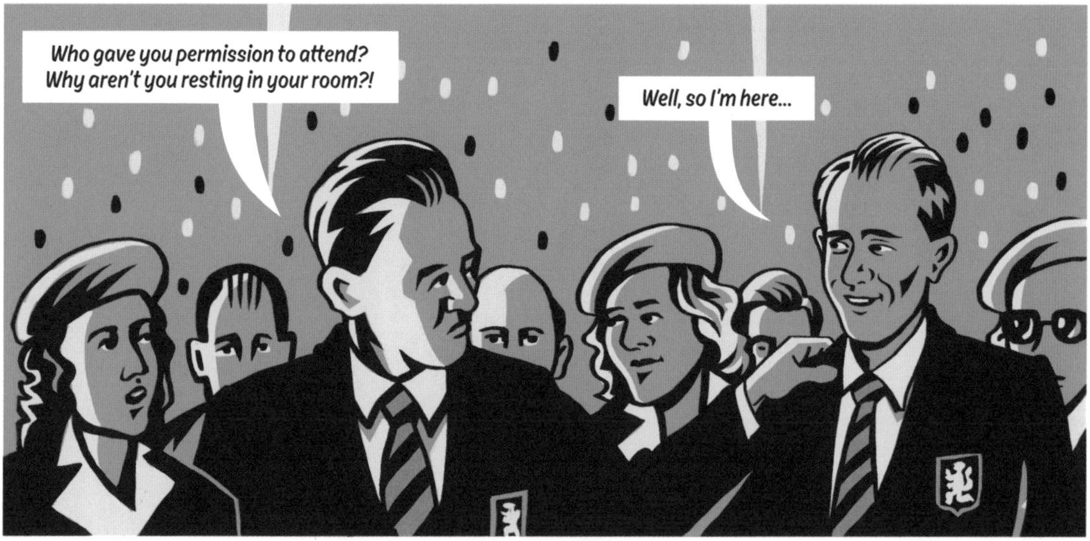
Who gave you permission to attend? Why aren't you resting in your room?!
Well, so I'm here...

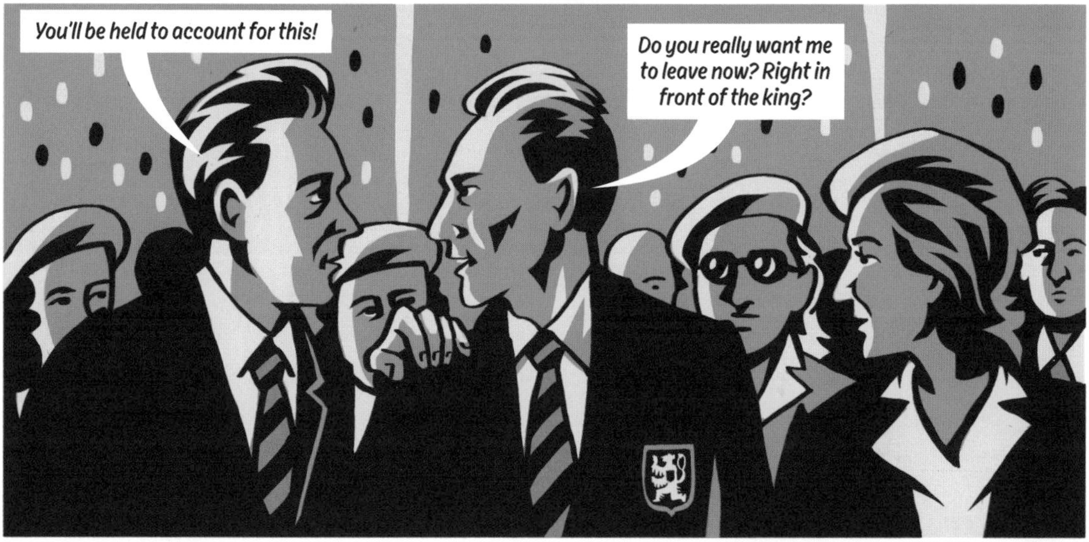
You'll be held to account for this!
Do you really want me to leave now? Right in front of the king?

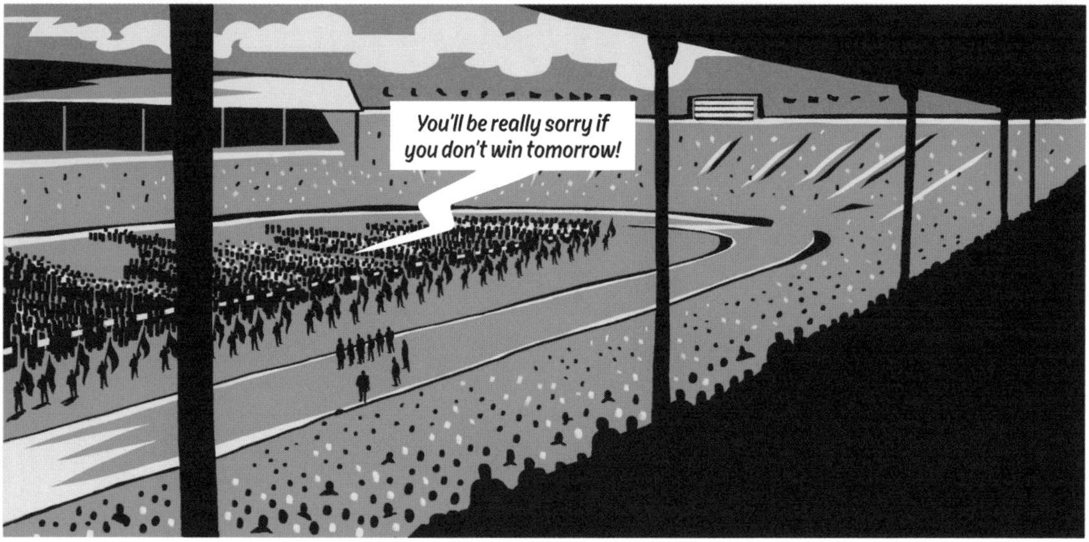
You'll be really sorry if you don't win tomorrow!

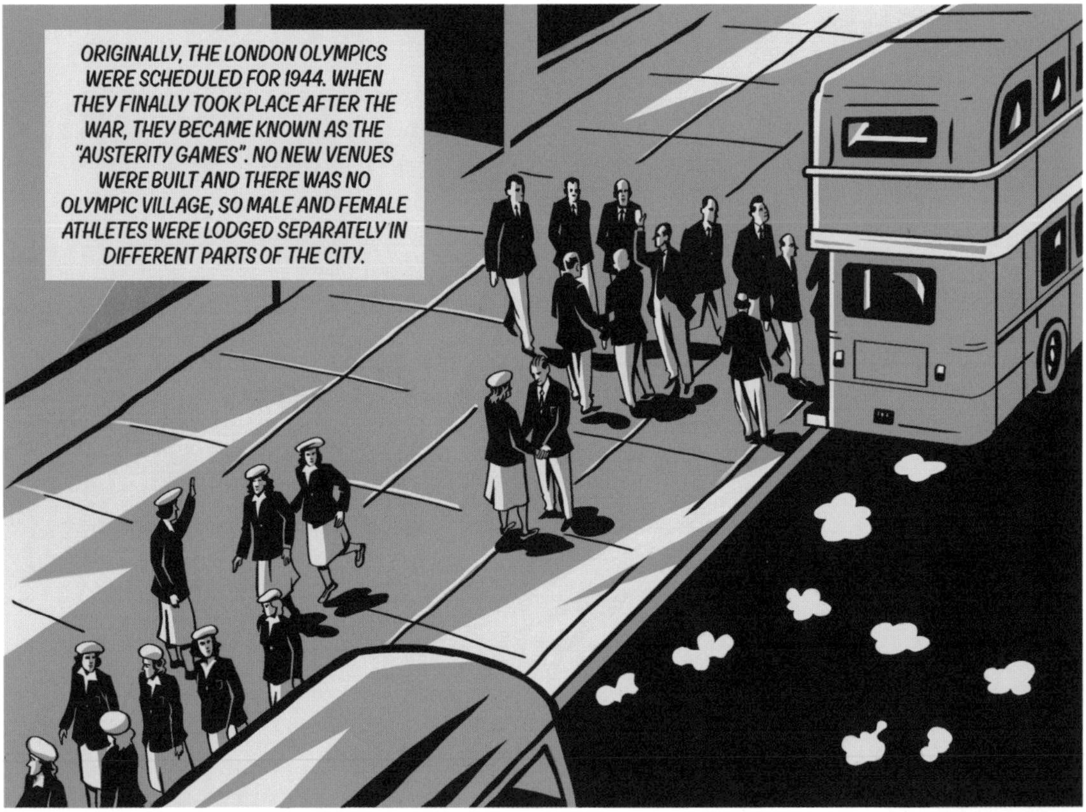
ORIGINALLY, THE LONDON OLYMPICS WERE SCHEDULED FOR 1944. WHEN THEY FINALLY TOOK PLACE AFTER THE WAR, THEY BECAME KNOWN AS THE "AUSTERITY GAMES". NO NEW VENUES WERE BUILT AND THERE WAS NO OLYMPIC VILLAGE, SO MALE AND FEMALE ATHLETES WERE LODGED SEPARATELY IN DIFFERENT PARTS OF THE CITY.

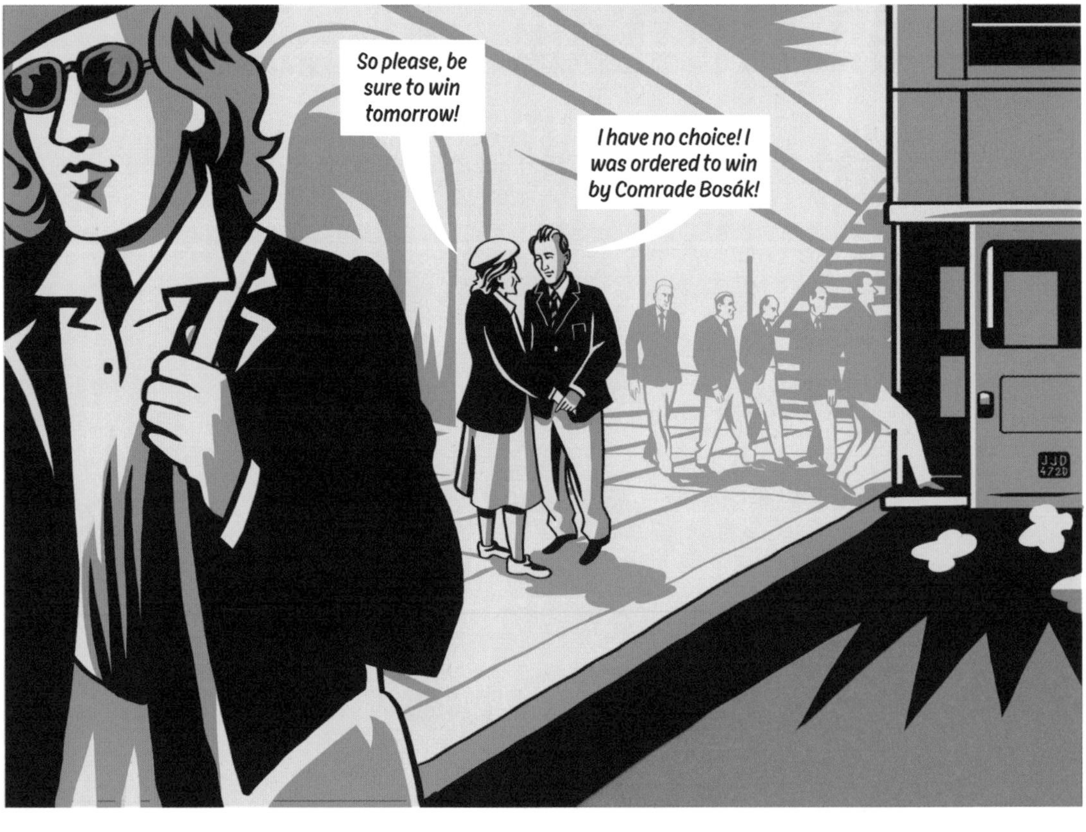
So please, be sure to win tomorrow!
I have no choice! I was ordered to win by Comrade Bosák!
JJD 472D

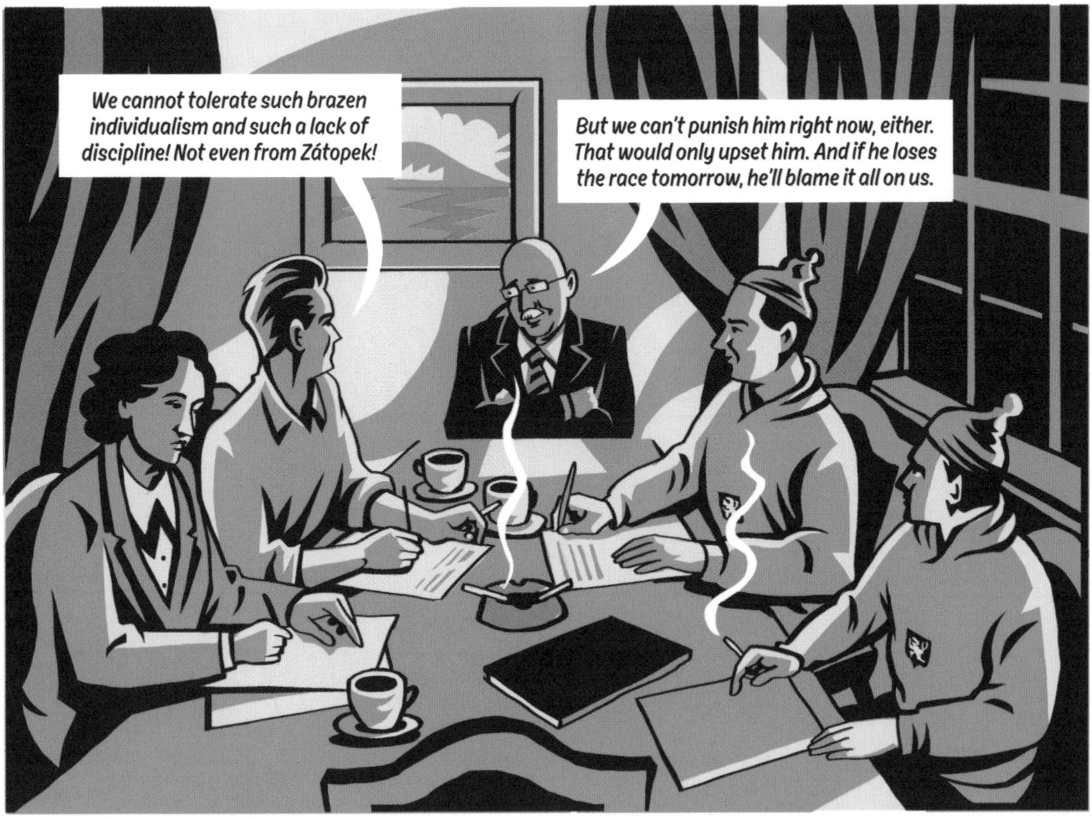
We cannot tolerate such brazen individualism and such a lack of discipline! Not even from Zátopek!
But we can't punish him right now, either. That would only upset him. And if he loses the race tomorrow, he'll blame it all on us.

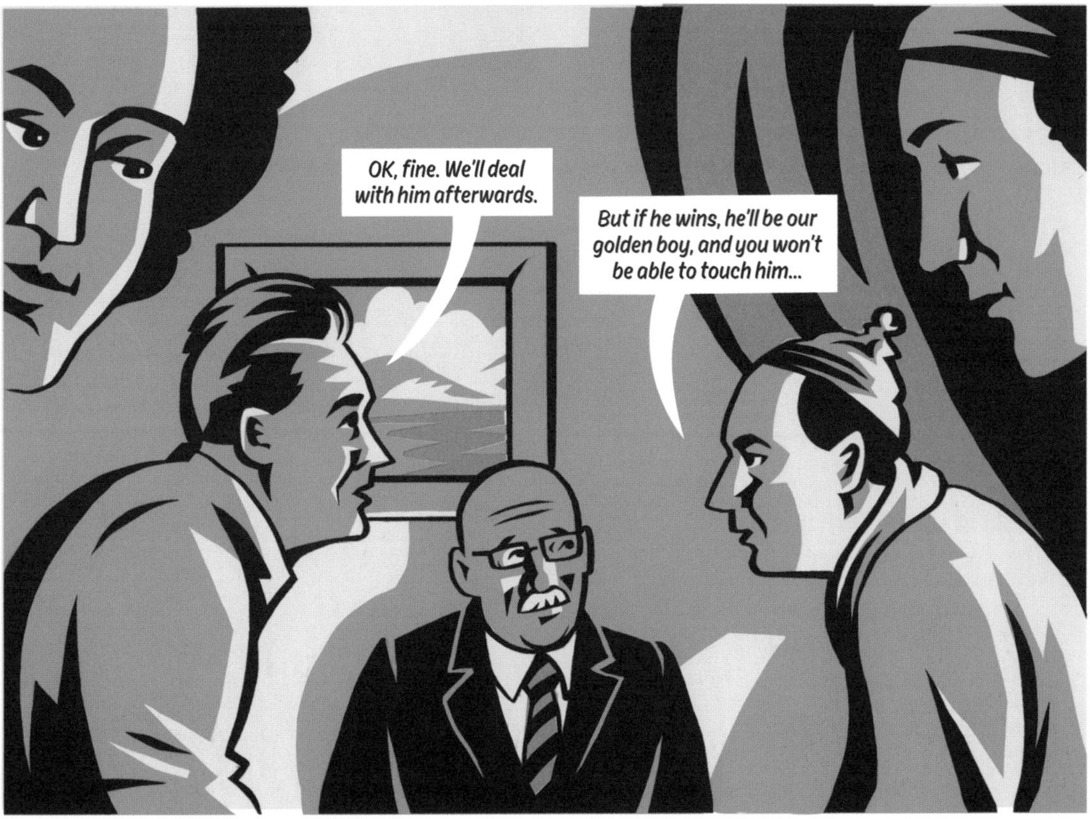
OK, fine. We'll deal with him afterwards.
But if he wins, he'll be our golden boy, and you won't be able to touch him...

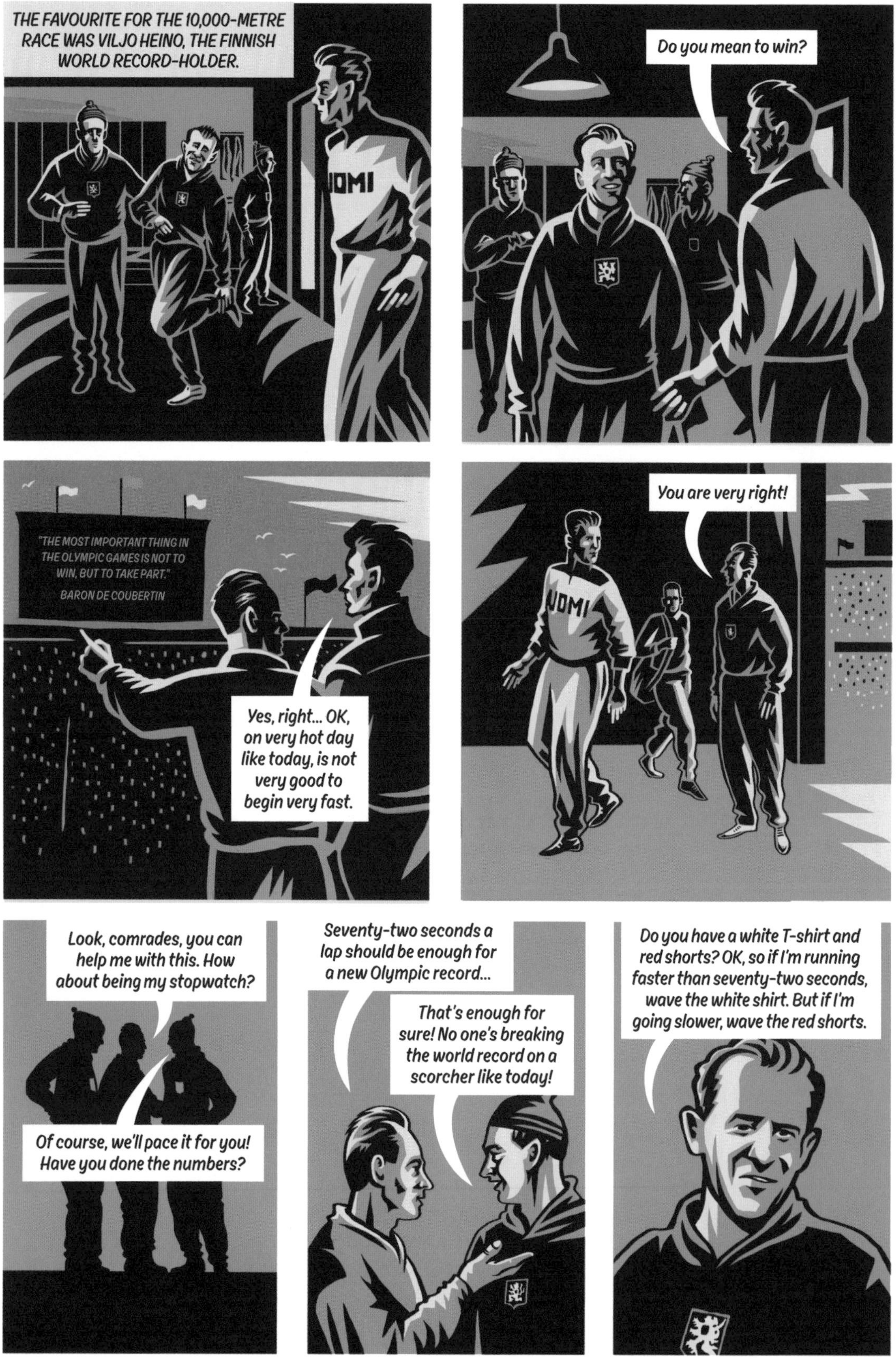
THE FAVOURITE FOR THE 10,000-METRE RACE WAS VILJO HEINO, THE FINNISH WORLD RECORD-HOLDER.
UOMI
Do you mean to win?
"THE MOST IMPORTANT THING IN THE OLYMPIC GAMES IS NOT TO WIN, BUT TO TAKE PART." BARON DE COUBERTIN
Yes, right... OK, on very hot day like today, is not very good to begin very fast.
You are very right!
UOMI
Look, comrades, you can help me with this. How about being my stopwatch?
Of course, we'll pace it for you! Have you done the numbers?
Seventy-two seconds a lap should be enough for a new Olympic record...
That's enough for sure! No one's breaking the world record on a scorcher like today!
Do you have a white T-shirt and red shorts? OK, so if I'm running faster than seventy-two seconds, wave the white shirt. But if I'm going slower, wave the red shorts.

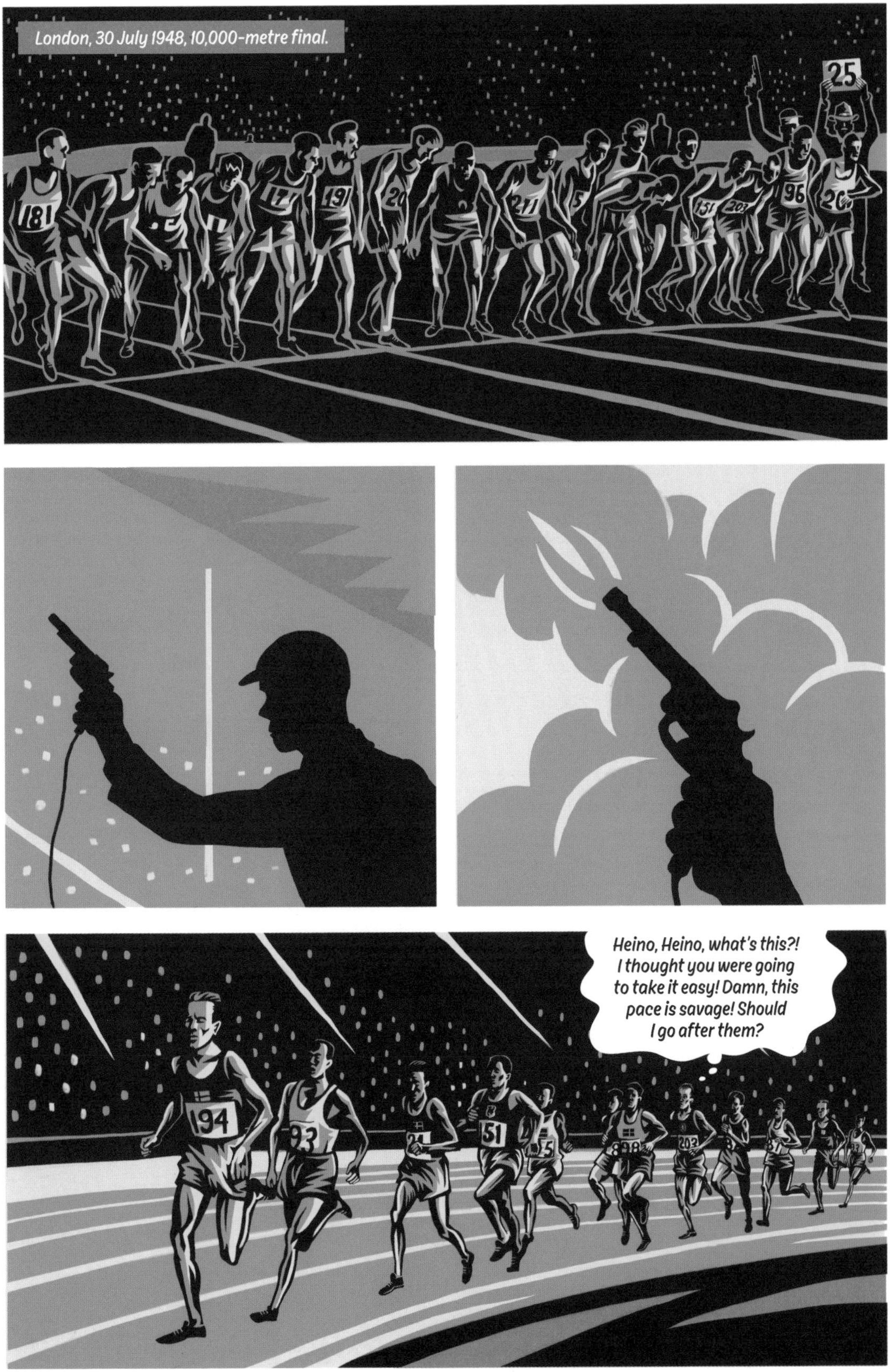
London, 30 July 1948, 10,000-metre final.
Heino, Heino, what's this?! I thought you were going to take it easy! Damn, this pace is savage! Should I go after them?

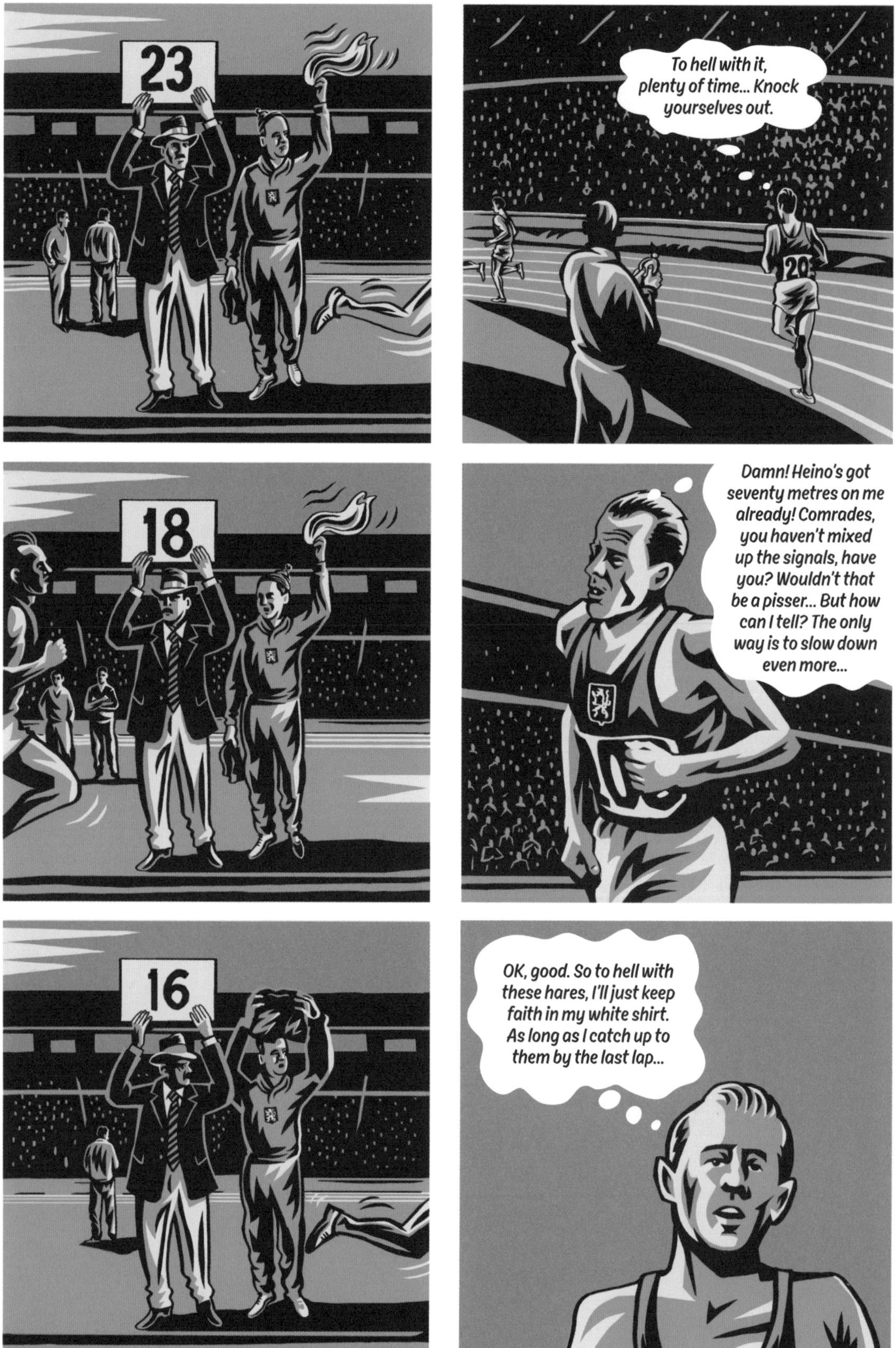
23
To hell with it, plenty of time... Knock yourselves out.
18
Damn! Heino's got seventy metres on me already! Comrades, you haven't mixed up the signals, have you? Wouldn't that be a pisser... But how can I tell? The only way is to slow down even more...
16
OK, good. So to hell with these hares, I'll just keep faith in my white shirt. As long as I catch up to them by the last lap...

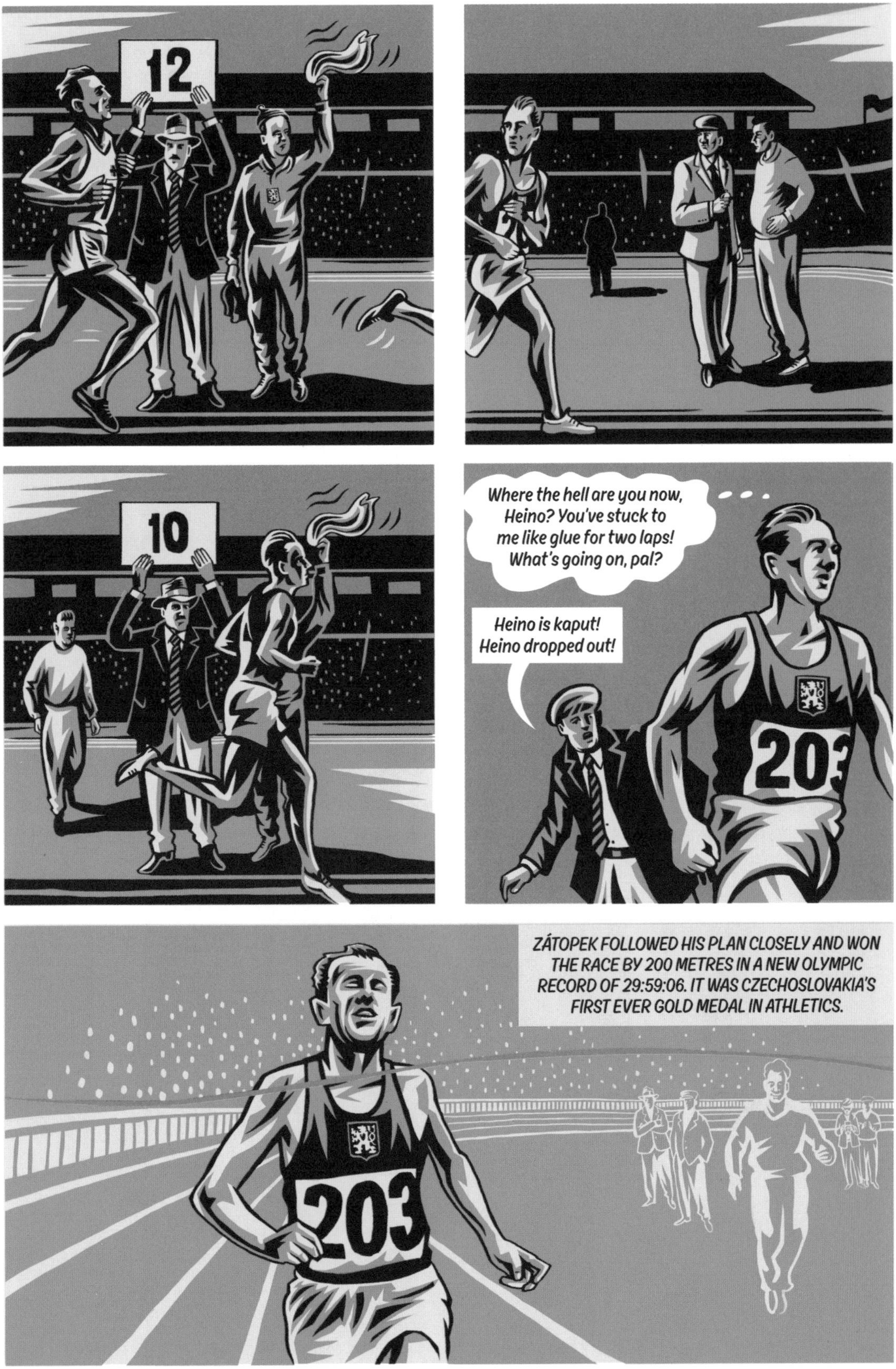
12
10
Where the hell are you now, Heino? You've stuck to me like glue for two laps! What's going on, pal?
Heino is kaput! Heino dropped out!
203
ZÁTOPEK FOLLOWED HIS PLAN CLOSELY AND WON THE RACE BY 200 METRES IN A NEW OLYMPIC RECORD OF 29:59:06. IT WAS CZECHOSLOVAKIA'S FIRST EVER GOLD MEDAL IN ATHLETICS.
203

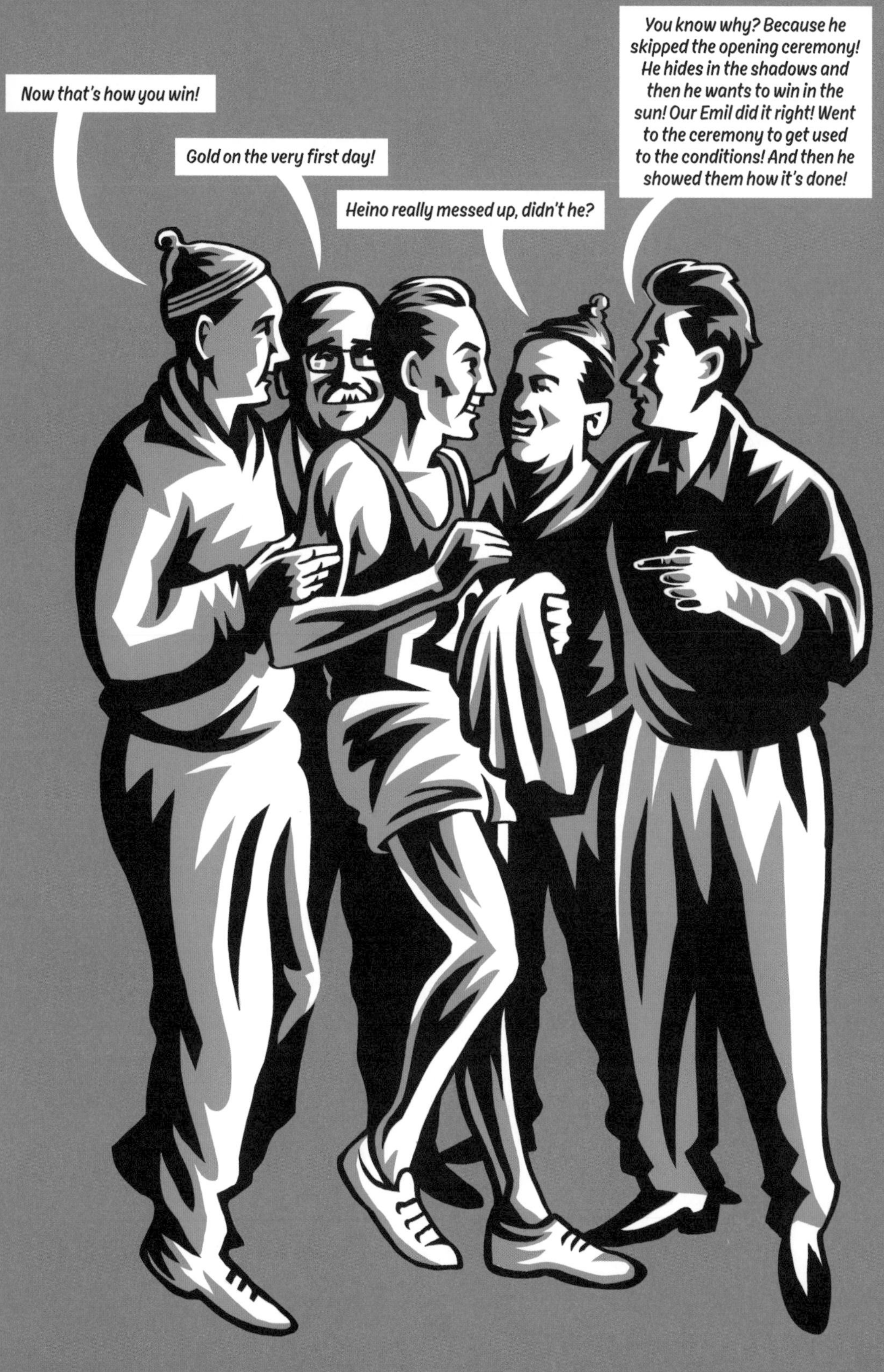

Now that's how you win!
Gold on the very first day!
Heino really messed up, didn't he?
You know why? Because he skipped the opening ceremony! He hides in the shadows and then he wants to win in the sun! Our Emil did it right! Went to the ceremony to get used to the conditions! And then he showed them how it's done!

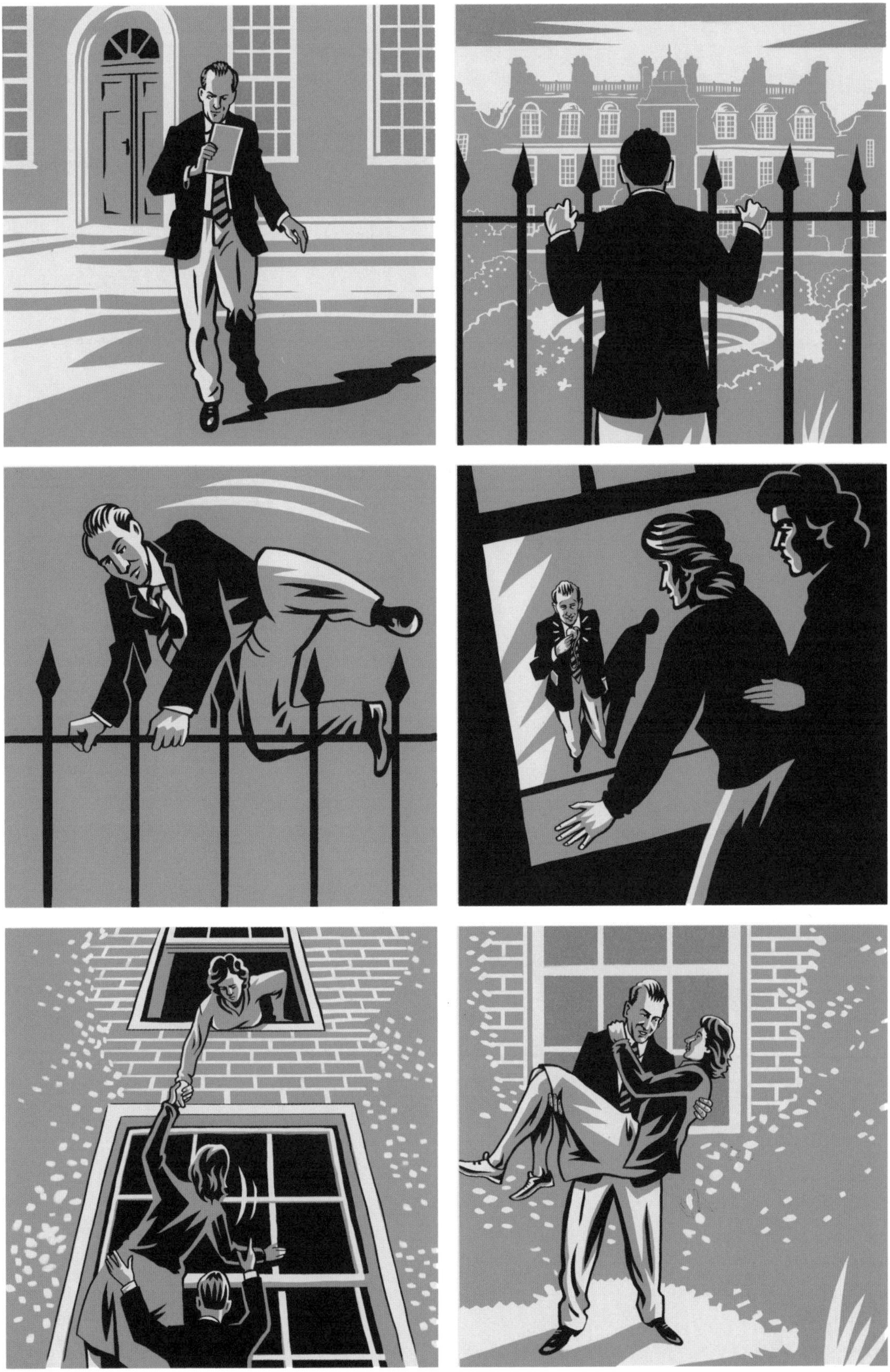

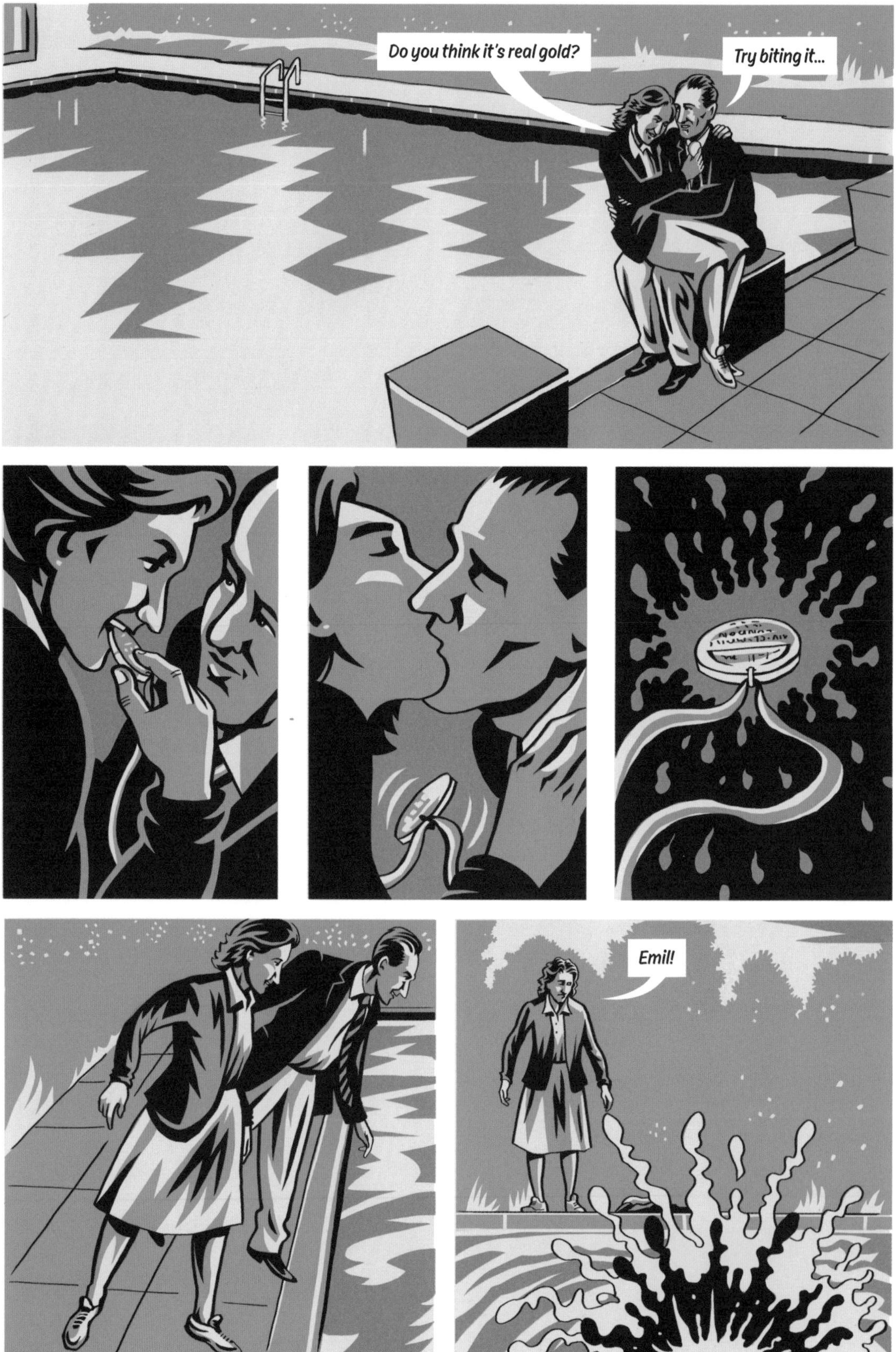
Do you think it's real gold?
Try biting it...
Emil!

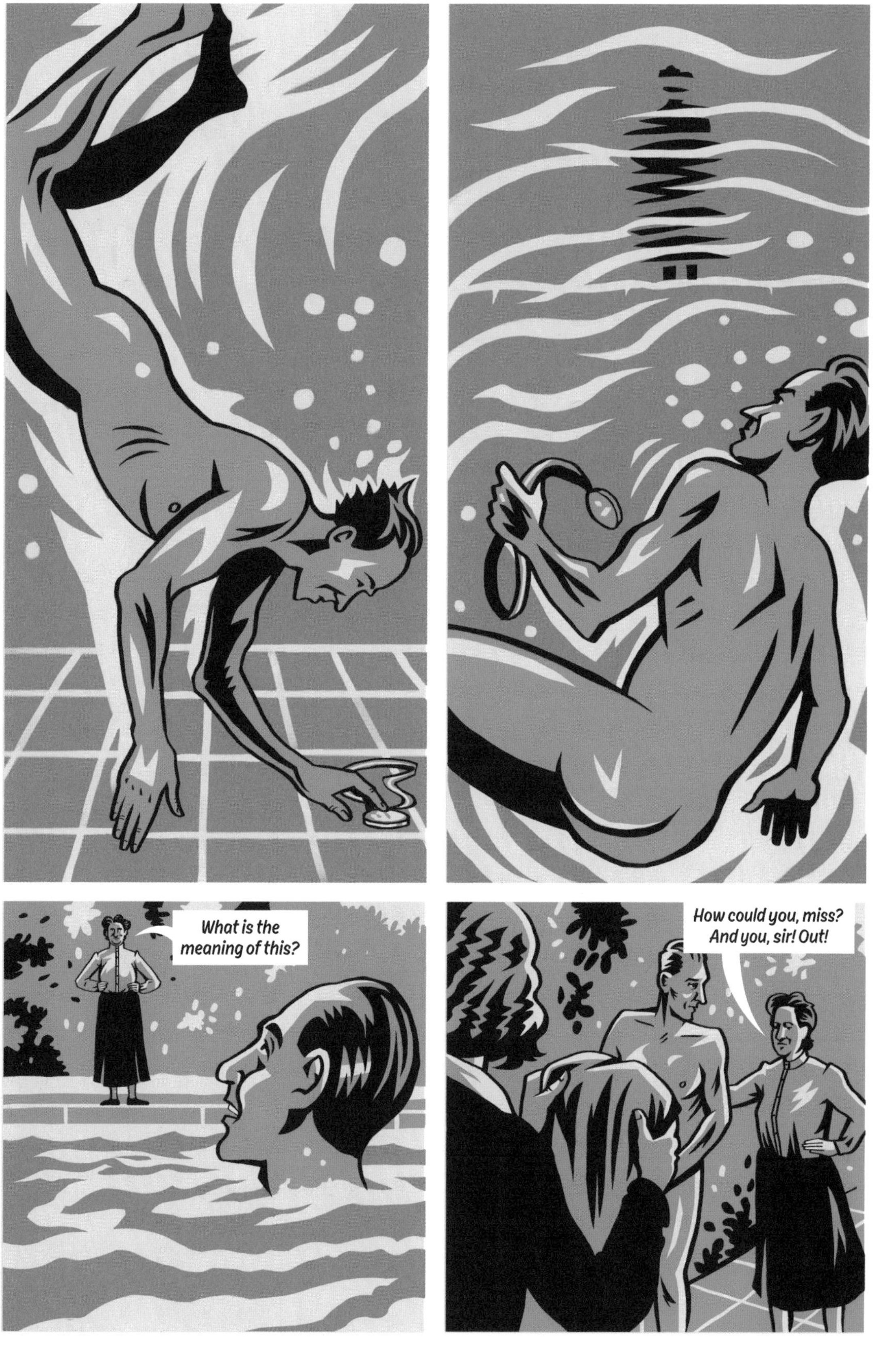
What is the meaning of this?
How could you, miss? And you, sir! Out!

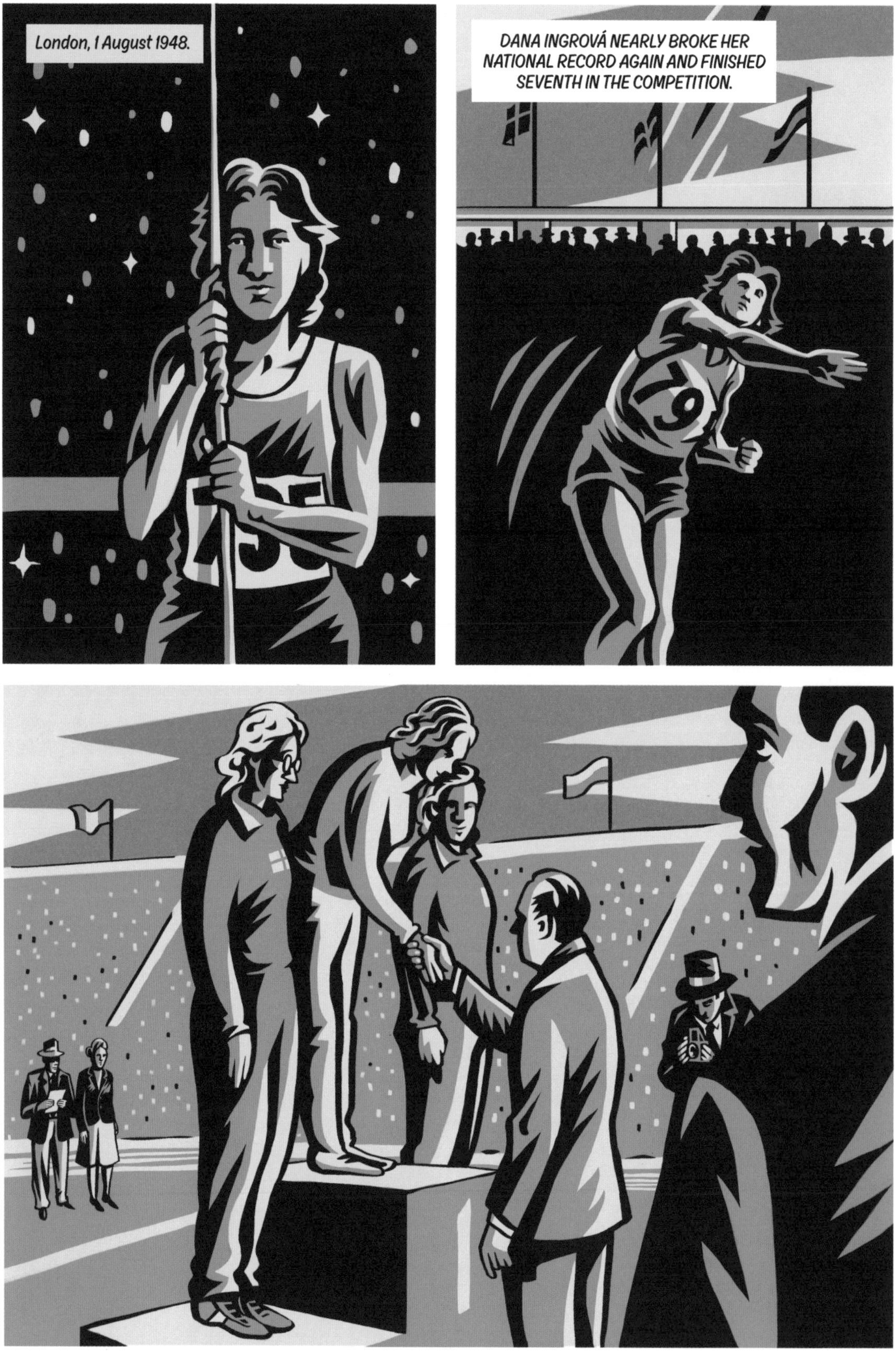
London, 1 August 1948.
DANA INGROVÁ NEARLY BROKE HER NATIONAL RECORD AGAIN AND FINISHED SEVENTH IN THE COMPETITION.

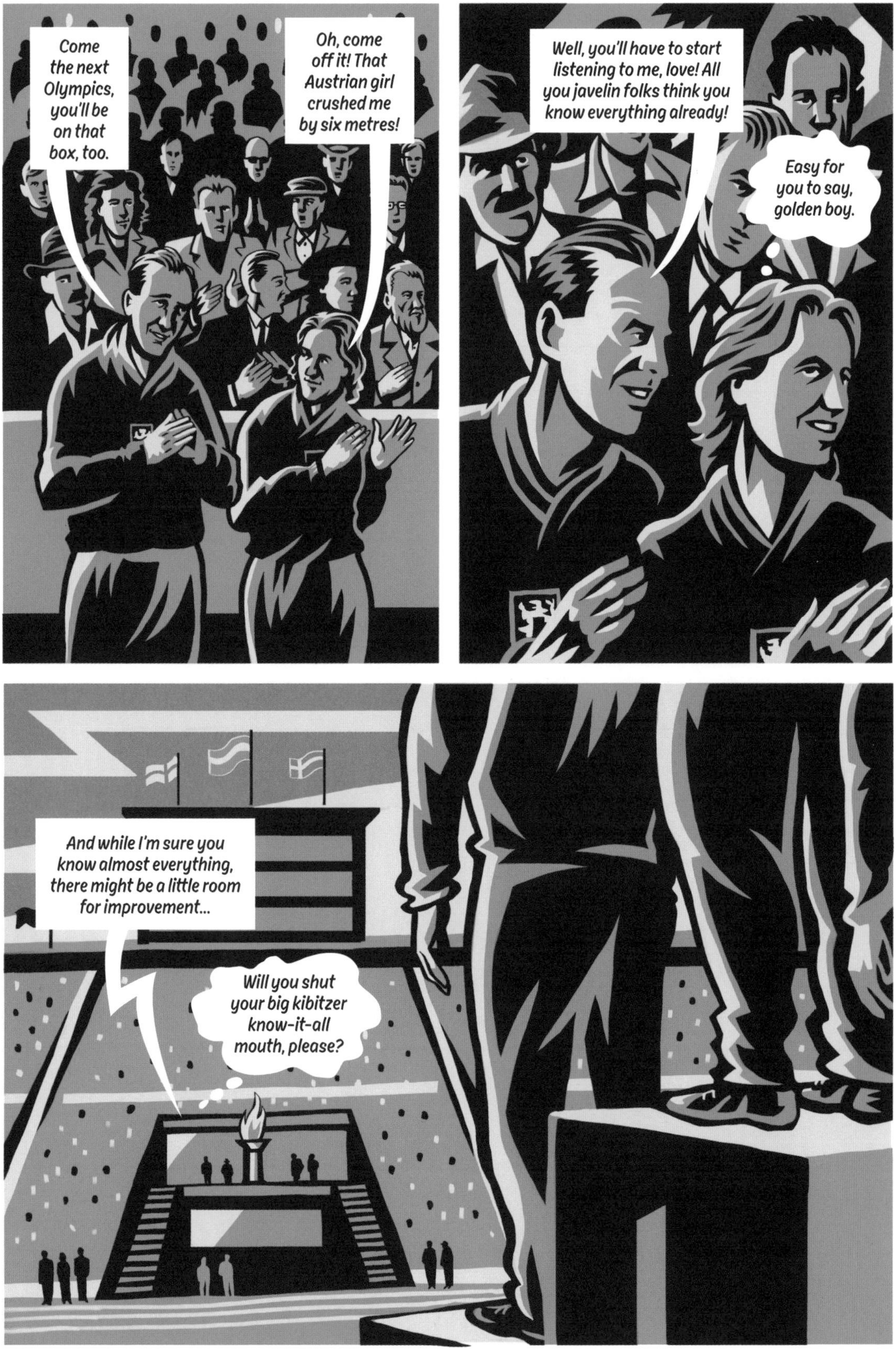
Come the next Olympics, you'll be on that box, too.
Oh, come off it! That Austrian girl crushed me by six metres!
Well, you'll have to start listening to me, love! All you javelin folks think you know everything already!
Easy for you to say, golden boy.
And while I'm sure you know almost everything, there might be a little room for improvement...
Will you shut your big kibitzer know-it-all mouth, please?

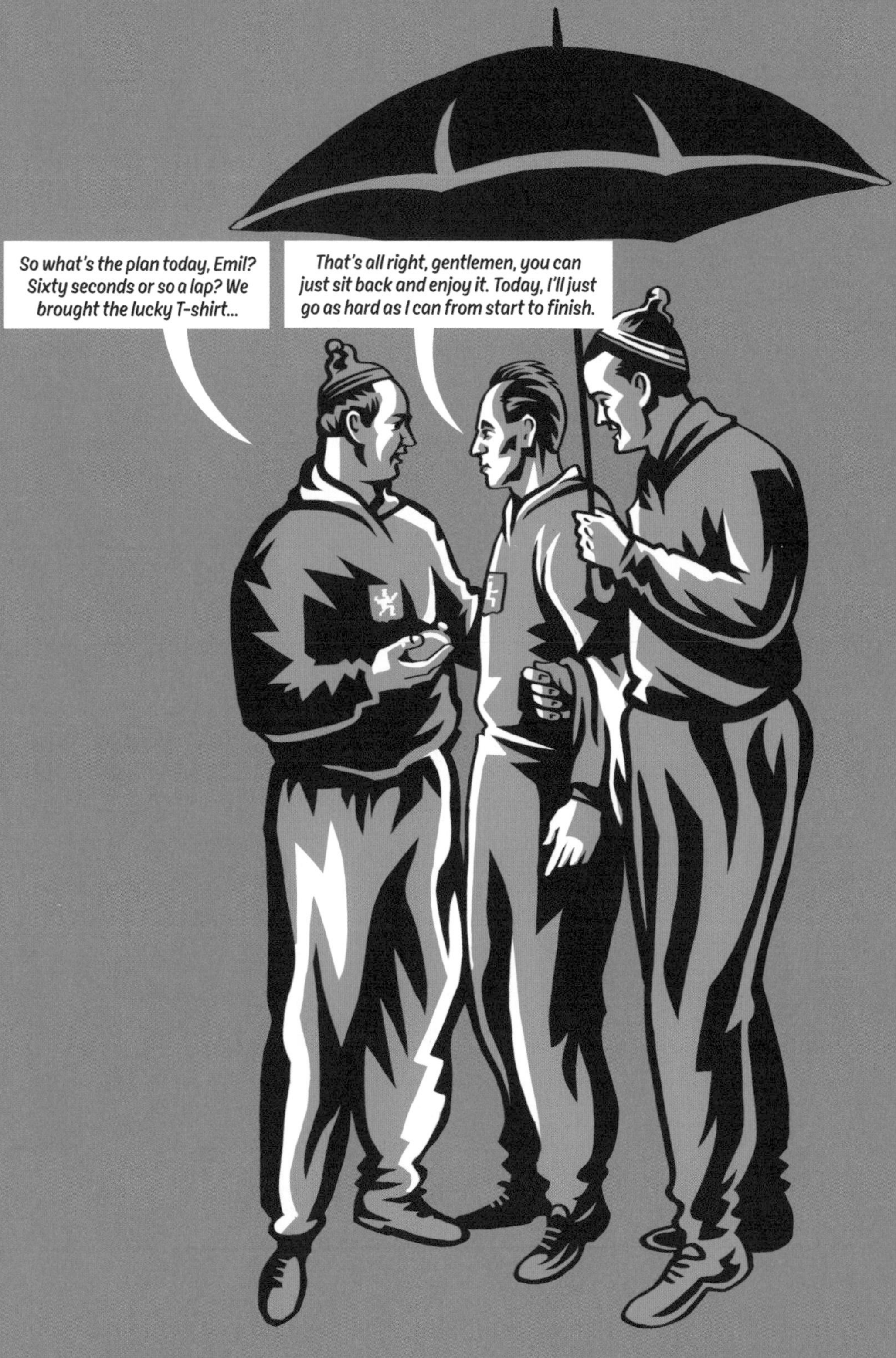
So what's the plan today, Emil? Sixty seconds or so a lap? We brought the lucky T-shirt...
That's all right, gentlemen, you can just sit back and enjoy it. Today, I'll just go as hard as I can from start to finish.

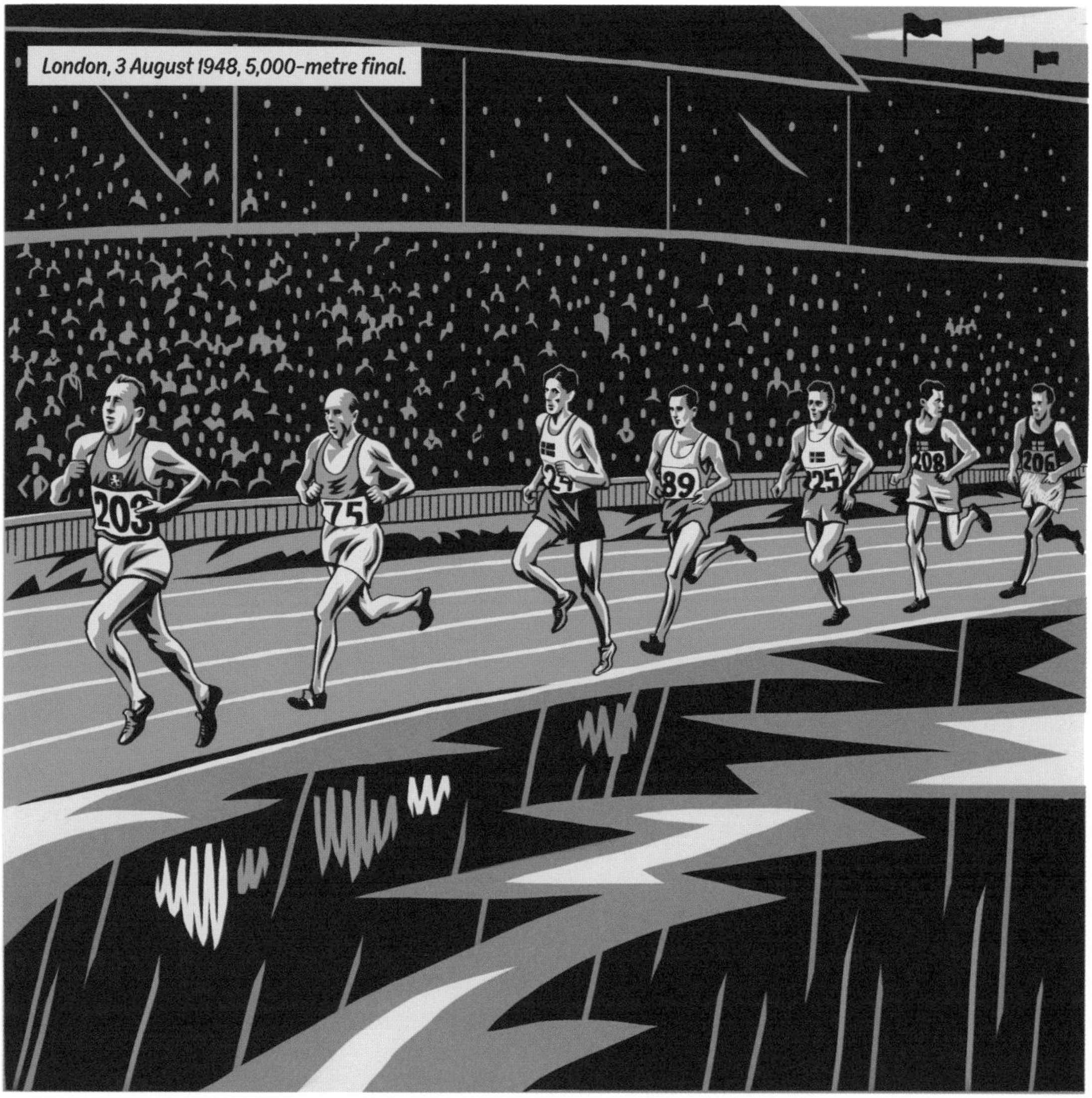
London, 3 August 1948, 5,000-metre final.
203
75
89
25
208
206

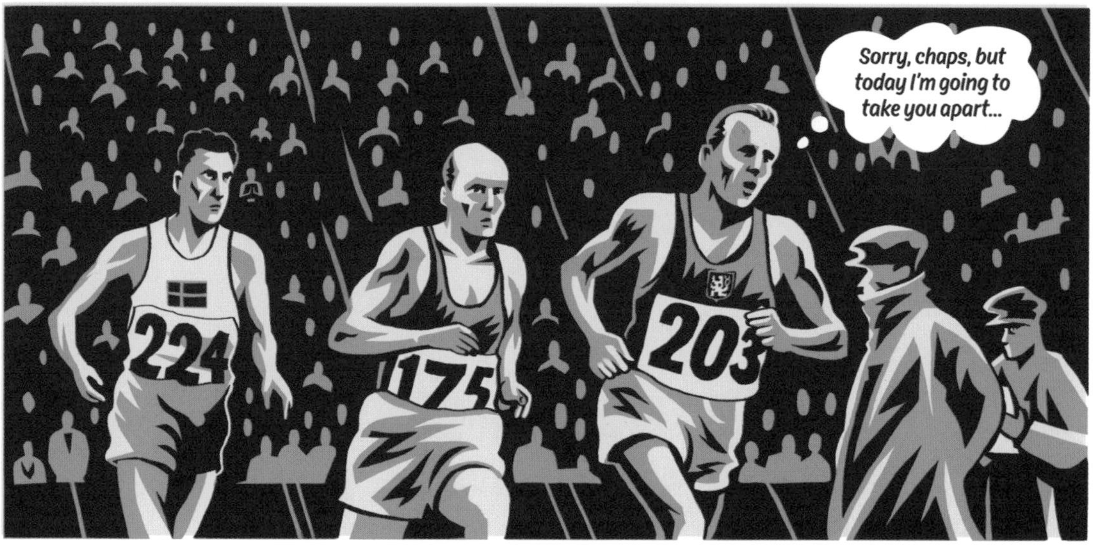
Sorry, chaps, but today I'm going to take you apart...
224
175
203

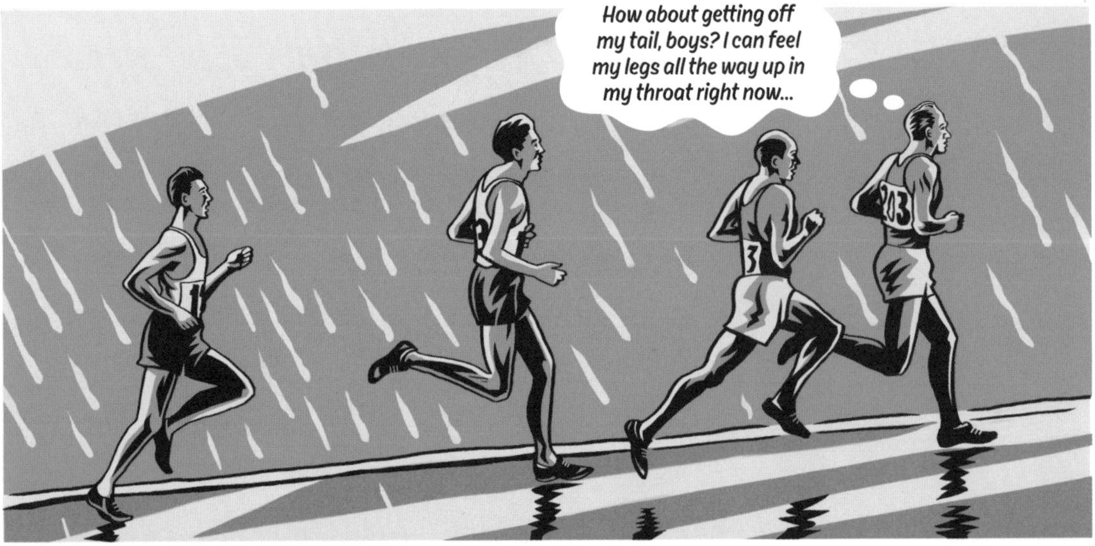
How about getting off my tail, boys? I can feel my legs all the way up in my throat right now...
203
3
2

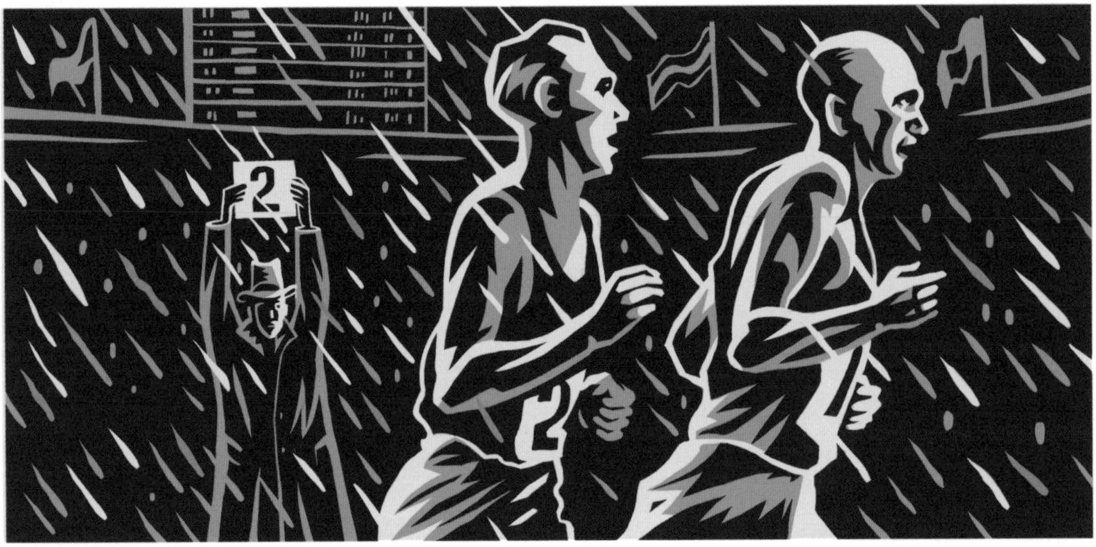
2
2

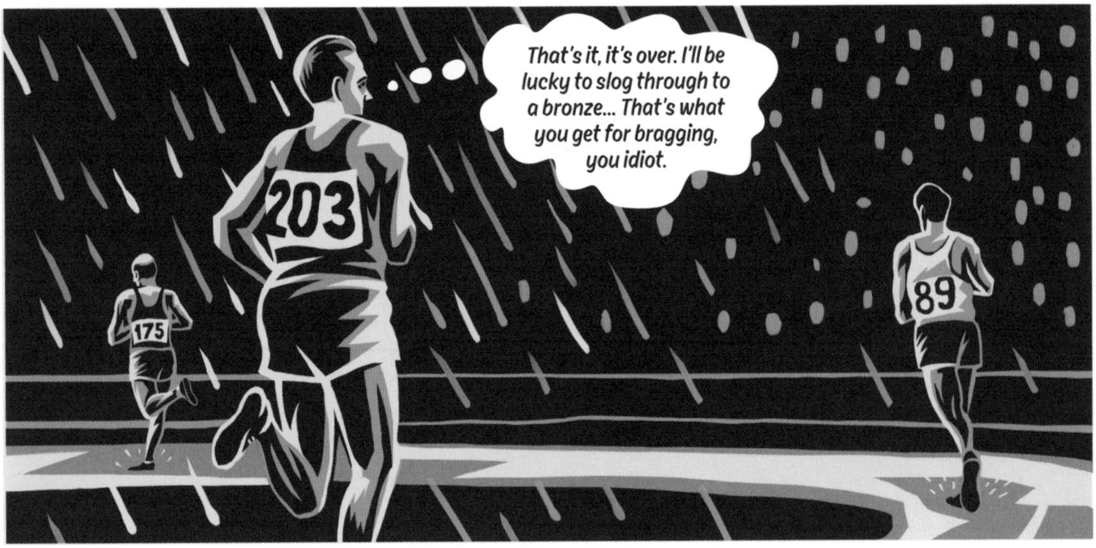
That's it, it's over. I'll be lucky to slog through to a bronze... That's what you get for bragging, you idiot.
203
175
89

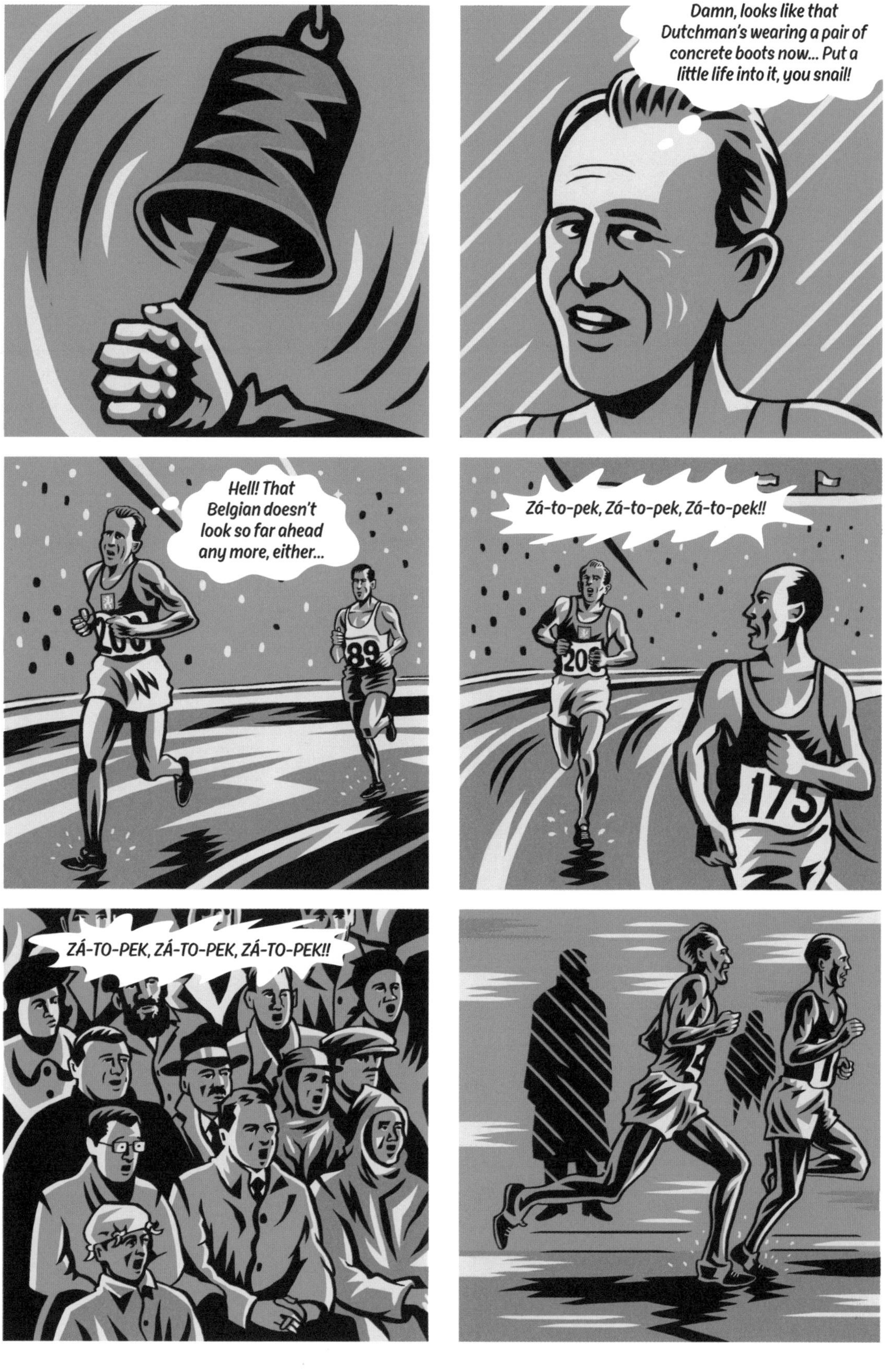
Damn, looks like that Dutchman's wearing a pair of concrete boots now... Put a little life into it, you snail!
Hell! That Belgian doesn't look so far ahead any more, either...
Zá-to-pek, Zá-to-pek, Zá-to-pek!!
ZÁ-TO-PEK, ZÁ-TO-PEK, ZÁ-TO-PEK!!

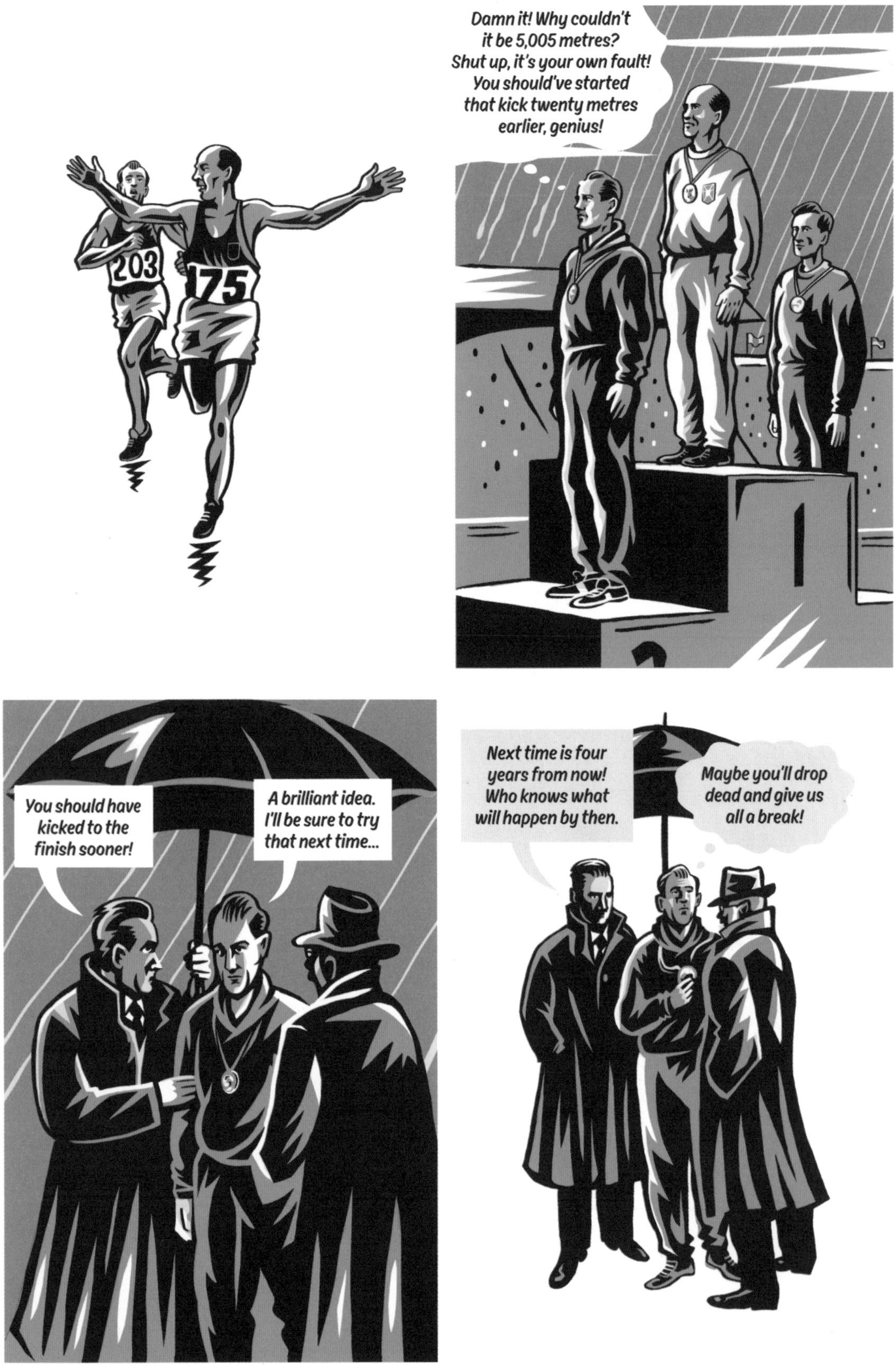
203
175
Damn it! Why couldn't it be 5,005 metres? Shut up, it's your own fault! You should've started that kick twenty metres earlier, genius!
You should have kicked to the finish sooner!
A brilliant idea. I'll be sure to try that next time...
Next time is four years from now! Who knows what will happen by then.
Maybe you'll drop dead and give us all a break!

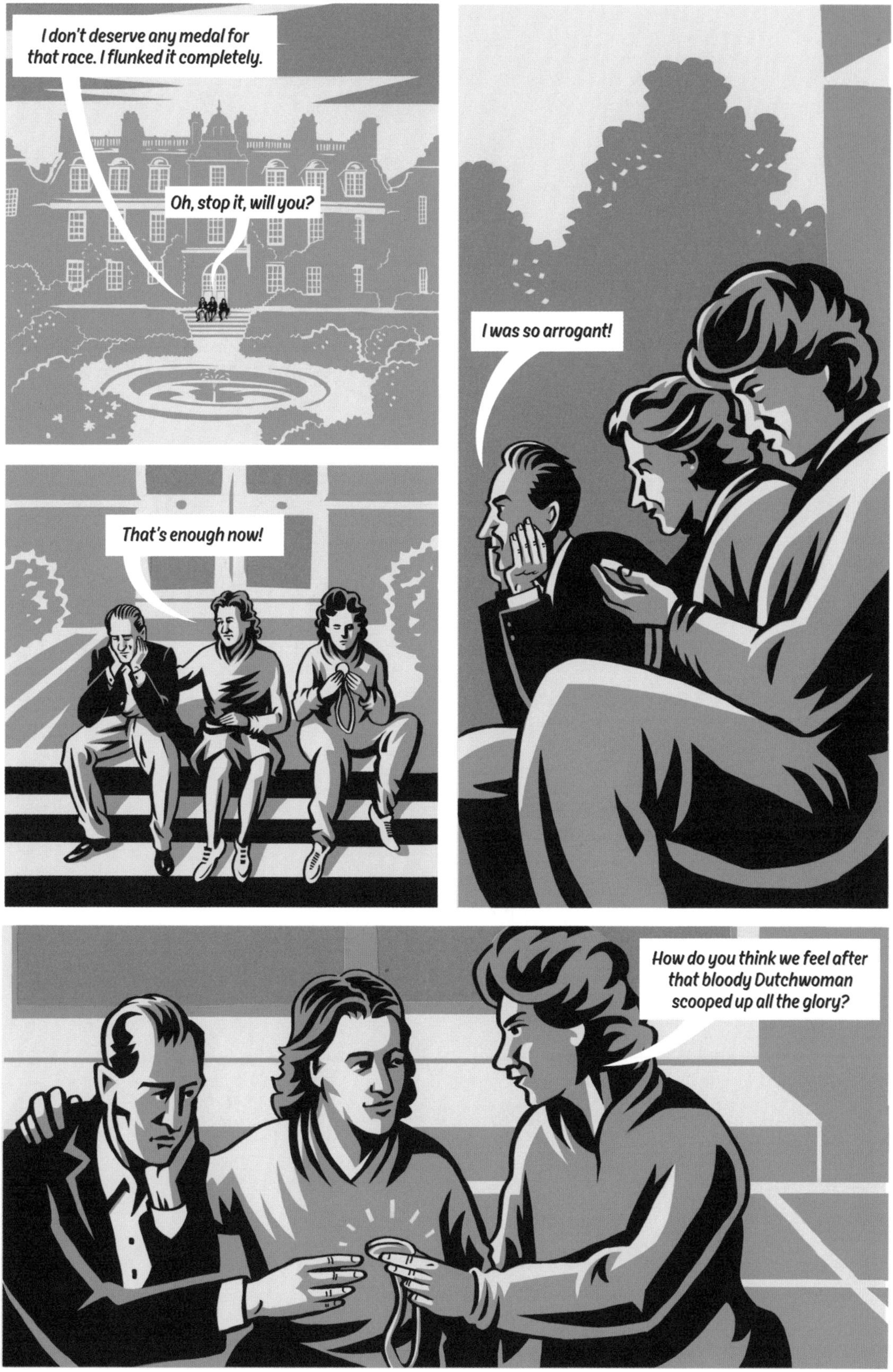
I don't deserve any medal for that race. I flunked it completely.
Oh, stop it, will you?
I was so arrogant!
That's enough now!
How do you think we feel after that bloody Dutchwoman scooped up all the glory?

THE STAR OF THE LONDON OLYMPICS WAS FANNY BLANKERS-KOEN, "THE FLYING HOUSEWIFE". THE THIRTY-YEAR-OLD MOTHER OF TWO WON THE 100- AND 200-METRE SPRINTS, THE 80-METRE HURDLES AND THE 4 X 100-METRE RELAY. (AT THAT TIME, 200 METRES WAS THE LONGEST DISTANCE AT WHICH WOMEN COULD COMPETE; IT WAS FEARED THAT LONGER DISTANCES WOULD TAX THEIR FRAGILE CONSTITUTIONS.) "THE FLYING HOUSEWIFE" WOULD PROBABLY HAVE WON MORE MEDALS IN LONDON, AS SHE WAS ALSO THE WORLD RECORD-HOLDER IN LONG JUMP AND HIGH JUMP. BUT IN THOSE DAYS, NO ATHLETE WAS ALLOWED TO COMPETE IN MORE THAN THREE INDIVIDUAL DISCIPLINES.

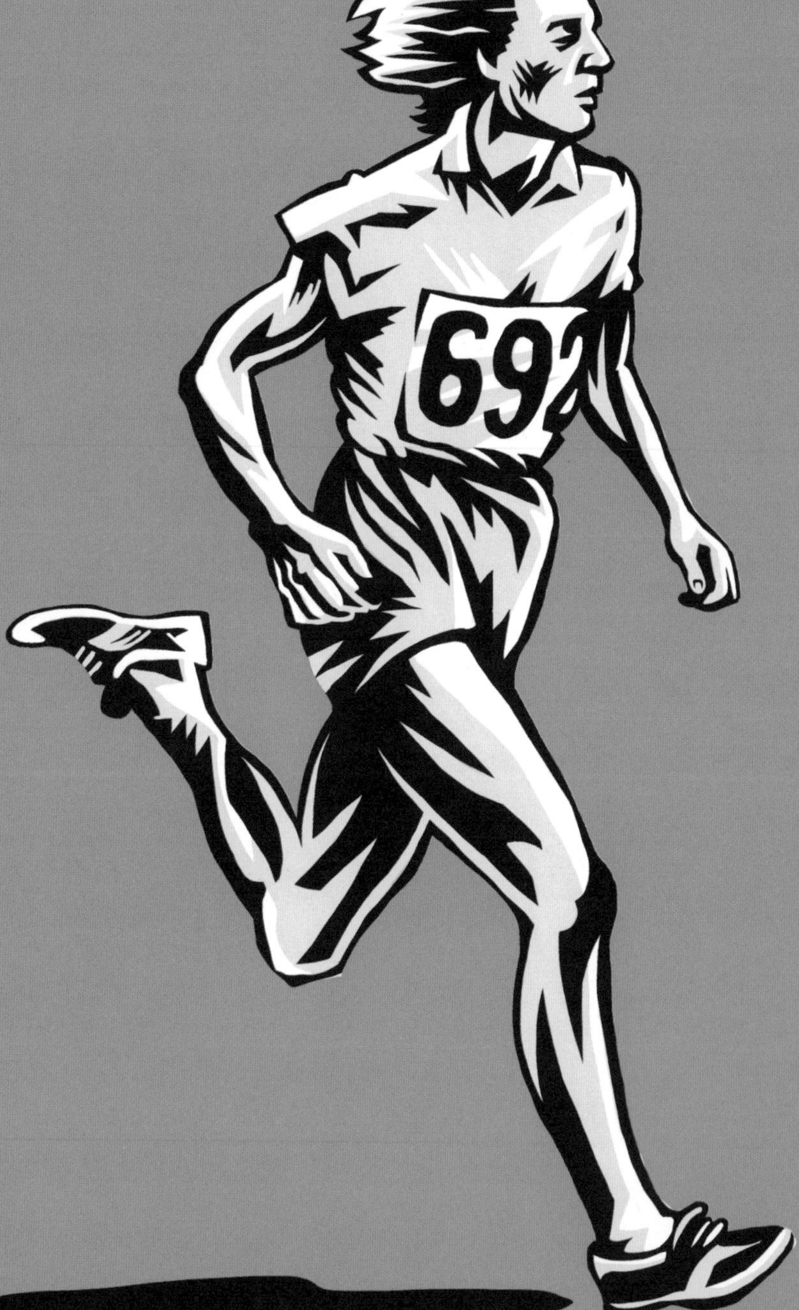
69

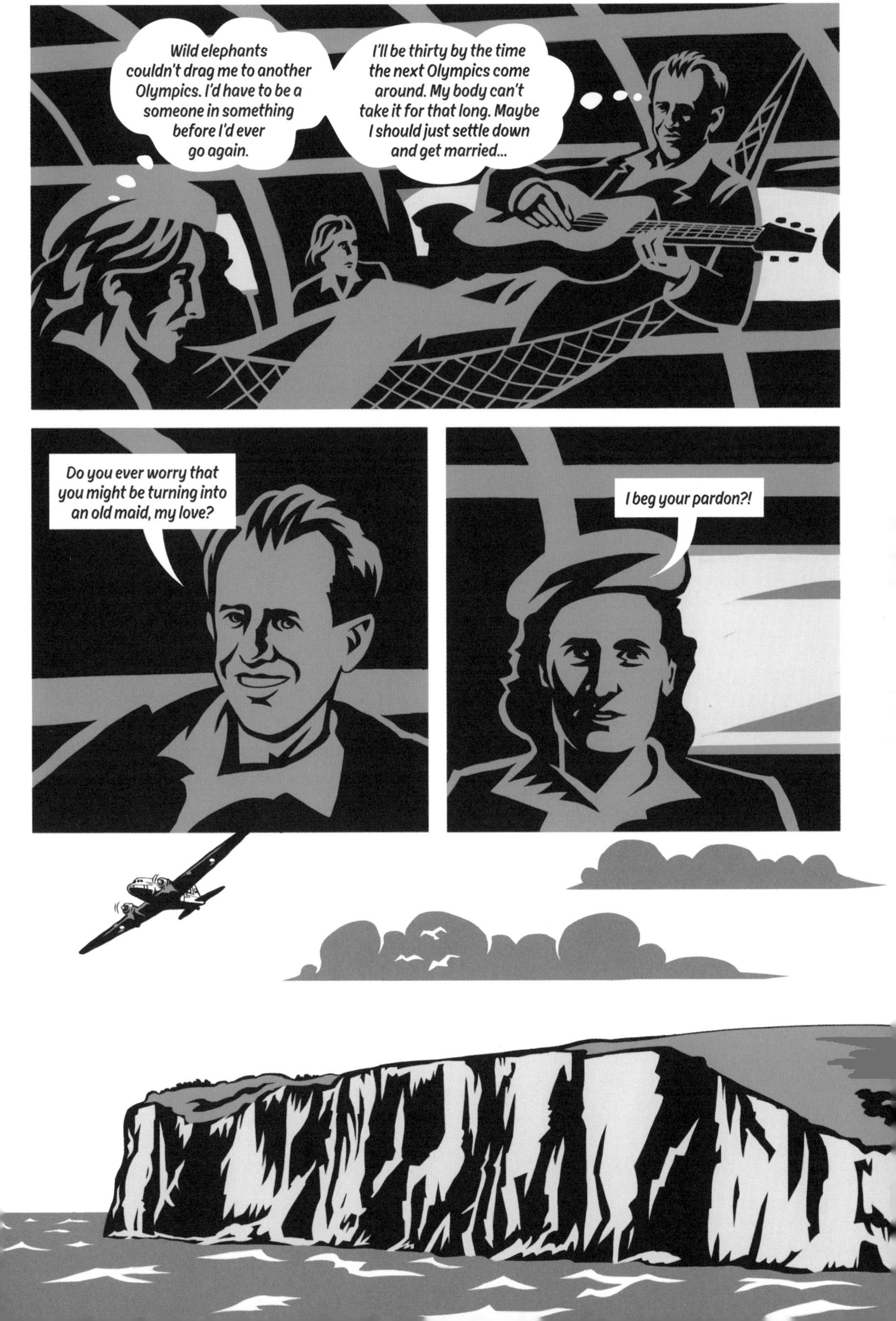
Wild elephants couldn't drag me to another Olympics. I'd have to be a someone in something before I'd ever go again.
I'll be thirty by the time the next Olympics come around. My body can't take it for that long. Maybe I should just settle down and get married...
Do you ever worry that you might be turning into an old maid, my love?
I beg your pardon?!

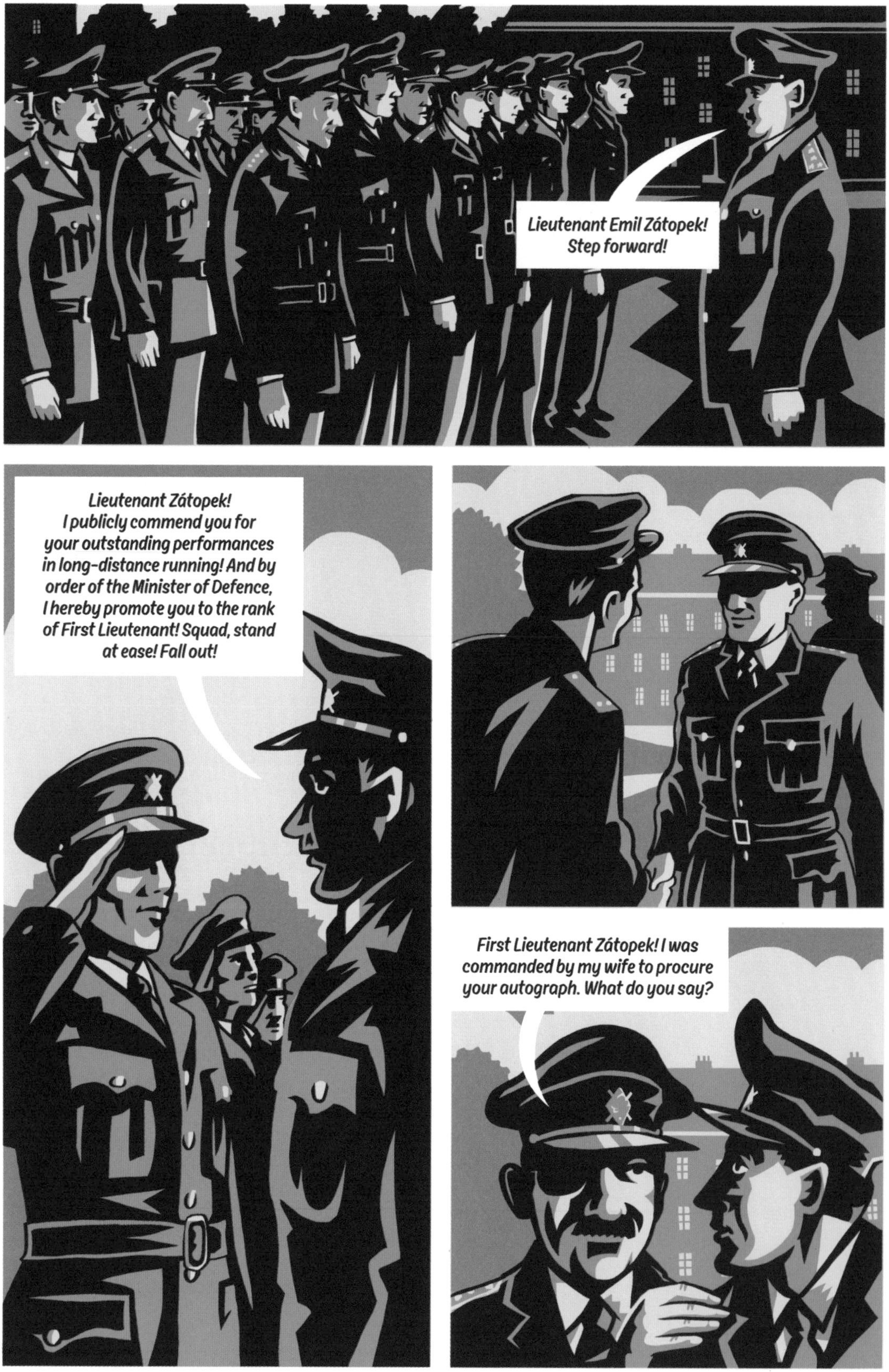
Lieutenant Emil Zátopek! Step forward!
Lieutenant Zátopek! I publicly commend you for your outstanding performances in long-distance running! And by order of the Minister of Defence, I hereby promote you to the rank of First Lieutenant! Squad, stand at ease! Fall out!
First Lieutenant Zátopek! I was commanded by my wife to procure your autograph. What do you say?

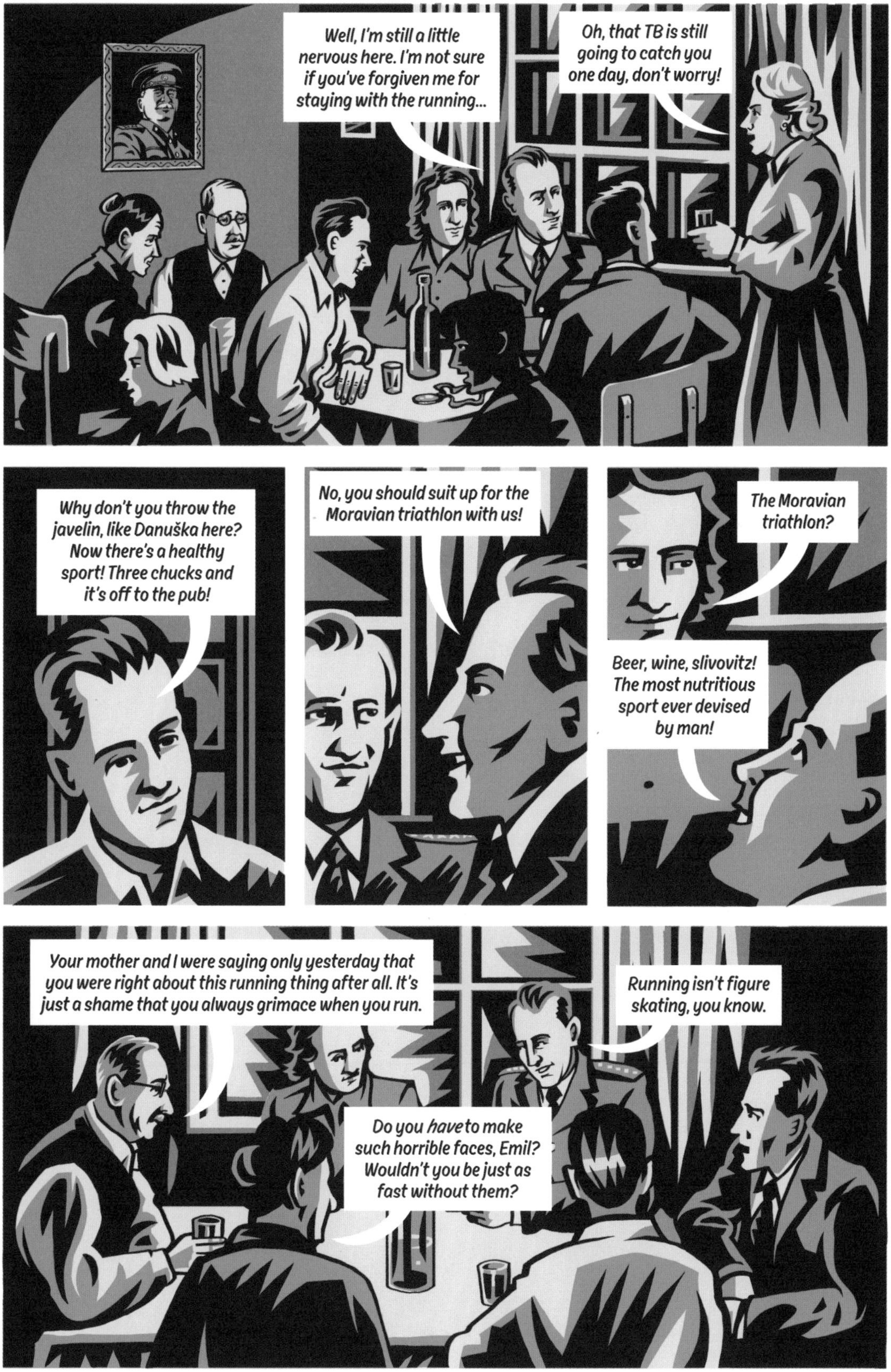

Well, I'm still a little nervous here. I'm not sure if you've forgiven me for staying with the running...
Oh, that TB is still going to catch you one day, don't worry!
Why don't you throw the javelin, like Danuška here? Now there's a healthy sport! Three chucks and it's off to the pub!
No, you should suit up for the Moravian triathlon with us!
The Moravian triathlon?
Beer, wine, slivovitz! The most nutritious sport ever devised by man!
Your mother and I were saying only yesterday that you were right about this running thing after all. It's just a shame that you always grimace when you run.
Running isn't figure skating, you know.
Do you *have* to make such horrible faces, Emil? Wouldn't you be just as fast without them?

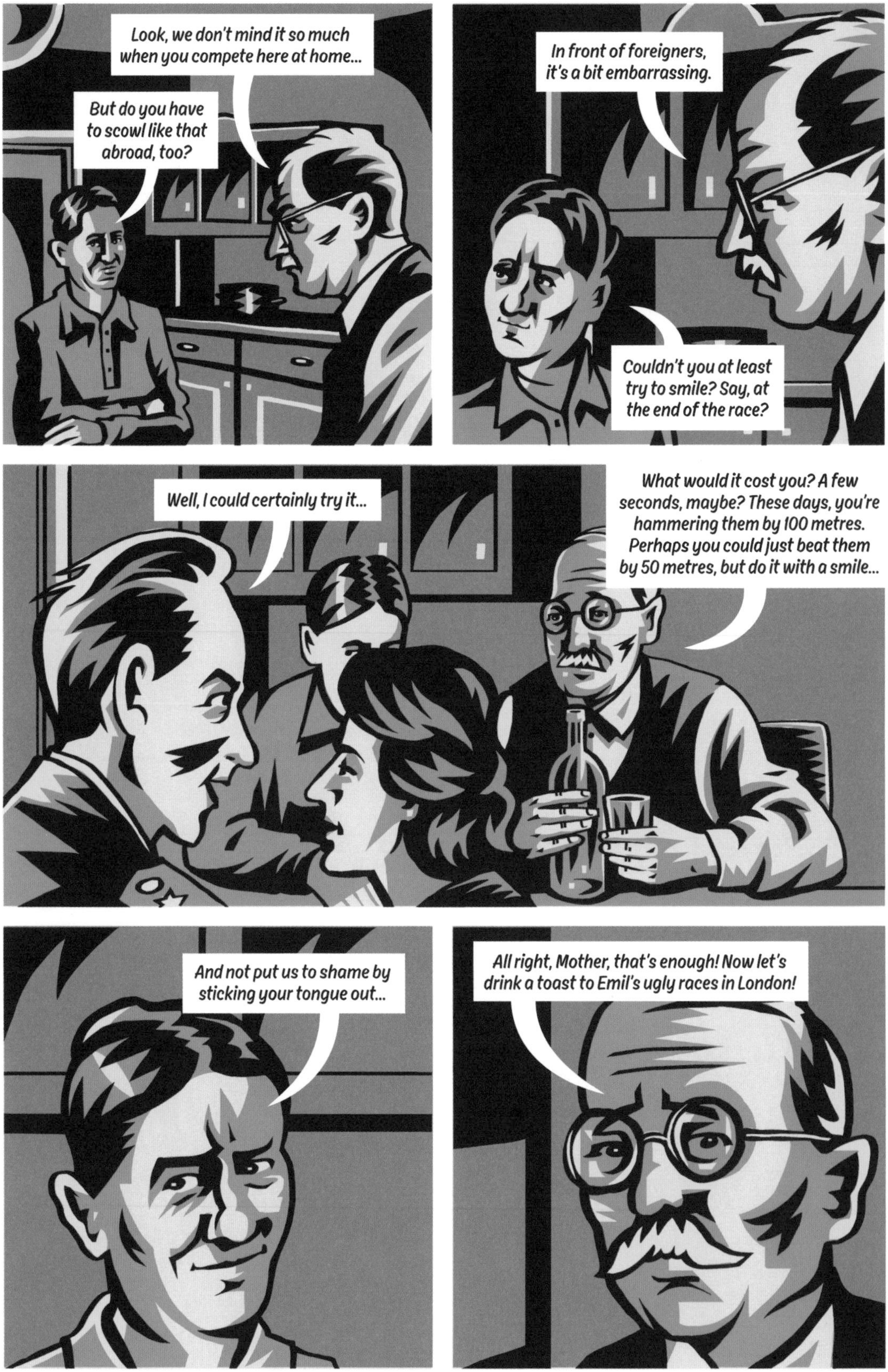
Look, we don't mind it so much when you compete here at home...
But do you have to scowl like that abroad, too?
In front of foreigners, it's a bit embarrassing.
Couldn't you at least try to smile? Say, at the end of the race?
Well, I could certainly try it...
What would it cost you? A few seconds, maybe? These days, you're hammering them by 100 metres. Perhaps you could just beat them by 50 metres, but do it with a smile...
And not put us to shame by sticking your tongue out...
All right, Mother, that's enough! Now let's drink a toast to Emil's ugly races in London!

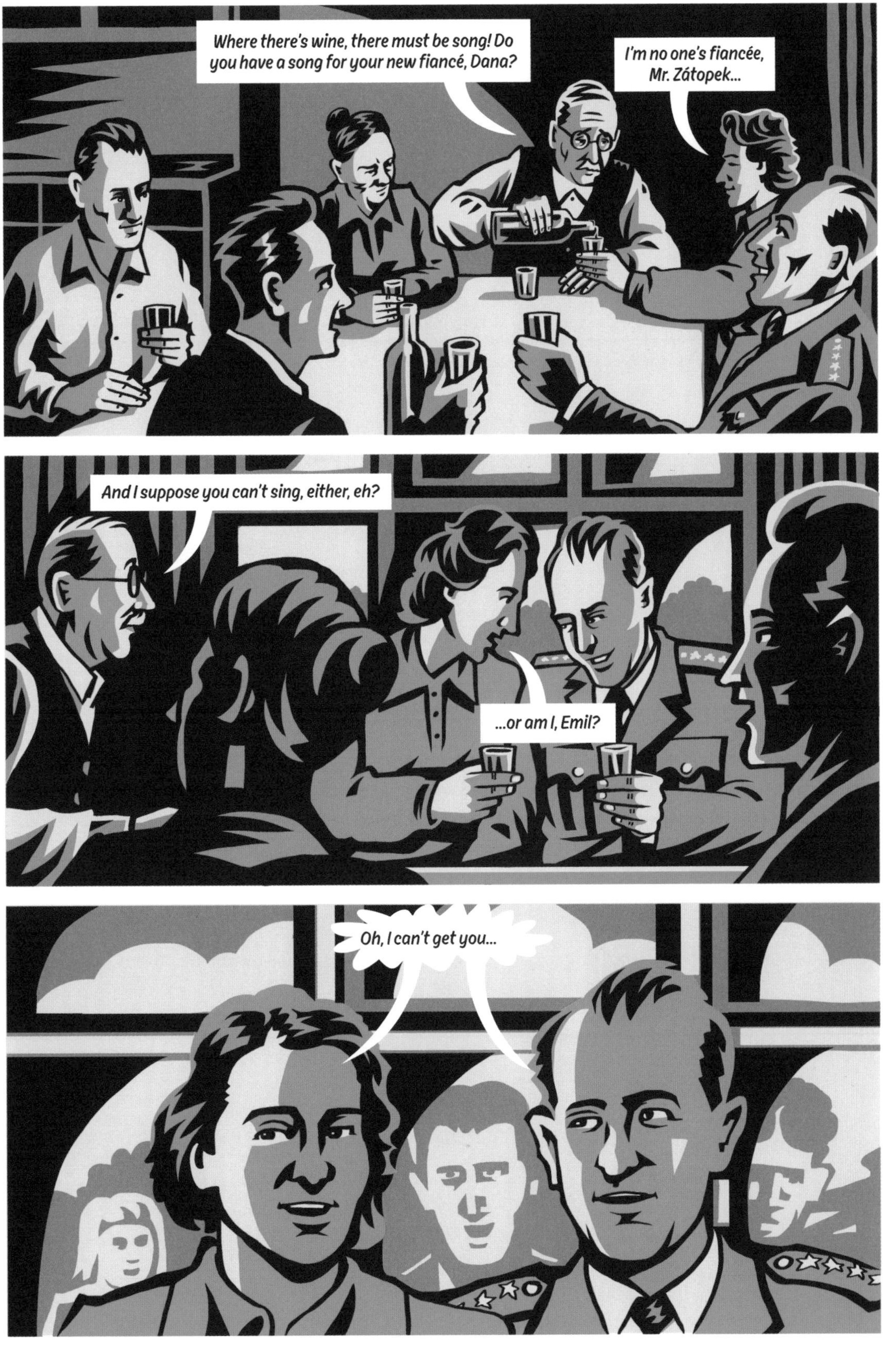
Where there's wine, there must be song! Do you have a song for your new fiancé, Dana?
I'm no one's fiancée, Mr. Zátopek...
And I suppose you can't sing, either, eh?
...or am I, Emil?
Oh, I can't get you...

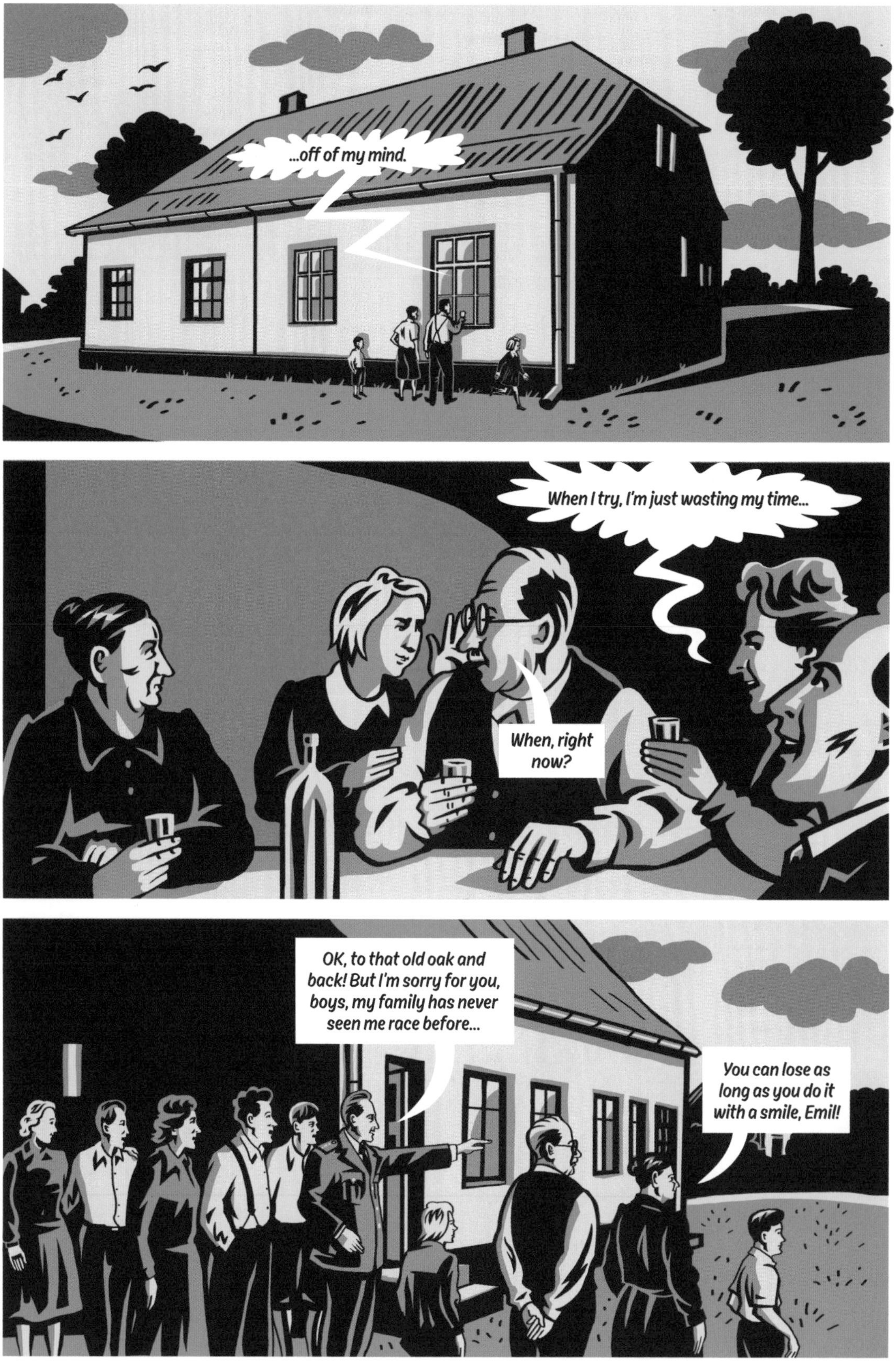
...off of my mind.
When I try, I'm just wasting my time...
When, right now?
OK, to that old oak and back! But I'm sorry for you, boys, my family has never seen me race before...
You can lose as long as you do it with a smile, Emil!

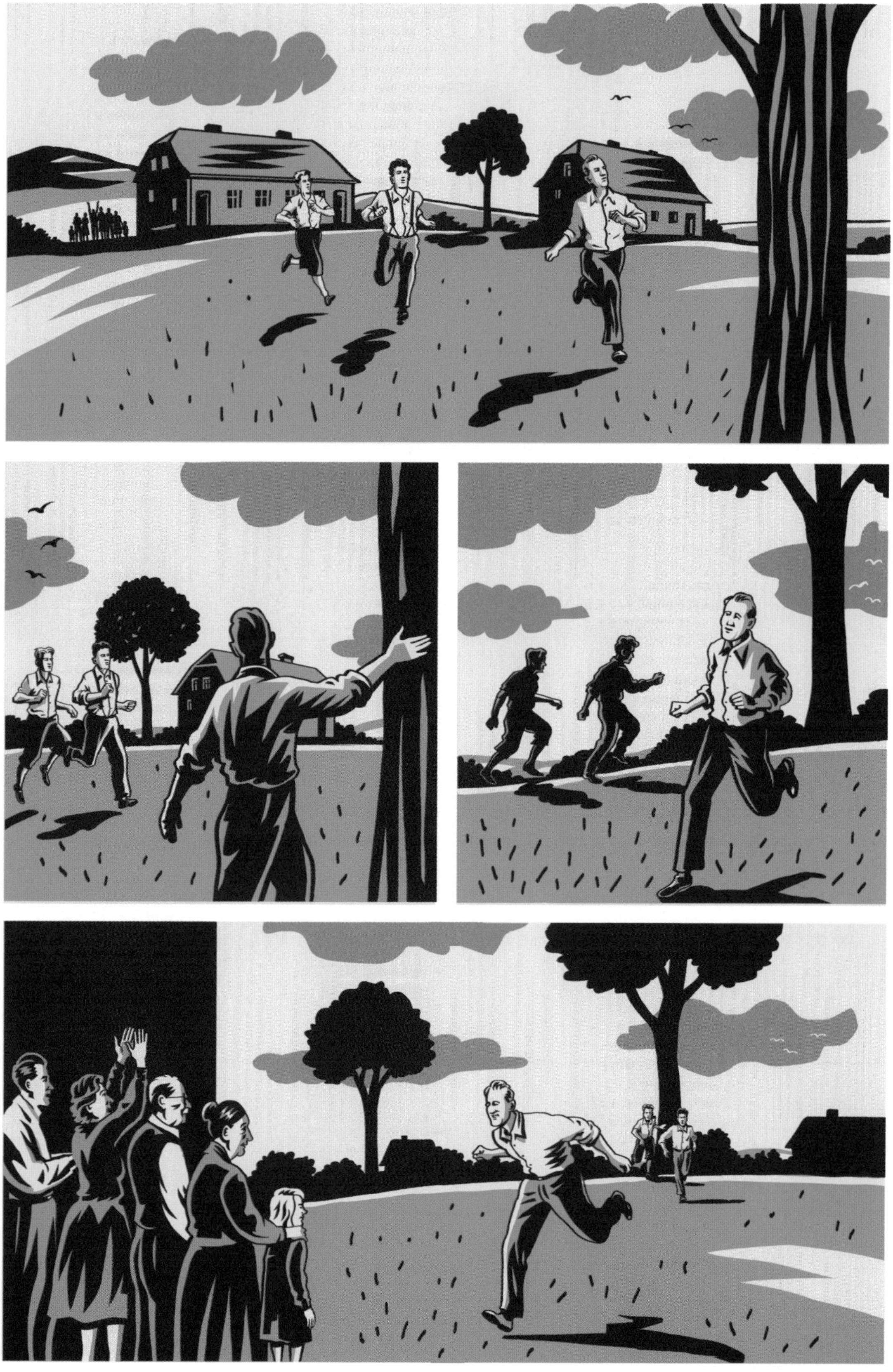

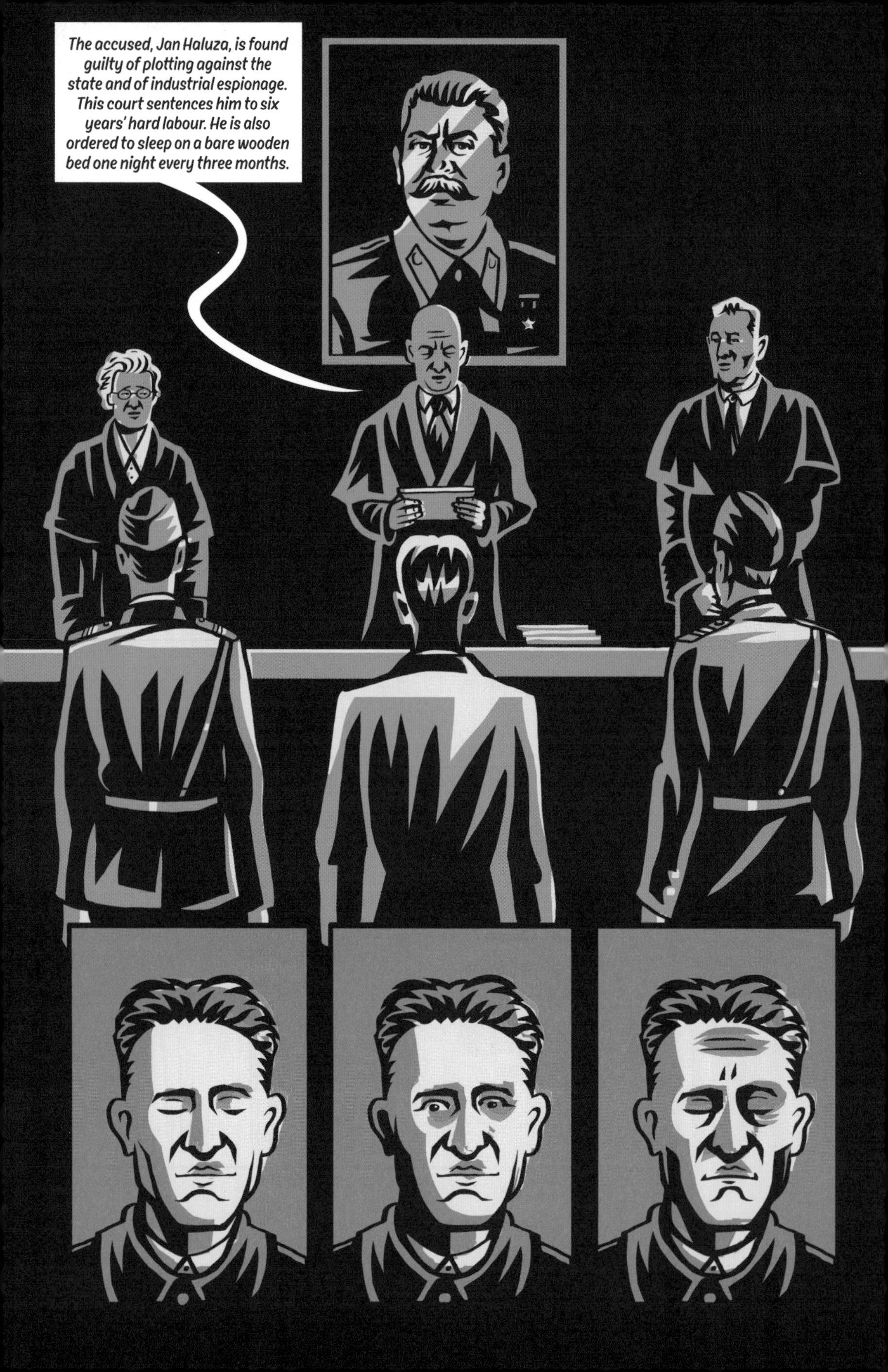
The accused, Jan Haluza, is found guilty of plotting against the state and of industrial espionage. This court sentences him to six years' hard labour. He is also ordered to sleep on a bare wooden bed one night every three months.

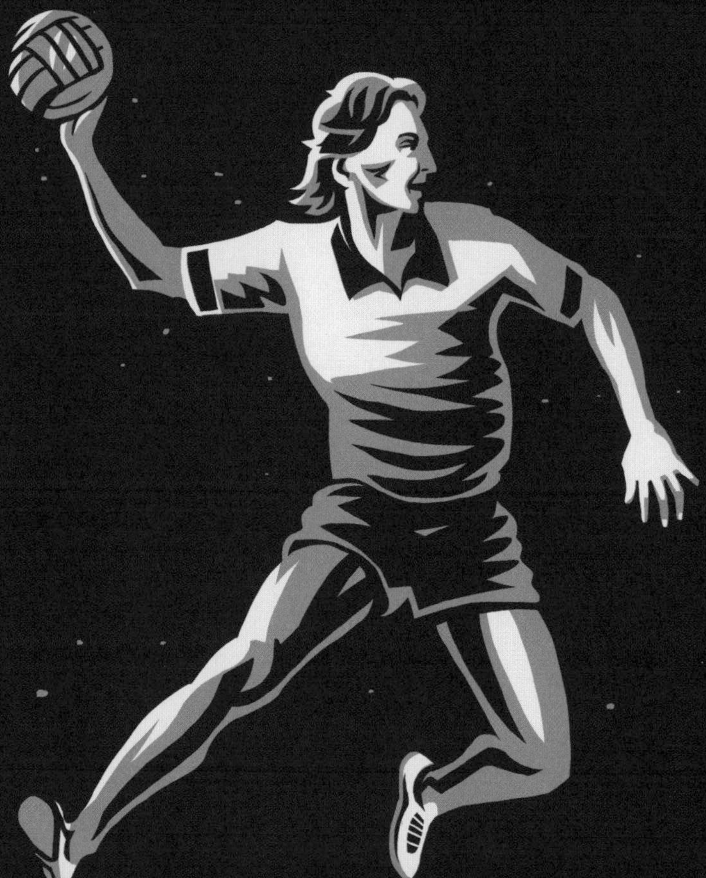

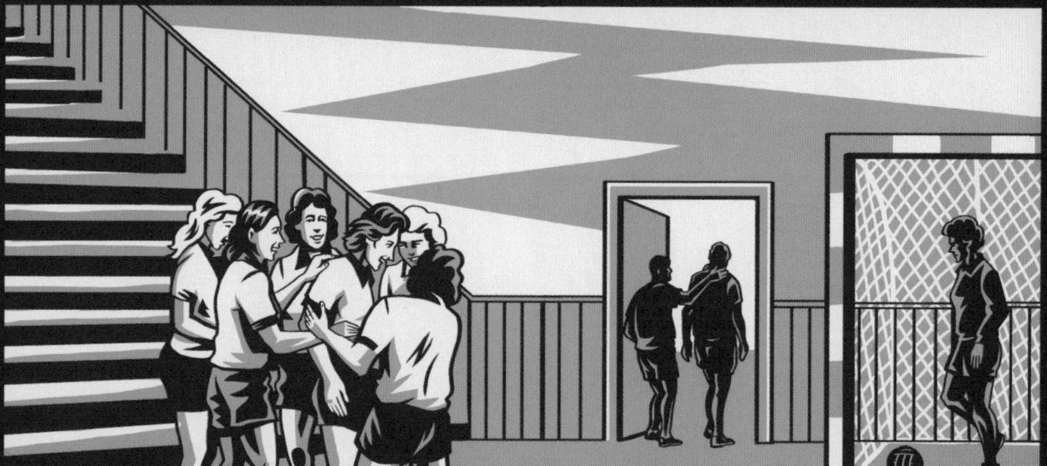

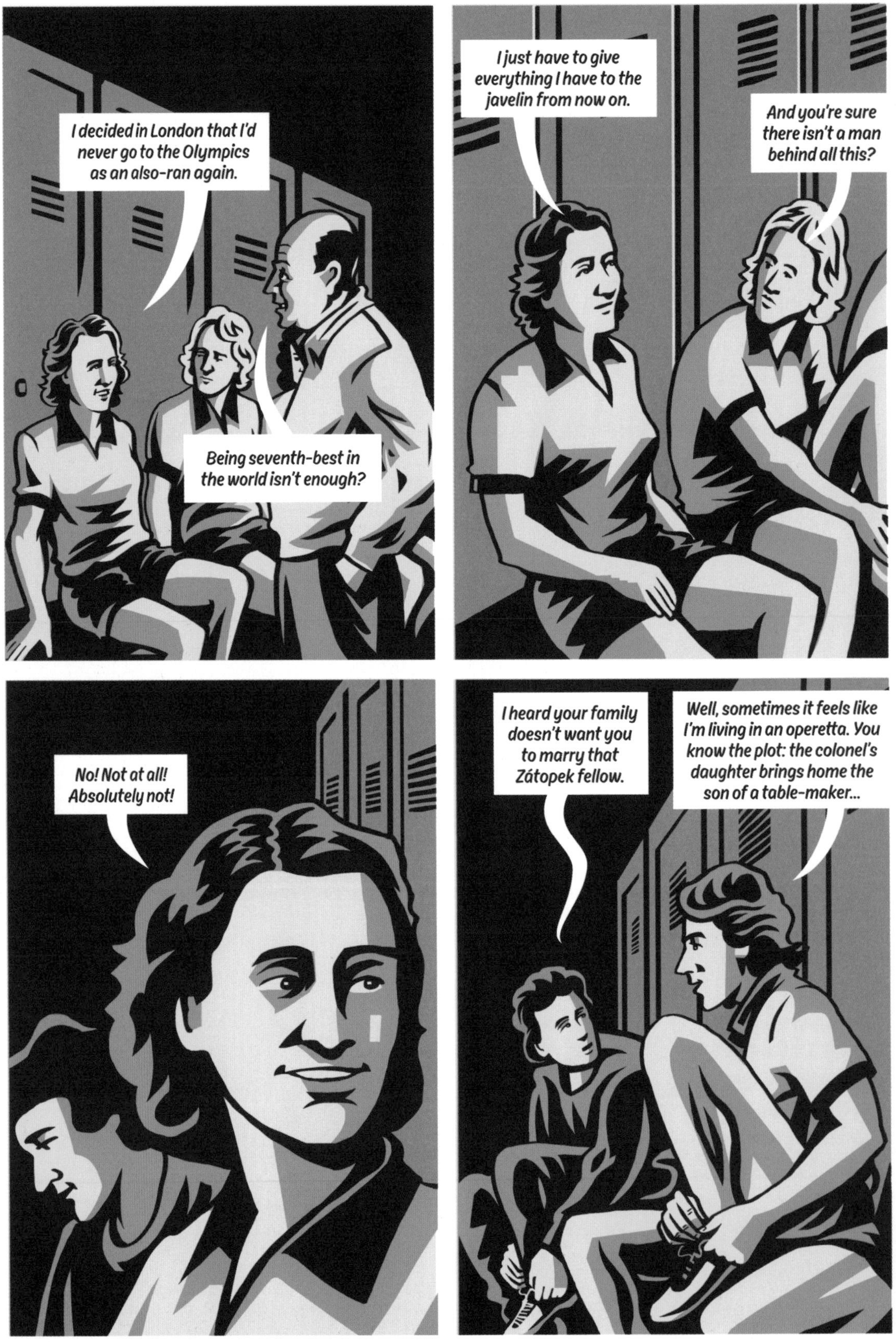
I decided in London that I'd never go to the Olympics as an also-ran again.
Being seventh-best in the world isn't enough?
I just have to give everything I have to the javelin from now on.
And you're sure there isn't a man behind all this?
No! Not at all! Absolutely not!
I heard your family doesn't want you to marry that Zátopek fellow.
Well, sometimes it feels like I'm living in an operetta. You know the plot: the colonel's daughter brings home the son of a table-maker...

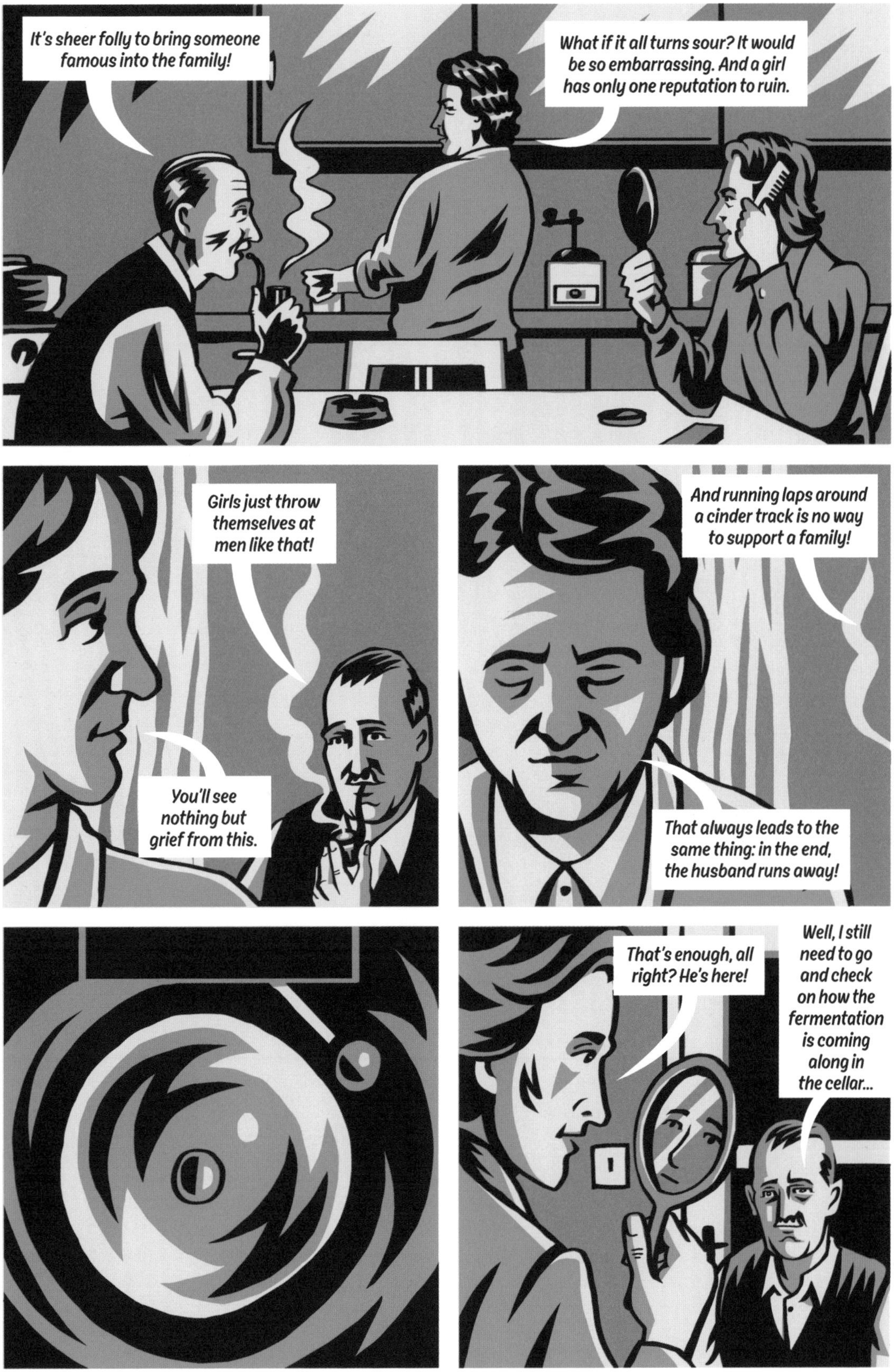
It's sheer folly to bring someone famous into the family!
What if it all turns sour? It would be so embarrassing. And a girl has only one reputation to ruin.
Girls just throw themselves at men like that!
You'll see nothing but grief from this.
And running laps around a cinder track is no way to support a family!
That always leads to the same thing: in the end, the husband runs away!
That's enough, all right? He's here!
Well, I still need to go and check on how the fermentation is coming along in the cellar...

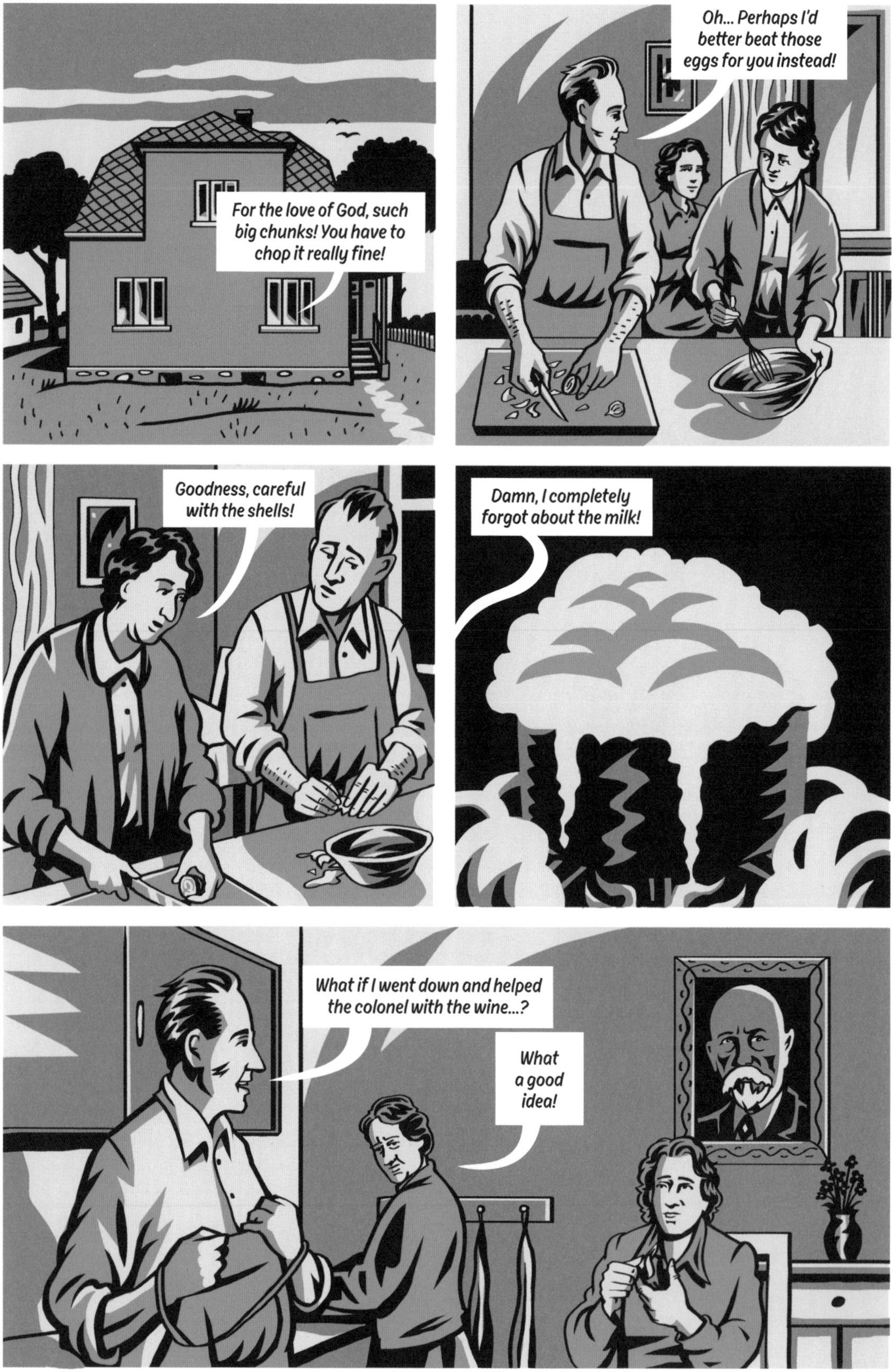
For the love of God, such big chunks! You have to chop it really fine!
Oh... Perhaps I'd better beat those eggs for you instead!
Goodness, careful with the shells!
Damn, I completely forgot about the milk!
What if I went down and helped the colonel with the wine...?
What a good idea!

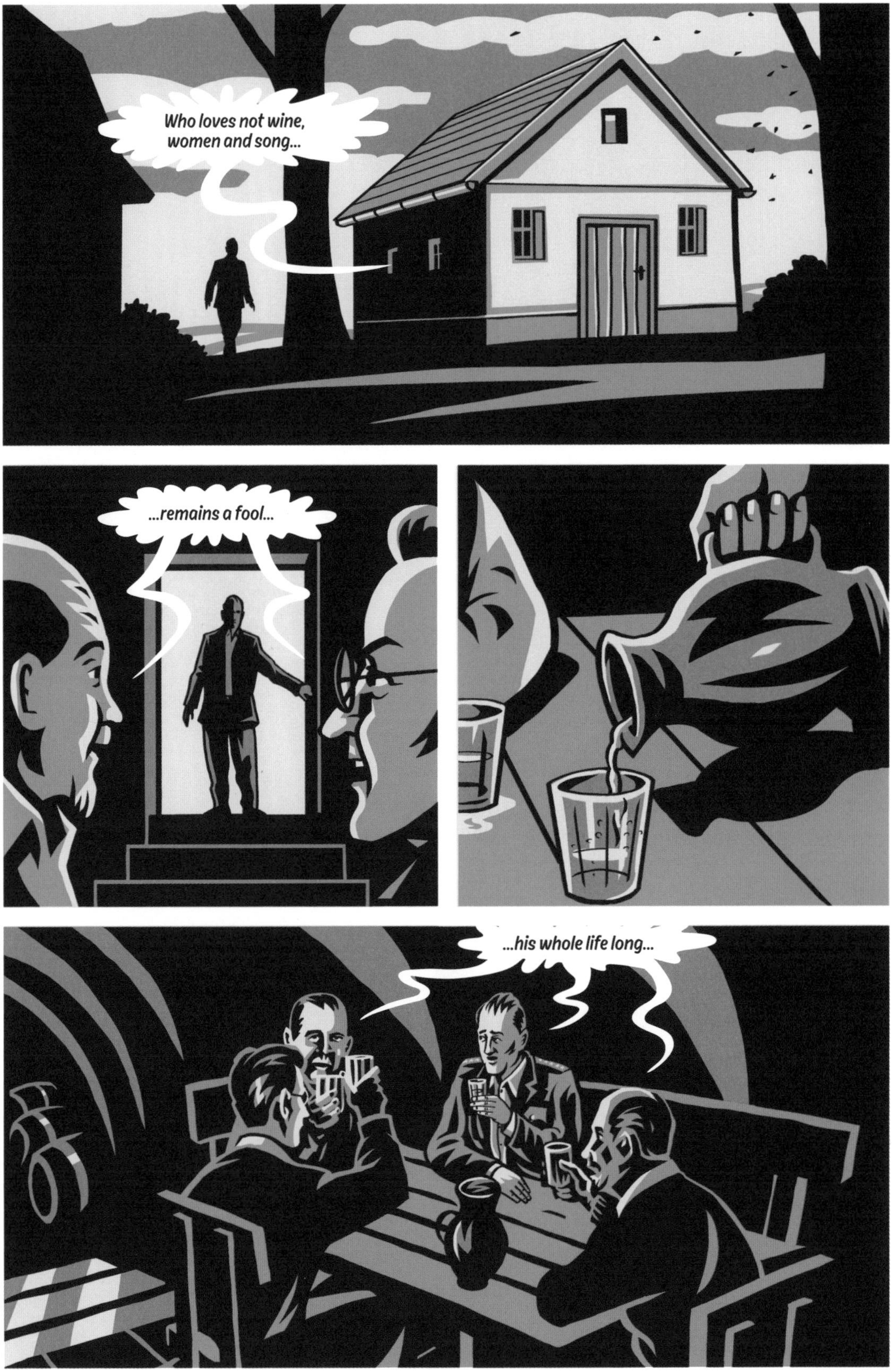
Who loves not wine, women and song...
...remains a fool...
...his whole life long...

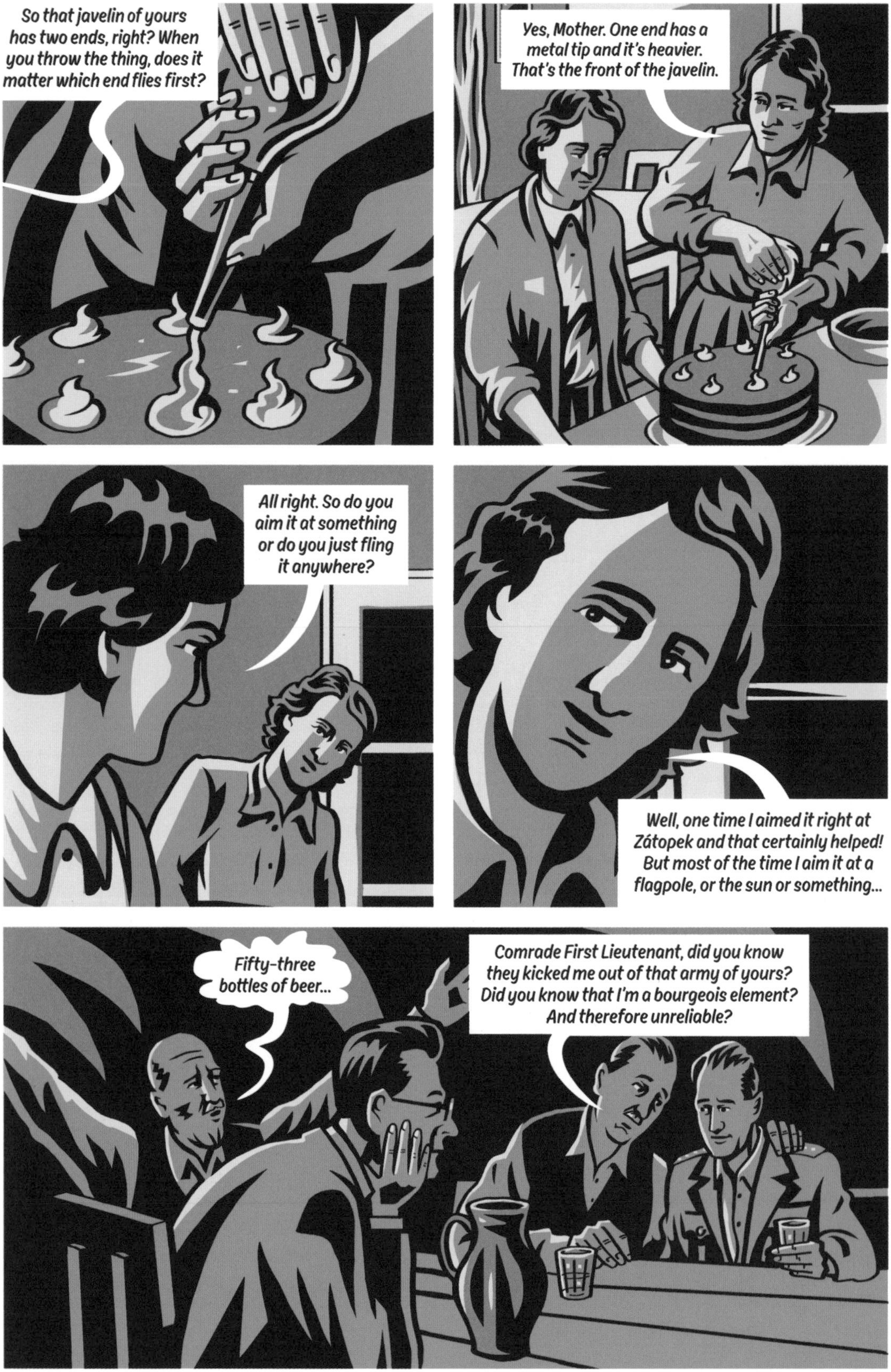
So that javelin of yours has two ends, right? When you throw the thing, does it matter which end flies first?
Yes, Mother. One end has a metal tip and it's heavier. That's the front of the javelin.
All right. So do you aim it at something or do you just fling it anywhere?
Well, one time I aimed it right at Zátopek and that certainly helped! But most of the time I aim it at a flagpole, or the sun or something...
Fifty-three bottles of beer...
Comrade First Lieutenant, did you know they kicked me out of that army of yours? Did you know that I'm a bourgeois element? And therefore unreliable?

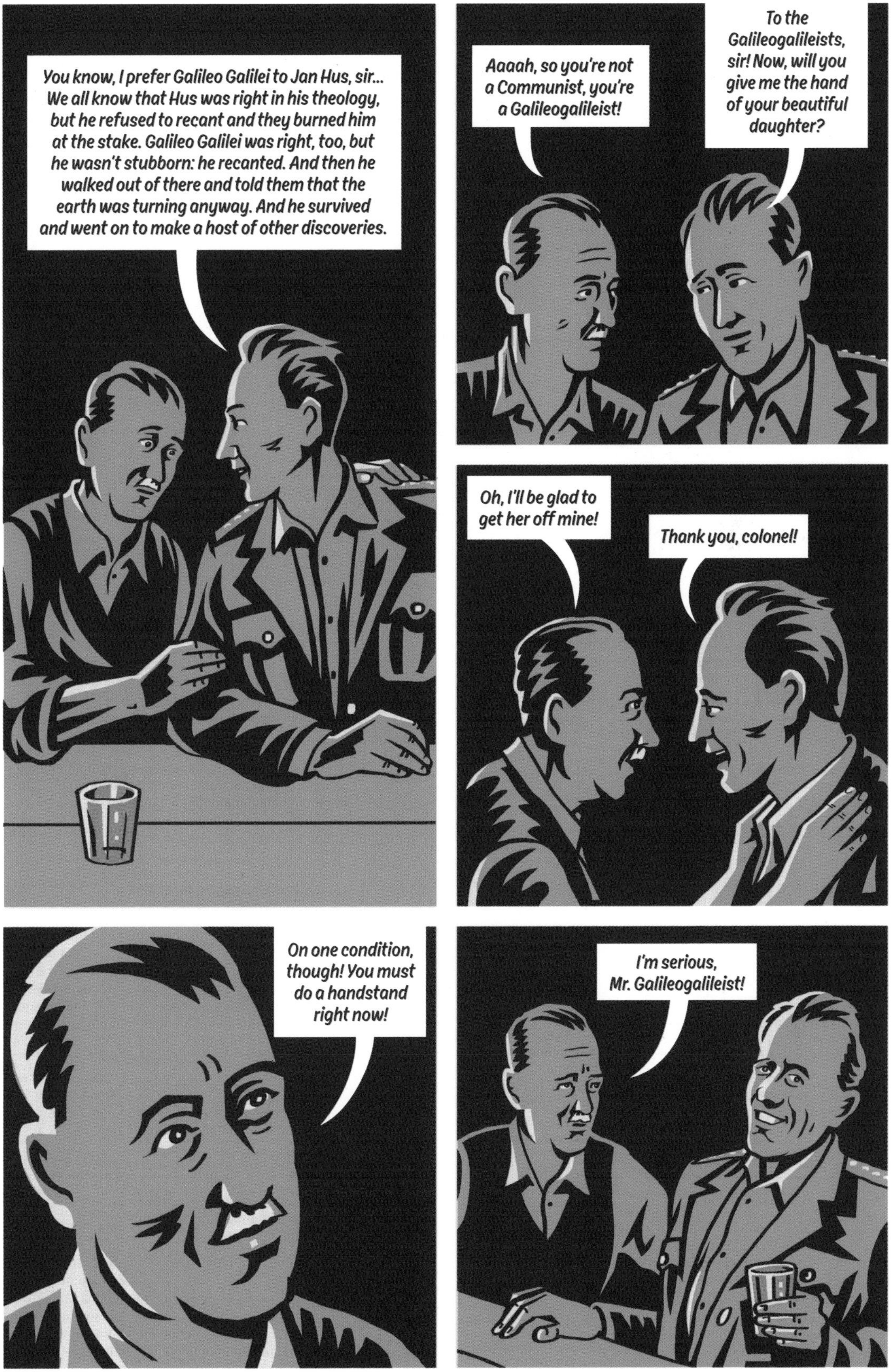
You know, I prefer Galileo Galilei to Jan Hus, sir... We all know that Hus was right in his theology, but he refused to recant and they burned him at the stake. Galileo Galilei was right, too, but he wasn't stubborn: he recanted. And then he walked out of there and told them that the earth was turning anyway. And he survived and went on to make a host of other discoveries.
Aaaah, so you're not a Communist, you're a Galileogalileist!
To the Galileogalileists, sir! Now, will you give me the hand of your beautiful daughter?
Oh, I'll be glad to get her off mine!
Thank you, colonel!
On one condition, though! You must do a handstand right now!
I'm serious, Mr. Galileogalileist!

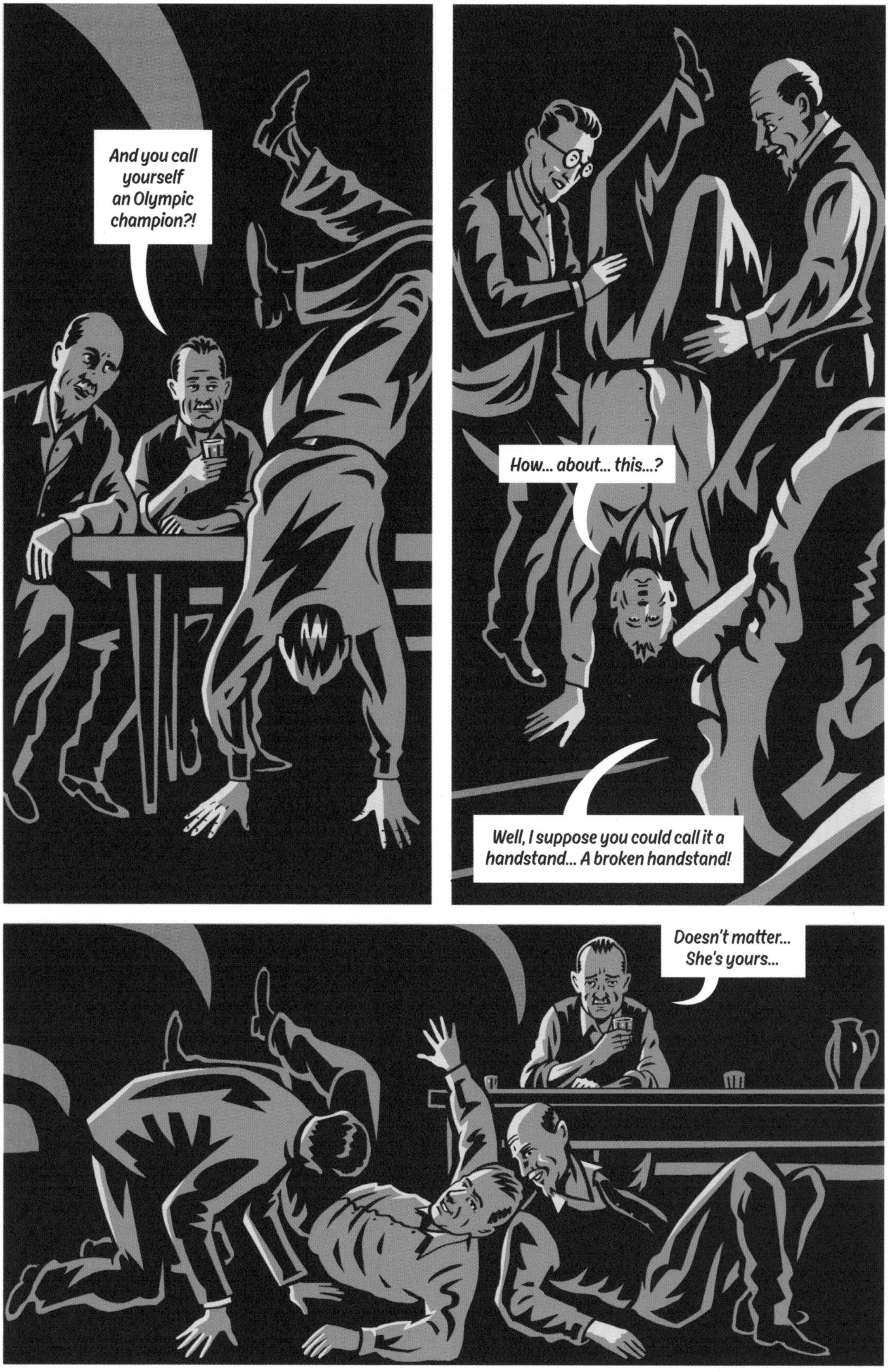
And you call yourself an Olympic champion?!
How... about... this...?
Well, I suppose you could call it a handstand... A broken handstand!
Doesn't matter... She's yours...

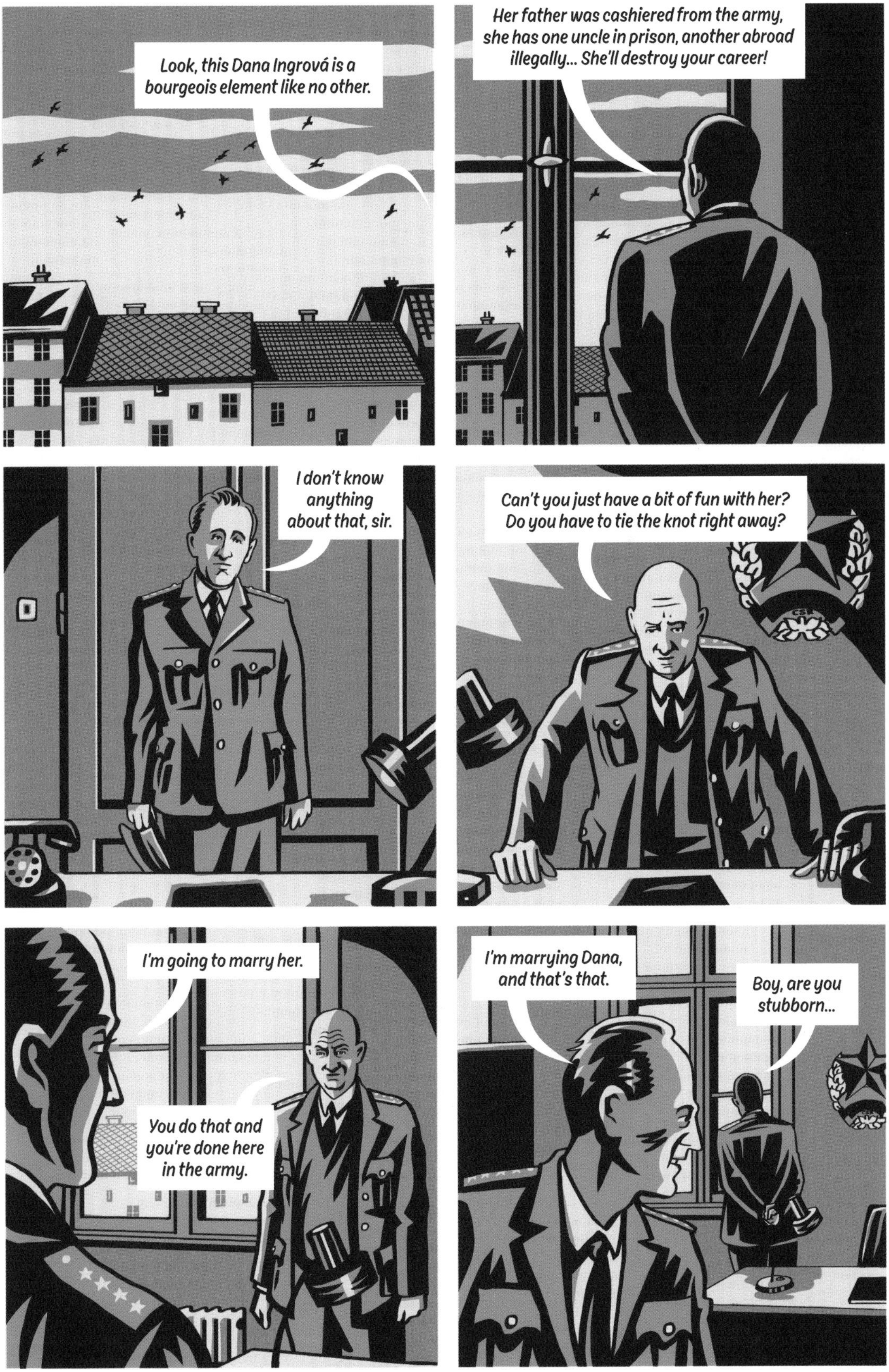
Look, this Dana Ingrová is a bourgeois element like no other.
Her father was cashiered from the army, she has one uncle in prison, another abroad illegally... She'll destroy your career!
I don't know anything about that, sir.
Can't you just have a bit of fun with her? Do you have to tie the knot right away?
I'm going to marry her.
You do that and you're done here in the army.
I'm marrying Dana, and that's that.
Boy, are you stubborn...

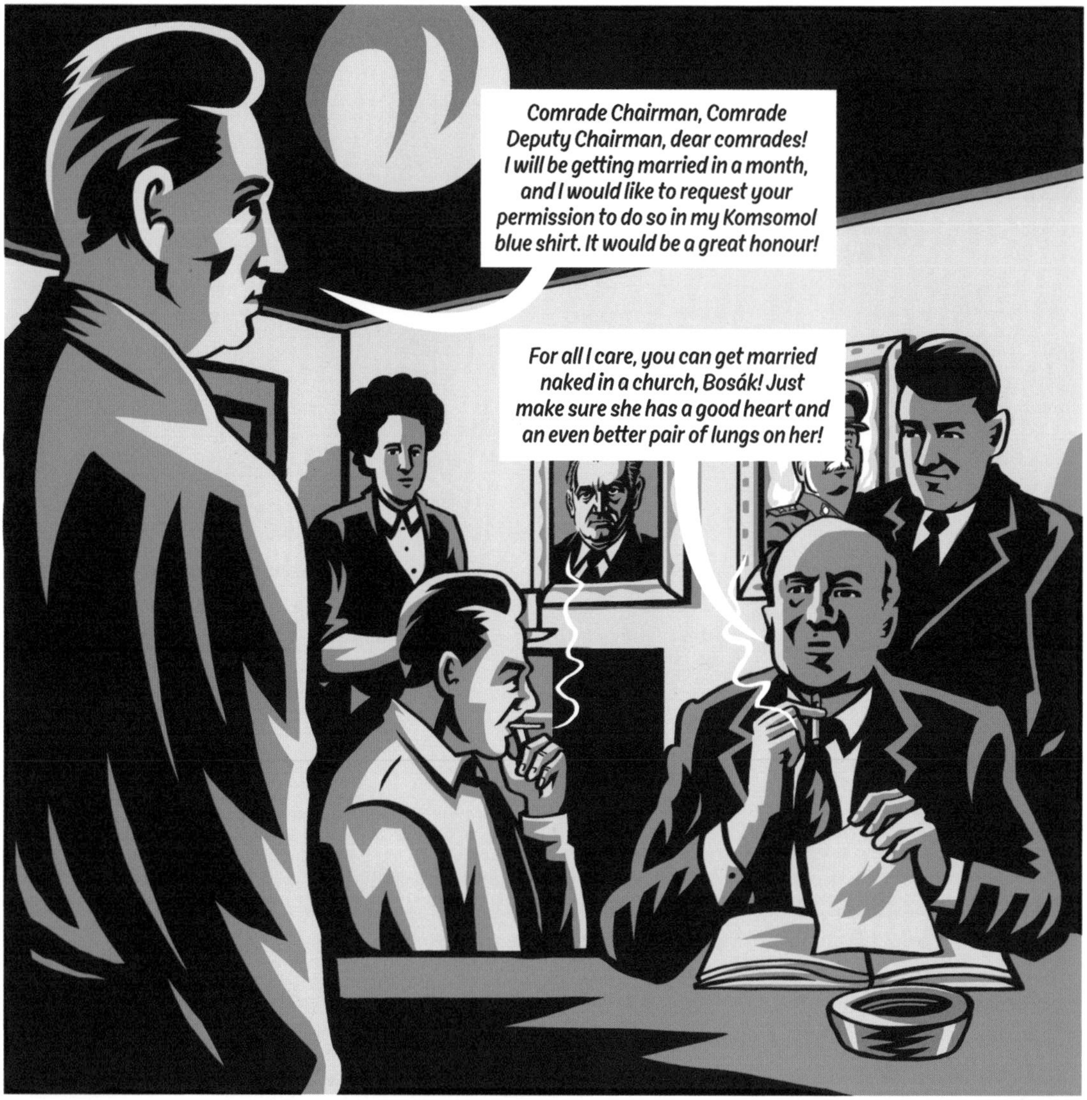
Comrade Chairman, Comrade Deputy Chairman, dear comrades! I will be getting married in a month, and I would like to request your permission to do so in my Komsomol blue shirt. It would be a great honour!
For all I care, you can get married naked in a church, Bosák! Just make sure she has a good heart and an even better pair of lungs on her!

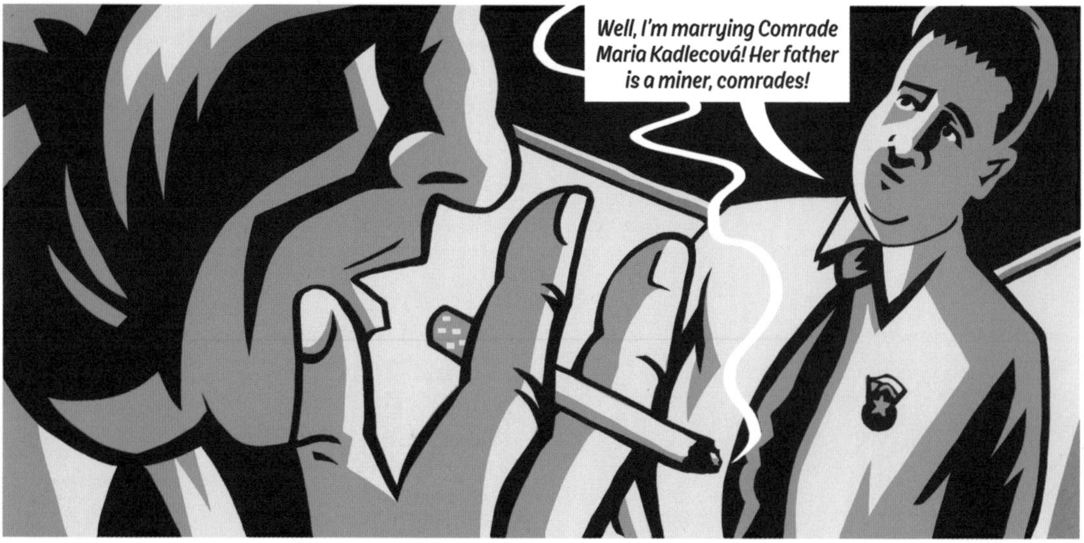
Well, I'm marrying Comrade Maria Kadlecová! Her father is a miner, comrades!

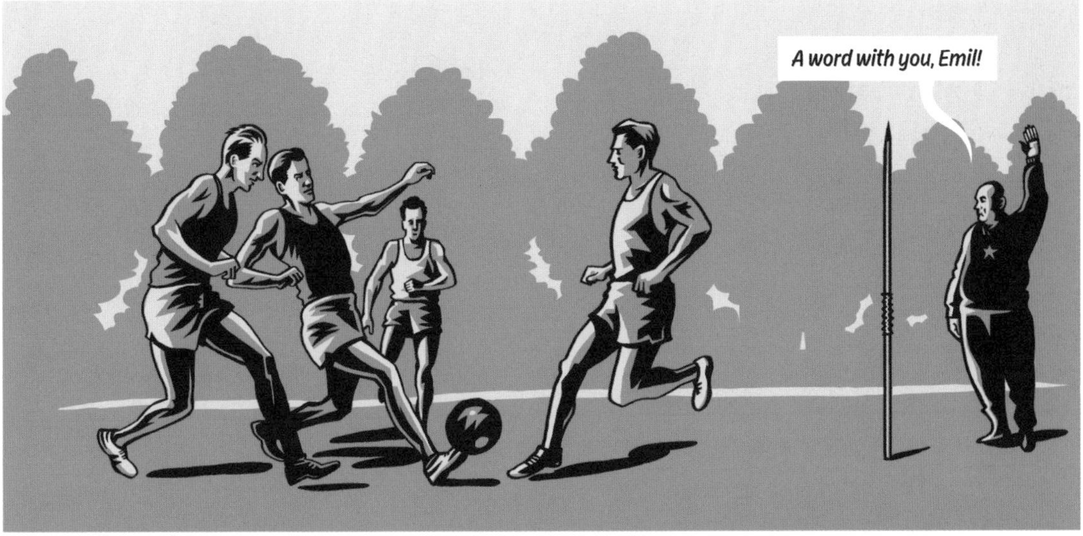
A word with you, Emil!

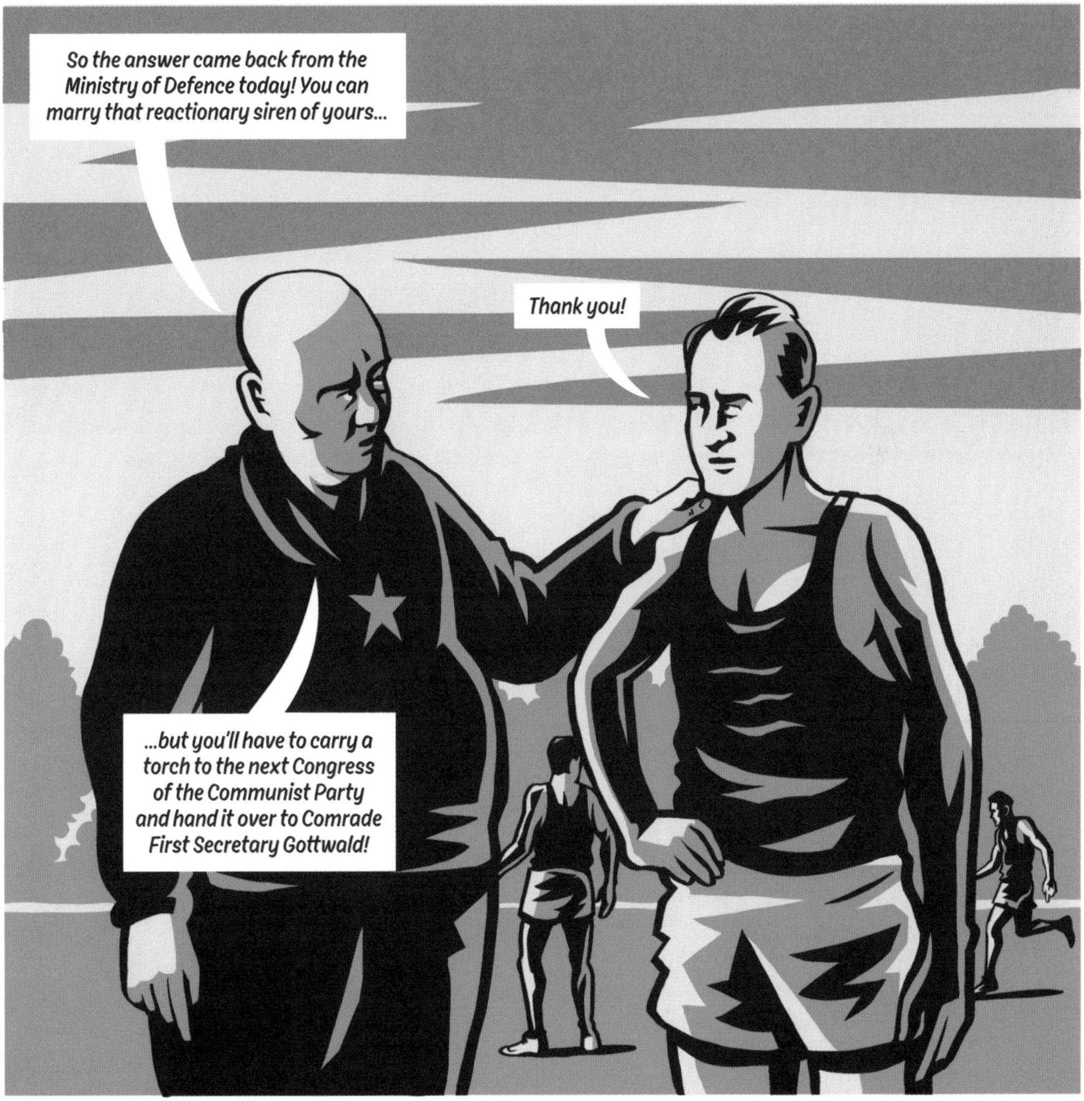
So the answer came back from the Ministry of Defence today! You can marry that reactionary siren of yours...
Thank you!
...but you'll have to carry a torch to the next Congress of the Communist Party and hand it over to Comrade First Secretary Gottwald!

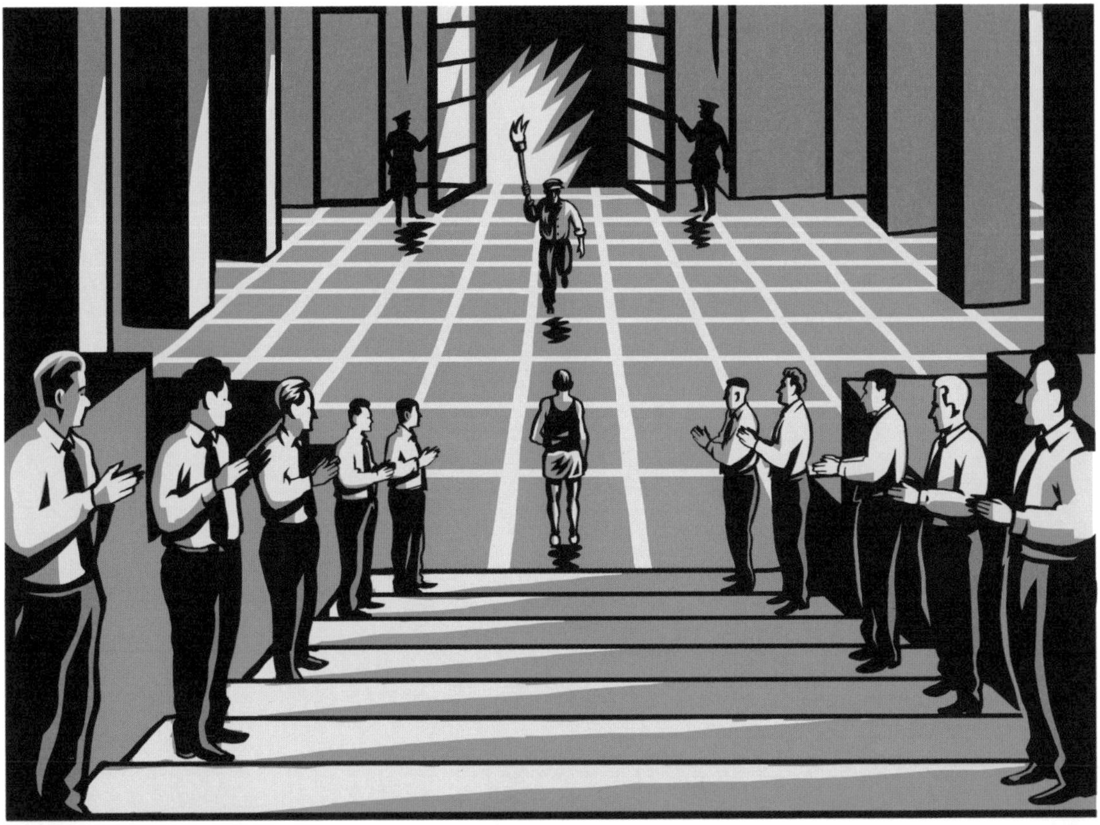

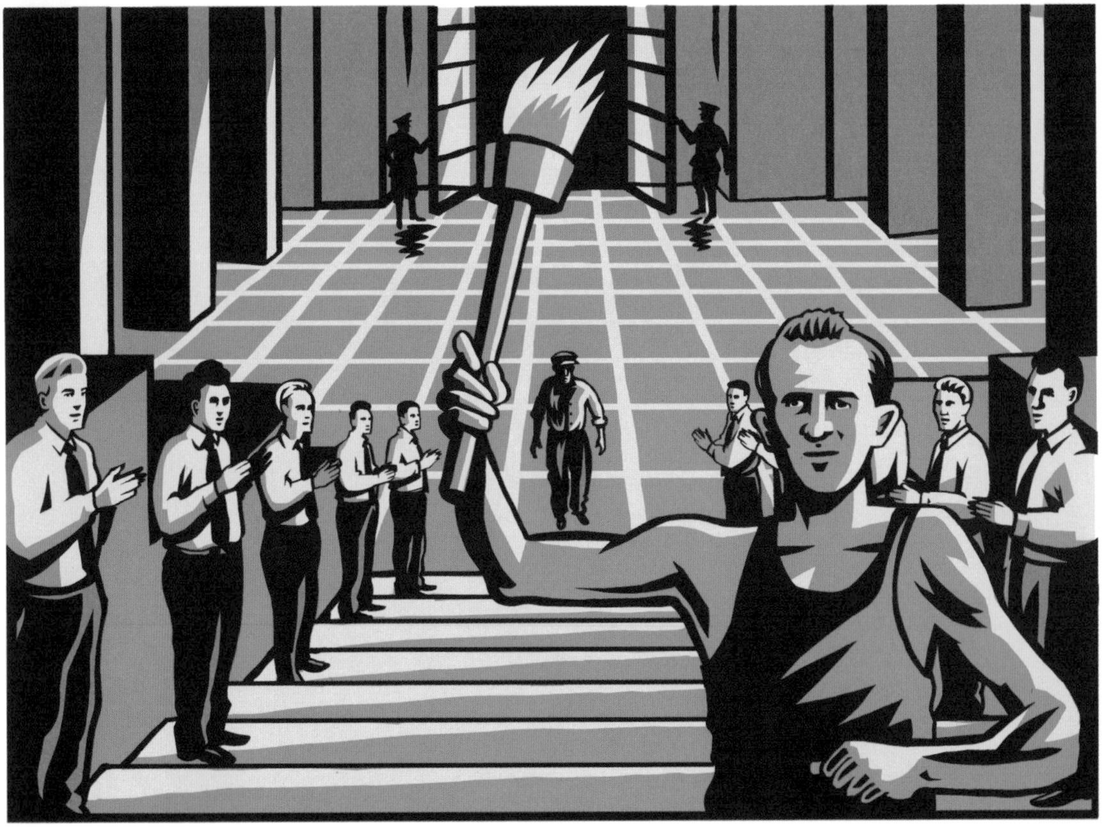

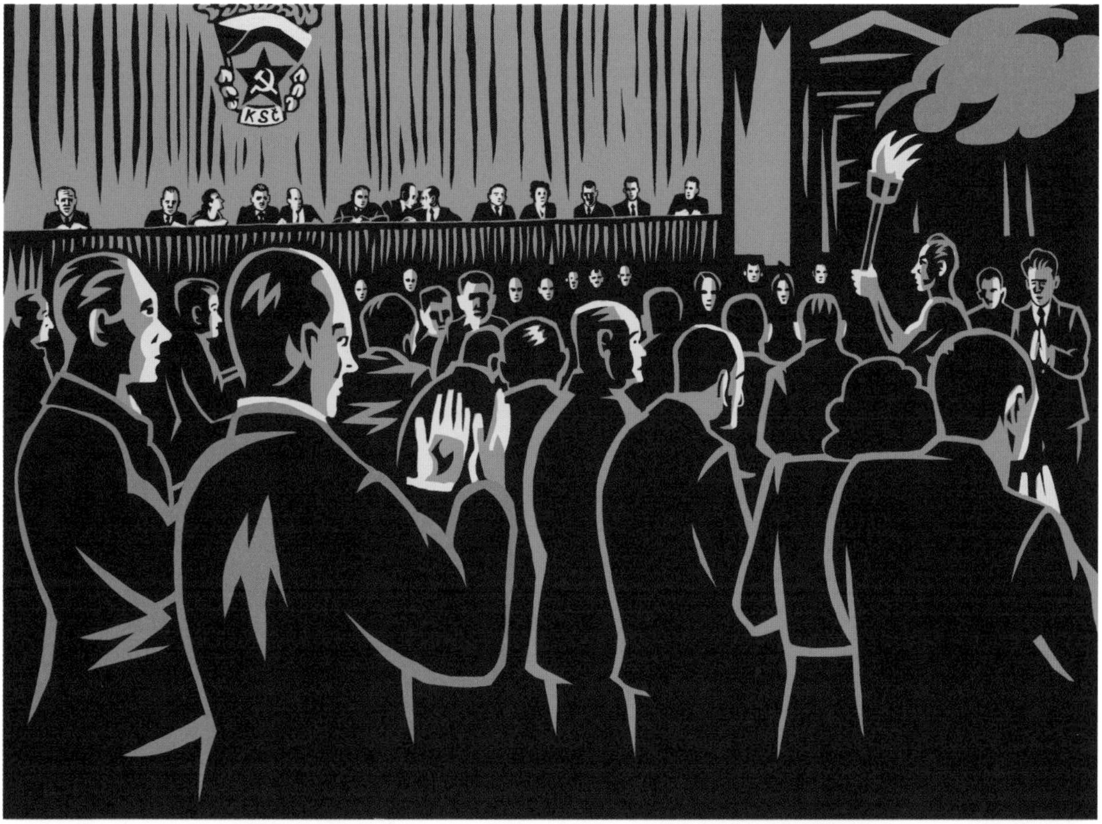
KSČ
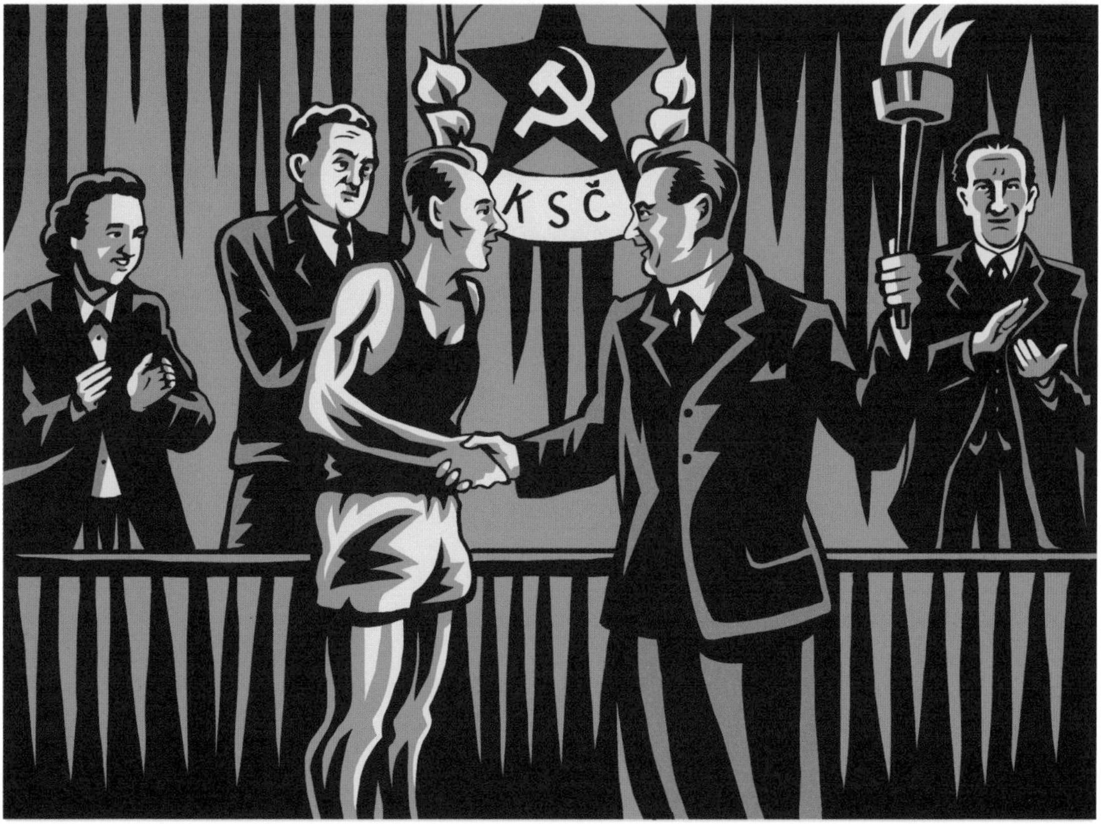
KSČ

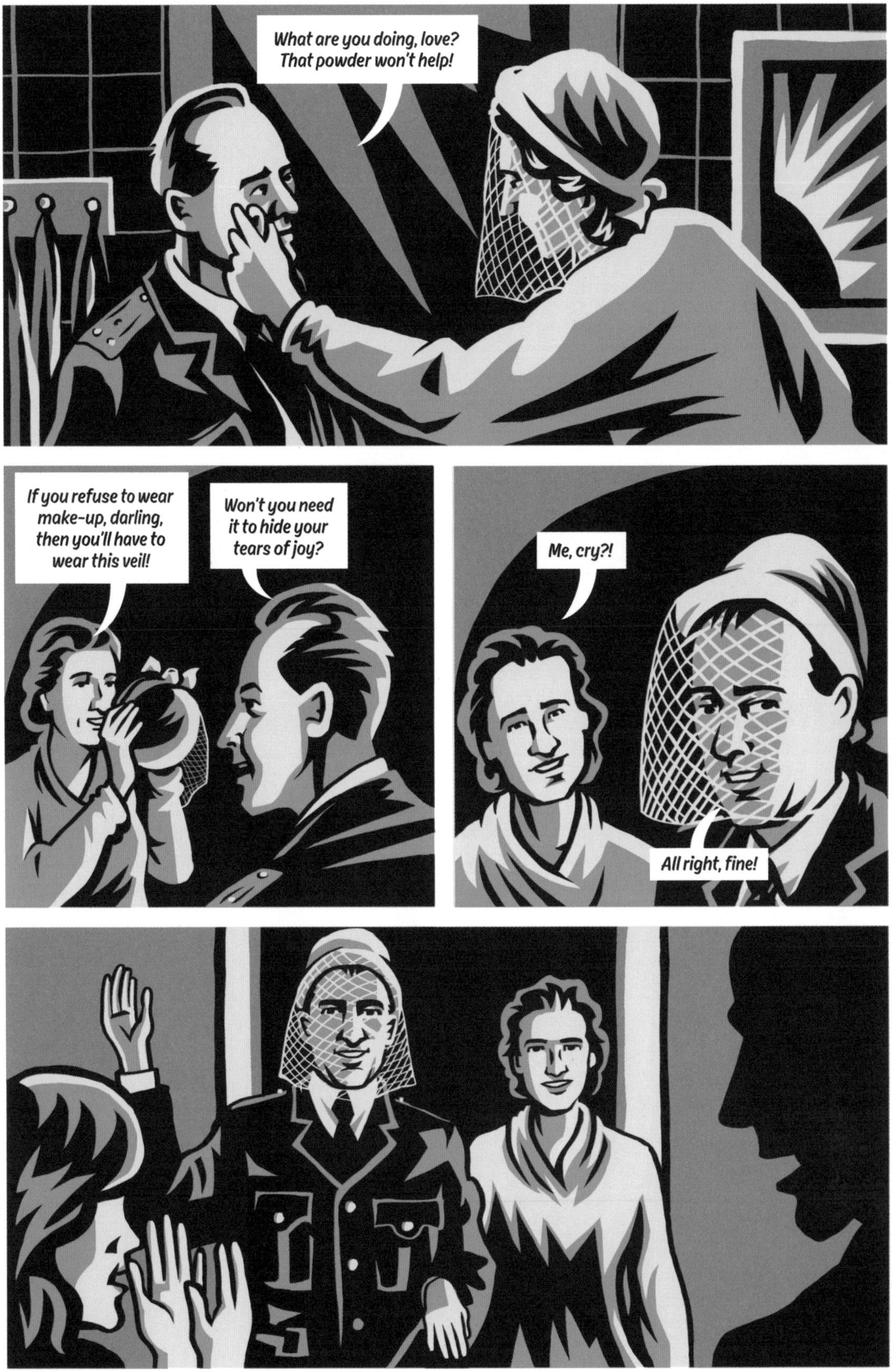
What are you doing, love? That powder won't help!
If you refuse to wear make-up, darling, then you'll have to wear this veil!
Won't you need it to hide your tears of joy?
Me, cry?!
All right, fine!

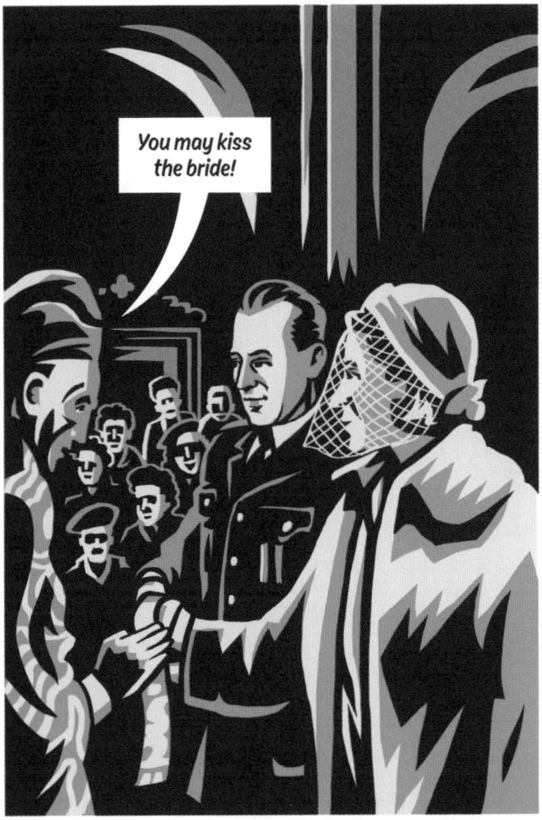
You may kiss the bride!

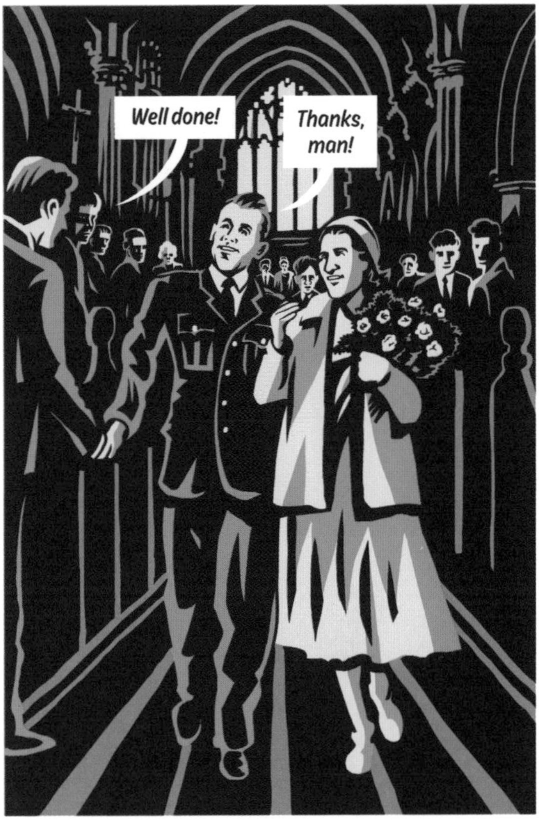
Well done!
Thanks, man!

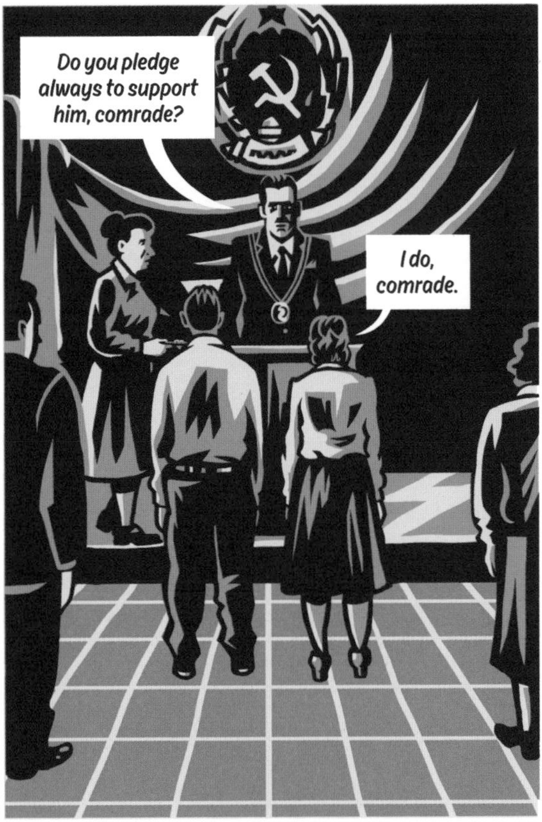
Do you pledge always to support him, comrade?
I do, comrade.

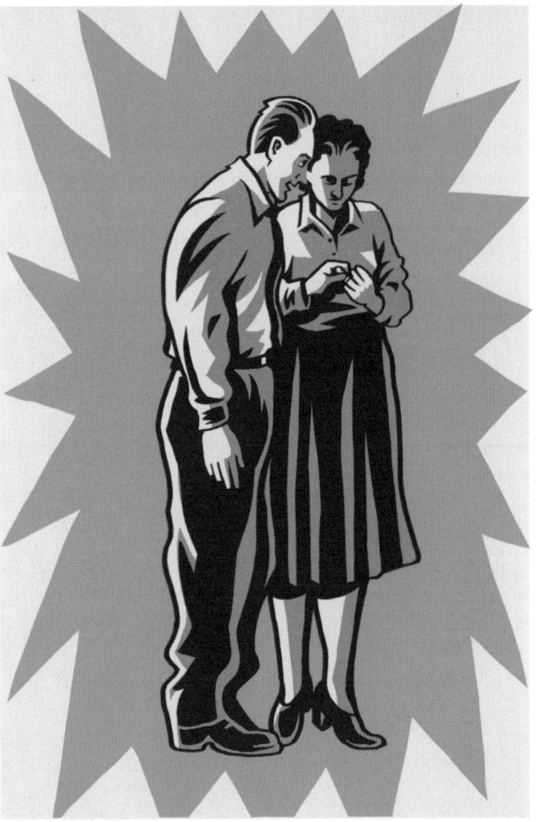

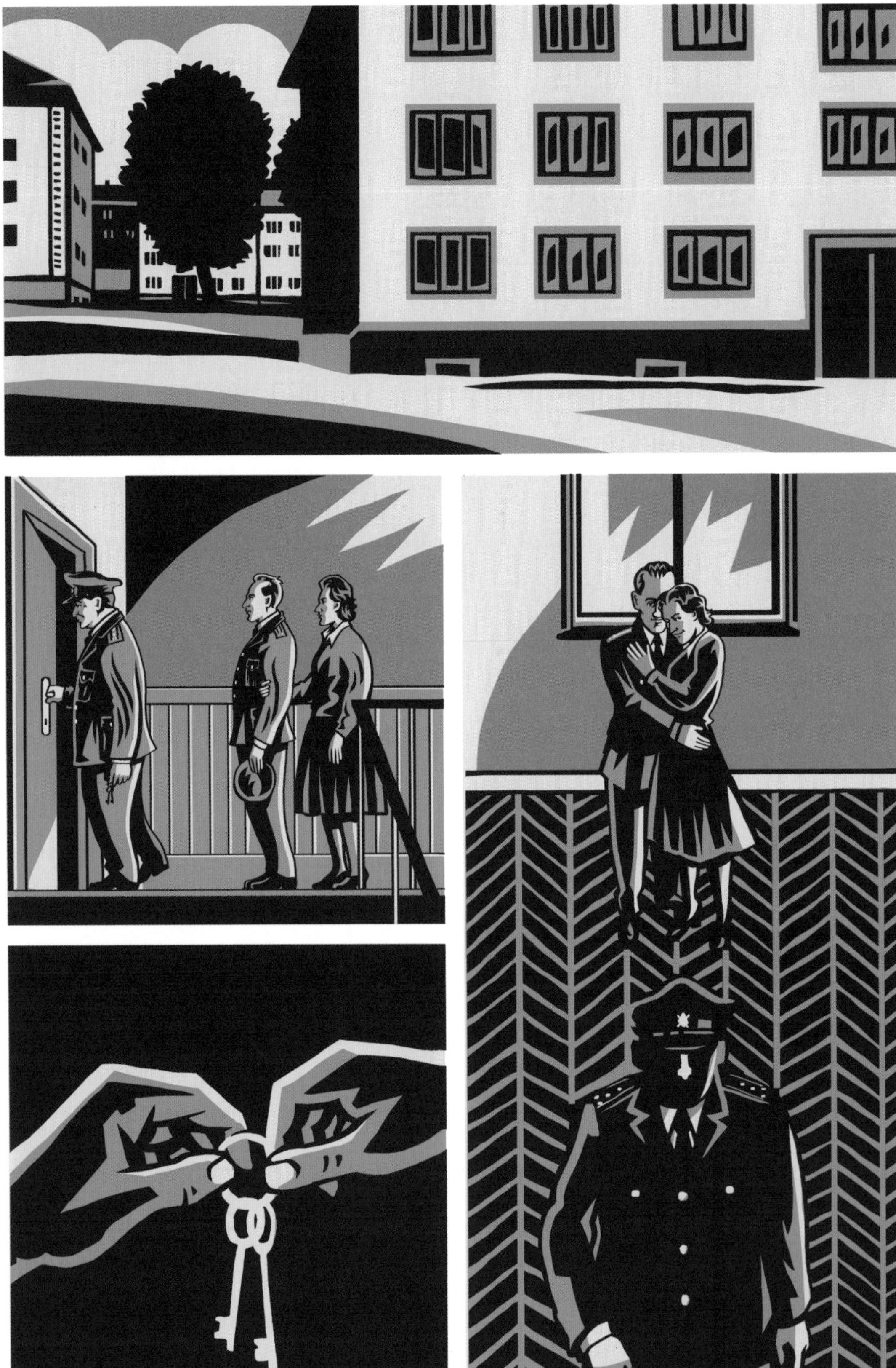

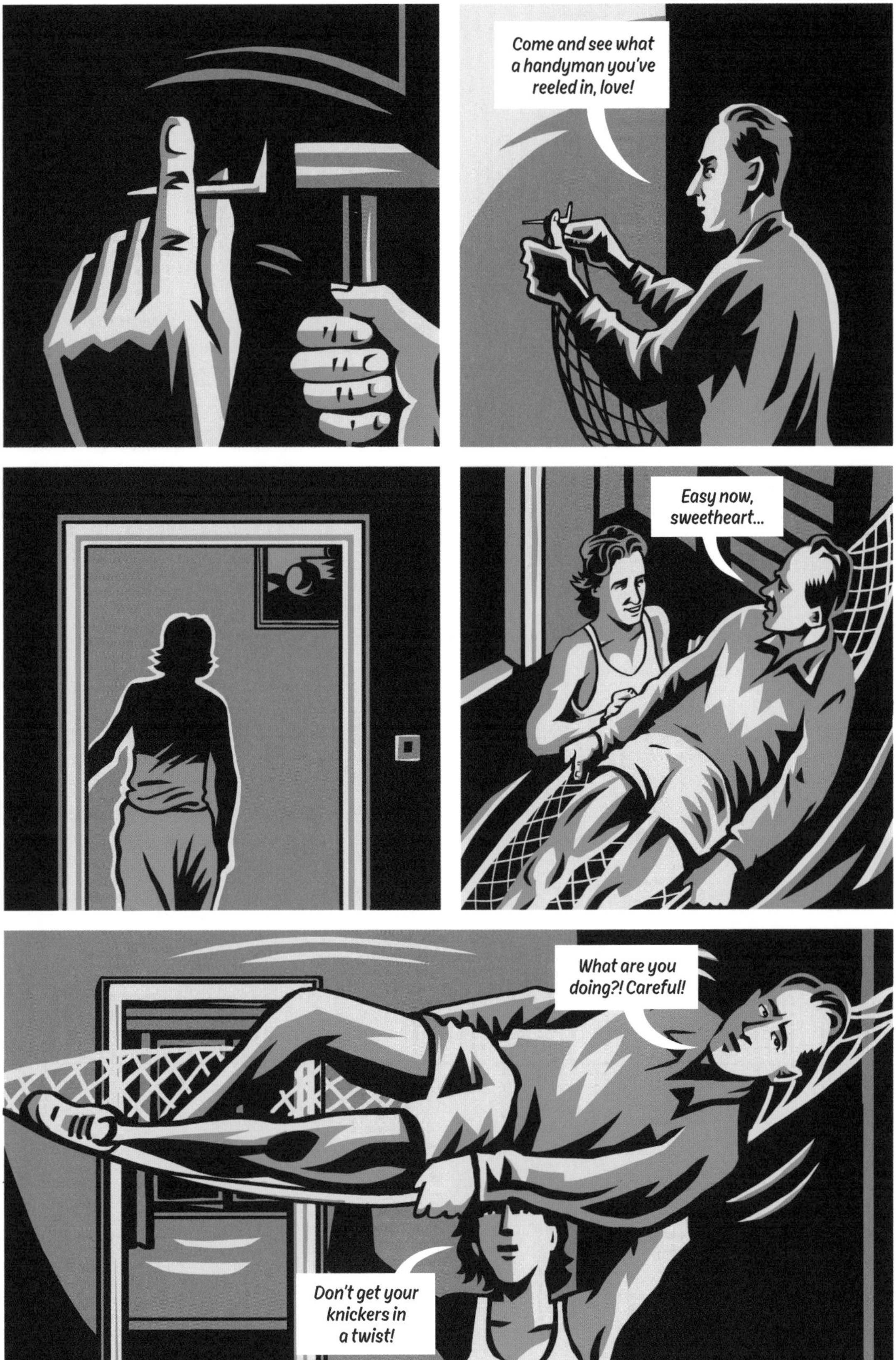
Come and see what a handyman you've reeled in, love!
Easy now, sweetheart...
What are you doing?! Careful!
Don't get your knickers in a twist!

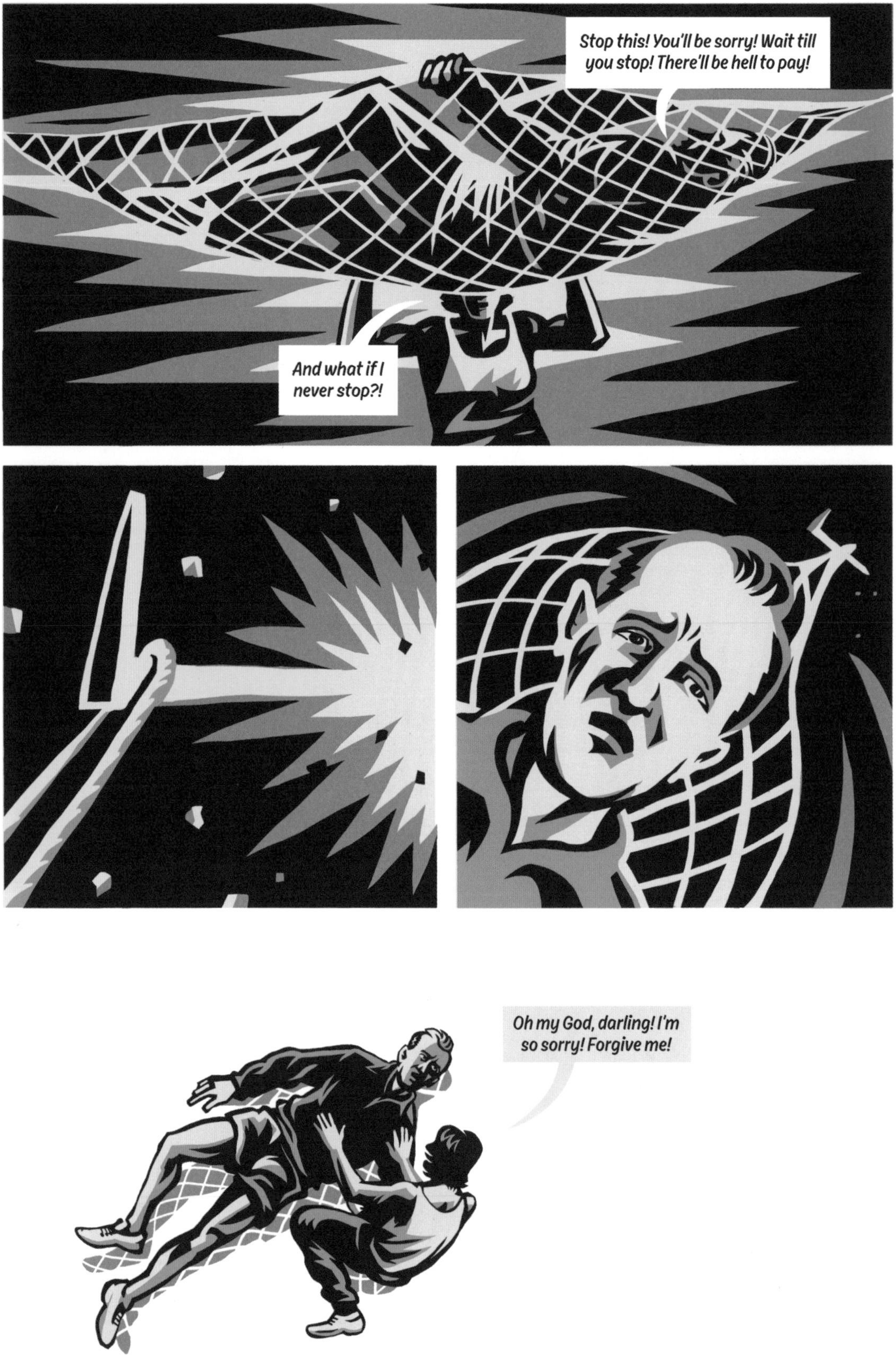
Stop this! You'll be sorry! Wait till you stop! There'll be hell to pay!
And what if I never stop?!
Oh my God, darling! I'm so sorry! Forgive me!

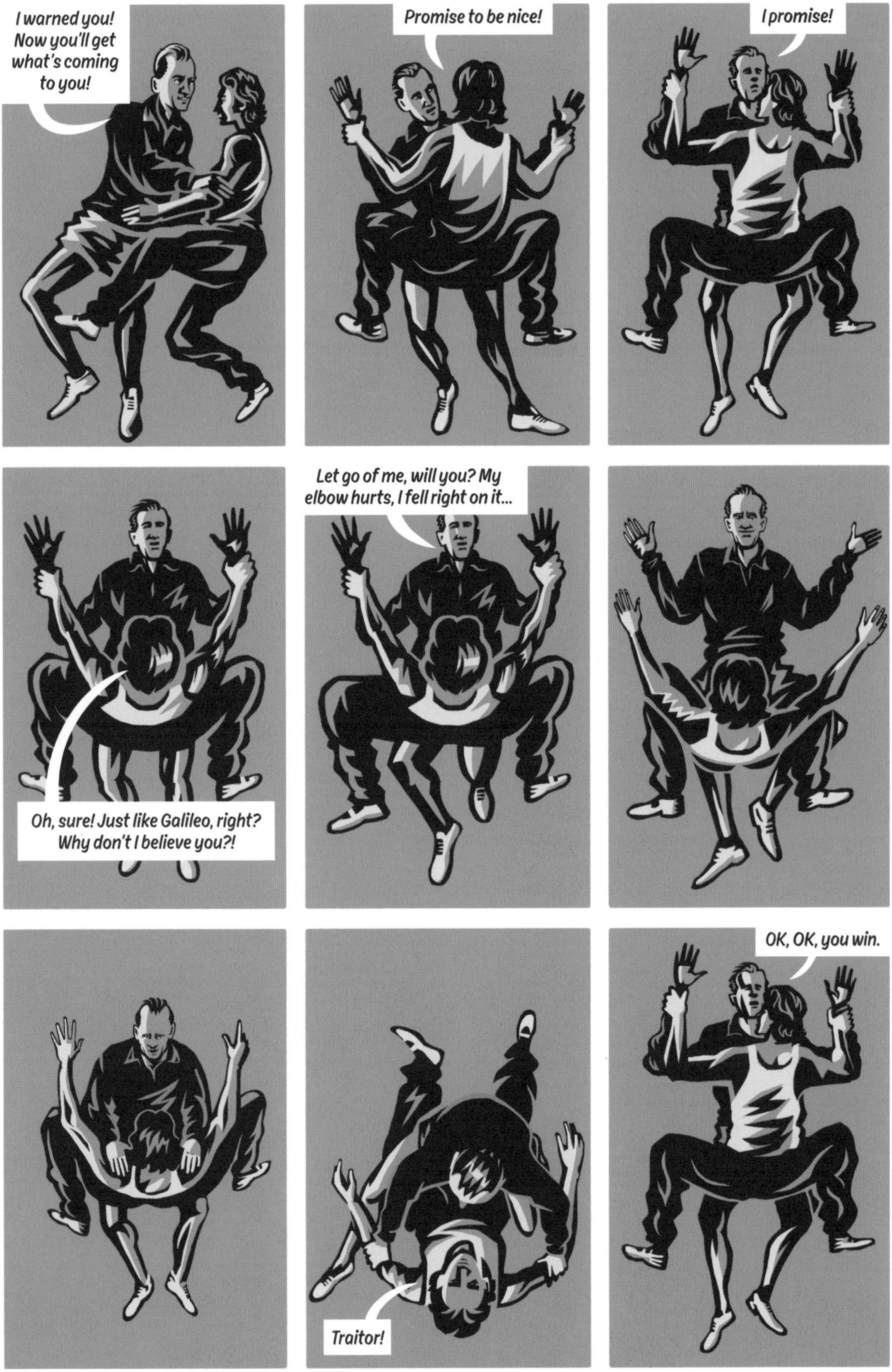
I warned you! Now you'll get what's coming to you!
Promise to be nice!
I promise!
Oh, sure! Just like Galileo, right? Why don't I believe you?!
Let go of me, will you? My elbow hurts, I fell right on it...
Traitor!
OK, OK, you win.

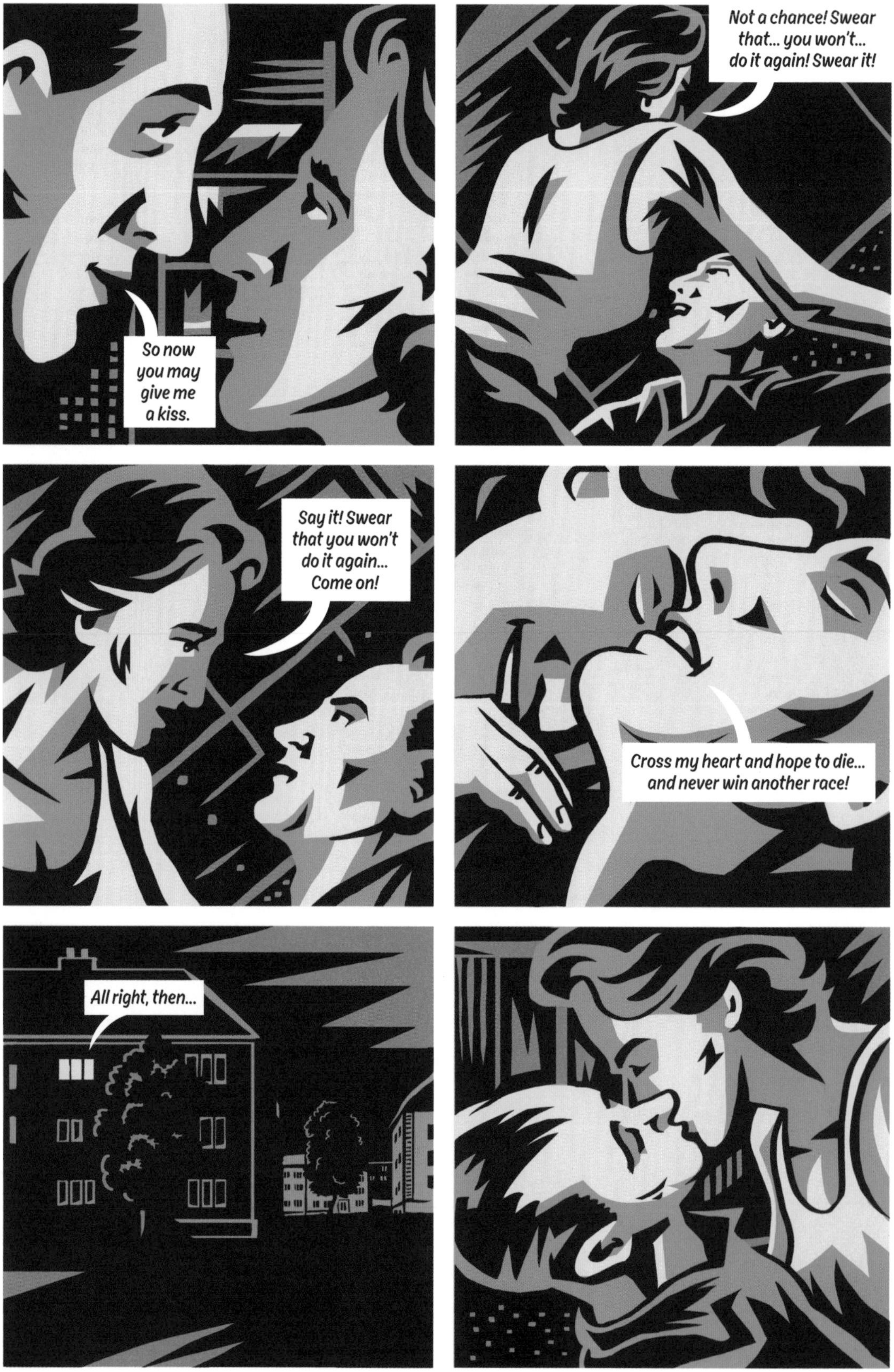
So now you may give me a kiss.
Not a chance! Swear that... you won't... do it again! Swear it!
Say it! Swear that you won't do it again... Come on!
Cross my heart and hope to die... and never win another race!
All right, then...

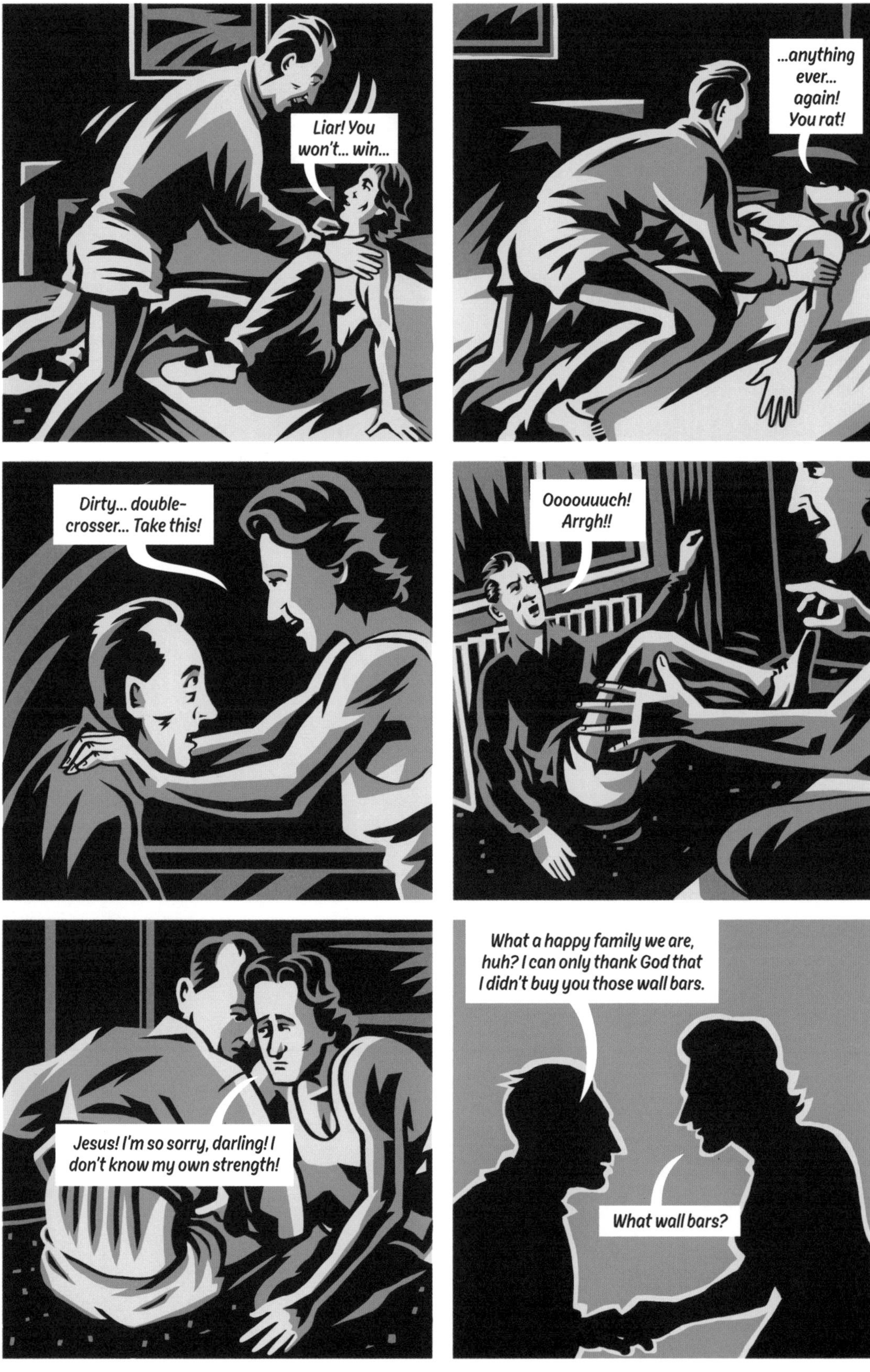
Liar! You won't... win...
...anything ever... again! You rat!
Dirty... double-crosser... Take this!
Oooouuuch! Arrgh!!
Jesus! I'm so sorry, darling! I don't know my own strength!
What a happy family we are, huh? I can only thank God that I didn't buy you those wall bars.
What wall bars?

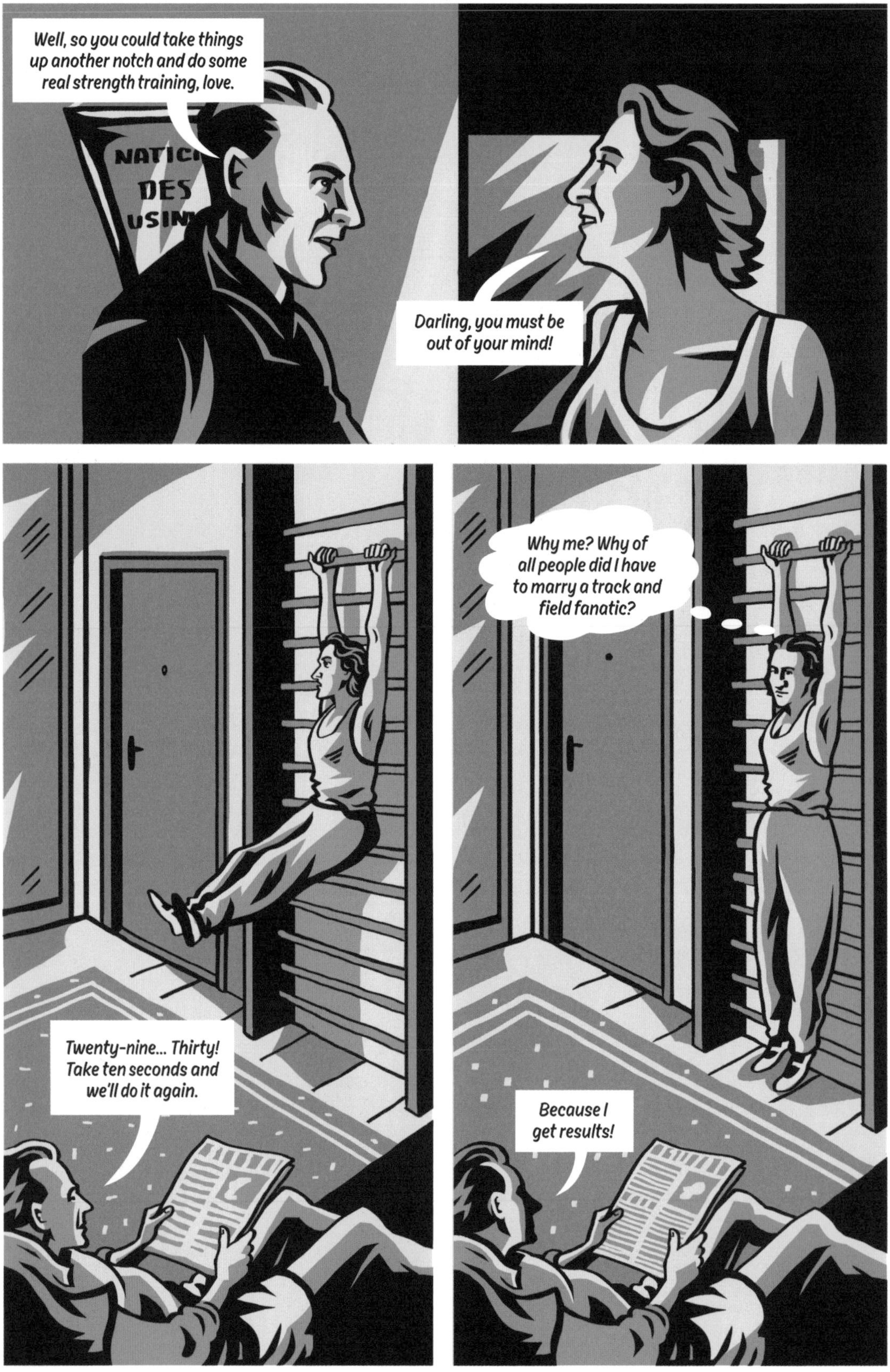
Well, so you could take things up another notch and do some real strength training, love.
NATIO DES USIN
Darling, you must be out of your mind!
Twenty-nine... Thirty! Take ten seconds and we'll do it again.
Why me? Why of all people did I have to marry a track and field fanatic?
Because I get results!

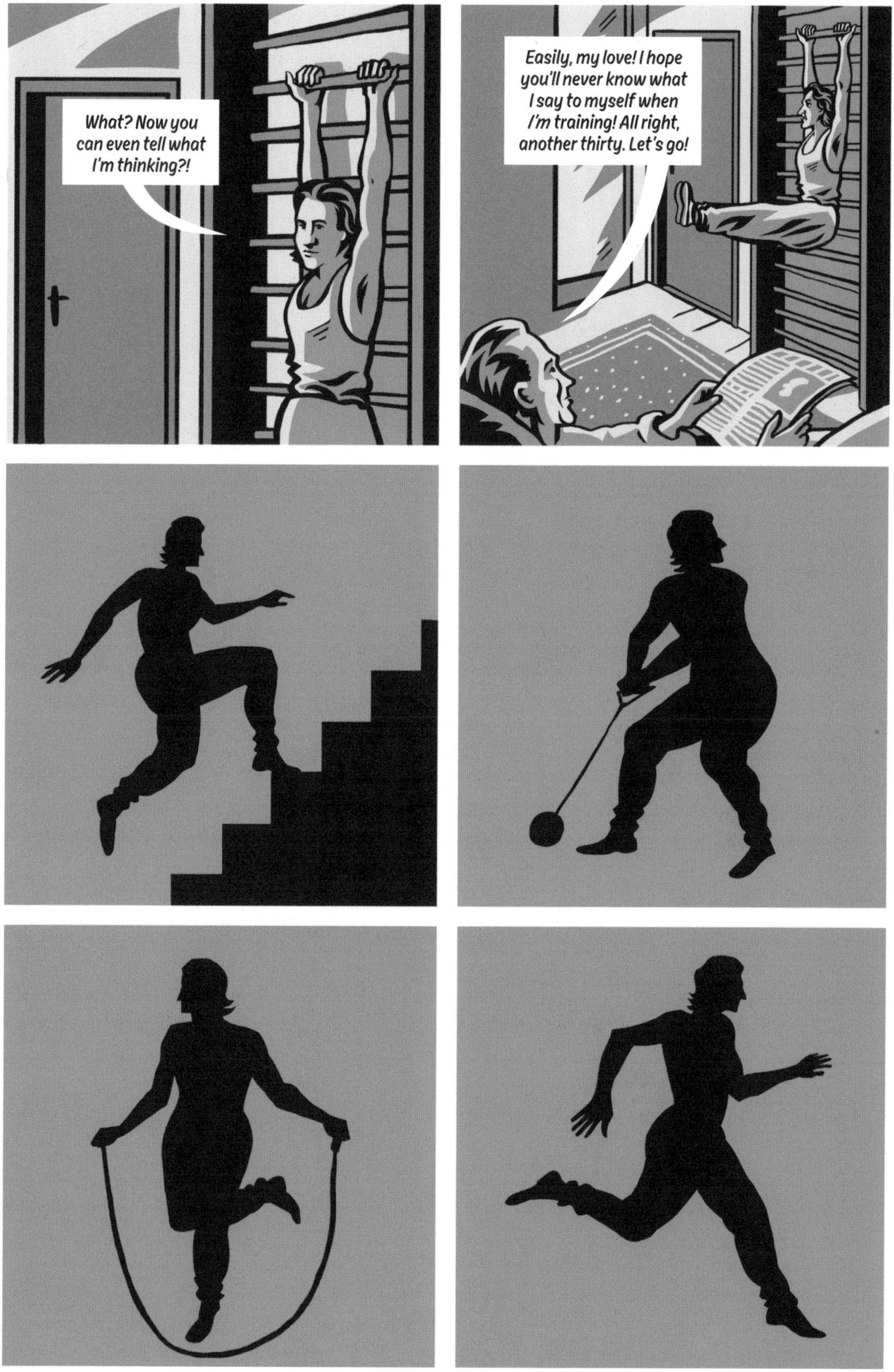
What? Now you can even tell what I'm thinking?!
Easily, my love! I hope you'll never know what I say to myself when *I'm* training! All right, another thirty. Let's go!

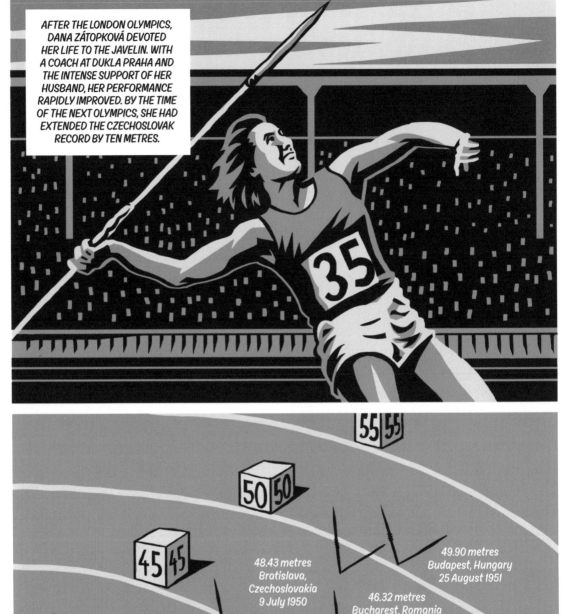

AFTER THE LONDON OLYMPICS, DANA ZÁTOPKOVÁ DEVOTED HER LIFE TO THE JAVELIN. WITH A COACH AT DUKLA PRAHA AND THE INTENSE SUPPORT OF HER HUSBAND, HER PERFORMANCE RAPIDLY IMPROVED. BY THE TIME OF THE NEXT OLYMPICS, SHE HAD EXTENDED THE CZECHOSLOVAK RECORD BY TEN METRES.

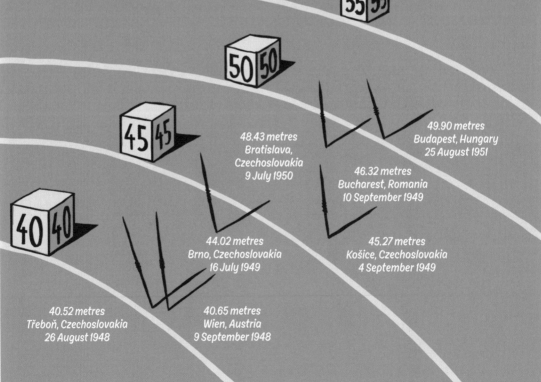

48.43 metres
Bratislava,
Czechoslovakia
9 July 1950

49.90 metres
Budapest, Hungary
25 August 1951

46.32 metres
Bucharest, Romania
10 September 1949

44.02 metres
Brno, Czechoslovakia
16 July 1949

45.27 metres
Košice, Czechoslovakia
4 September 1949

40.52 metres
Třeboň, Czechoslovakia
26 August 1948

40.65 metres
Wien, Austria
9 September 1948

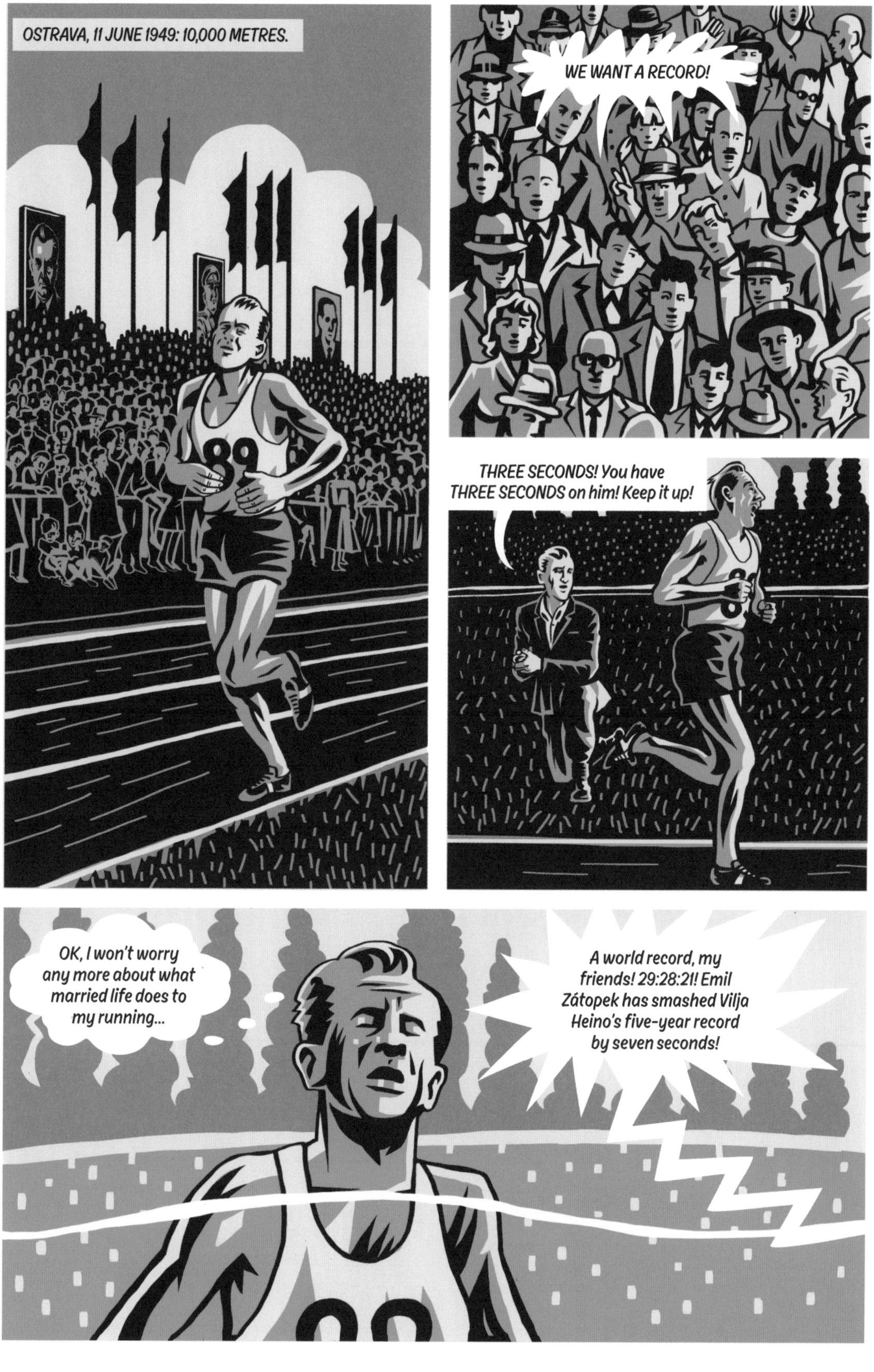
OSTRAVA, 11 JUNE 1949: 10,000 METRES.
WE WANT A RECORD!
THREE SECONDS! You have THREE SECONDS on him! Keep it up!
OK, I won't worry any more about what married life does to my running...
A world record, my friends! 29:28:21! Emil Zátopek has smashed Vilja Heino's five-year record by seven seconds!

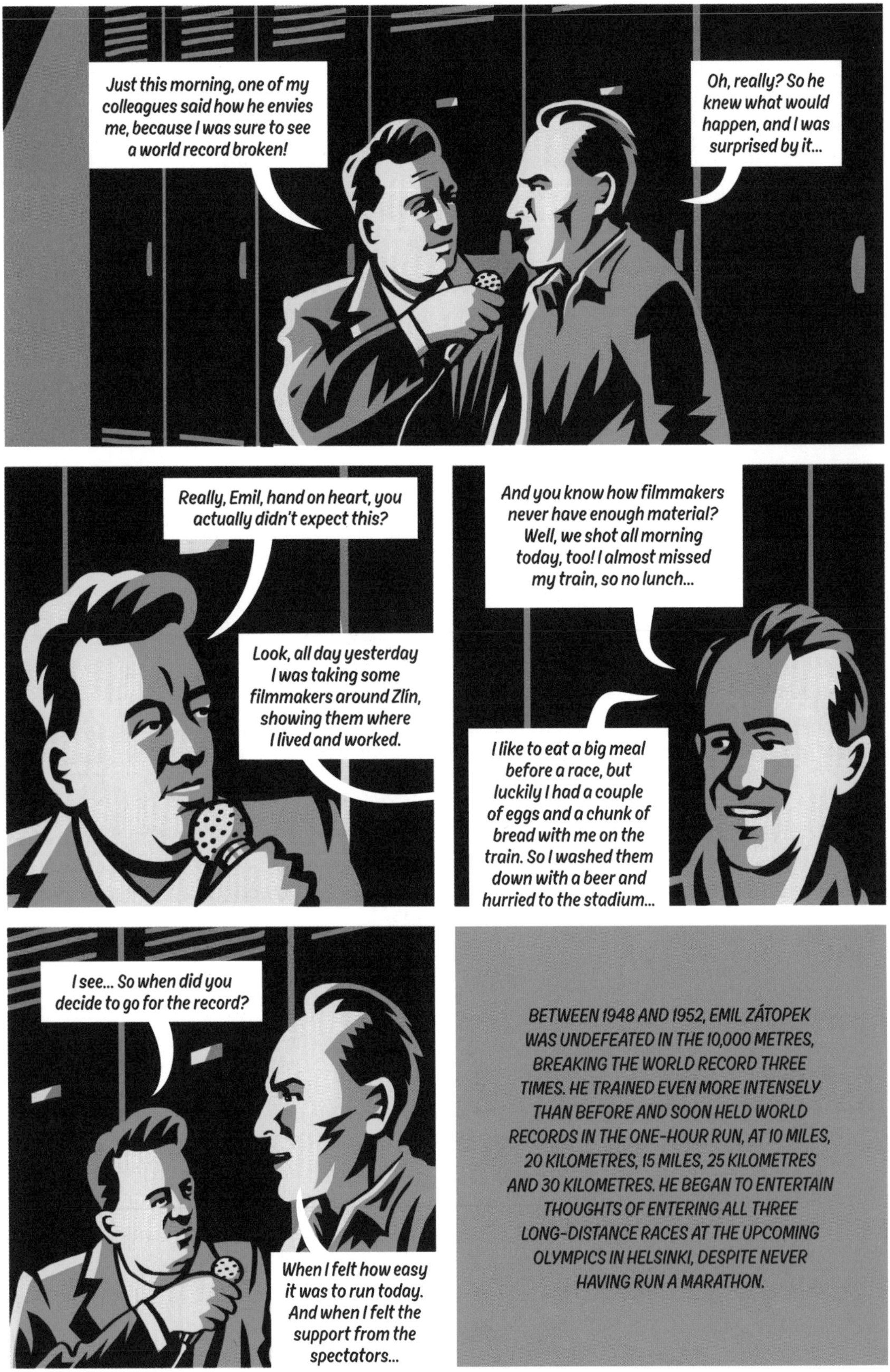
Just this morning, one of my colleagues said how he envies me, because I was sure to see a world record broken!
Oh, really? So he knew what would happen, and I was surprised by it...
Really, Emil, hand on heart, you actually didn't expect this?
Look, all day yesterday I was taking some filmmakers around Zlín, showing them where I lived and worked.
And you know how filmmakers never have enough material? Well, we shot all morning today, too! I almost missed my train, so no lunch...
I like to eat a big meal before a race, but luckily I had a couple of eggs and a chunk of bread with me on the train. So I washed them down with a beer and hurried to the stadium...
I see... So when did you decide to go for the record?
When I felt how easy it was to run today. And when I felt the support from the spectators...
BETWEEN 1948 AND 1952, EMIL ZÁTOPEK WAS UNDEFEATED IN THE 10,000 METRES, BREAKING THE WORLD RECORD THREE TIMES. HE TRAINED EVEN MORE INTENSELY THAN BEFORE AND SOON HELD WORLD RECORDS IN THE ONE-HOUR RUN, AT 10 MILES, 20 KILOMETRES, 15 MILES, 25 KILOMETRES AND 30 KILOMETRES. HE BEGAN TO ENTERTAIN THOUGHTS OF ENTERING ALL THREE LONG-DISTANCE RACES AT THE UPCOMING OLYMPICS IN HELSINKI, DESPITE NEVER HAVING RUN A MARATHON.

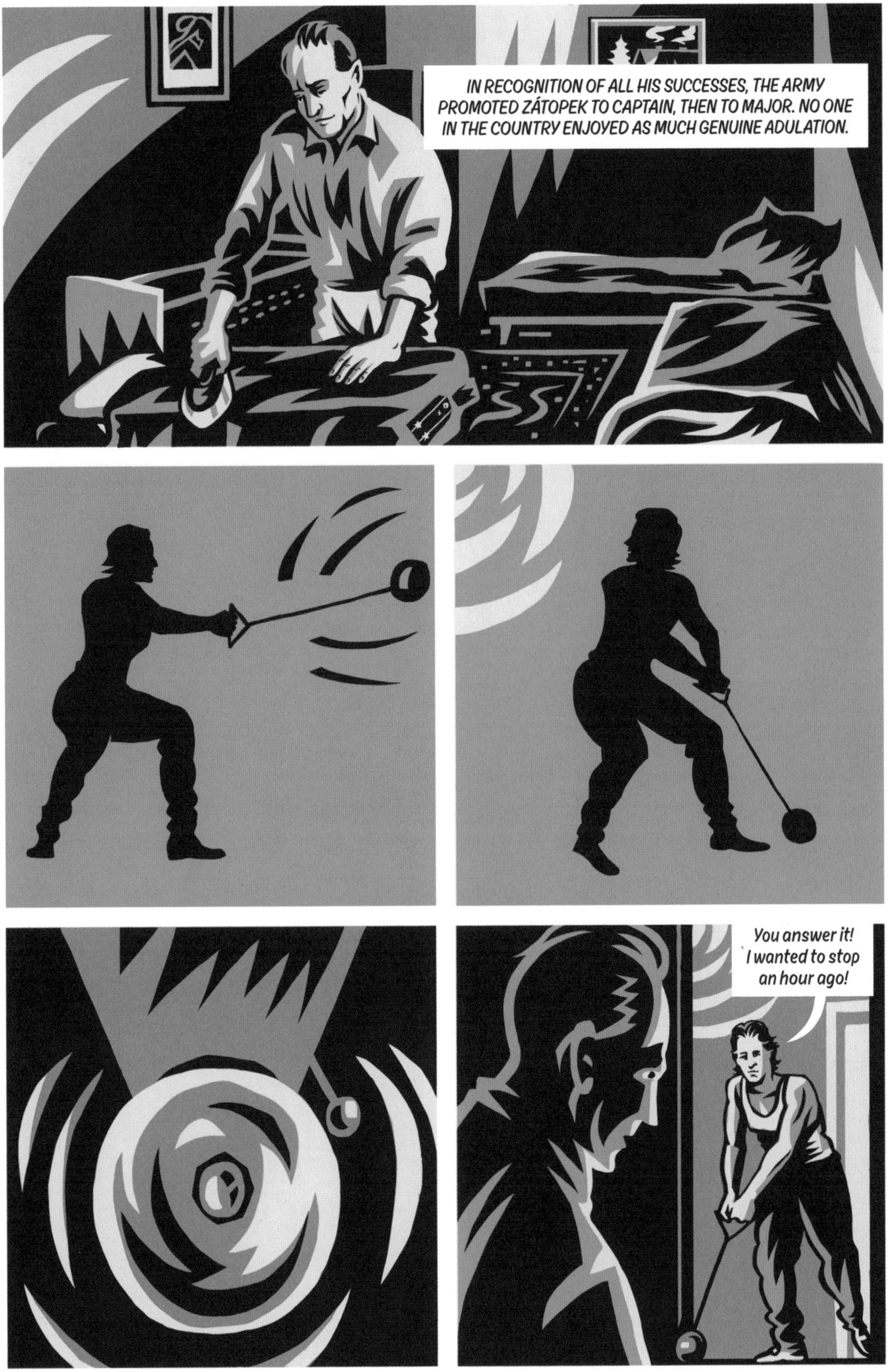
IN RECOGNITION OF ALL HIS SUCCESSES, THE ARMY PROMOTED ZÁTOPEK TO CAPTAIN, THEN TO MAJOR. NO ONE IN THE COUNTRY ENJOYED AS MUCH GENUINE ADULATION.
You answer it! I wanted to stop an hour ago!

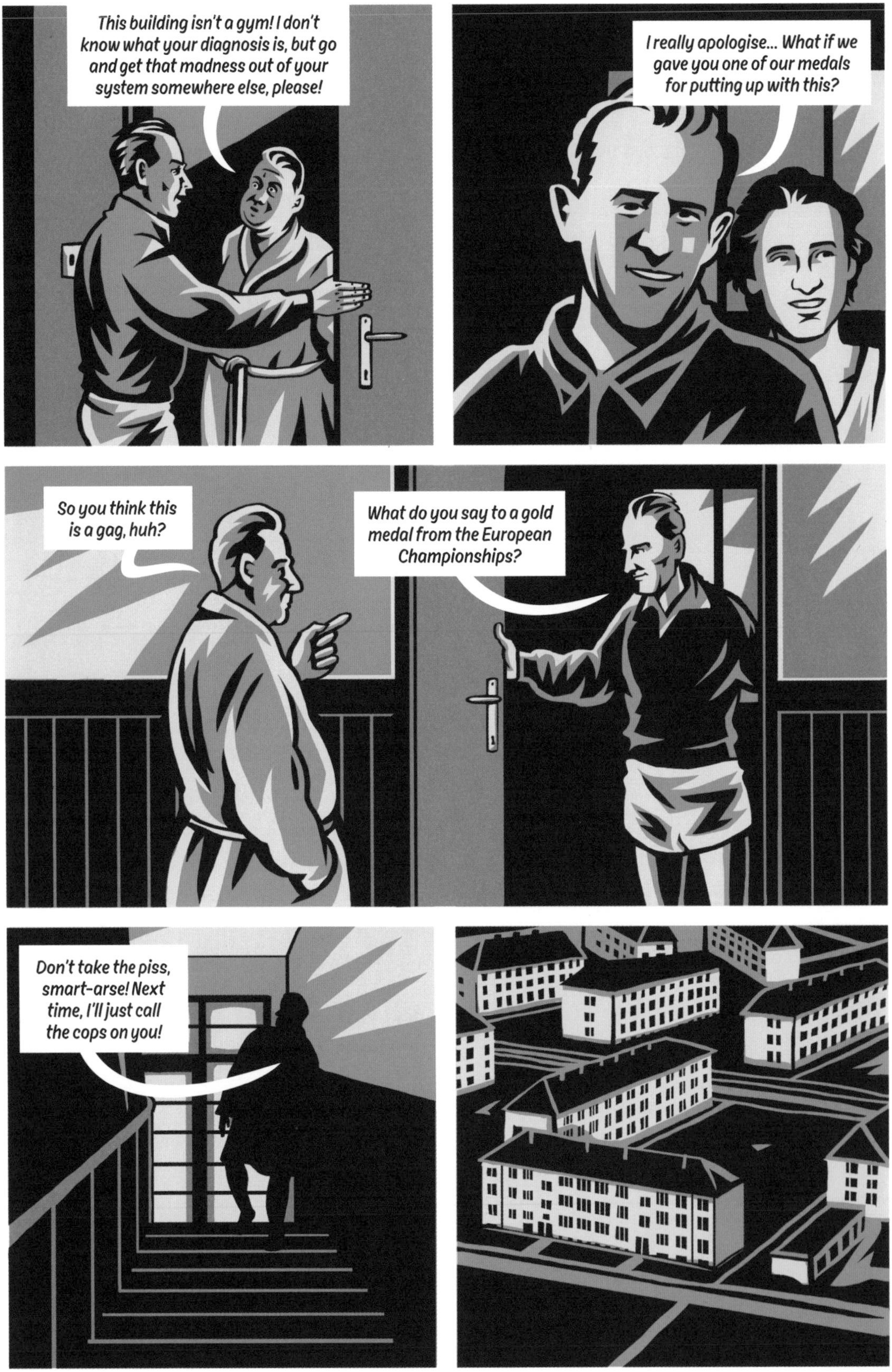
This building isn't a gym! I don't know what your diagnosis is, but go and get that madness out of your system somewhere else, please!
I really apologise... What if we gave you one of our medals for putting up with this?
So you think this is a gag, huh?
What do you say to a gold medal from the European Championships?
Don't take the piss, smart-arse! Next time, I'll just call the cops on you!

Houšťka Park, near Prague, Czechoslovakia, 1952.

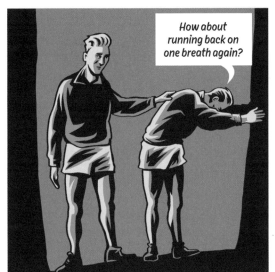

How about running back on one breath again?

Sorry... I've gone way beyond my training plan for today.

Your coach will never know, who'll tell him?

I'll tell him myself.

They said you hold on to his apron strings for dear life! All right, I'm doing it on one breath. I've got nothing left to throw up now anyhow!

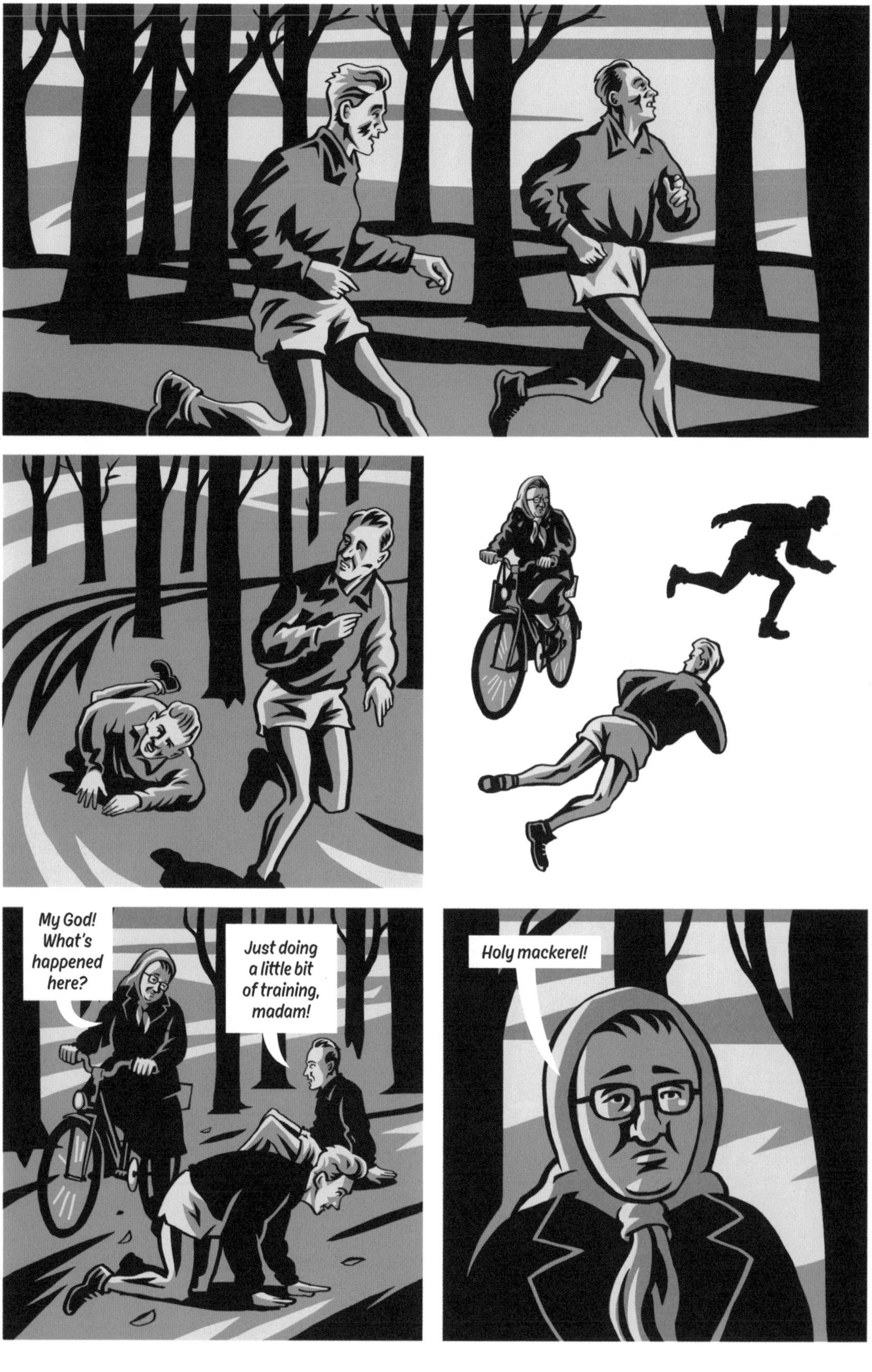
My God! What's happened here?
Just doing a little bit of training, madam!
Holy mackerel!

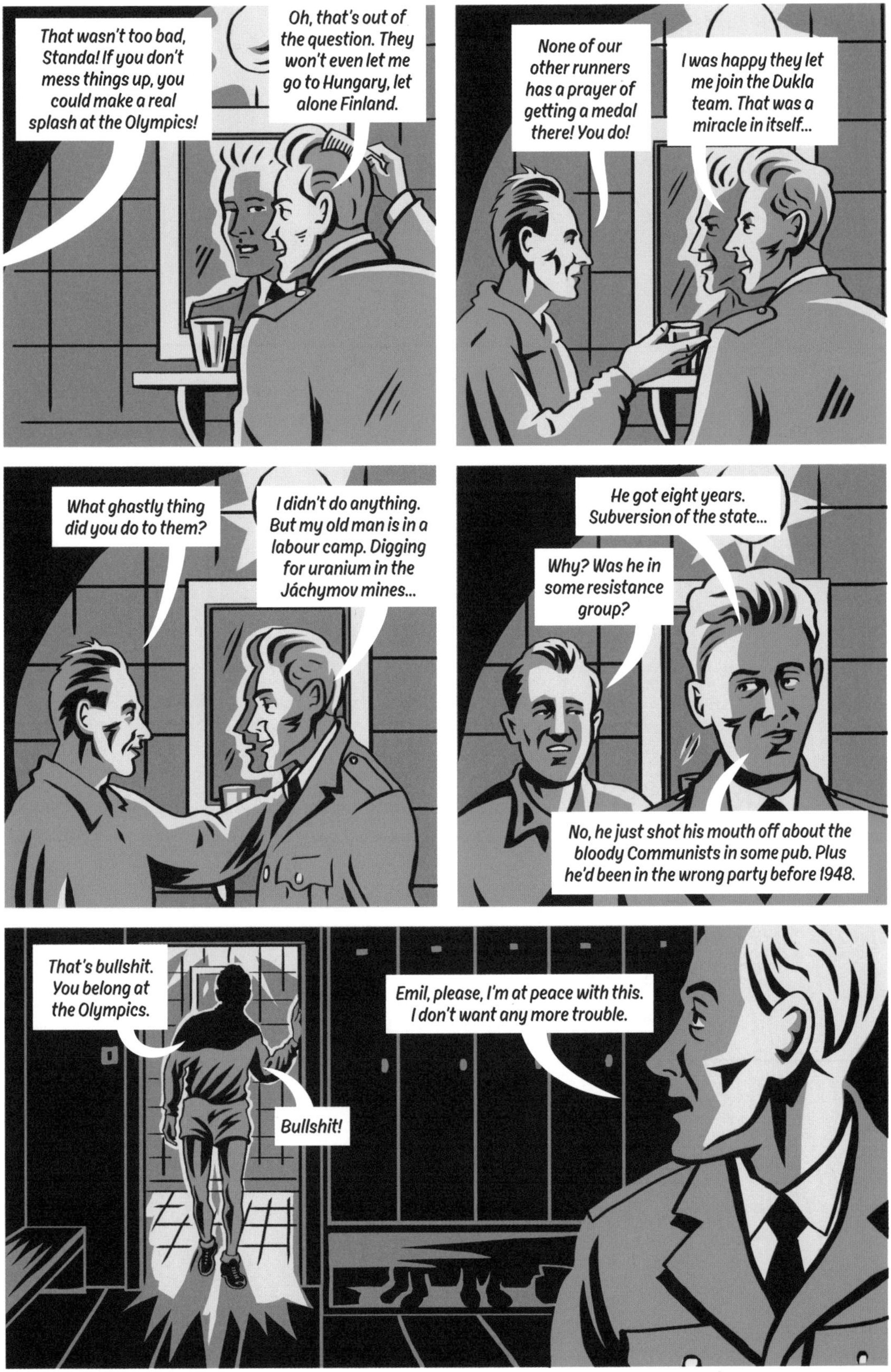
That wasn't too bad, Standa! If you don't mess things up, you could make a real splash at the Olympics!
Oh, that's out of the question. They won't even let me go to Hungary, let alone Finland.
None of our other runners has a prayer of getting a medal there! You do!
I was happy they let me join the Dukla team. That was a miracle in itself...
What ghastly thing did you do to them?
I didn't do anything. But my old man is in a labour camp. Digging for uranium in the Jáchymov mines...
He got eight years. Subversion of the state...
Why? Was he in some resistance group?
No, he just shot his mouth off about the bloody Communists in some pub. Plus he'd been in the wrong party before 1948.
That's bullshit. You belong at the Olympics.
Bullshit!
Emil, please, I'm at peace with this. I don't want any more trouble.

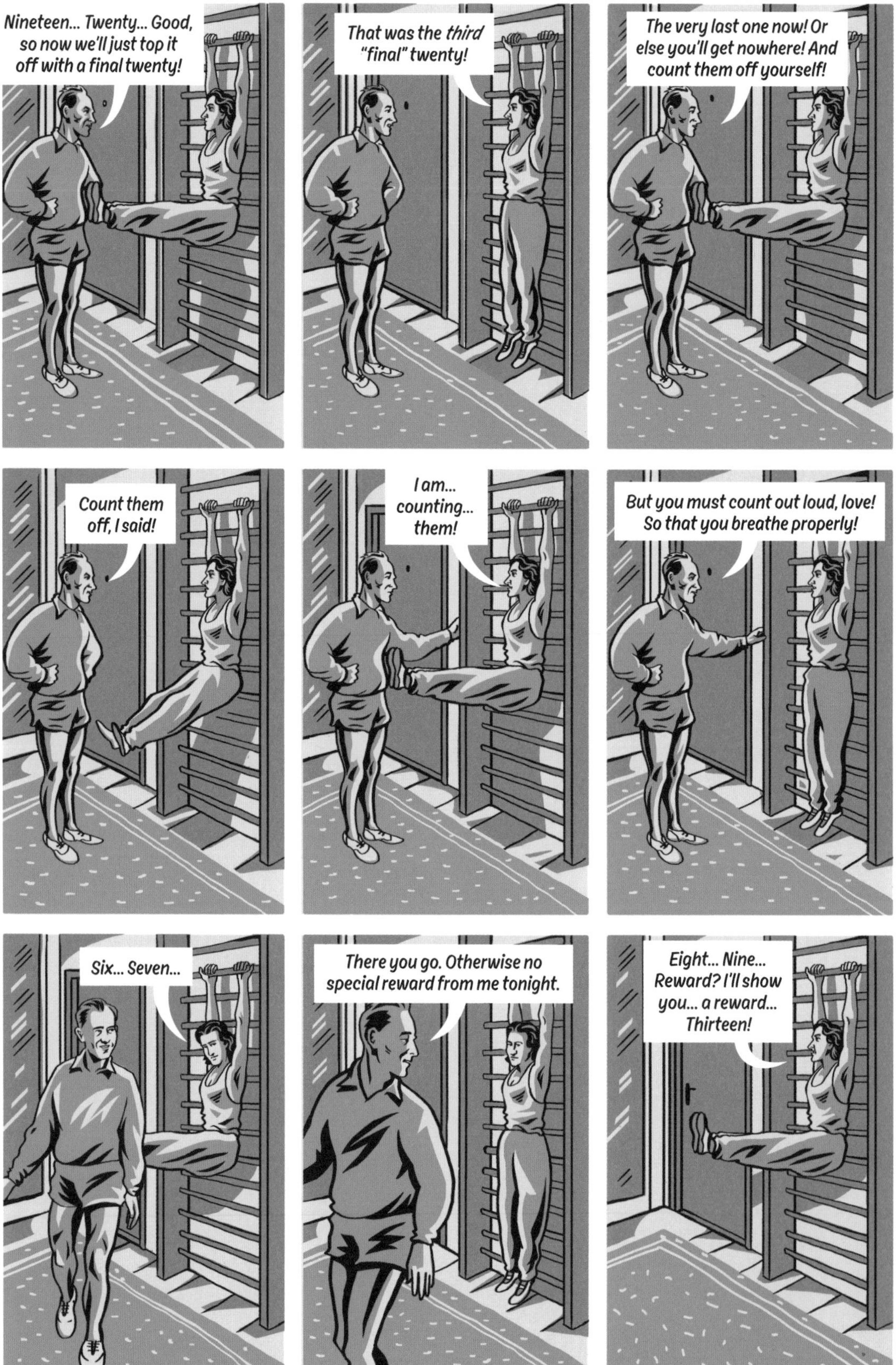
Nineteen... Twenty... Good, so now we'll just top it off with a final twenty!
That was the *third* "final" twenty!
The very last one now! Or else you'll get nowhere! And count them off yourself!
Count them off, I said!
I am... counting... them!
But you must count out loud, love! So that you breathe properly!
Six... Seven...
There you go. Otherwise no special reward from me tonight.
Eight... Nine... Reward? I'll show you... a reward... Thirteen!

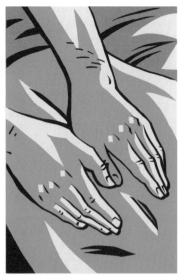

Owww!

Standa's barely training at all, and he still ran the 1,500 metres in 3:47! He ought to make the podium in Helsinki!

Oh, just drop it, will you?

Someone has to speak up for him! He's as shy as a debutante! I've already made an appointment at the Athletic Association.

Ouch!

Darling, have you lost your mind? This is bound to end in disaster! For you and for him!

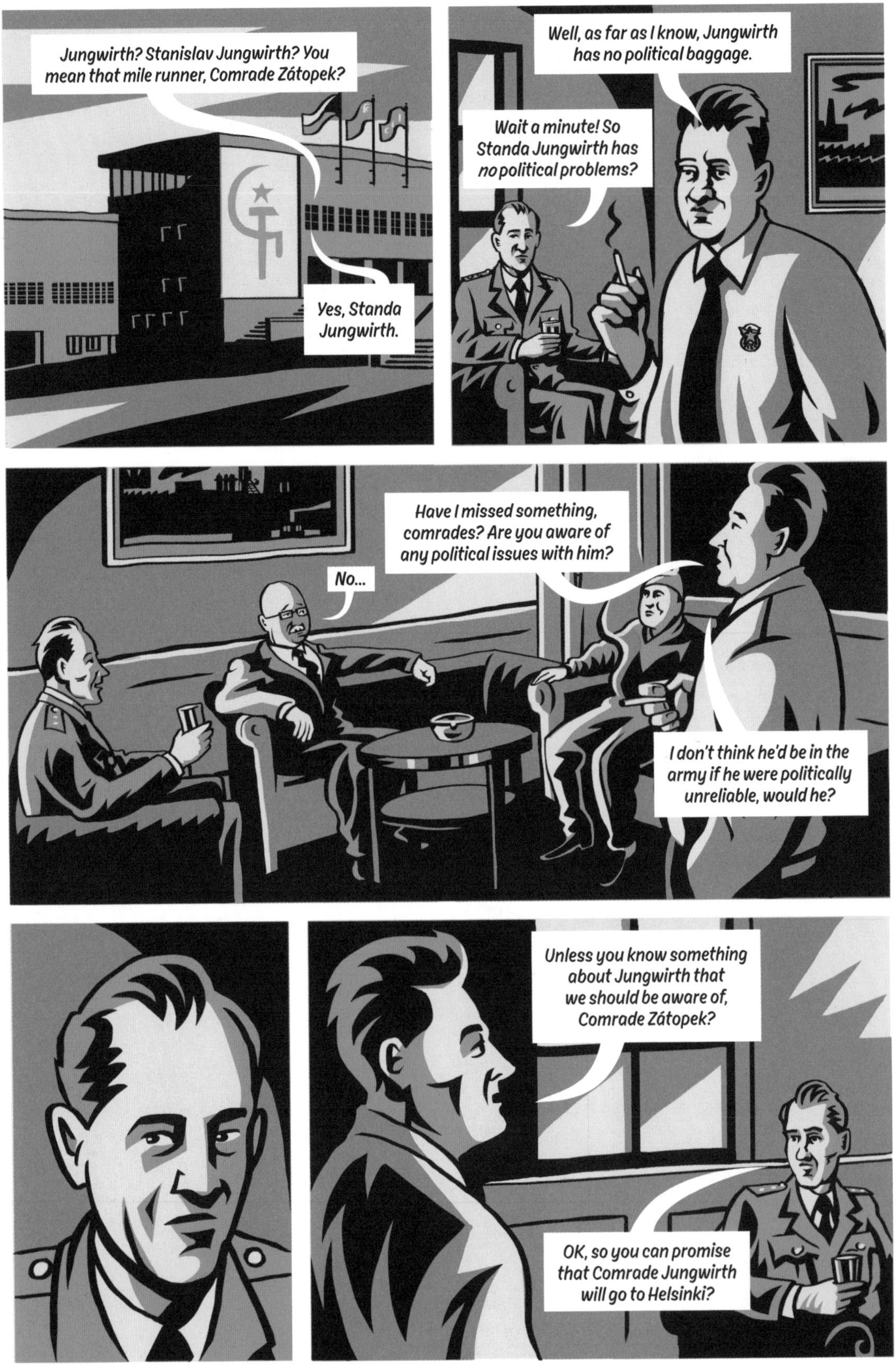
Jungwirth? Stanislav Jungwirth? You mean that mile runner, Comrade Zátopek?
Yes, Standa Jungwirth.
Well, as far as I know, Jungwirth has no political baggage.
Wait a minute! So Standa Jungwirth has *no* political problems?
Have I missed something, comrades? Are you aware of any political issues with him?
No...
I don't think he'd be in the army if he were politically unreliable, would he?
Unless you know something about Jungwirth that we should be aware of, Comrade Zátopek?
OK, so you can promise that Comrade Jungwirth will go to Helsinki?

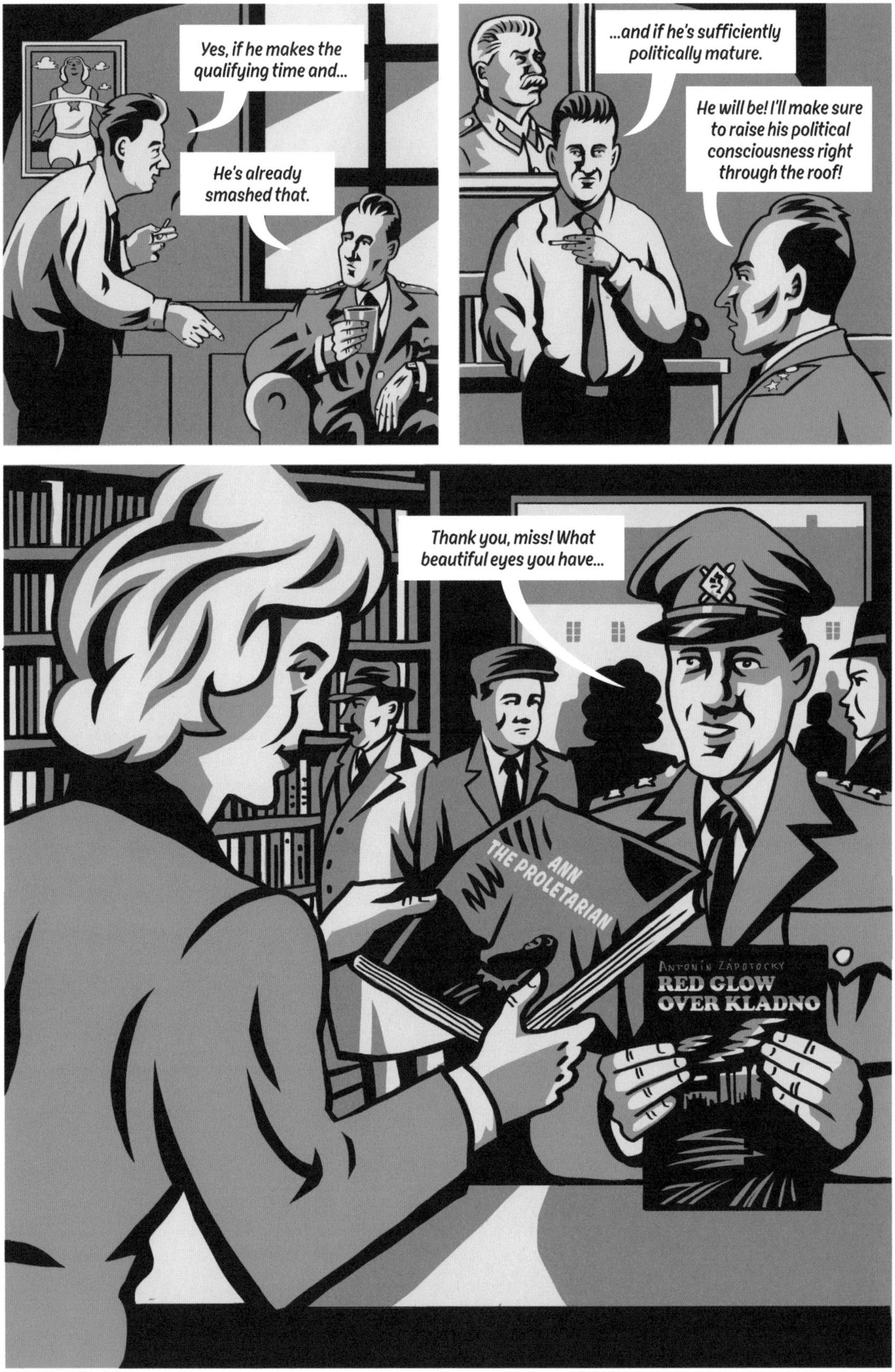
Yes, if he makes the qualifying time and...
He's already smashed that.
...and if he's sufficiently politically mature.
He will be! I'll make sure to raise his political consciousness right through the roof!
Thank you, miss! What beautiful eyes you have...
ANN THE PROLETARIAN
ANTONÍN ZÁPOTOCKY
RED GLOW OVER KLADNO

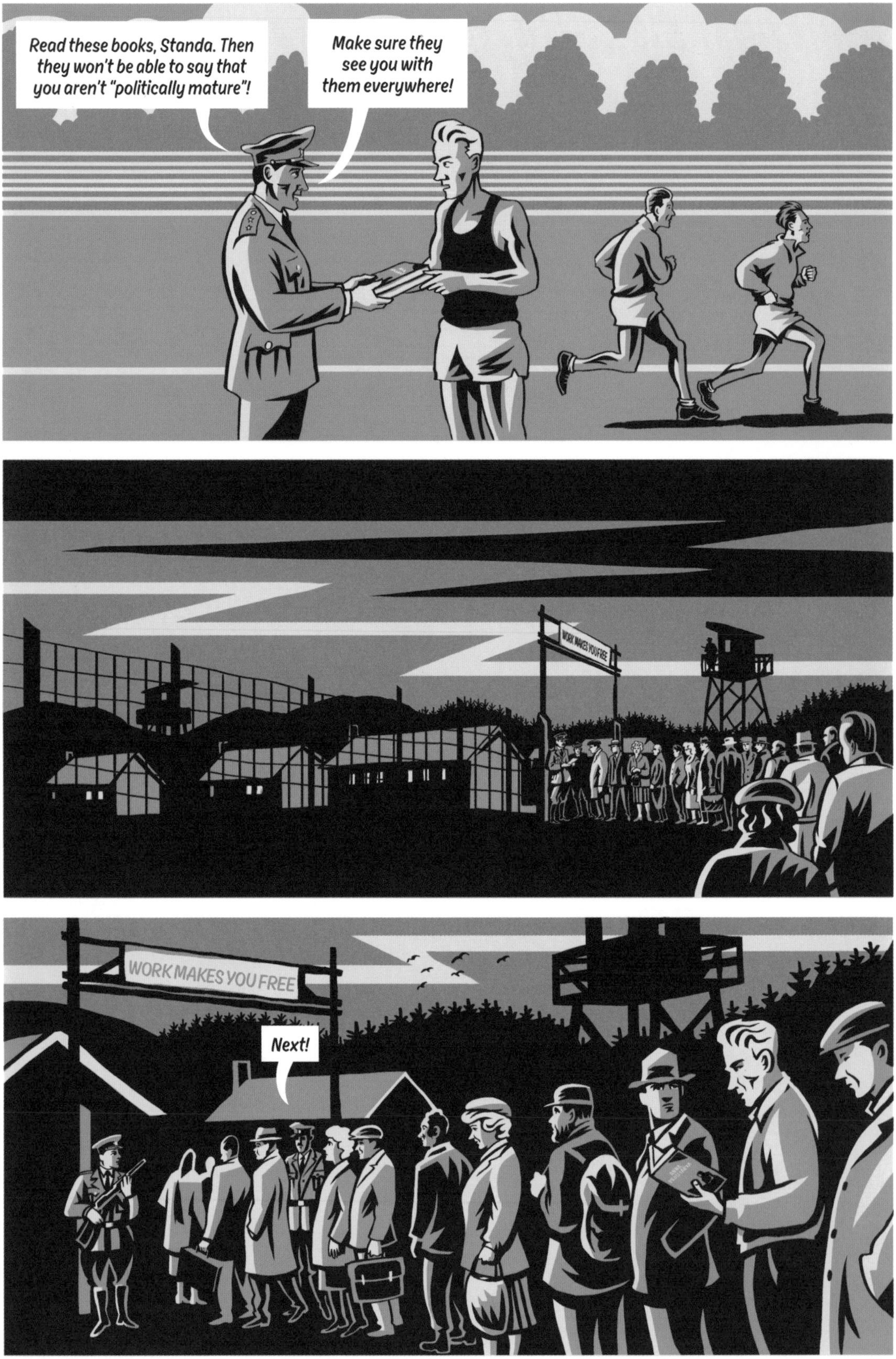

Read these books, Standa. Then they won't be able to say that you aren't "politically mature"!
Make sure they see you with them everywhere!
WORK MAKES YOU FREE
WORK MAKES YOU FREE
Next!

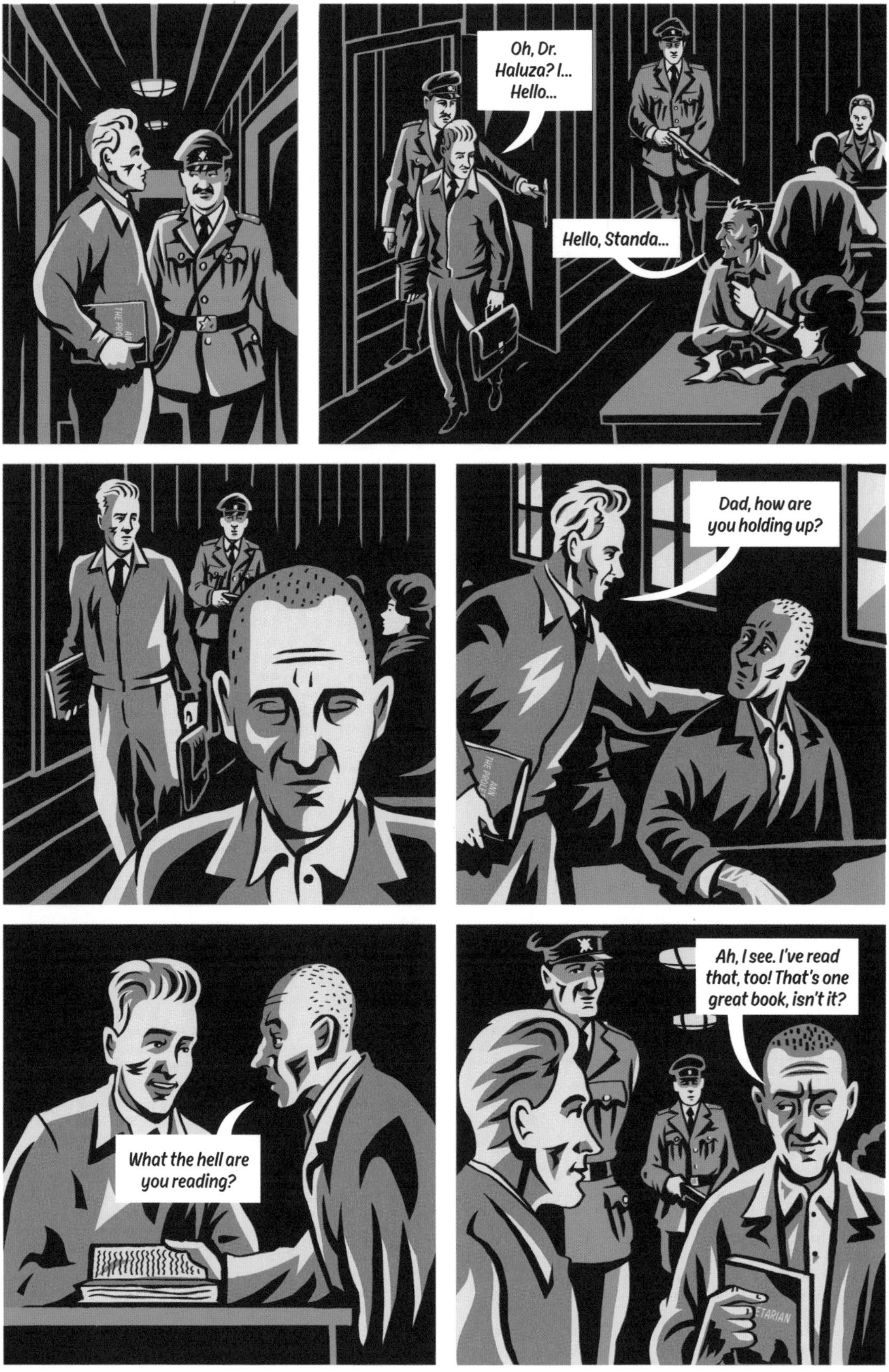
Oh, Dr. Haluza? I... Hello...
Hello, Standa...
Dad, how are you holding up?
What the hell are you reading?
Ah, I see. I've read that, too! That's one great book, isn't it?

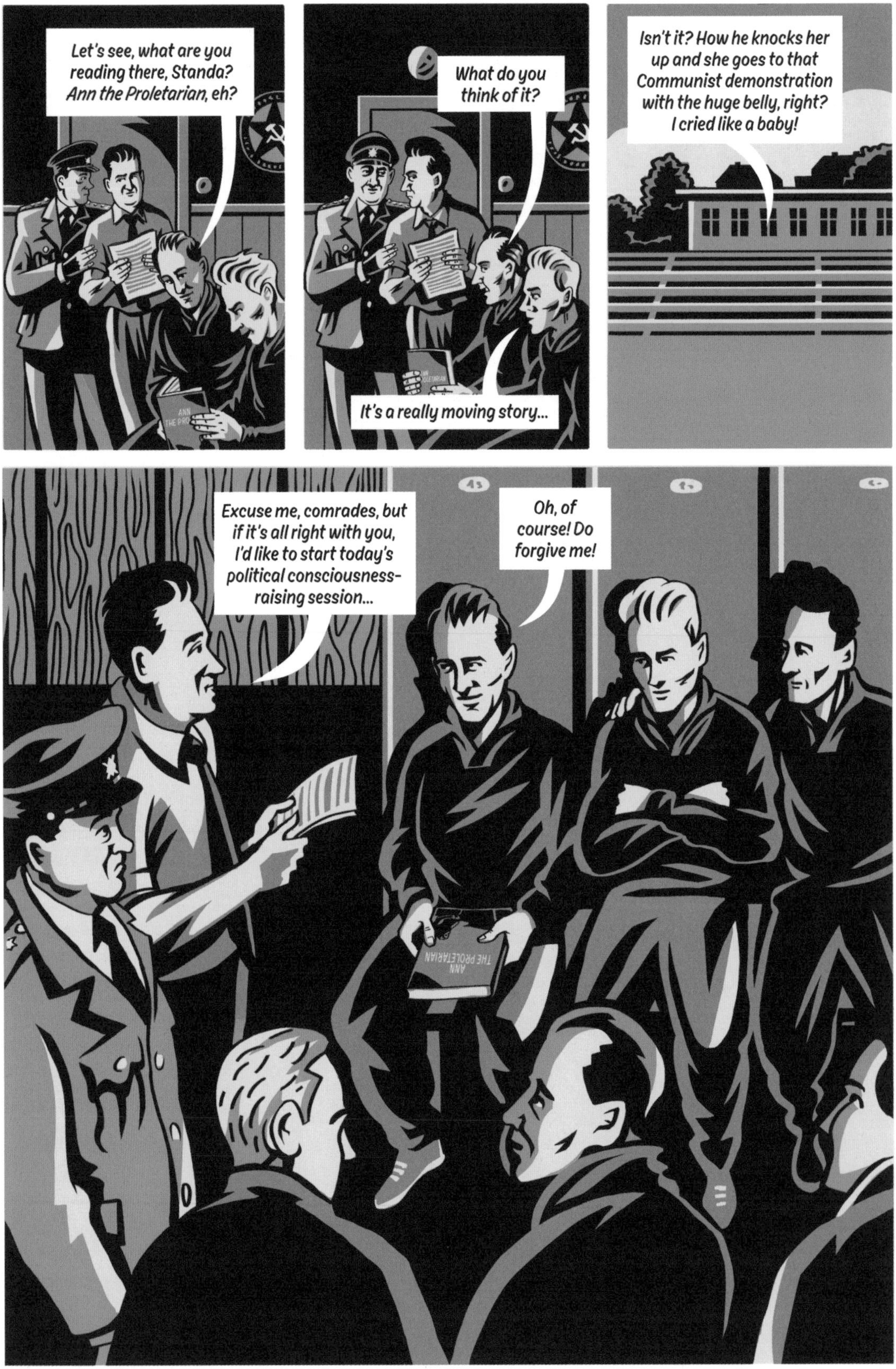
Let's see, what are you reading there, Standa? Ann the Proletarian, eh?
ANN THE PRO
What do you think of it?
It's a really moving story...
Isn't it? How he knocks her up and she goes to that Communist demonstration with the huge belly, right? I cried like a baby!
Excuse me, comrades, but if it's all right with you, I'd like to start today's political consciousness-raising session...
Oh, of course! Do forgive me!
ANN THE PROLETARIAN

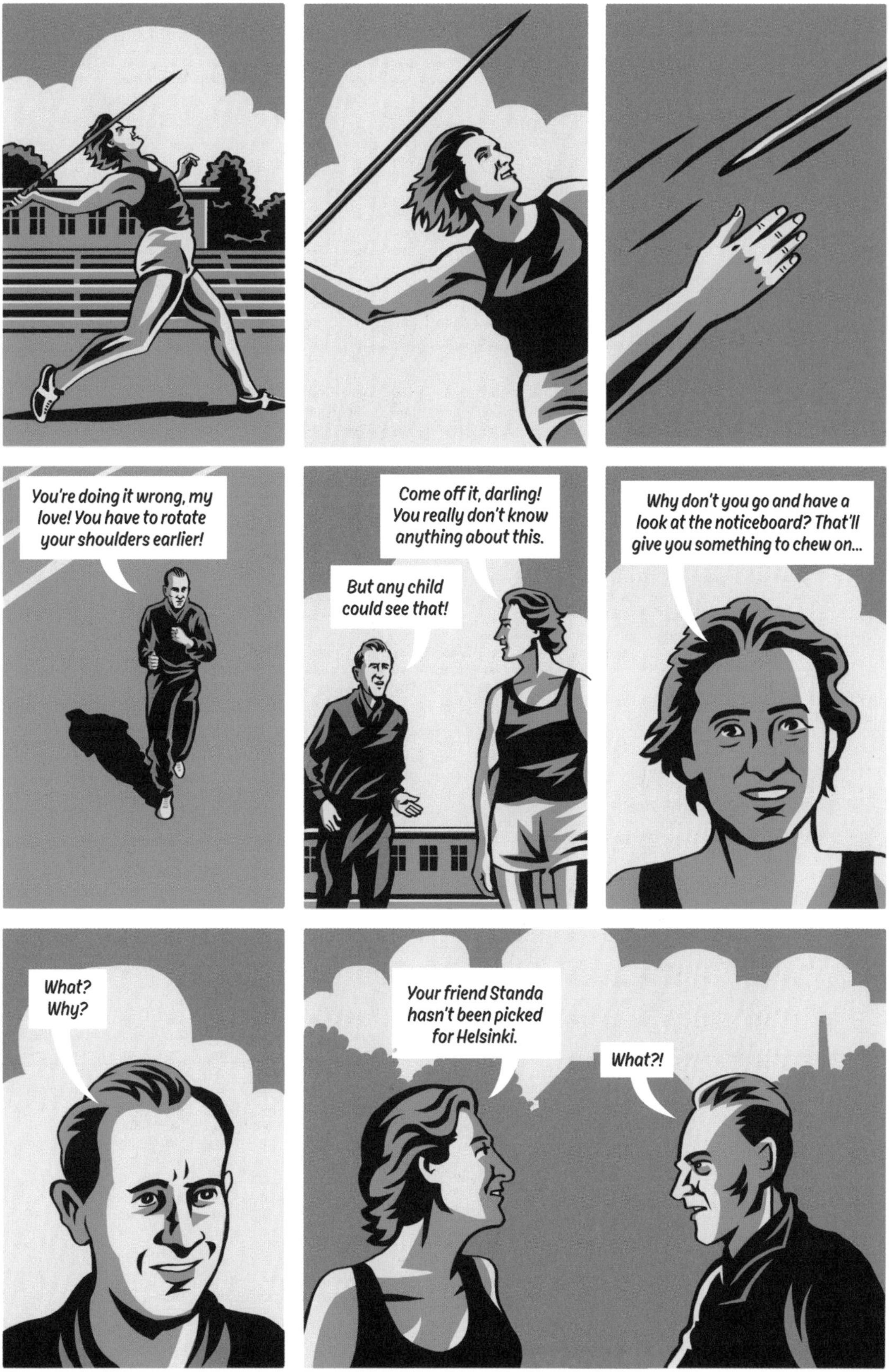
You're doing it wrong, my love! You have to rotate your shoulders earlier!
Come off it, darling! You really don't know anything about this.
But any child could see that!
Why don't you go and have a look at the noticeboard? That'll give you something to chew on...
What? Why?
Your friend Standa hasn't been picked for Helsinki.
What?!

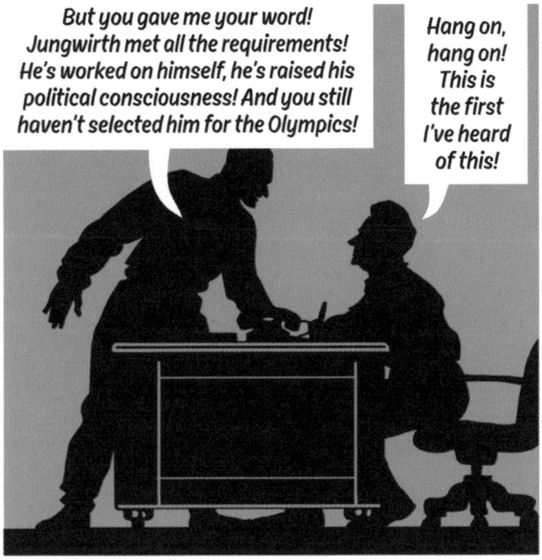
But you gave me your word! Jungwirth met all the requirements! He's worked on himself, he's raised his political consciousness! And you still haven't selected him for the Olympics!
Hang on, hang on! This is the first I've heard of this!

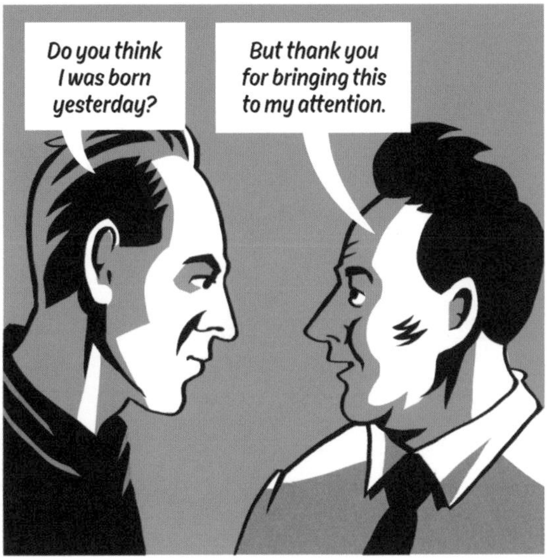
Do you think I was born yesterday?
But thank you for bringing this to my attention.

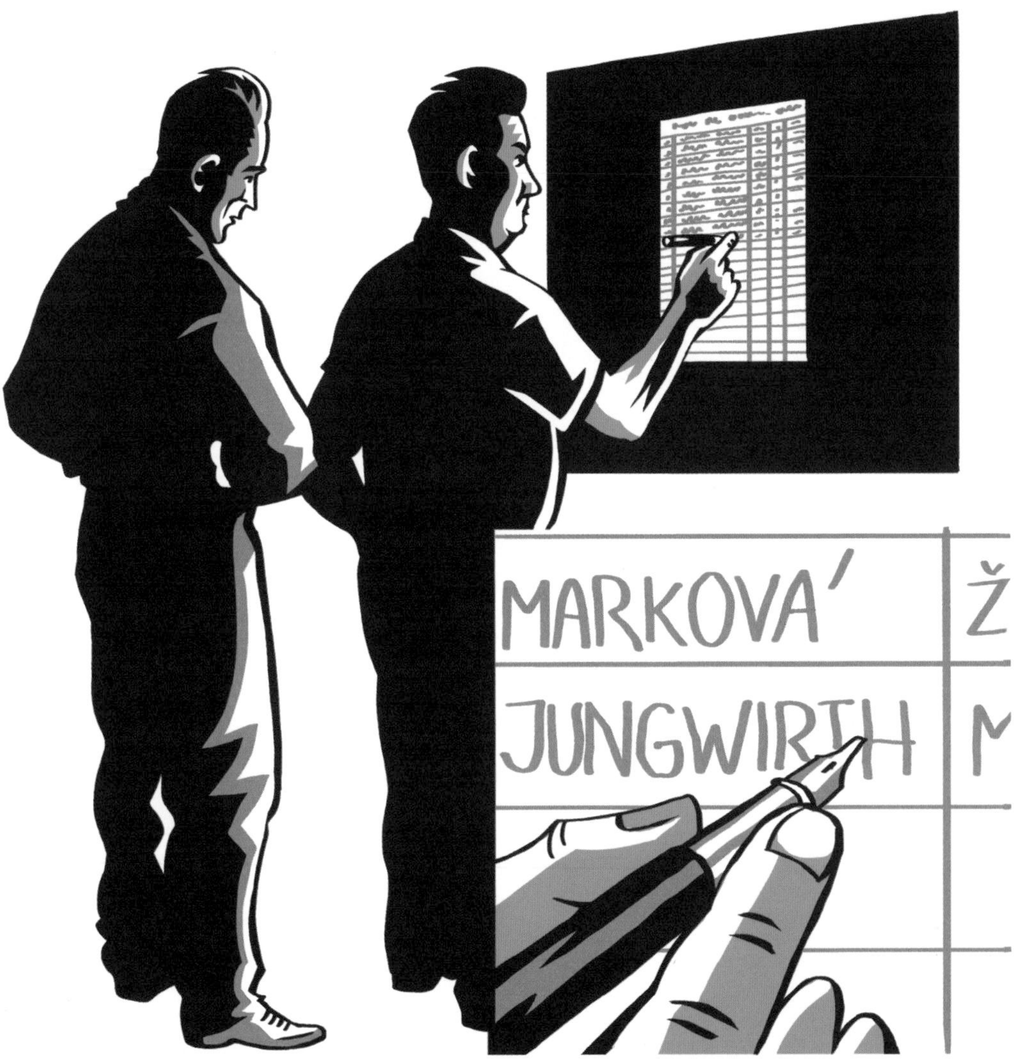
MARKOVA'
JUNGWIRTH

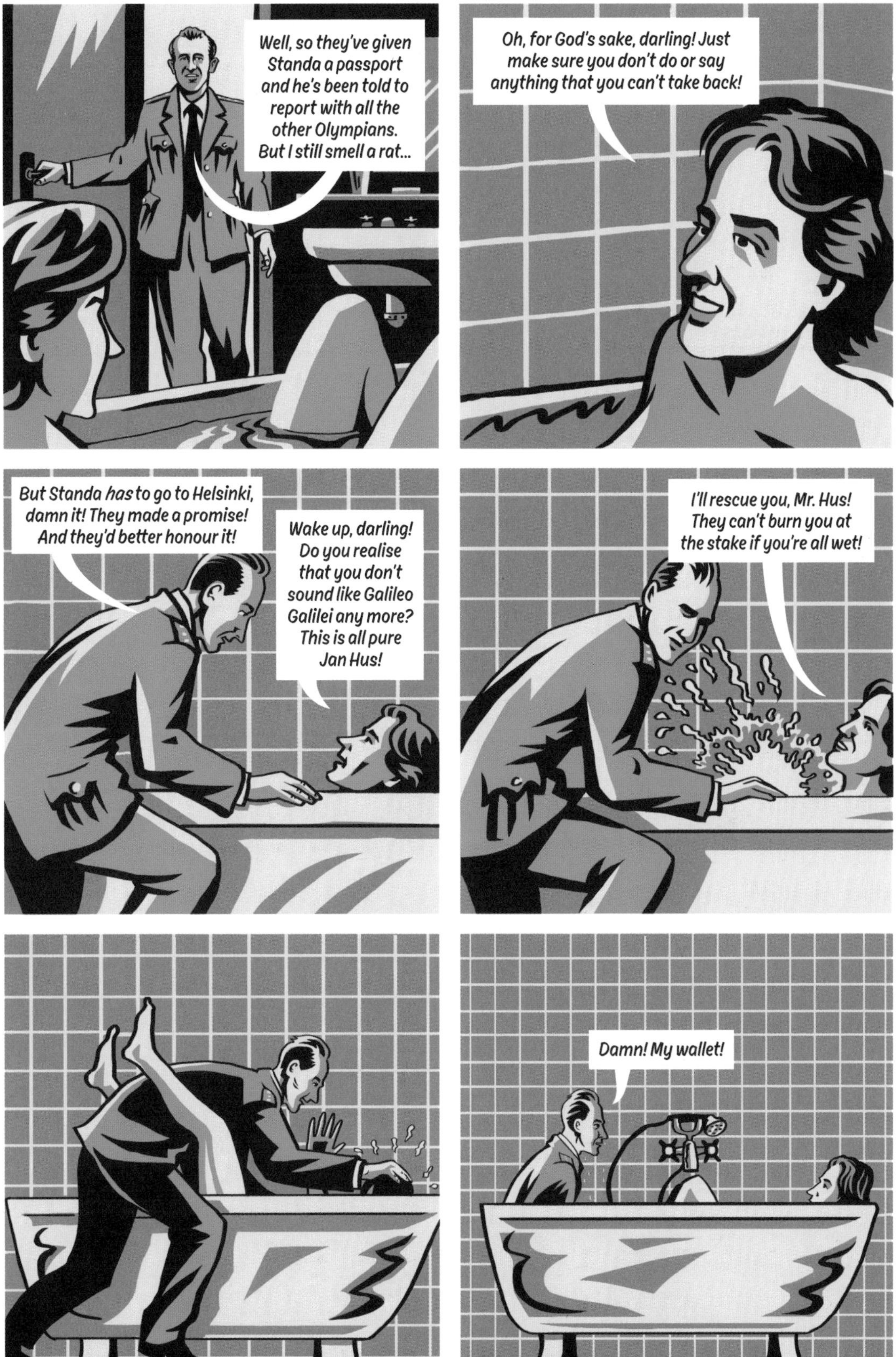
Well, so they've given Standa a passport and he's been told to report with all the other Olympians. But I still smell a rat...
Oh, for God's sake, darling! Just make sure you don't do or say anything that you can't take back!
But Standa *has* to go to Helsinki, damn it! They made a promise! And they'd better honour it!
Wake up, darling! Do you realise that you don't sound like Galileo Galilei any more? This is all pure Jan Hus!
I'll rescue you, Mr. Hus! They can't burn you at the stake if you're all wet!
Damn! My wallet!

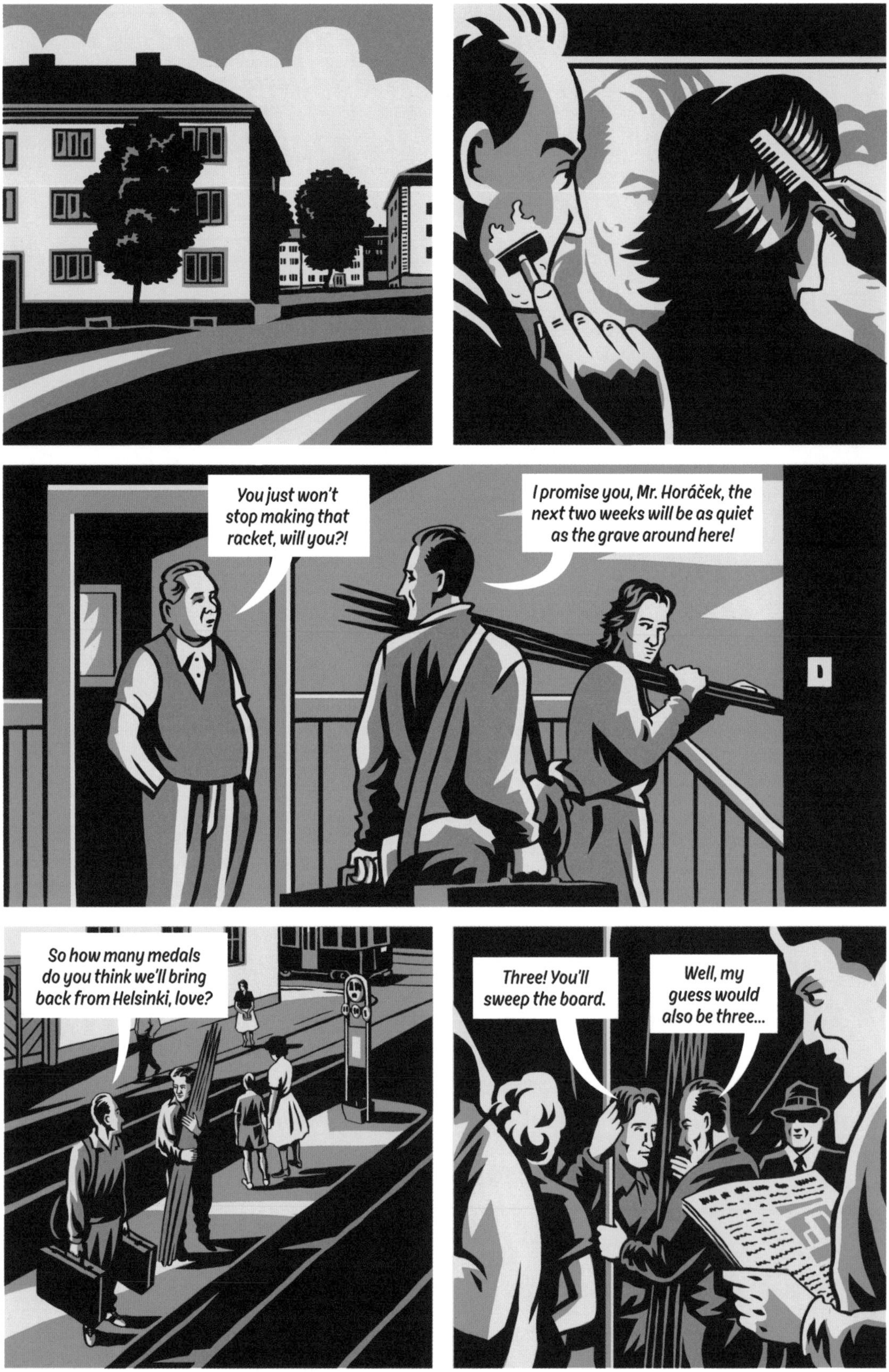
You just won't stop making that racket, will you?!
I promise you, Mr. Horáček, the next two weeks will be as quiet as the grave around here!
So how many medals do you think we'll bring back from Helsinki, love?
Three! You'll sweep the board.
Well, my guess would also be three...

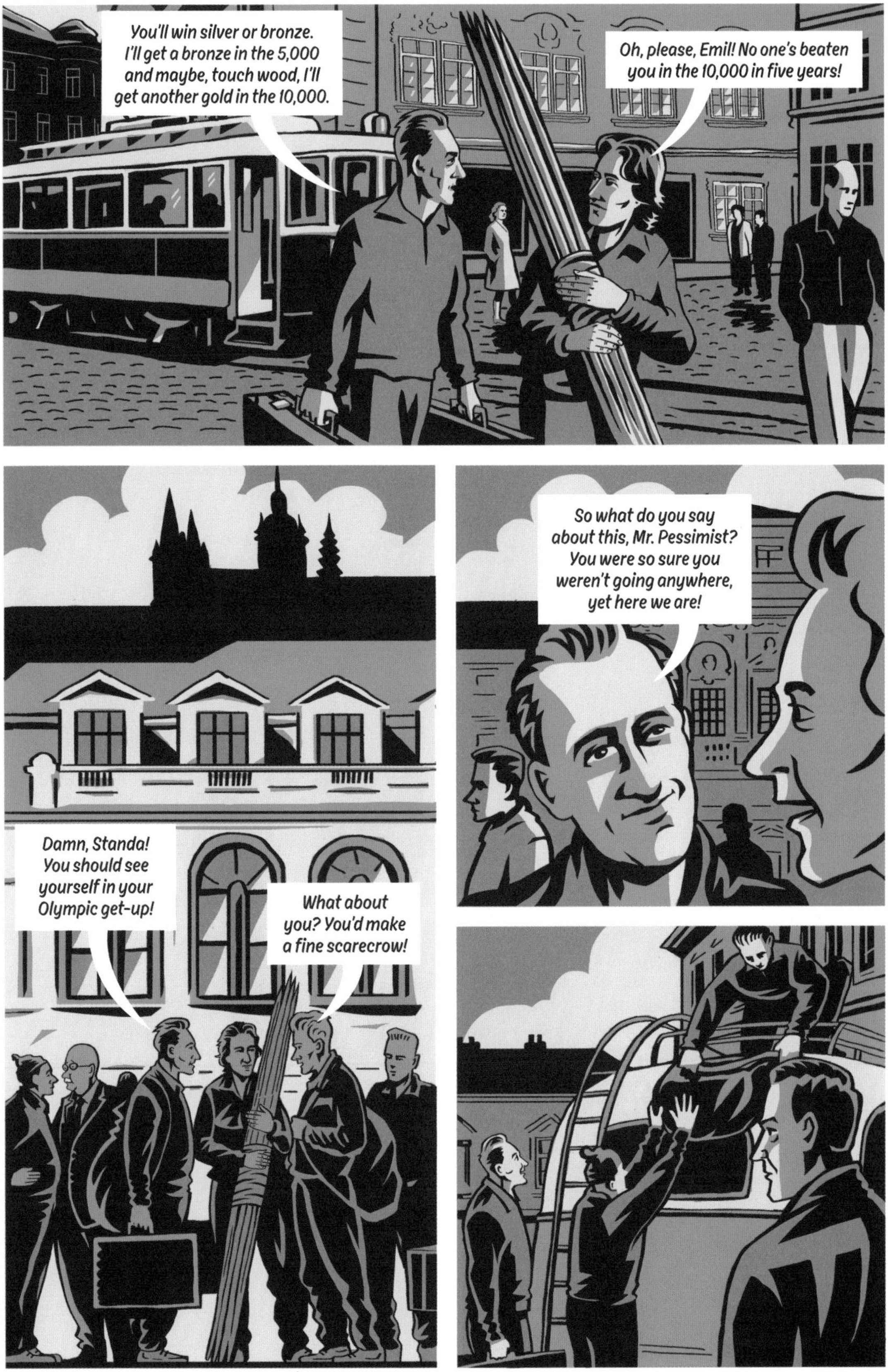
You'll win silver or bronze. I'll get a bronze in the 5,000 and maybe, touch wood, I'll get another gold in the 10,000.
Oh, please, Emil! No one's beaten you in the 10,000 in five years!
Damn, Standa! You should see yourself in your Olympic get-up!
What about you? You'd make a fine scarecrow!
So what do you say about this, Mr. Pessimist? You were so sure you weren't going anywhere, yet here we are!

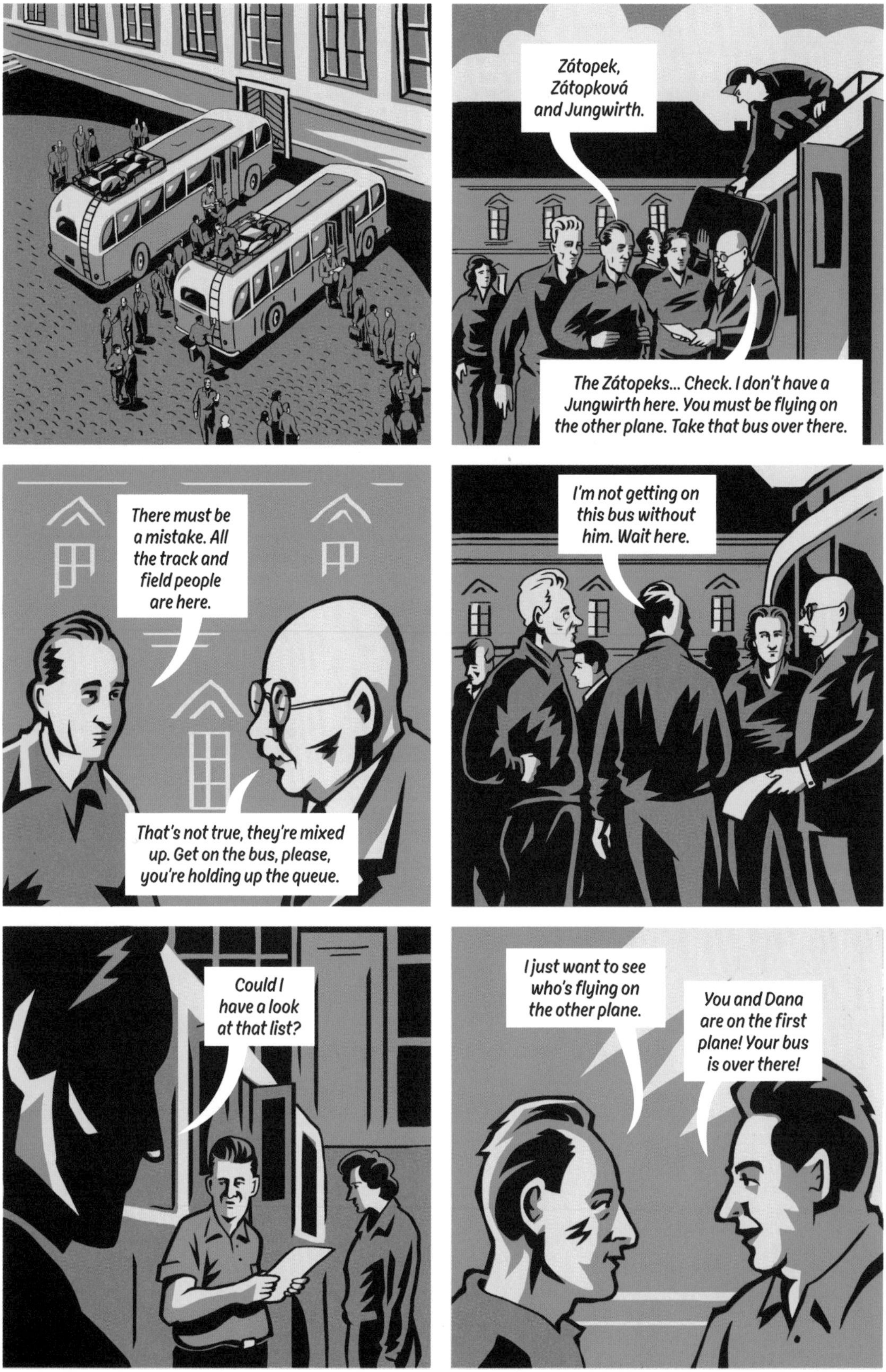
Zátopek, Zátopková and Jungwirth.
The Zátopeks... Check. I don't have a Jungwirth here. You must be flying on the other plane. Take that bus over there.
There must be a mistake. All the track and field people are here.
That's not true, they're mixed up. Get on the bus, please, you're holding up the queue.
I'm not getting on this bus without him. Wait here.
Could I have a look at that list?
I just want to see who's flying on the other plane.
You and Dana are on the first plane! Your bus is over there!

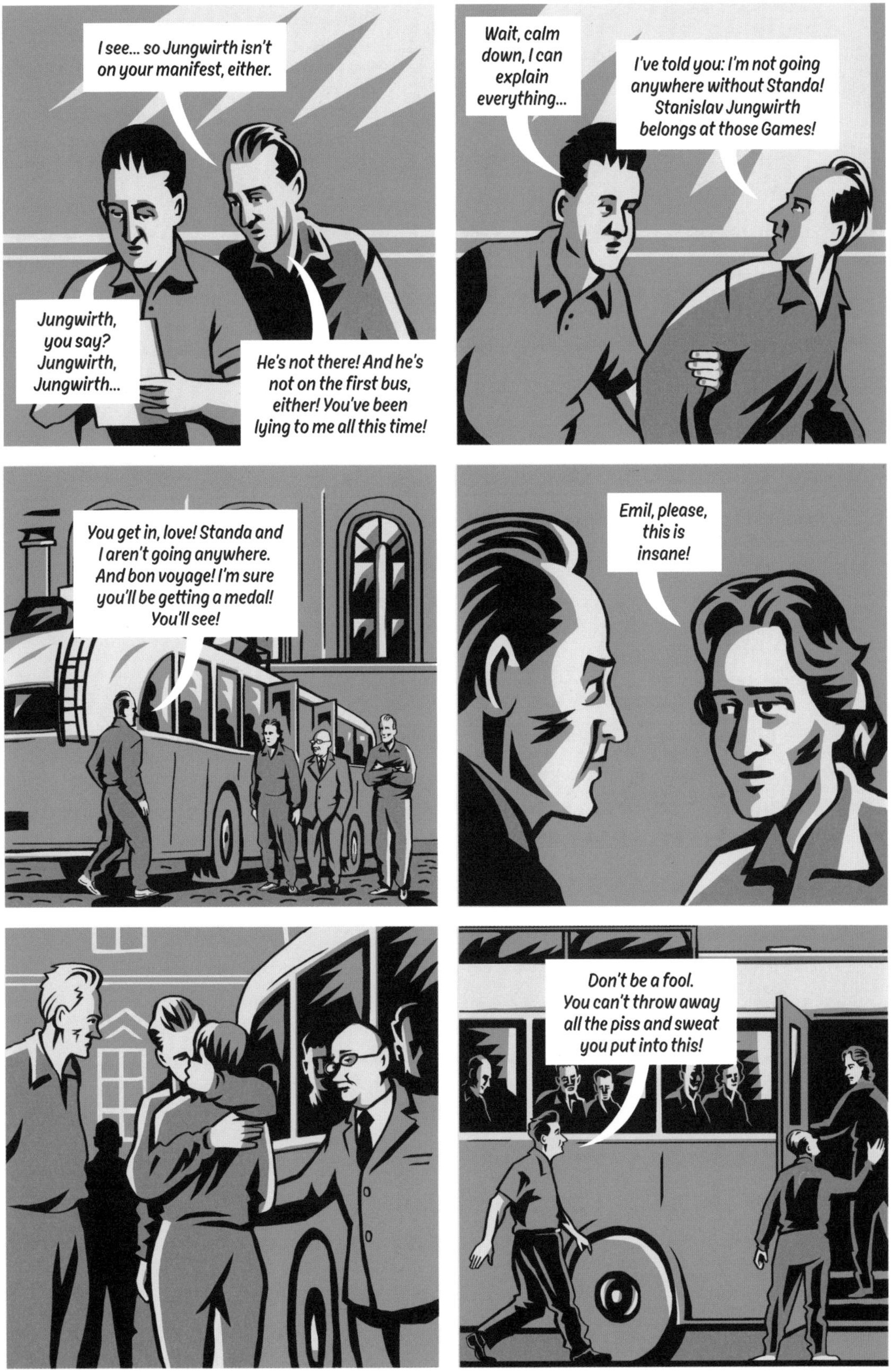
I see... so Jungwirth isn't on your manifest, either.
Jungwirth, you say? Jungwirth, Jungwirth...
He's not there! And he's not on the first bus, either! You've been lying to me all this time!
Wait, calm down, I can explain everything...
I've told you: I'm not going anywhere without Standa! Stanislav Jungwirth belongs at those Games!
You get in, love! Standa and I aren't going anywhere. And bon voyage! I'm sure you'll be getting a medal! You'll see!
Emil, please, this is insane!
Don't be a fool. You can't throw away all the piss and sweat you put into this!

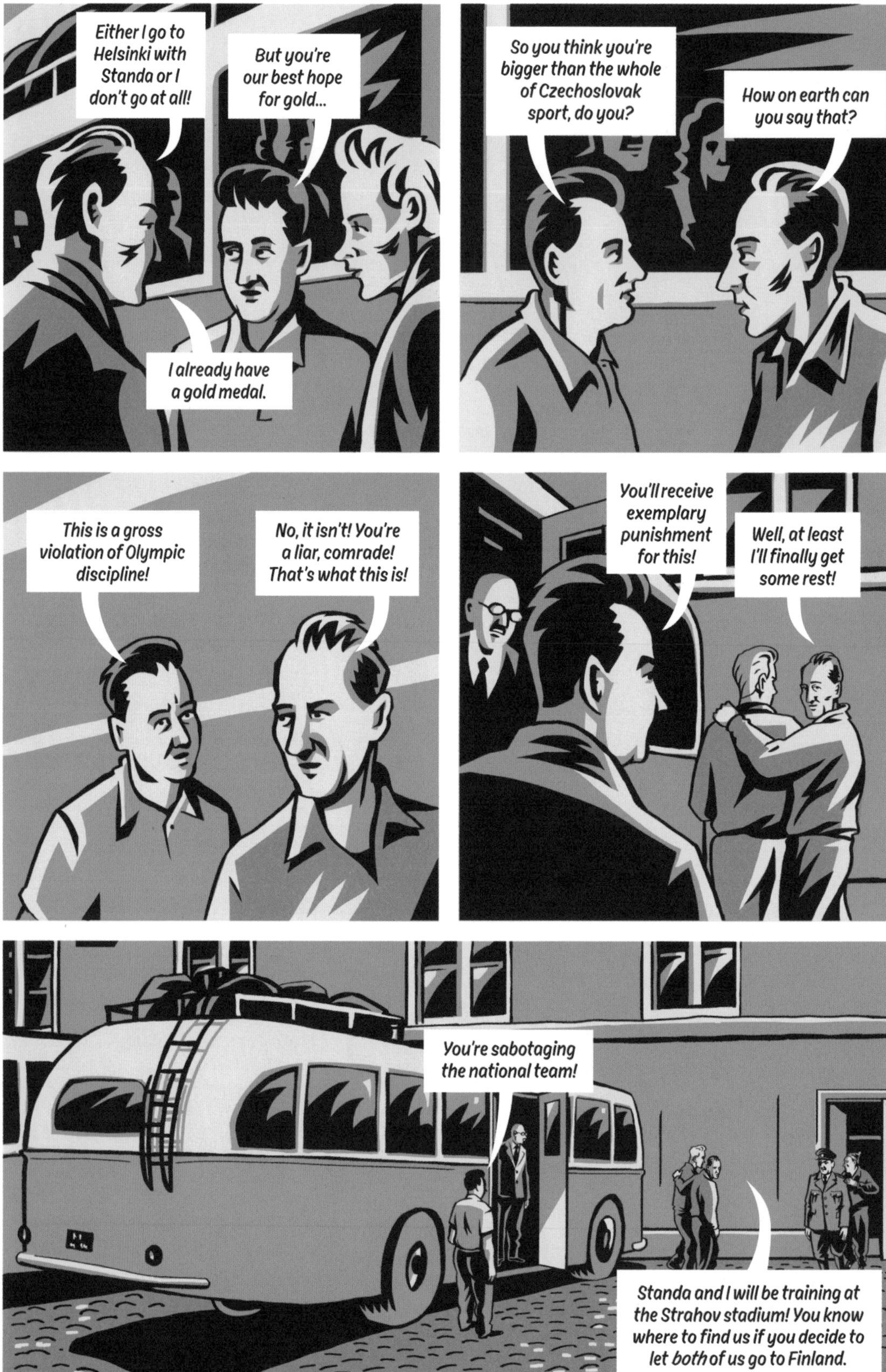
Either I go to Helsinki with Standa or I don't go at all!
But you're our best hope for gold...
I already have a gold medal.
So you think you're bigger than the whole of Czechoslovak sport, do you?
How on earth can you say that?
This is a gross violation of Olympic discipline!
No, it isn't! You're a liar, comrade! That's what this is!
You'll receive exemplary punishment for this!
Well, at least I'll finally get some rest!
You're sabotaging the national team!
Standa and I will be training at the Strahov stadium! You know where to find us if you decide to let *both* of us go to Finland.

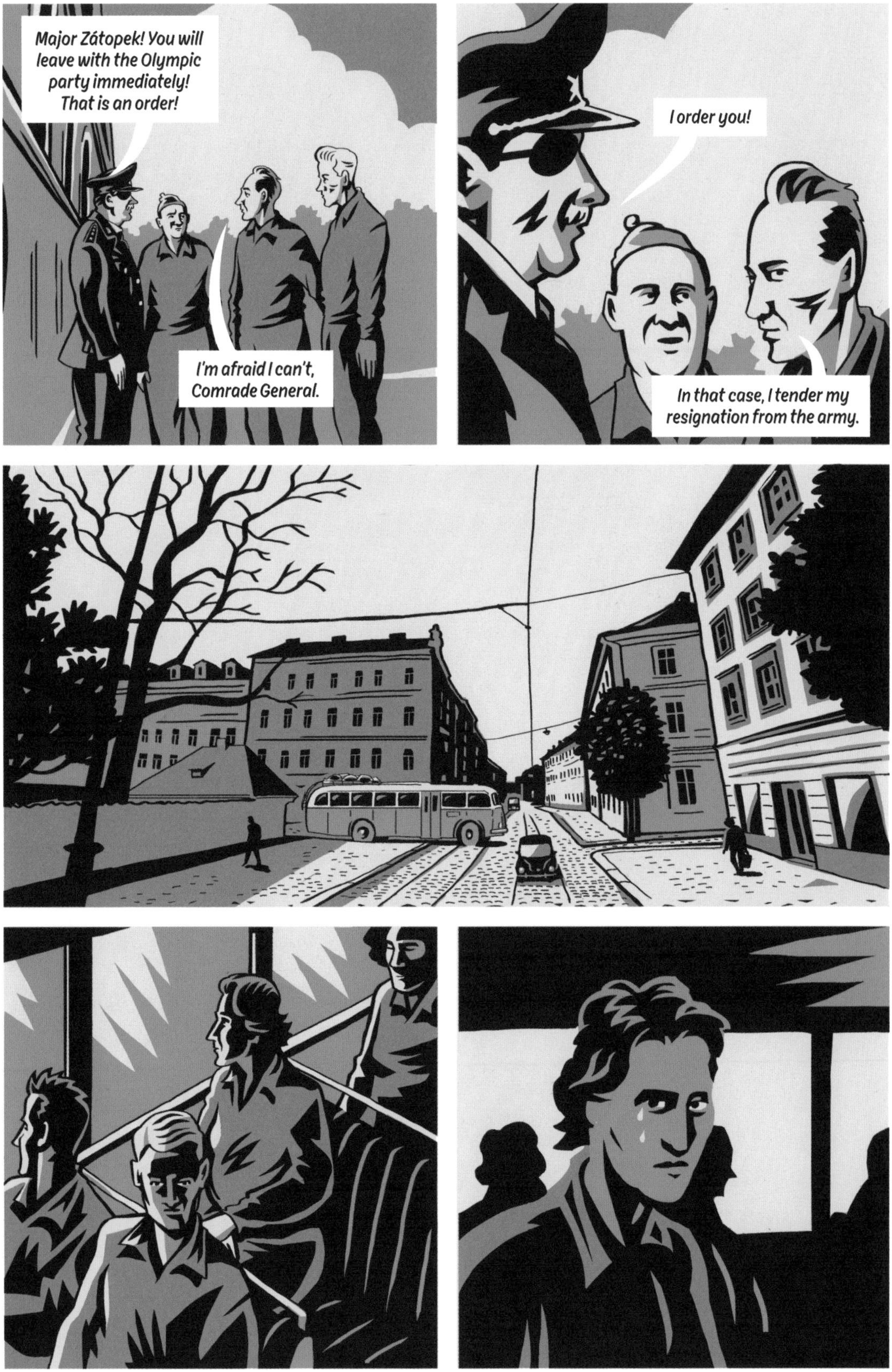
Major Zátopek! You will leave with the Olympic party immediately! That is an order!
I'm afraid I can't, Comrade General.
I order you!
In that case, I tender my resignation from the army.

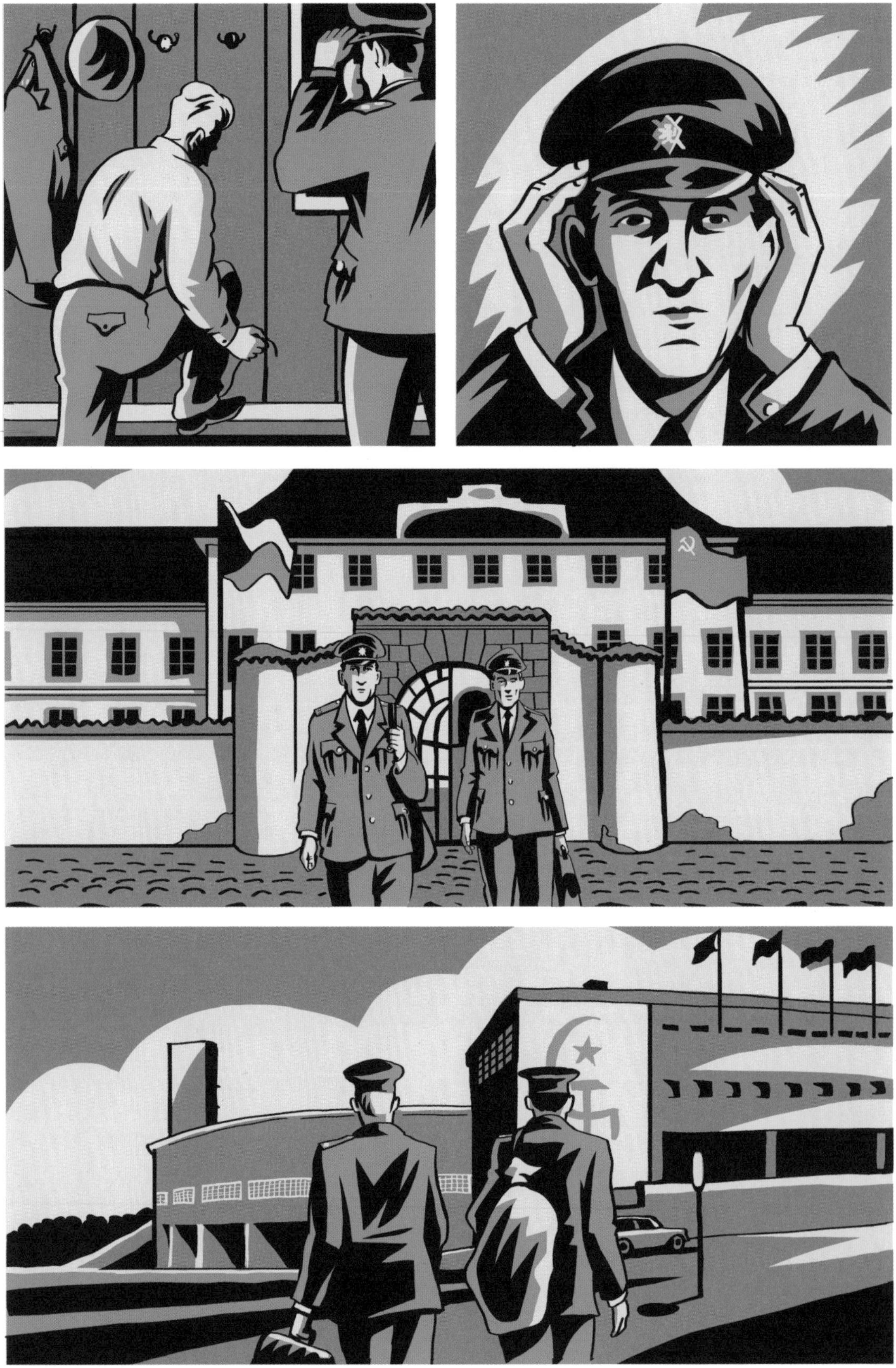

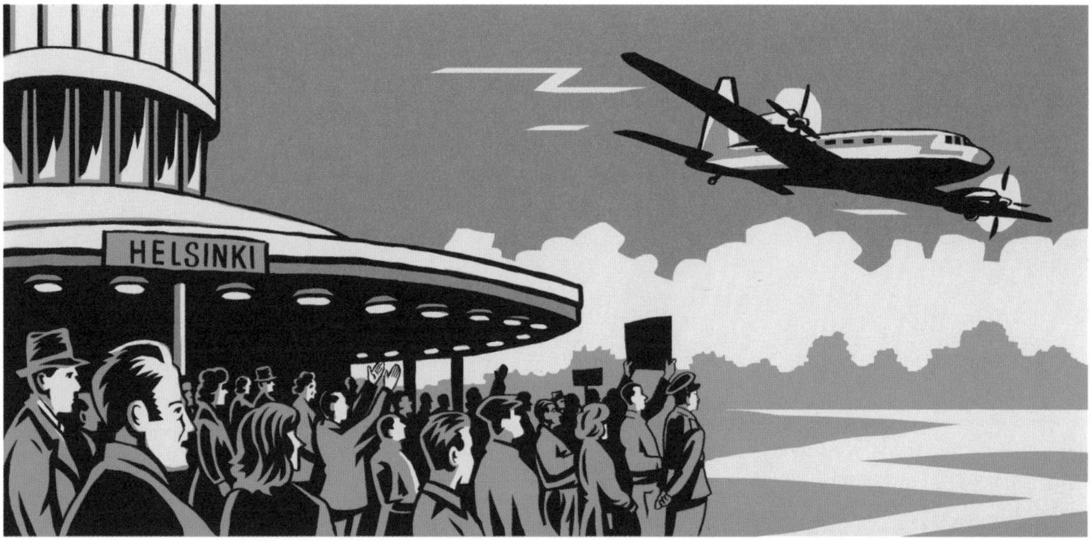
HELSINKI

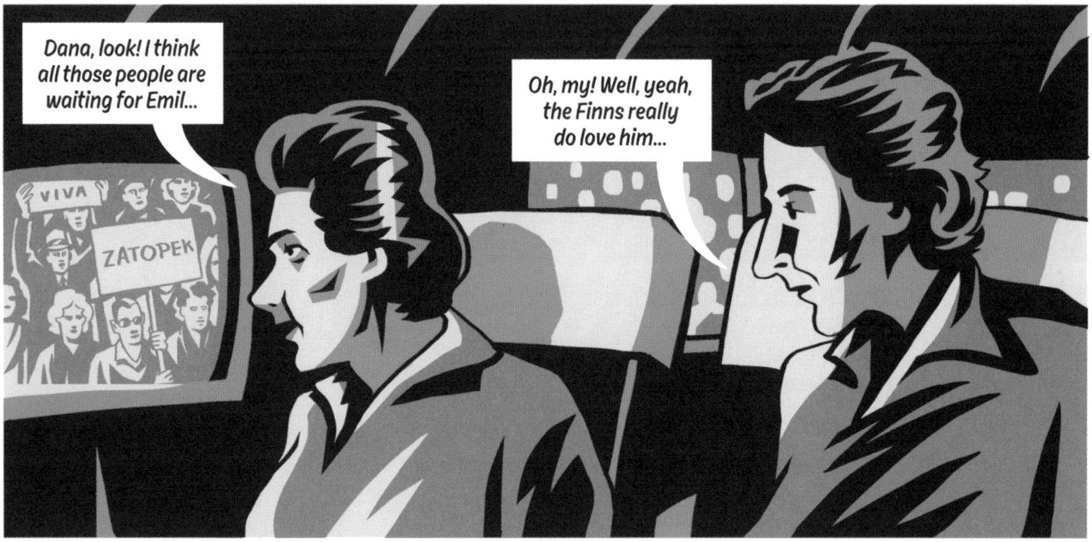
Dana, look! I think all those people are waiting for Emil...
VIVA
ZATOPEK
Oh, my! Well, yeah, the Finns really do love him...

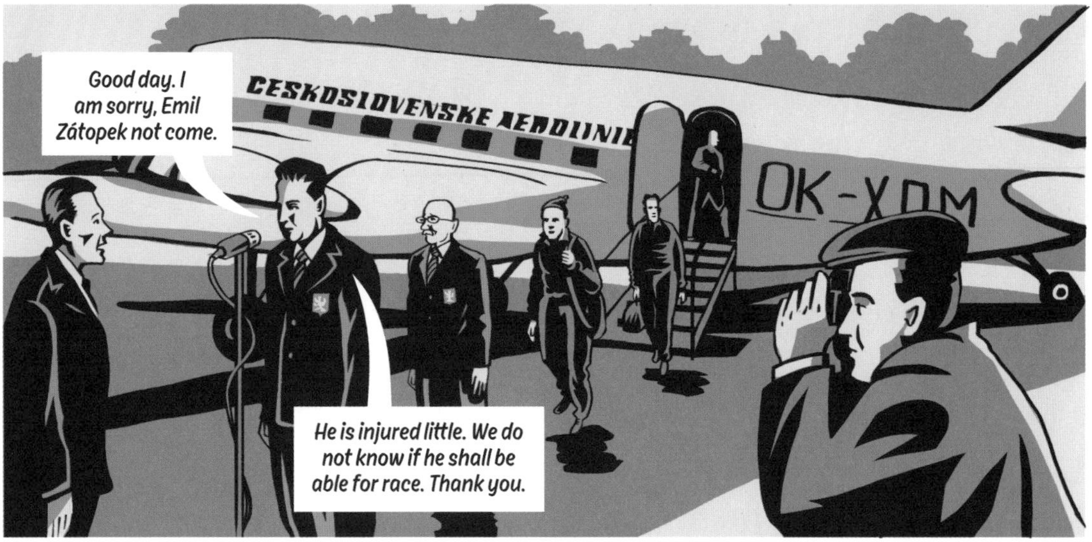
Good day. I am sorry, Emil Zátopek not come.
OK-XDM
He is injured little. We do not know if he shall be able for race. Thank you.

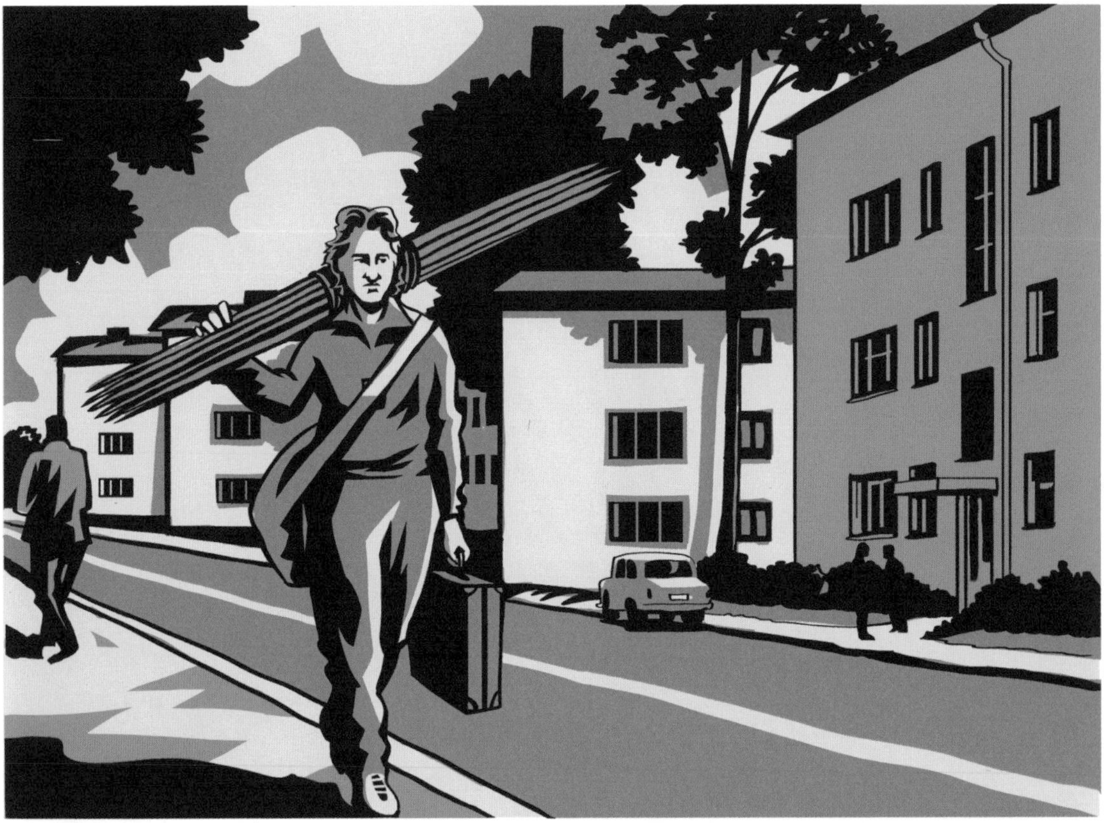

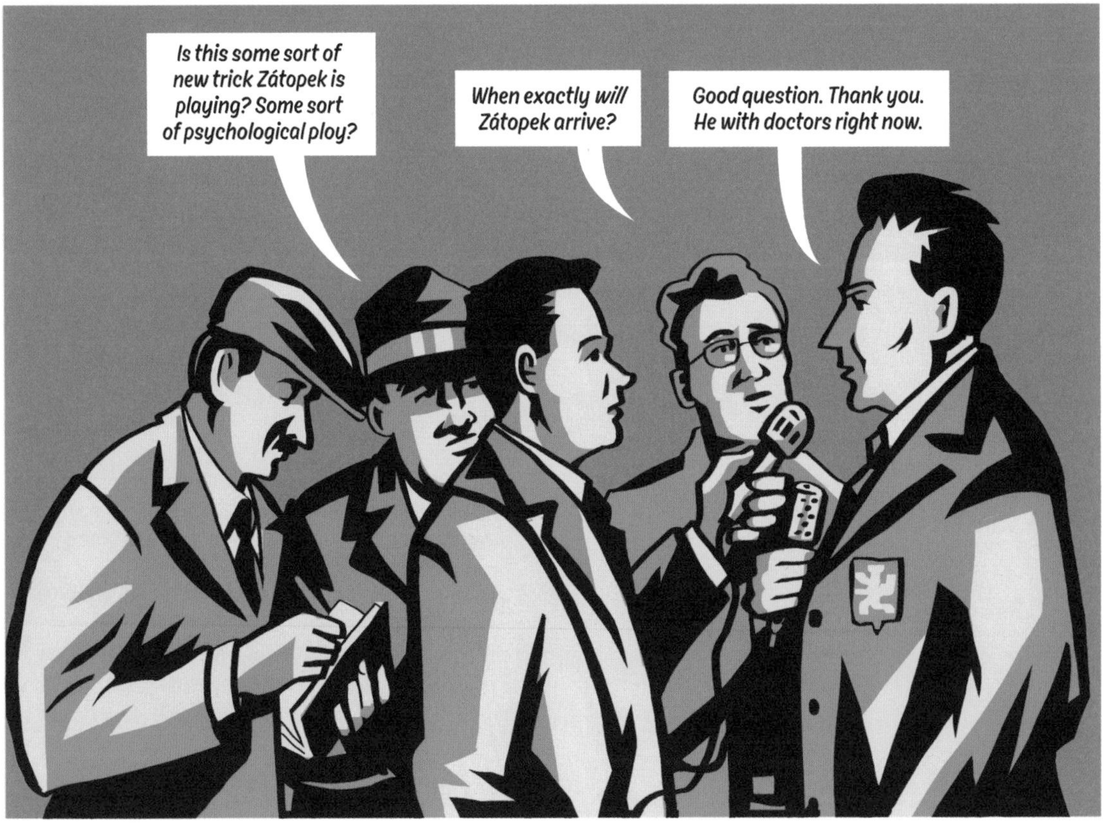
Is this some sort of new trick Zátopek is playing? Some sort of psychological ploy?
When exactly *will* Zátopek arrive?
Good question. Thank you. He with doctors right now.

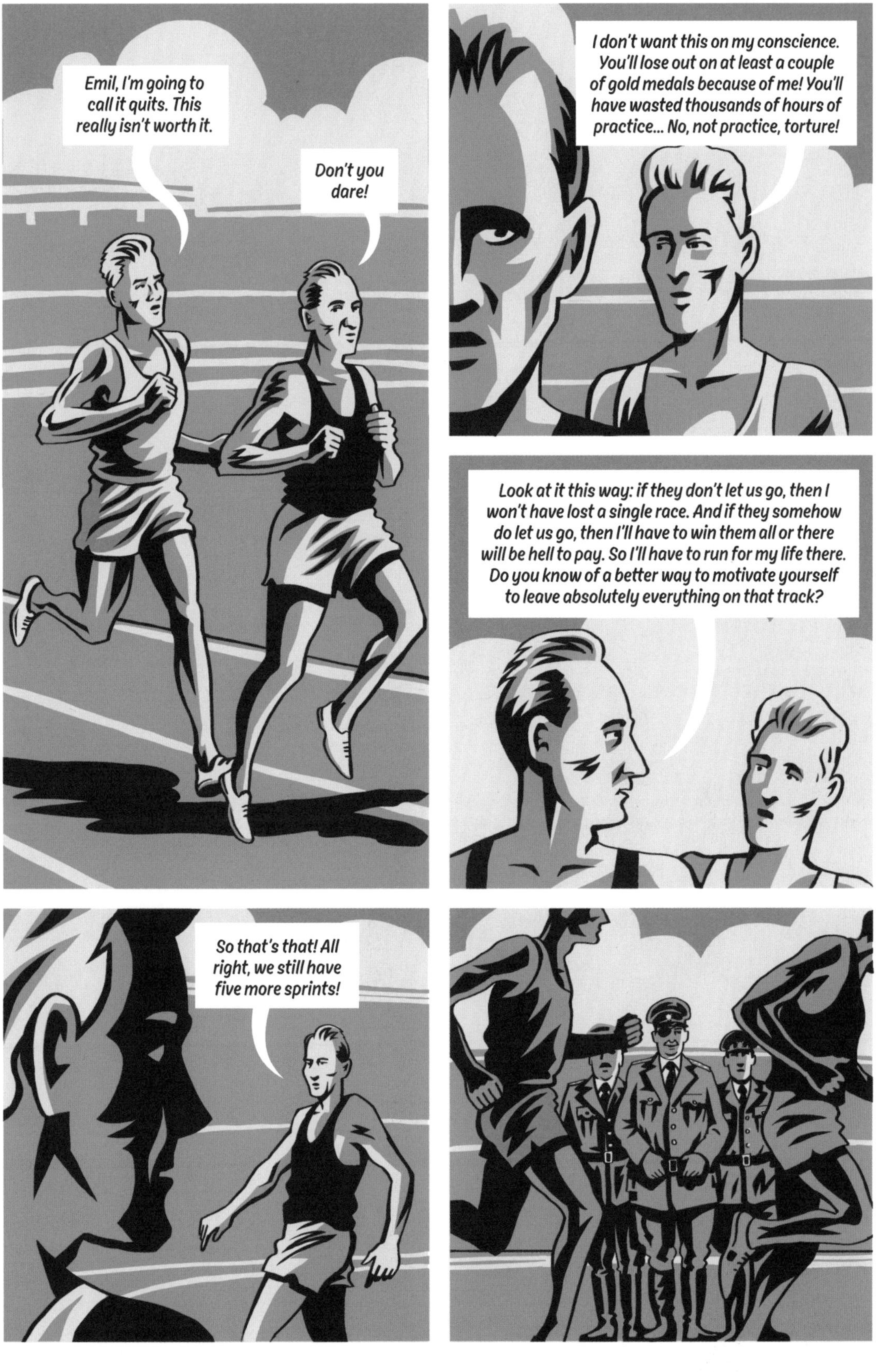
Emil, I'm going to call it quits. This really isn't worth it.
Don't you dare!
I don't want this on my conscience. You'll lose out on at least a couple of gold medals because of me! You'll have wasted thousands of hours of practice... No, not practice, torture!
Look at it this way: if they don't let us go, then I won't have lost a single race. And if they somehow do let us go, then I'll have to win them all or there will be hell to pay. So I'll have to run for my life there. Do you know of a better way to motivate yourself to leave absolutely everything on that track?
So that's that! All right, we still have five more sprints!

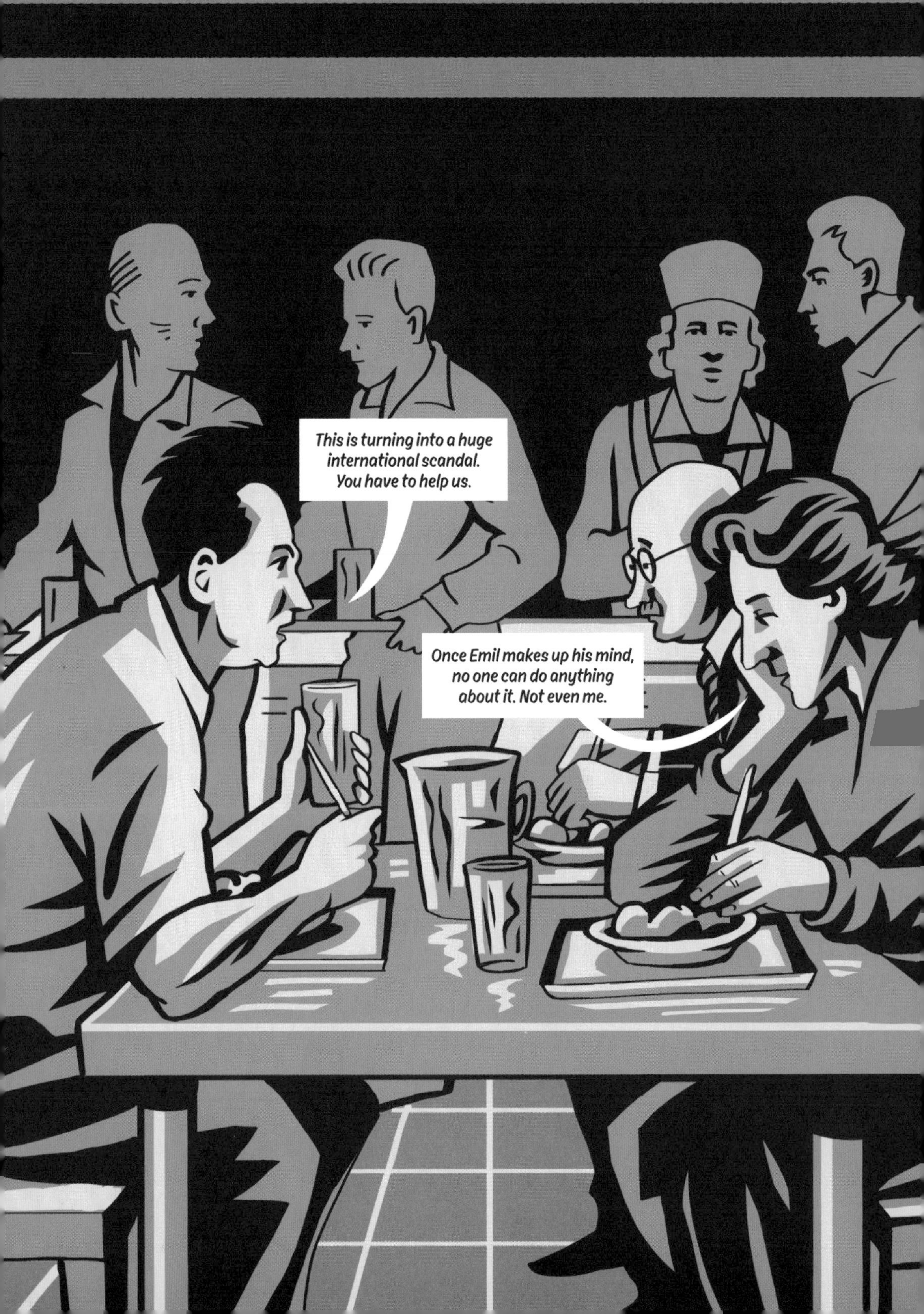
This is turning into a huge international scandal. You have to help us.
Once Emil makes up his mind, no one can do anything about it. Not even me.

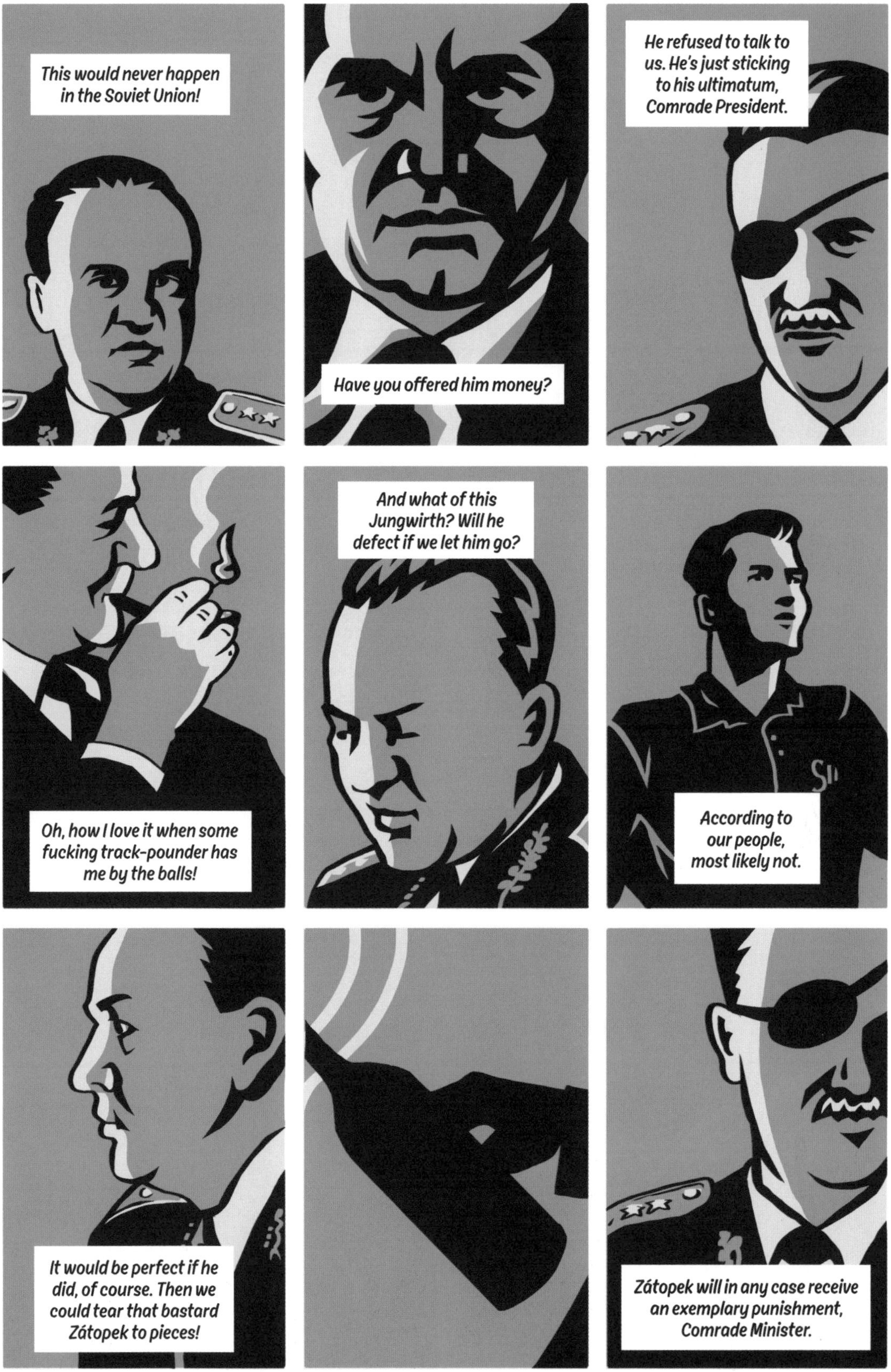
This would never happen in the Soviet Union!
Have you offered him money?
He refused to talk to us. He's just sticking to his ultimatum, Comrade President.
Oh, how I love it when some fucking track-pounder has me by the balls!
And what of this Jungwirth? Will he defect if we let him go?
According to our people, most likely not.
It would be perfect if he did, of course. Then we could tear that bastard Zátopek to pieces!
Zátopek will in any case receive an exemplary punishment, Comrade Minister.

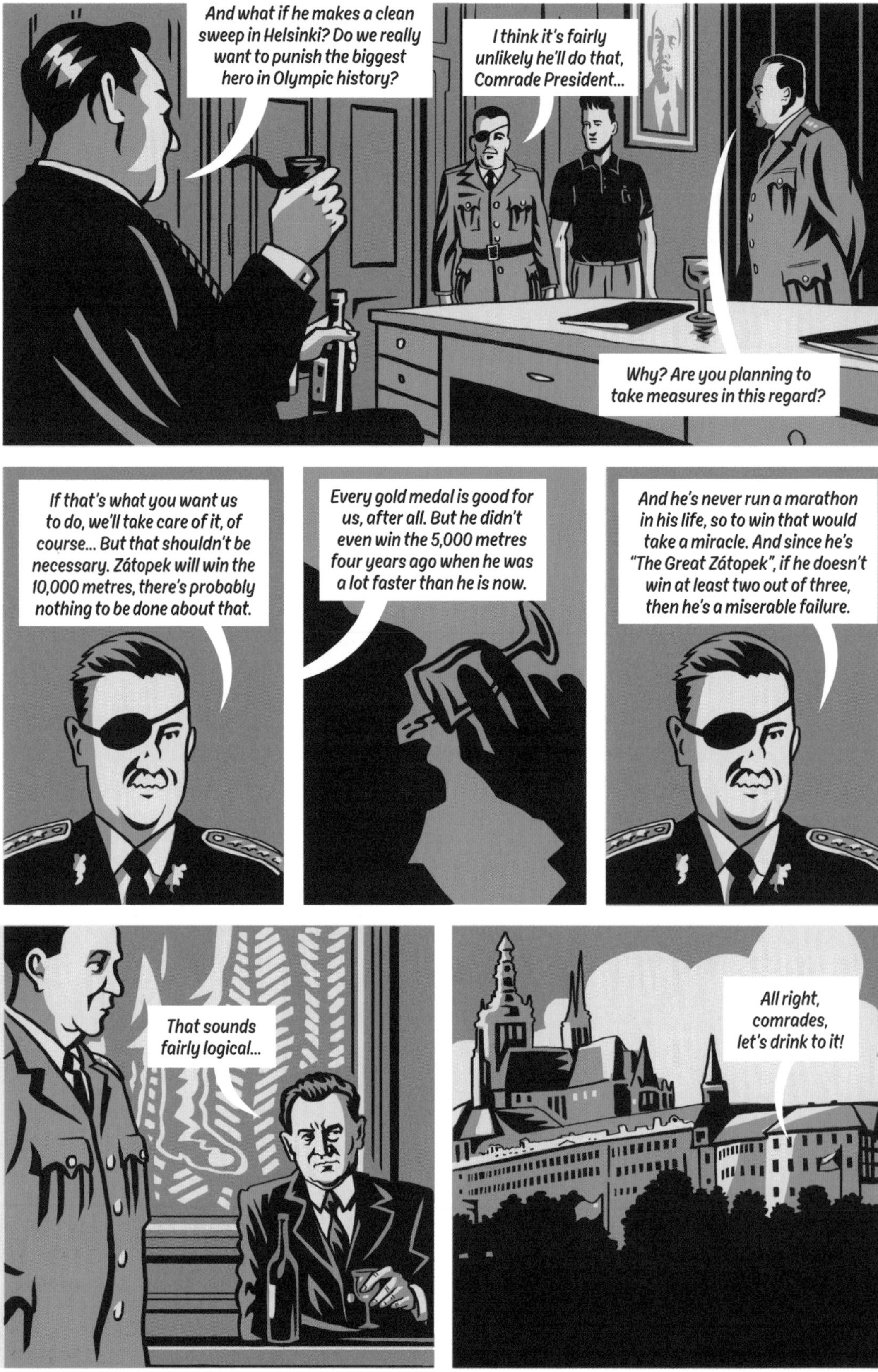
And what if he makes a clean sweep in Helsinki? Do we really want to punish the biggest hero in Olympic history?
I think it's fairly unlikely he'll do that, Comrade President...
Why? Are you planning to take measures in this regard?
If that's what you want us to do, we'll take care of it, of course... But that shouldn't be necessary. Zátopek will win the 10,000 metres, there's probably nothing to be done about that.
Every gold medal is good for us, after all. But he didn't even win the 5,000 metres four years ago when he was a lot faster than he is now.
And he's never run a marathon in his life, so to win that would take a miracle. And since he's "The Great Zátopek", if he doesn't win at least two out of three, then he's a miserable failure.
That sounds fairly logical...
All right, comrades, let's drink to it!

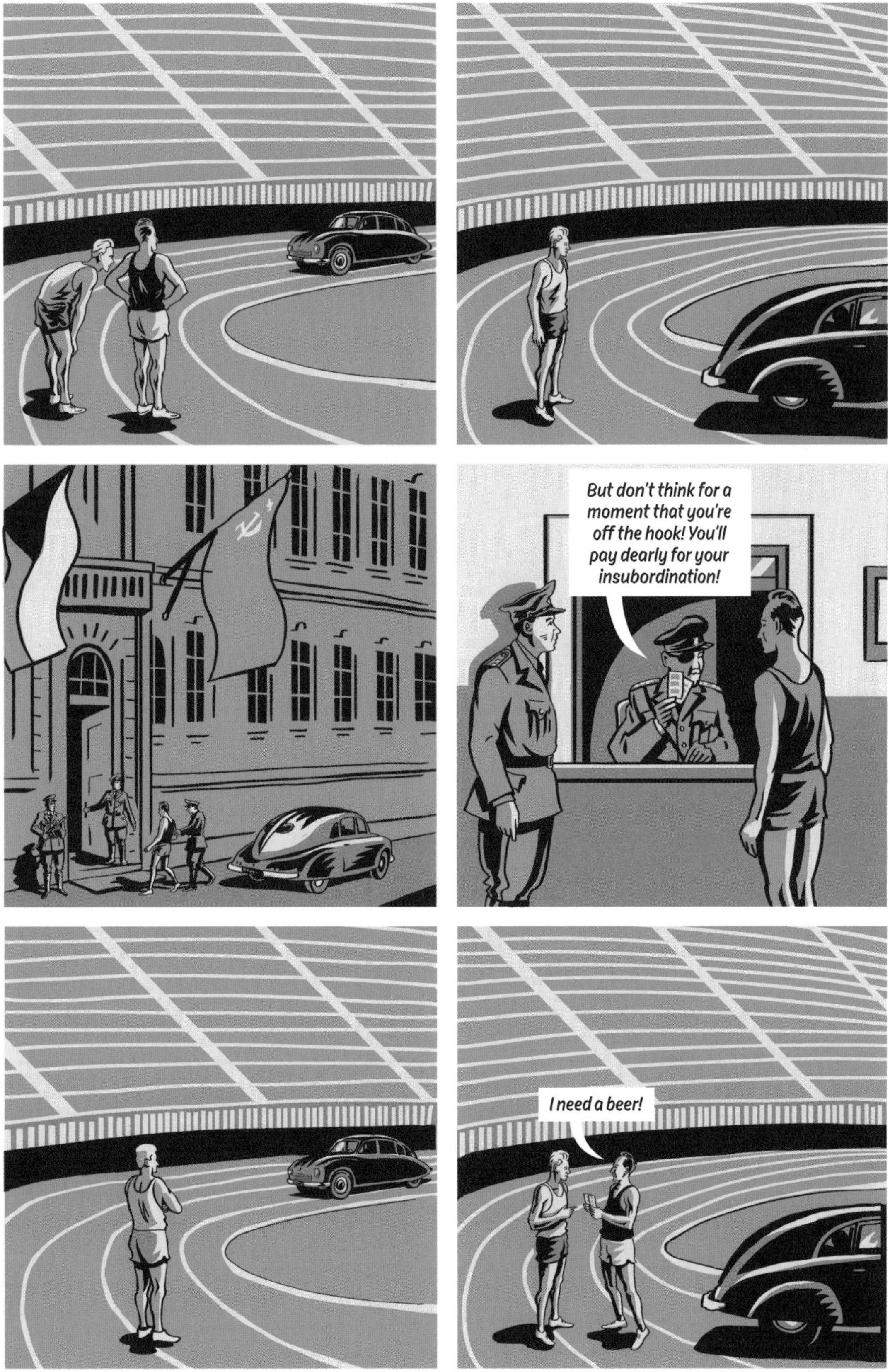
But don't think for a moment that you're off the hook! You'll pay dearly for your insubordination!
I need a beer!

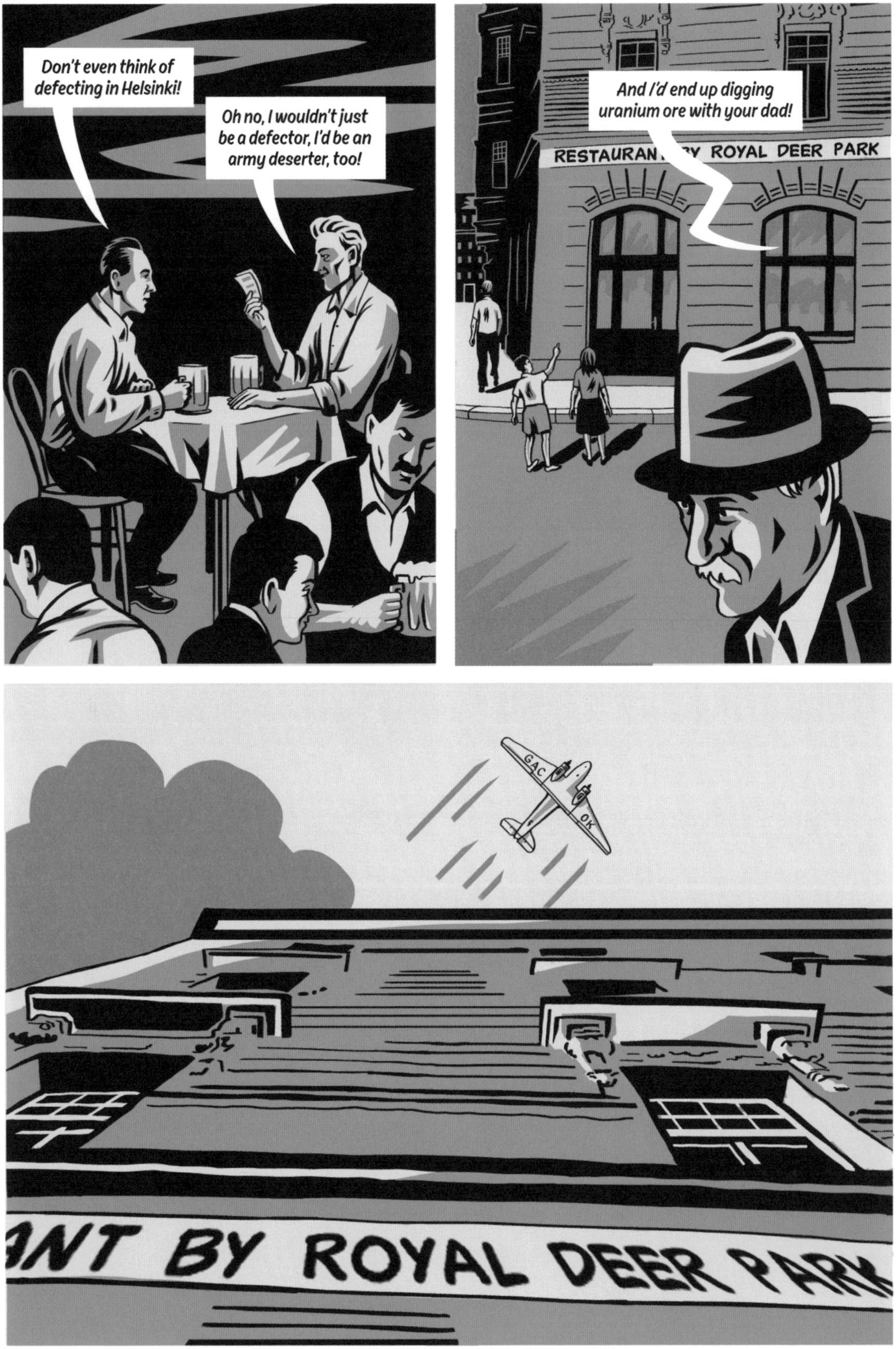
Don't even think of defecting in Helsinki!
Oh no, I wouldn't just be a defector, I'd be an army deserter, too!
And I'd end up digging uranium ore with your dad!
RESTAURAN Y ROYAL DEER PARK
GAC
OK
NT BY ROYAL DEER PARK

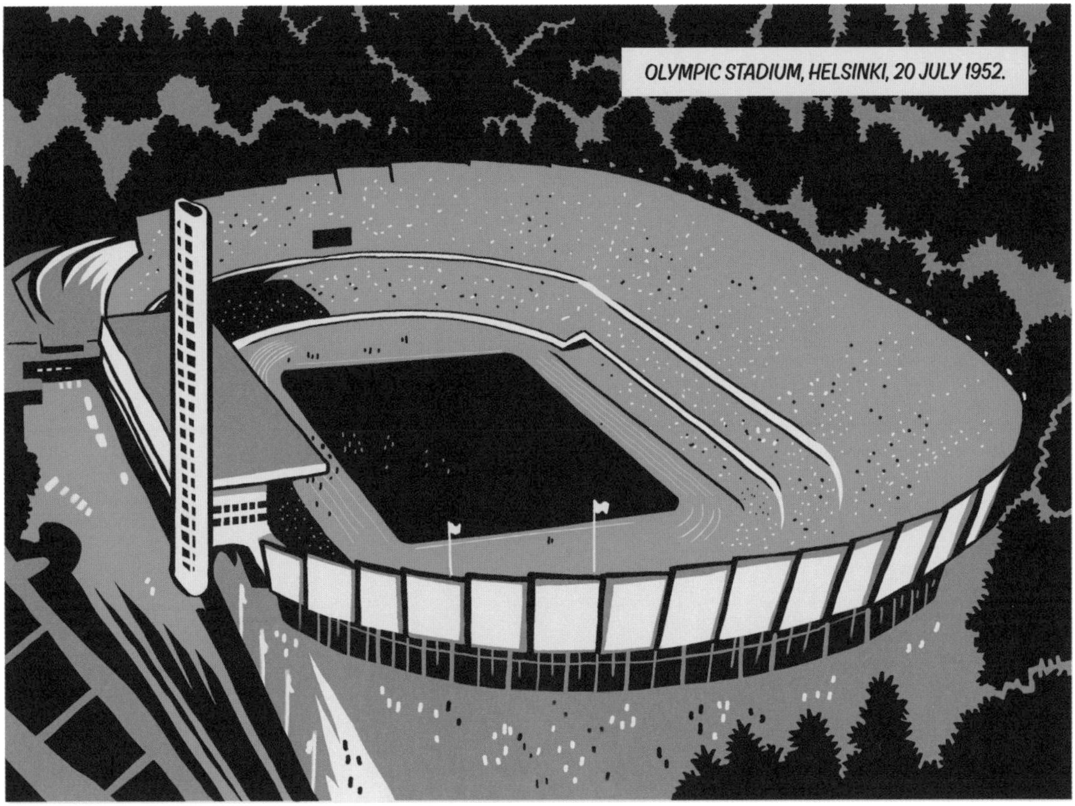
OLYMPIC STADIUM, HELSINKI, 20 JULY 1952.

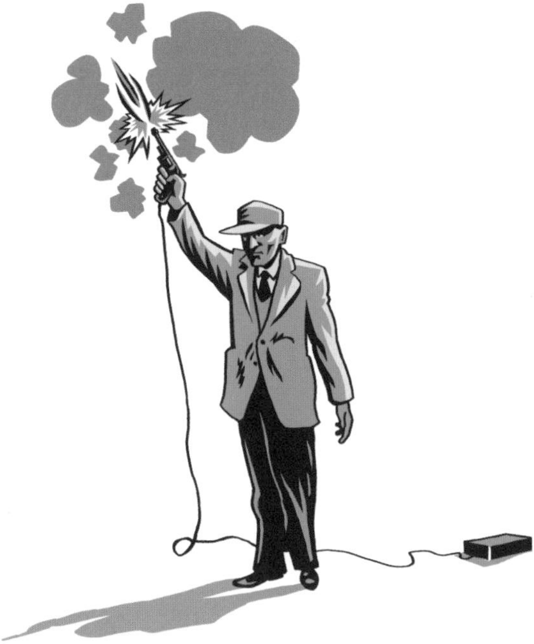

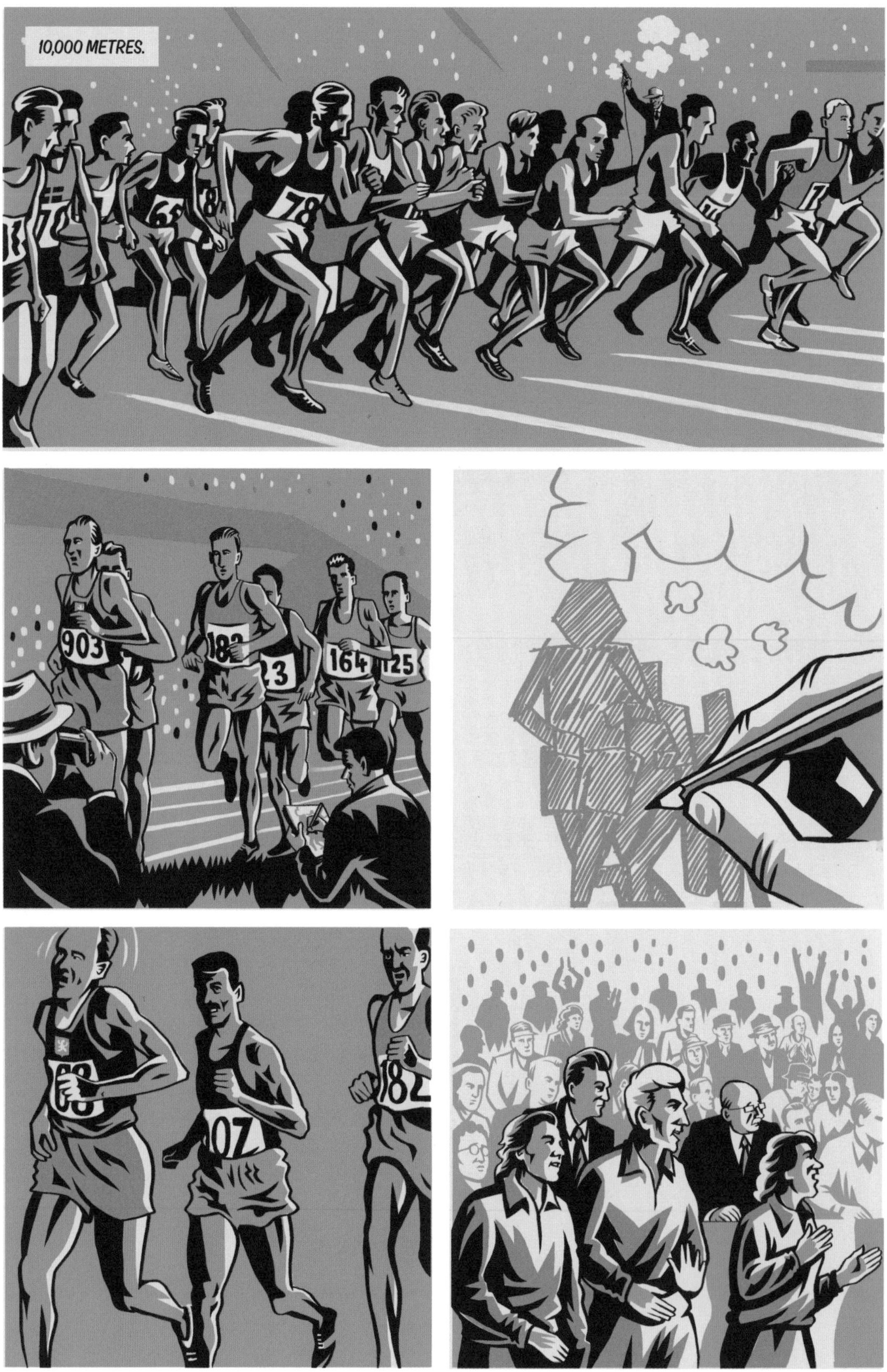
10,000 METRES.

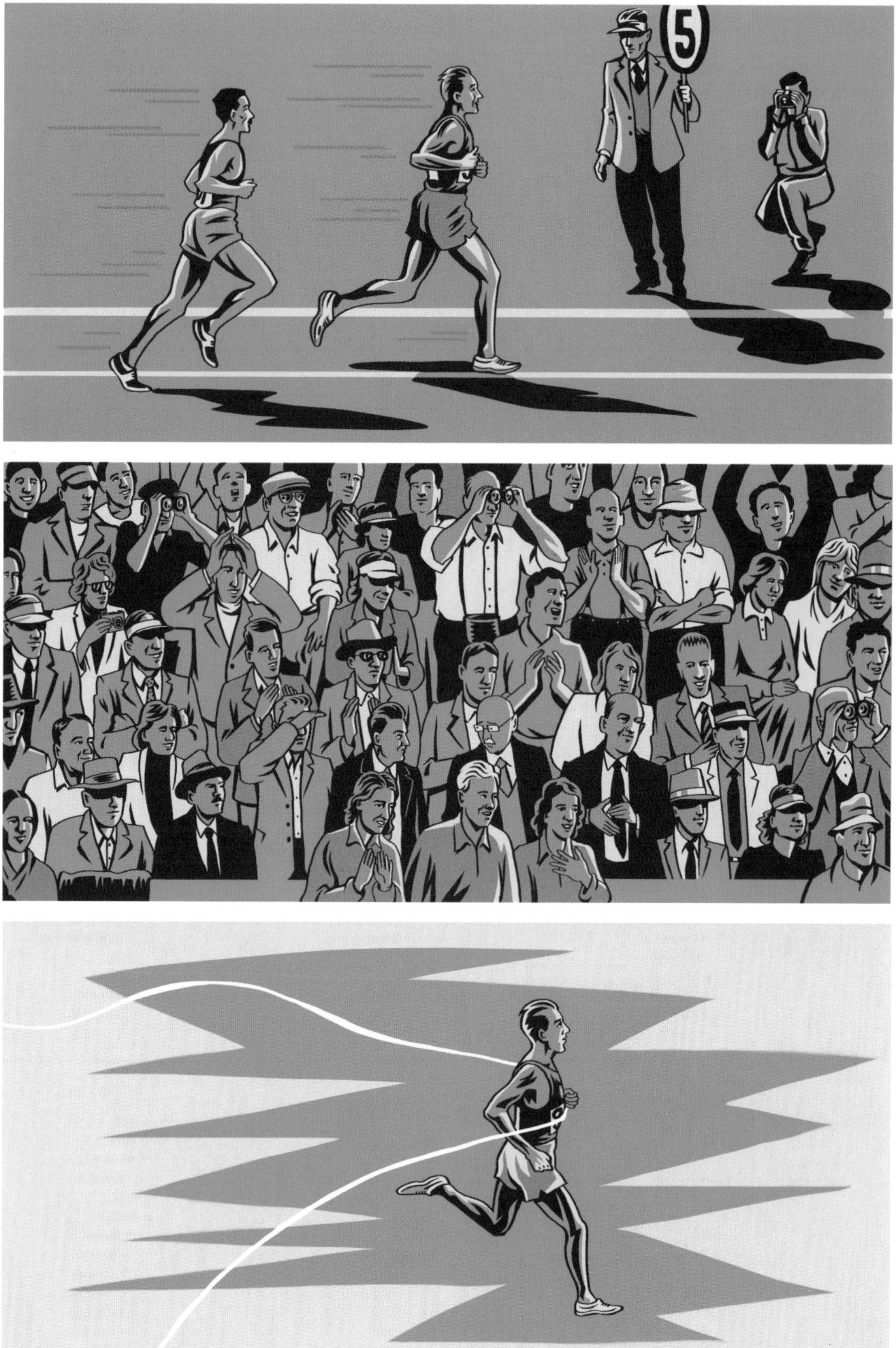
5

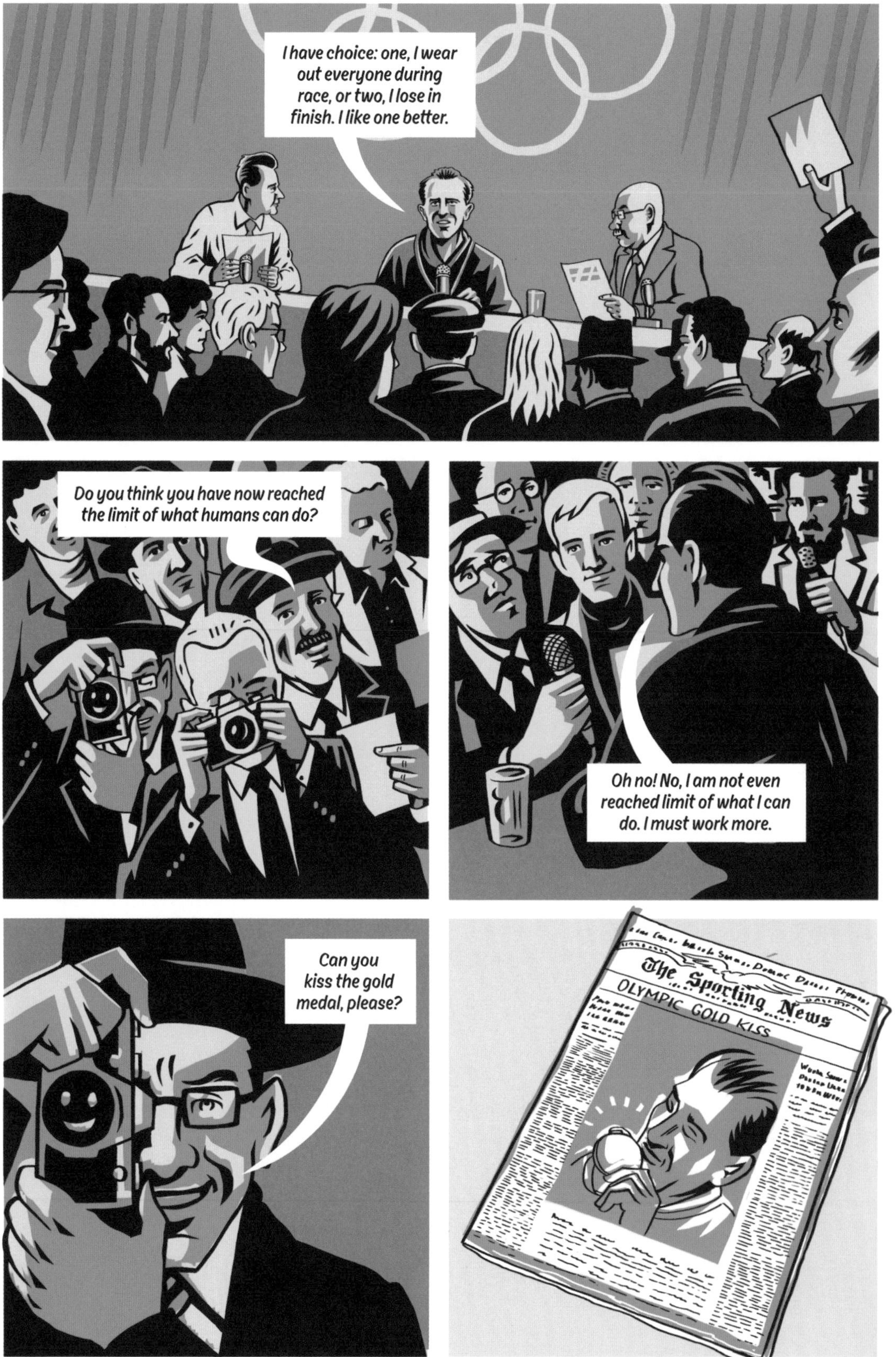
I have choice: one, I wear out everyone during race, or two, I lose in finish. I like one better.
Do you think you have now reached the limit of what humans can do?
Oh no! No, I am not even reached limit of what I can do. I must work more.
Can you kiss the gold medal, please?
The Sporting News
OLYMPIC GOLD KISS

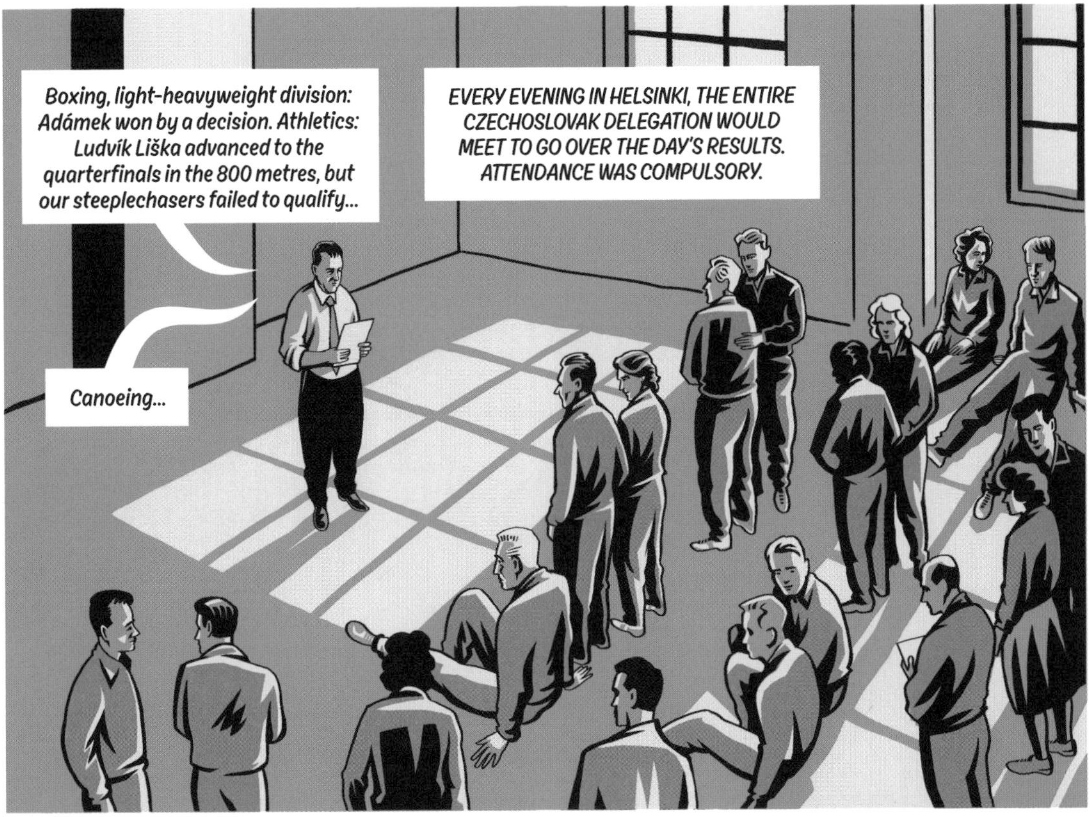
EVERY EVENING IN HELSINKI, THE ENTIRE CZECHOSLOVAK DELEGATION WOULD MEET TO GO OVER THE DAY'S RESULTS. ATTENDANCE WAS COMPULSORY.
Boxing, light-heavyweight division: Adámek won by a decision. Athletics: Ludvík Liška advanced to the quarterfinals in the 800 metres, but our steeplechasers failed to qualify...
Canoeing...

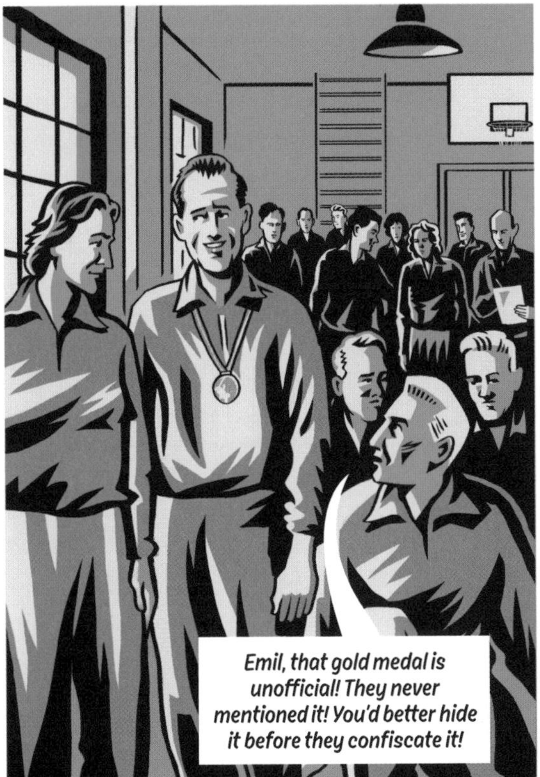
Emil, that gold medal is unofficial! They never mentioned it! You'd better hide it before they confiscate it!

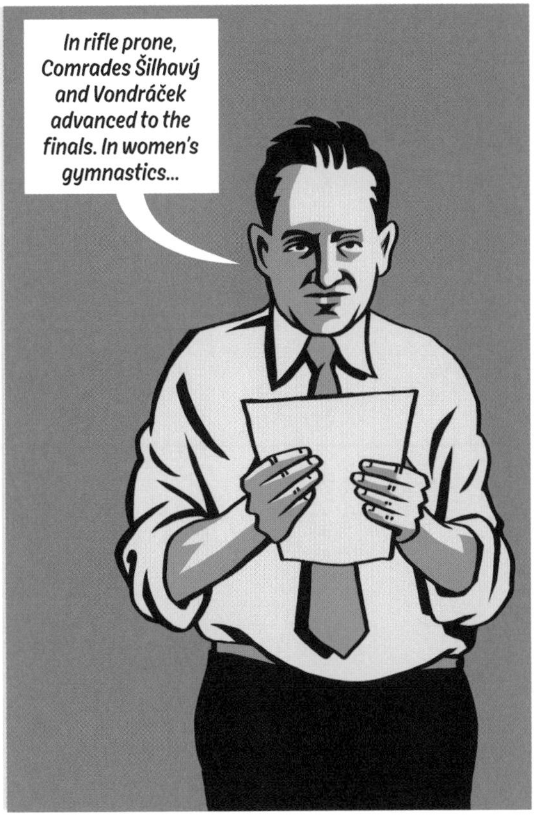
In rifle prone, Comrades Šilhavý and Vondráček advanced to the finals. In women's gymnastics...

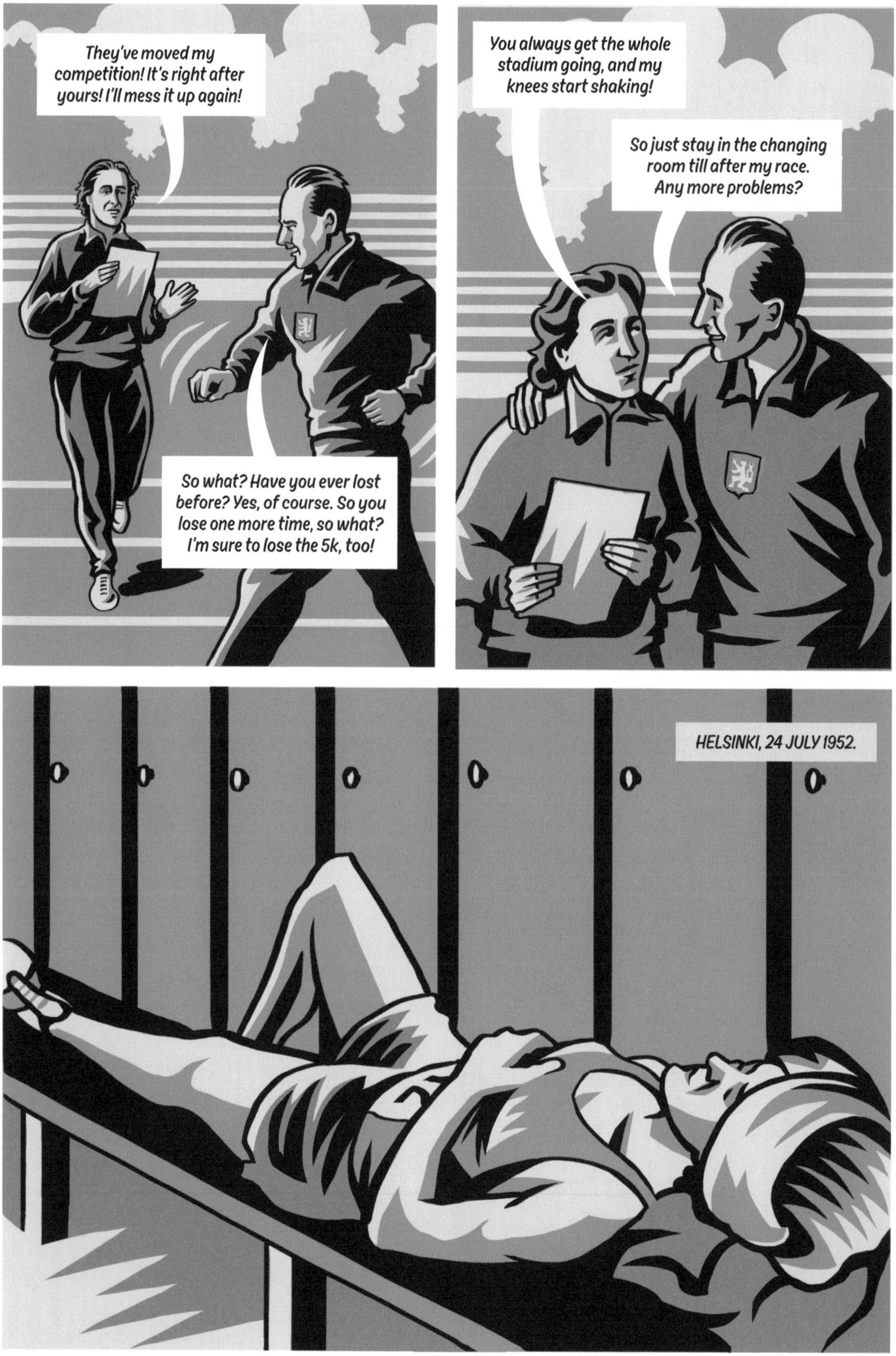
They've moved my competition! It's right after yours! I'll mess it up again!
So what? Have you ever lost before? Yes, of course. So you lose one more time, so what? I'm sure to lose the 5k, too!
You always get the whole stadium going, and my knees start shaking!
So just stay in the changing room till after my race. Any more problems?
HELSINKI, 24 JULY 1952.

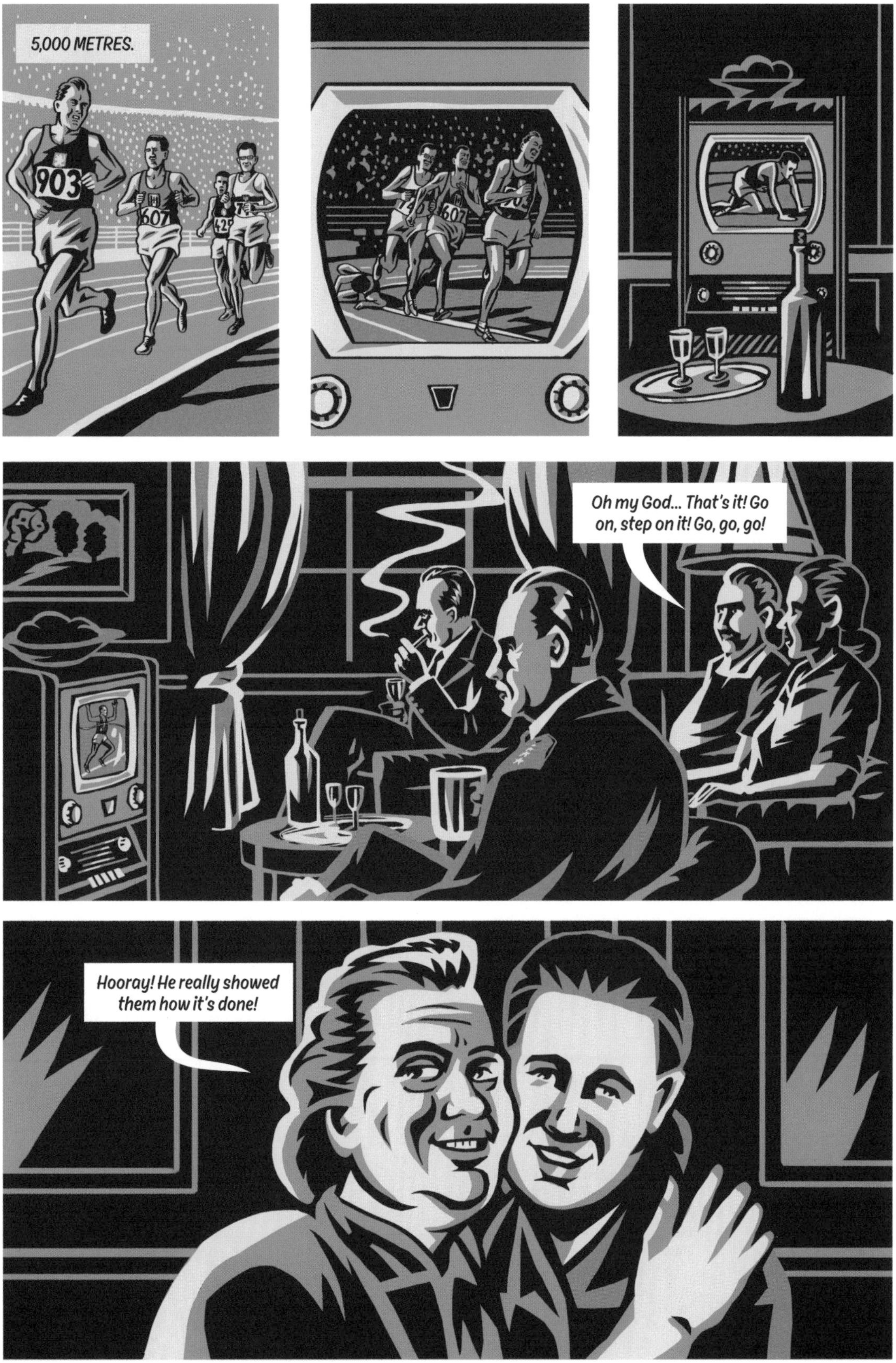
5,000 METRES.
Oh my God... That's it! Go on, step on it! Go, go, go!
Hooray! He really showed them how it's done!

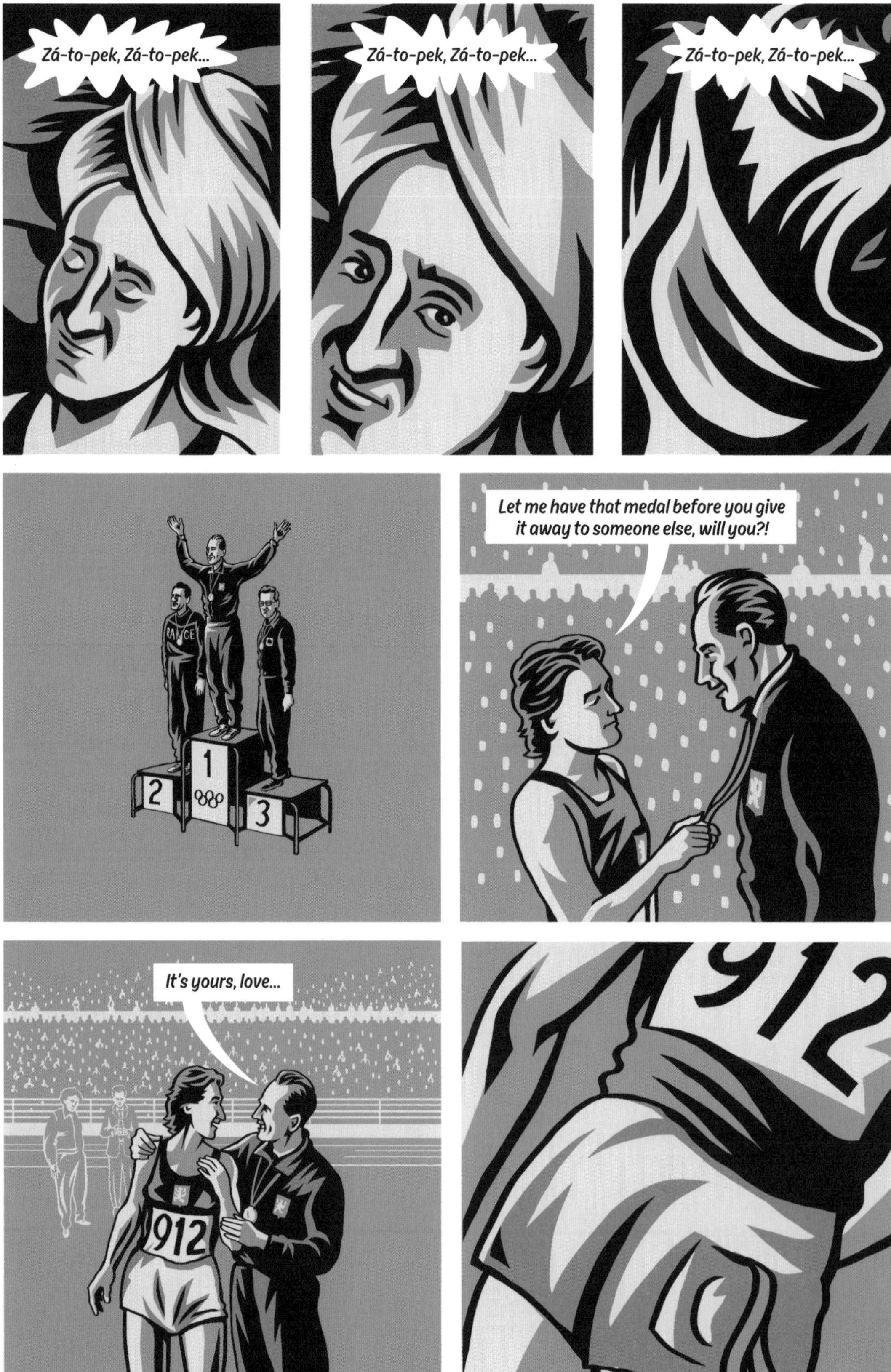
Zá-to-pek, Zá-to-pek...
Zá-to-pek, Zá-to-pek...
Zá-to-pek, Zá-to-pek...
Let me have that medal before you give it away to someone else, will you?!
It's yours, love...

WITH HER FIRST ATTEMPT IN HELSINKI, DANA ZÁTOPKOVÁ SURPASSED 50 METRES FOR THE FIRST TIME IN HER LIFE. WITH 50.47 METRES, SHE SET A NEW CZECHOSLOVAK RECORD.

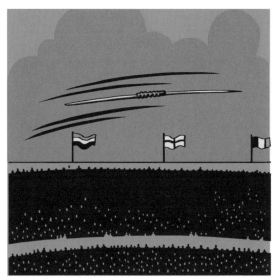

Holy shit, fifty and change! Might be enough for a medal! Wouldn't that be incredible?! What are you jabbering about? Don't even think about that or you'll jinx it! All right, all right, I'll pipe down...

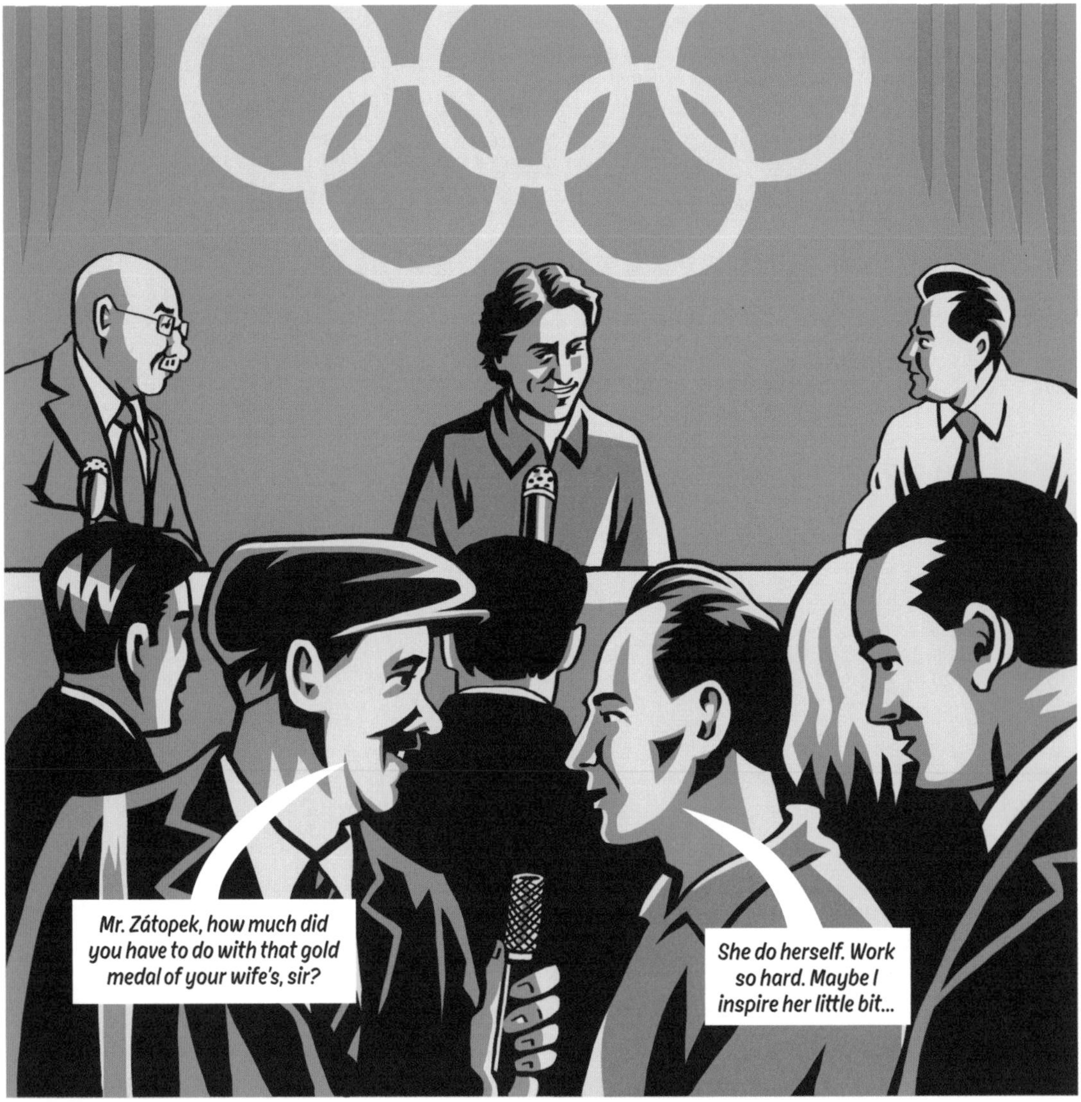
Mr. Zátopek, how much did you have to do with that gold medal of your wife's, sir?
She do herself. Work so hard. Maybe I inspire her little bit...

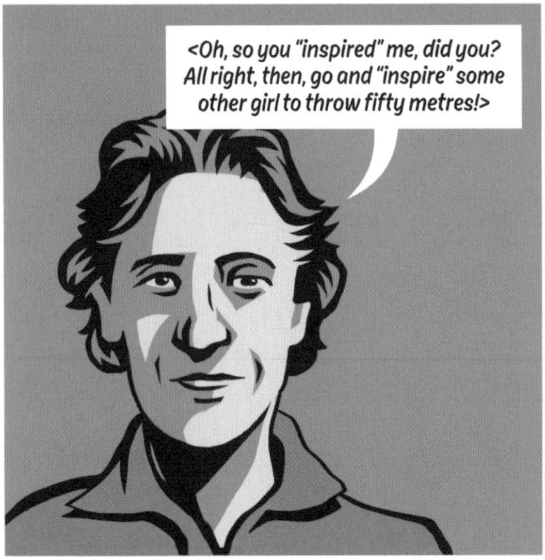
<Oh, so you "inspired" me, did you? All right, then, go and "inspire" some other girl to throw fifty metres!>

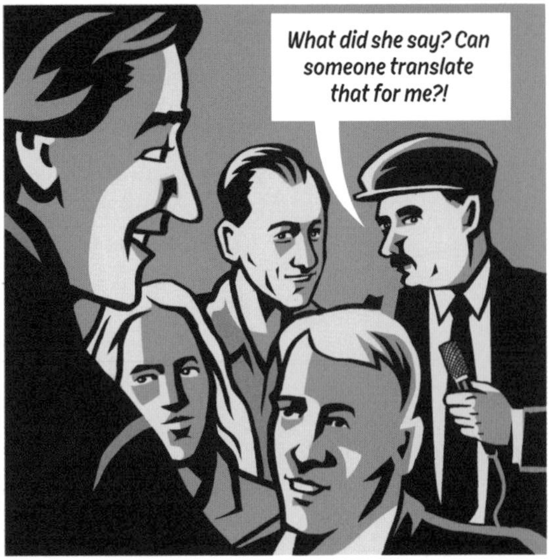
What did she say? Can someone translate that for me?!

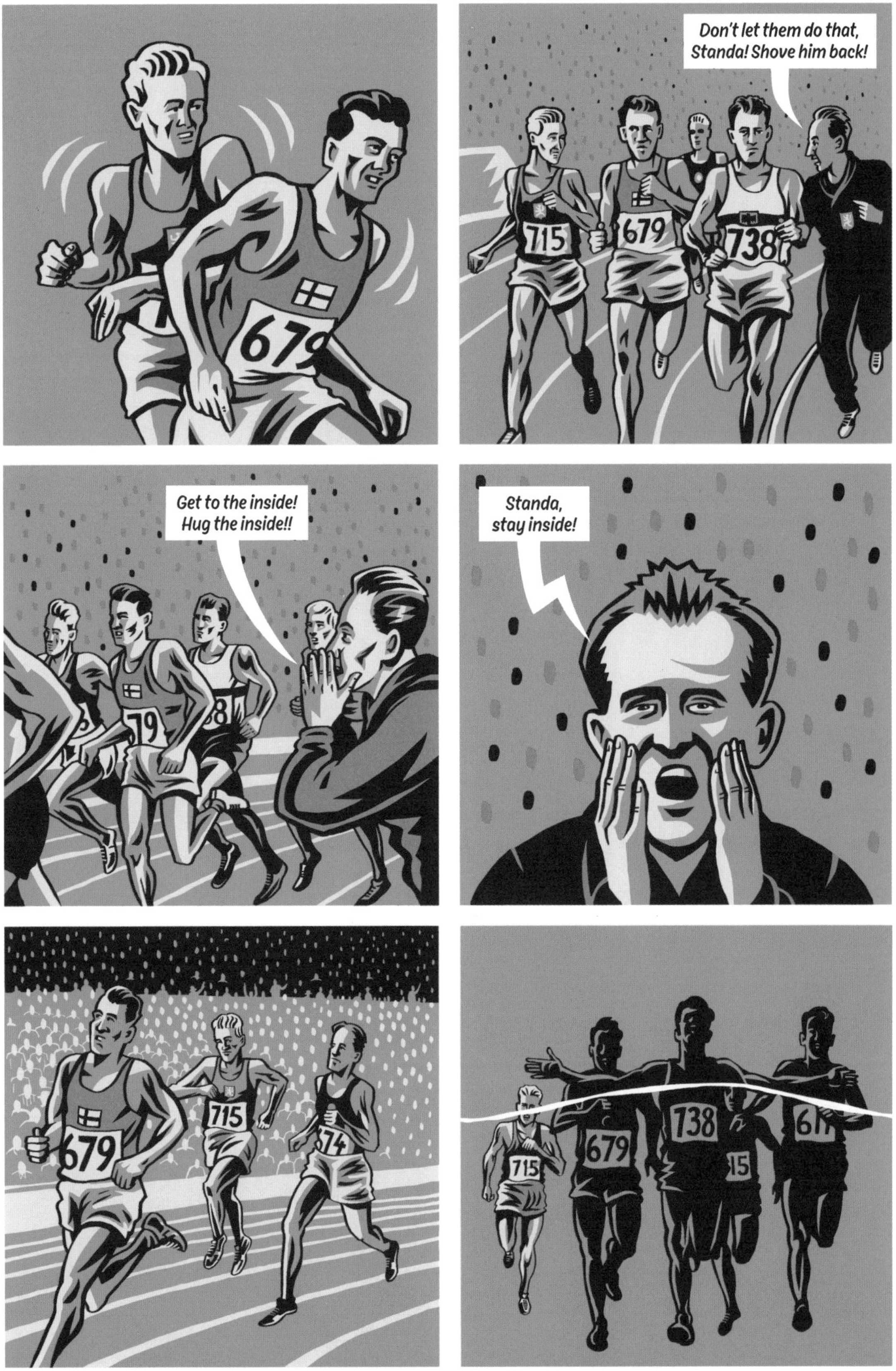
Don't let them do that, Standa! Shove him back!
Get to the inside! Hug the inside!!
Standa, stay inside!

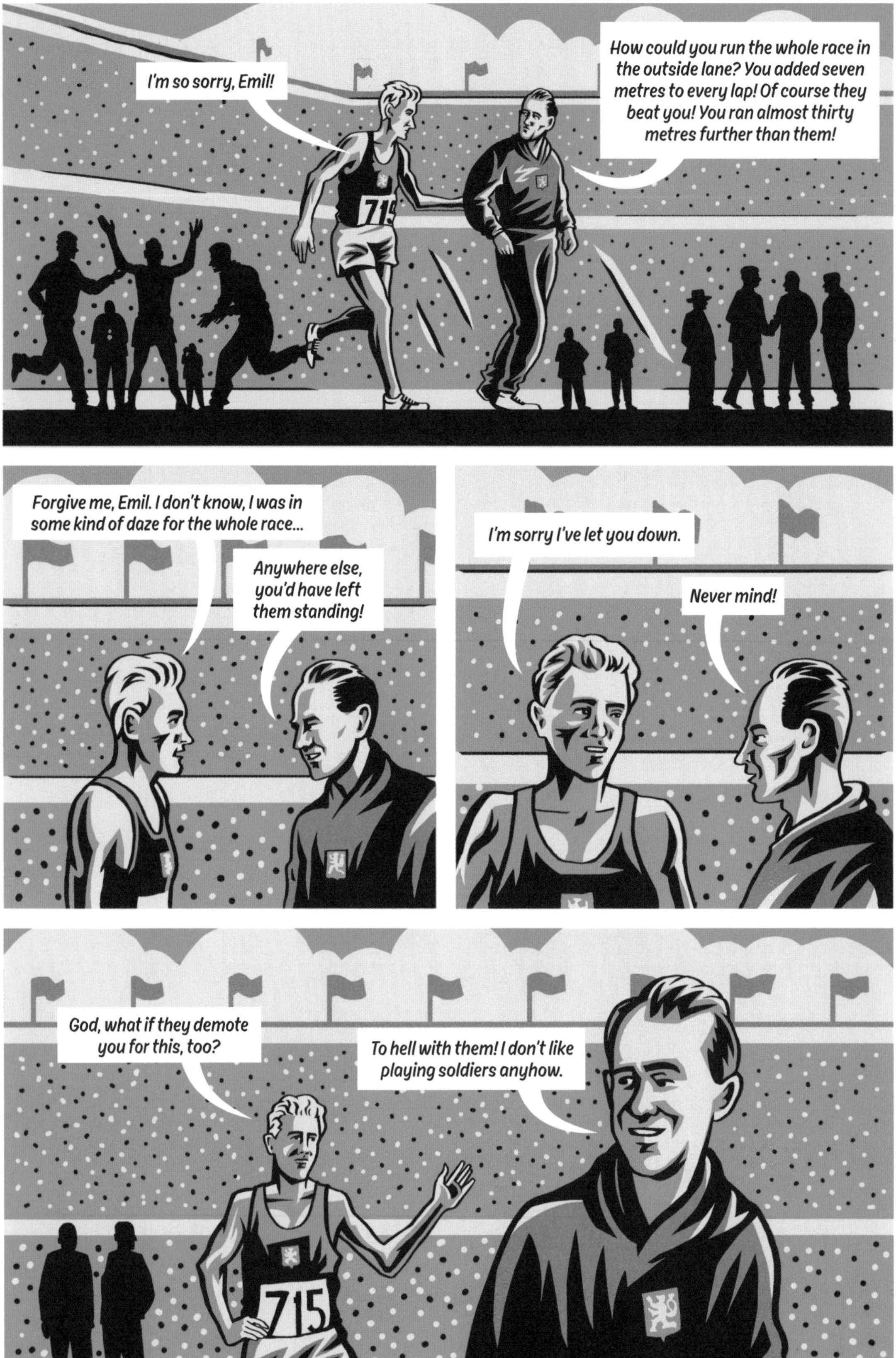
I'm so sorry, Emil!
How could you run the whole race in the outside lane? You added seven metres to every lap! Of course they beat you! You ran almost thirty metres further than them!
715
Forgive me, Emil. I don't know, I was in some kind of daze for the whole race...
Anywhere else, you'd have left them standing!
I'm sorry I've let you down.
Never mind!
God, what if they demote you for this, too?
To hell with them! I don't like playing soldiers anyhow.
715

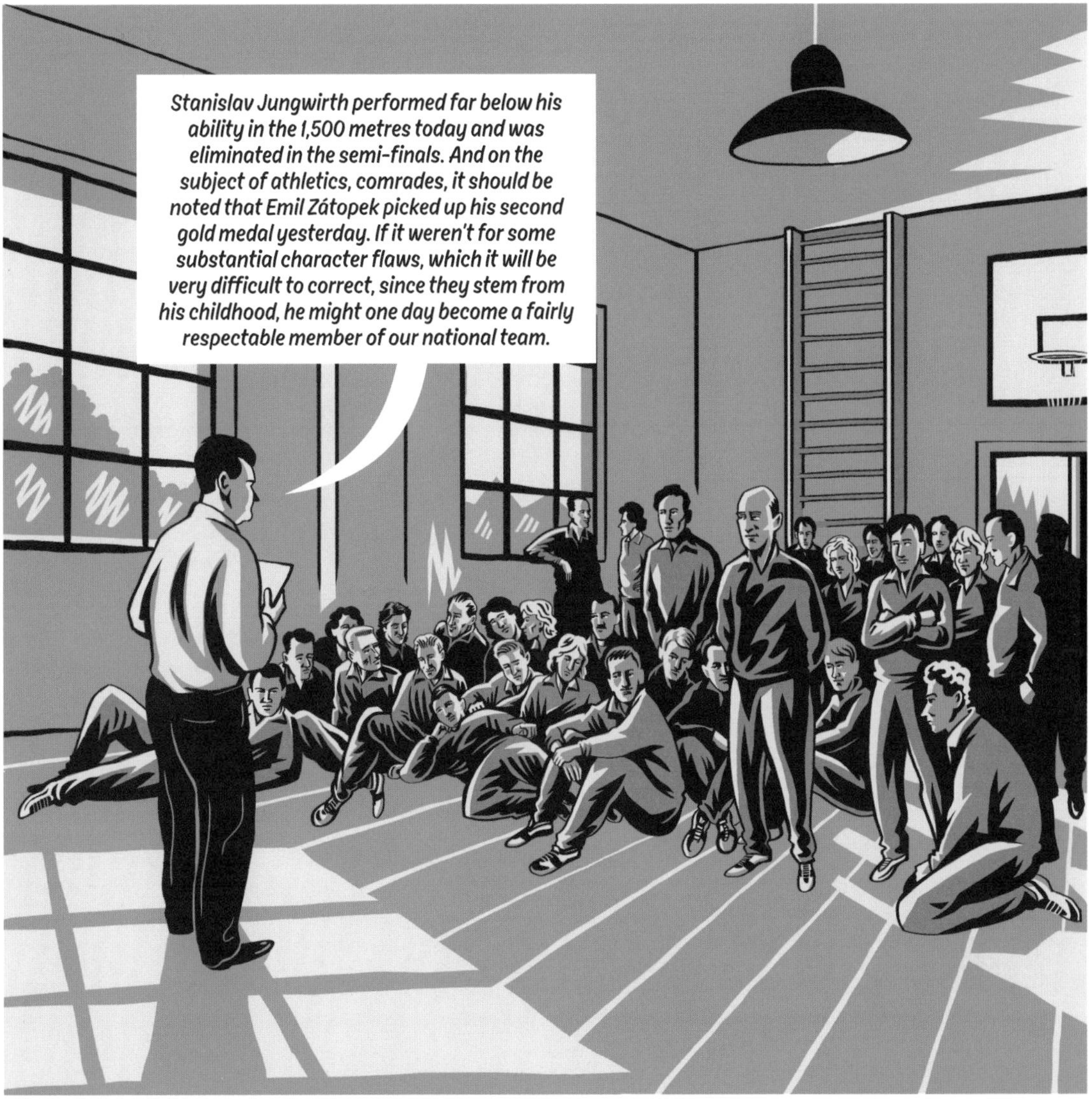
Stanislav Jungwirth performed far below his ability in the 1,500 metres today and was eliminated in the semi-finals. And on the subject of athletics, comrades, it should be noted that Emil Zátopek picked up his second gold medal yesterday. If it weren't for some substantial character flaws, which it will be very difficult to correct, since they stem from his childhood, he might one day become a fairly respectable member of our national team.

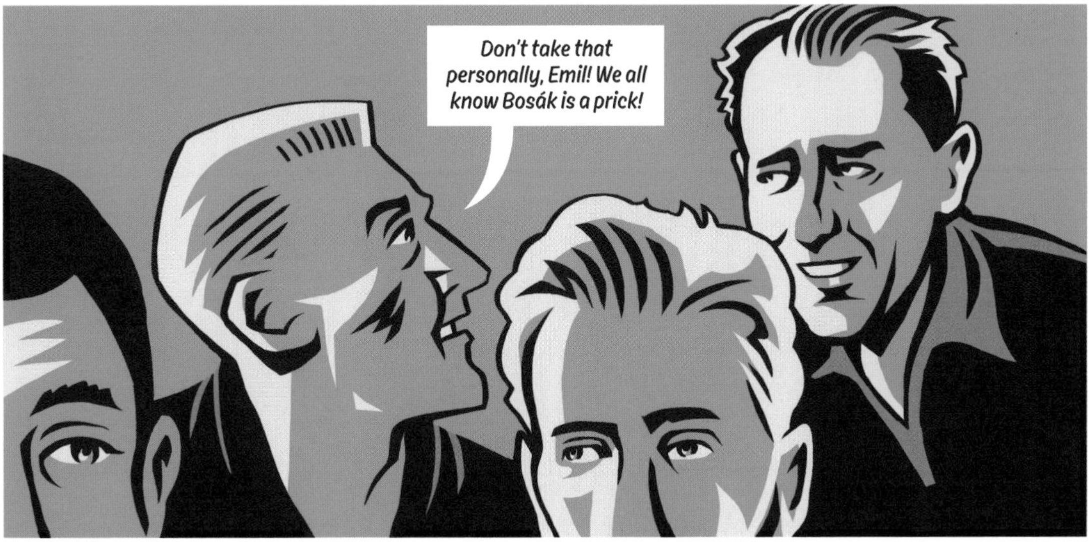
Don't take that personally, Emil! We all know Bosák is a prick!

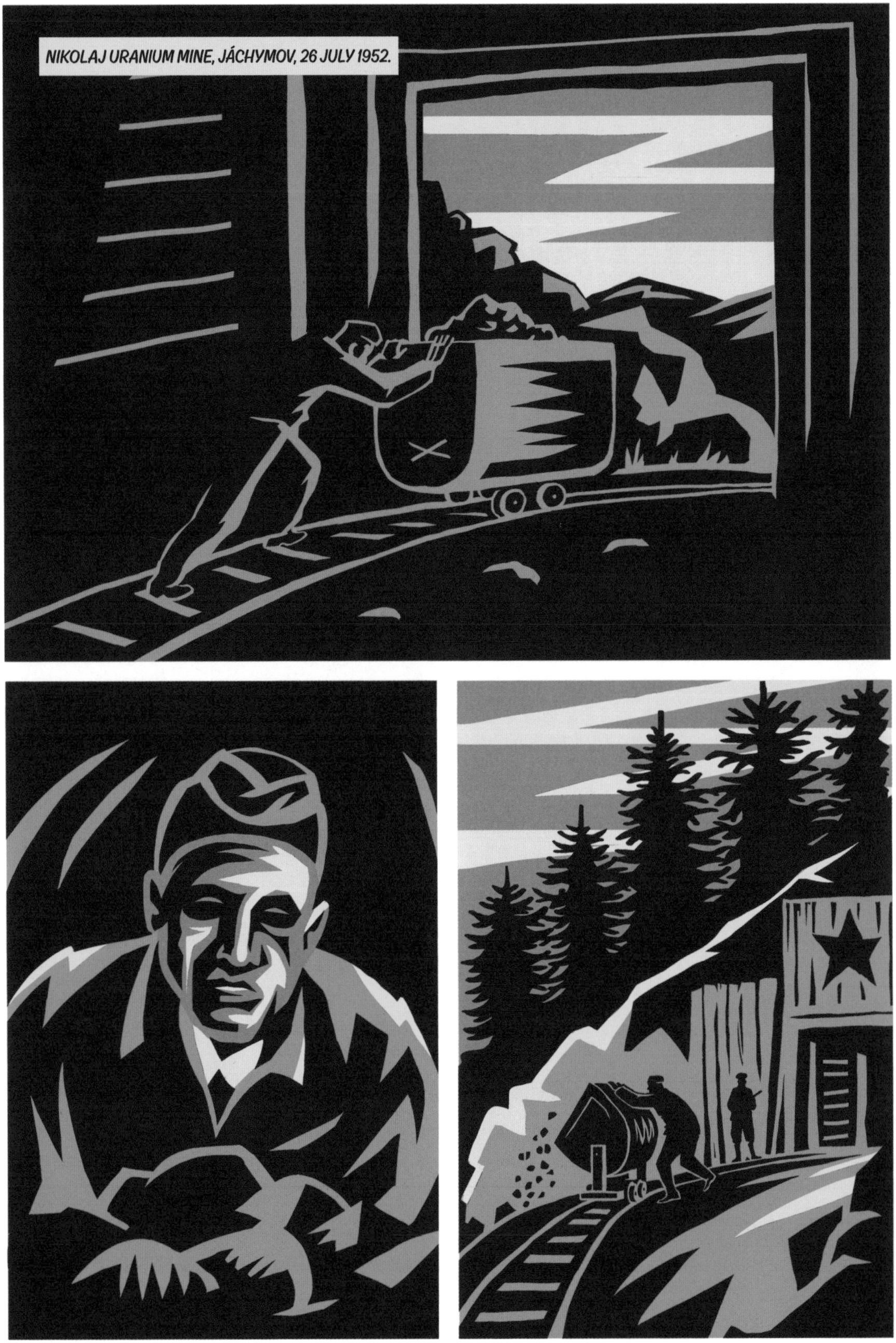
NIKOLAJ URANIUM MINE, JÁCHYMOV, 26 JULY 1952.

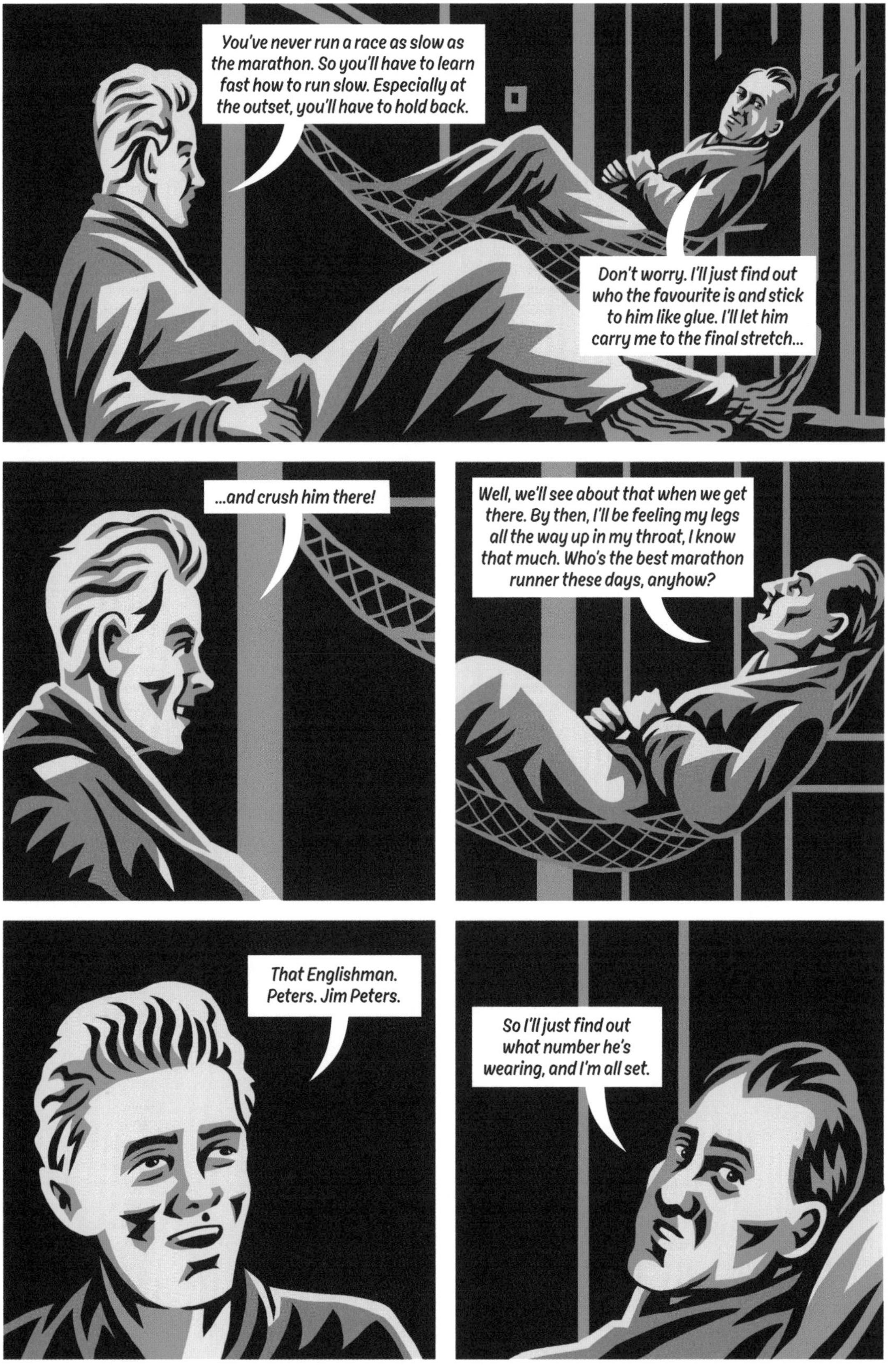
You've never run a race as slow as the marathon. So you'll have to learn fast how to run slow. Especially at the outset, you'll have to hold back.
Don't worry. I'll just find out who the favourite is and stick to him like glue. I'll let him carry me to the final stretch...
...and crush him there!
Well, we'll see about that when we get there. By then, I'll be feeling my legs all the way up in my throat, I know that much. Who's the best marathon runner these days, anyhow?
That Englishman. Peters. Jim Peters.
So I'll just find out what number he's wearing, and I'm all set.

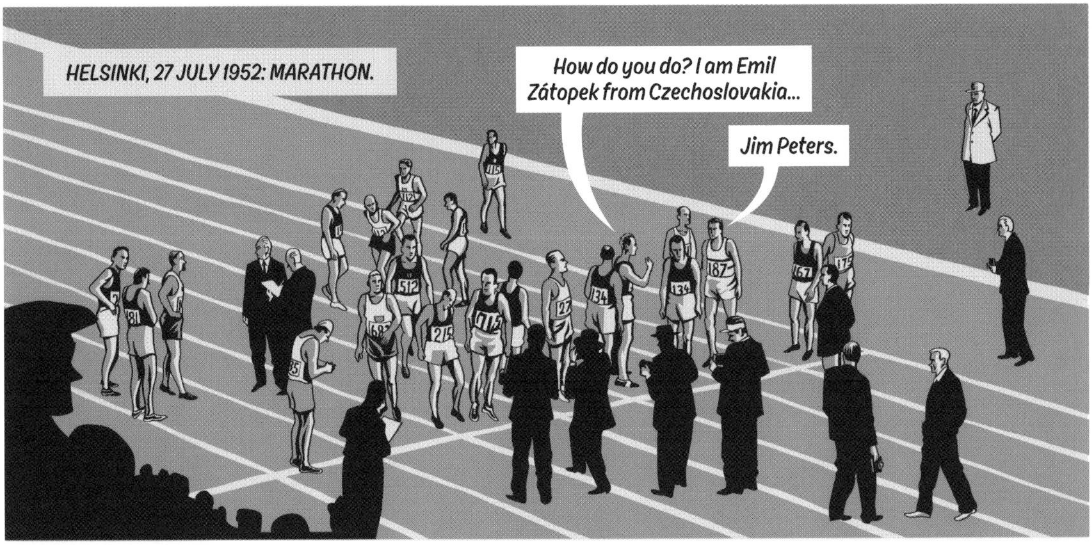
HELSINKI, 27 JULY 1952: MARATHON.
How do you do? I am Emil Zátopek from Czechoslovakia...
Jim Peters.

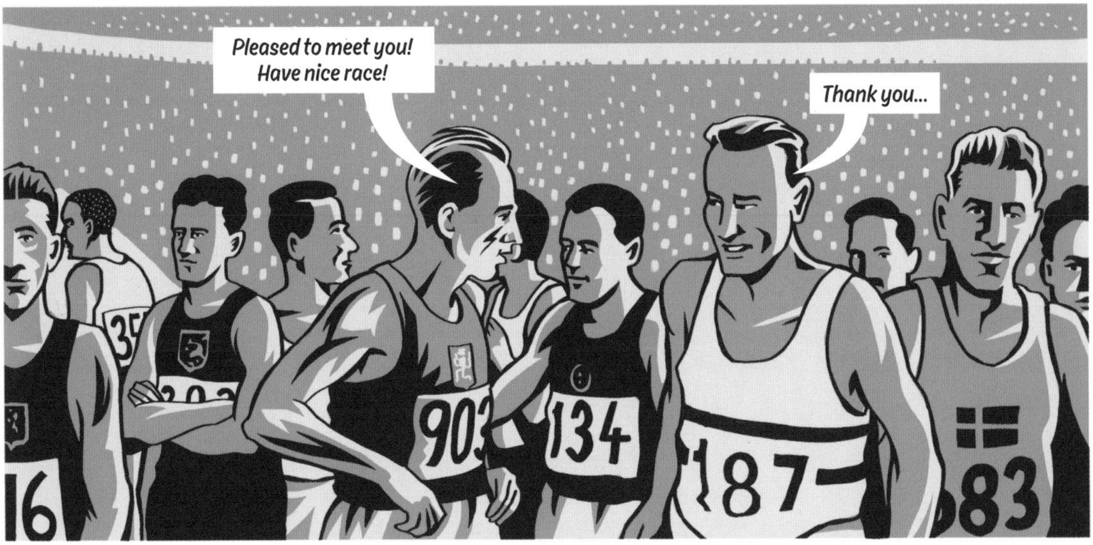
Pleased to meet you! Have nice race!
Thank you...

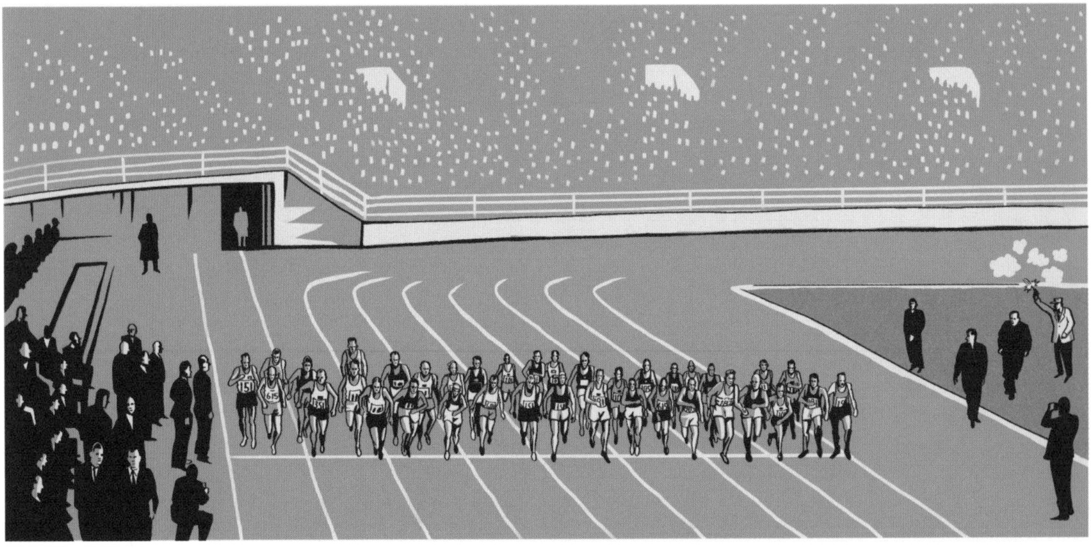

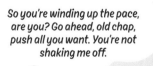So you're winding up the pace, are you? Go ahead, old chap, push all you want. You're not shaking me off.

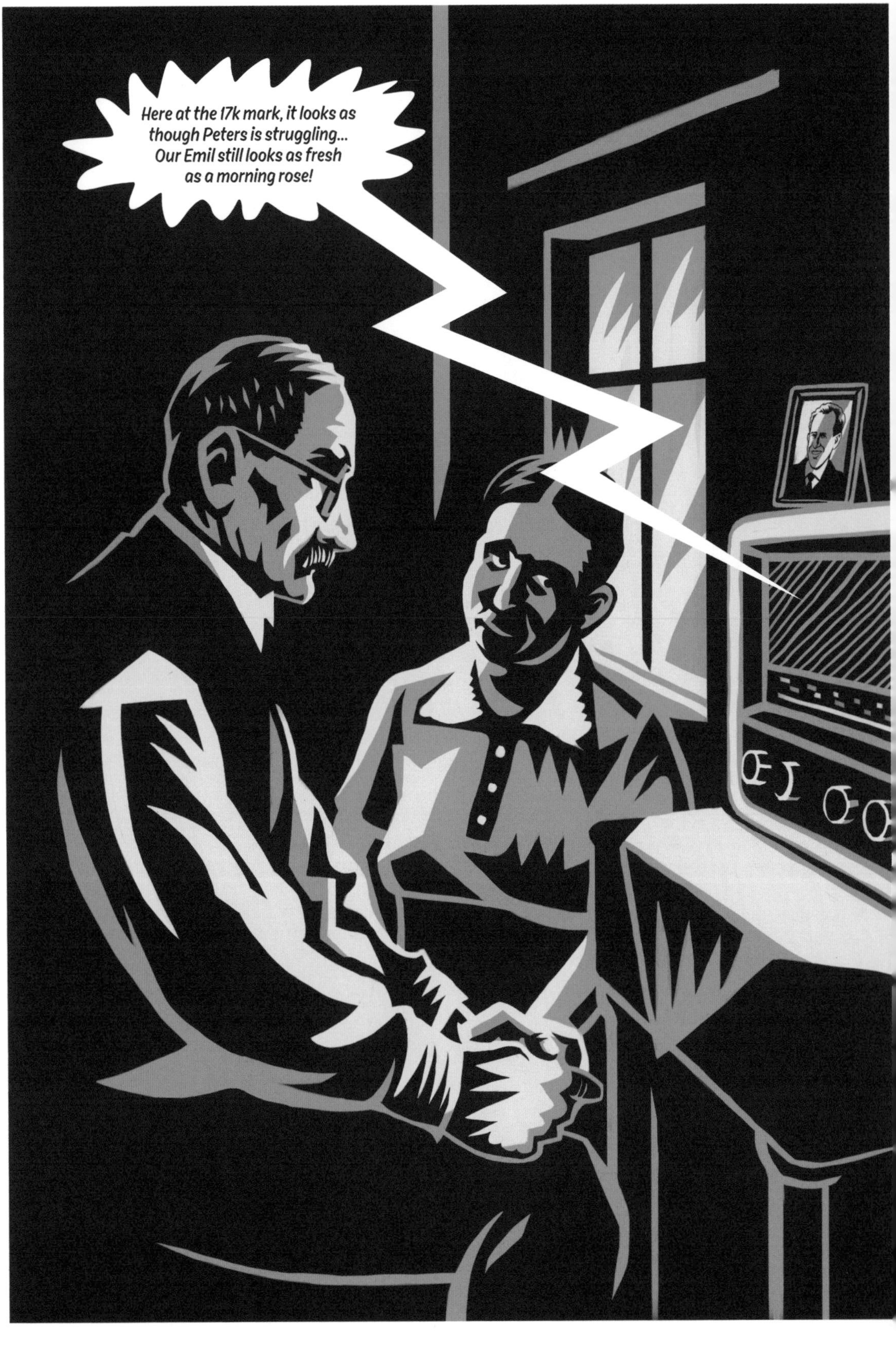
Here at the 17k mark, it looks as though Peters is struggling... Our Emil still looks as fresh as a morning rose!

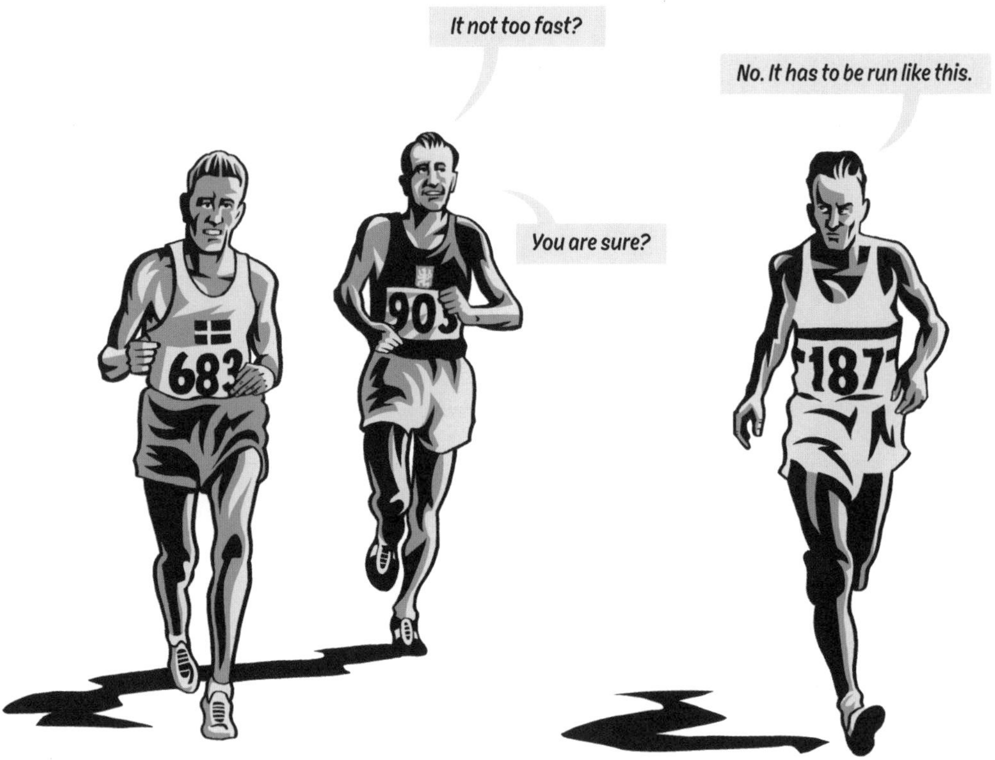
It not too fast?
You are sure?
No. It has to be run like this.
683
903
187

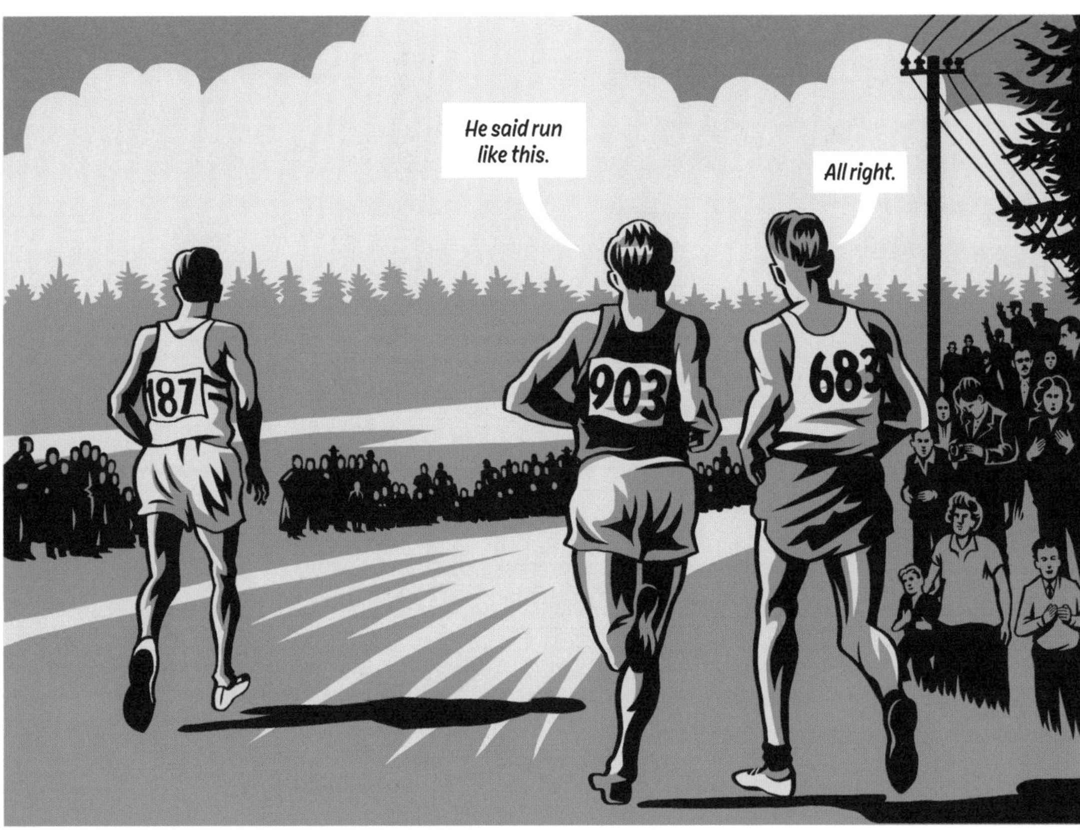
He said run
like this.
All right.
187
903
683

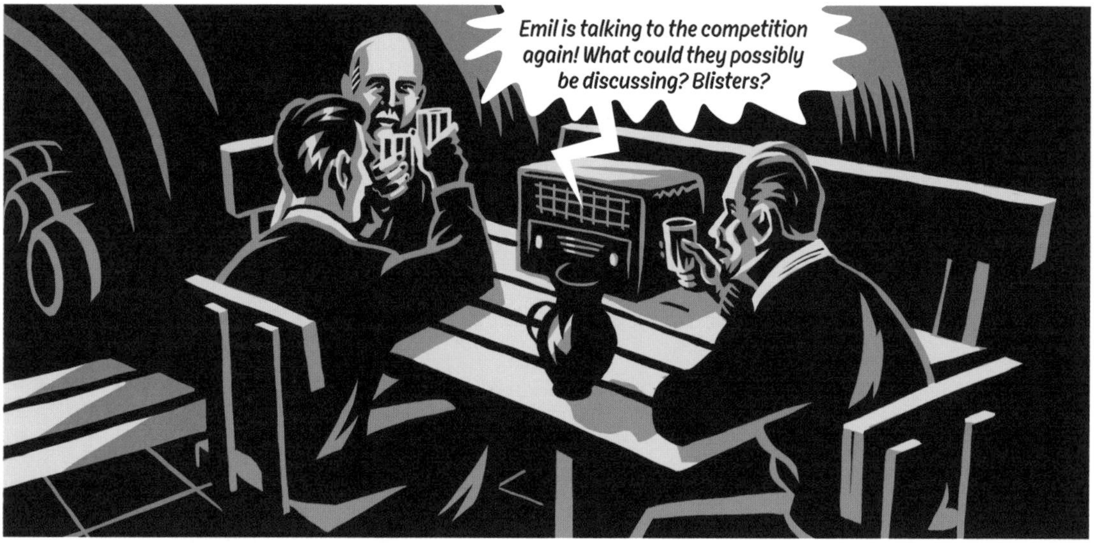
Emil is talking to the competition again! What could they possibly be discussing? Blisters?

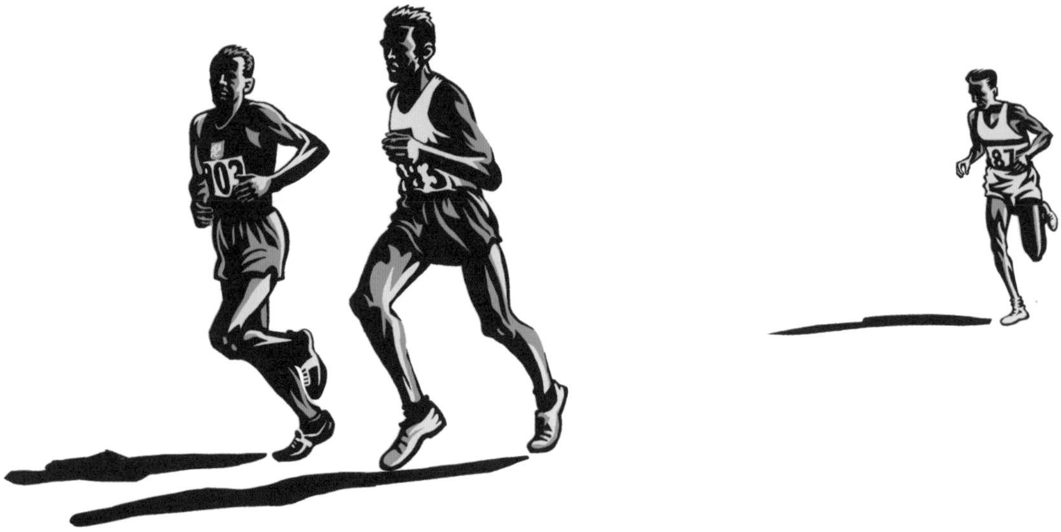

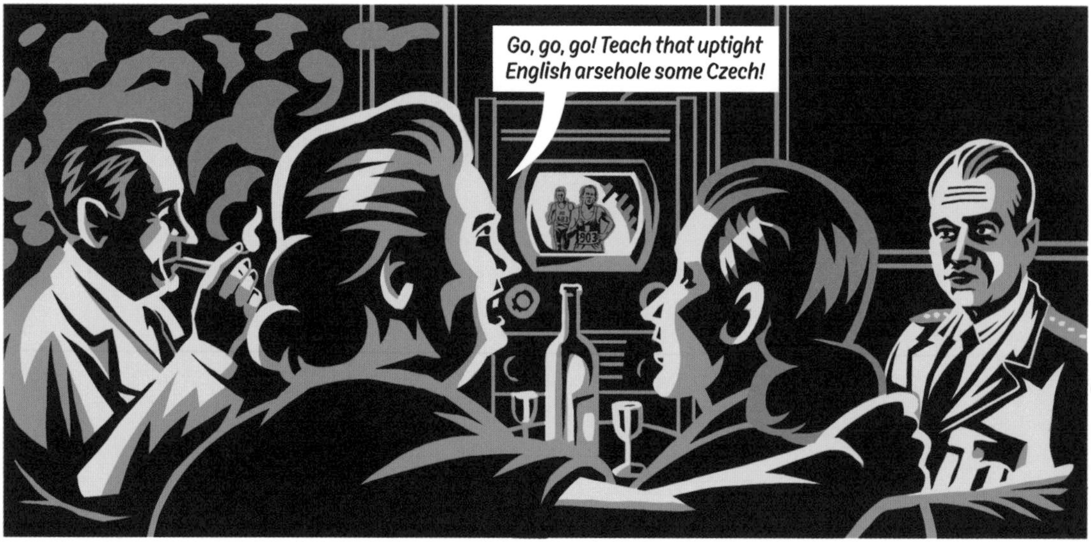
Go, go, go! Teach that uptight English arsehole some Czech!

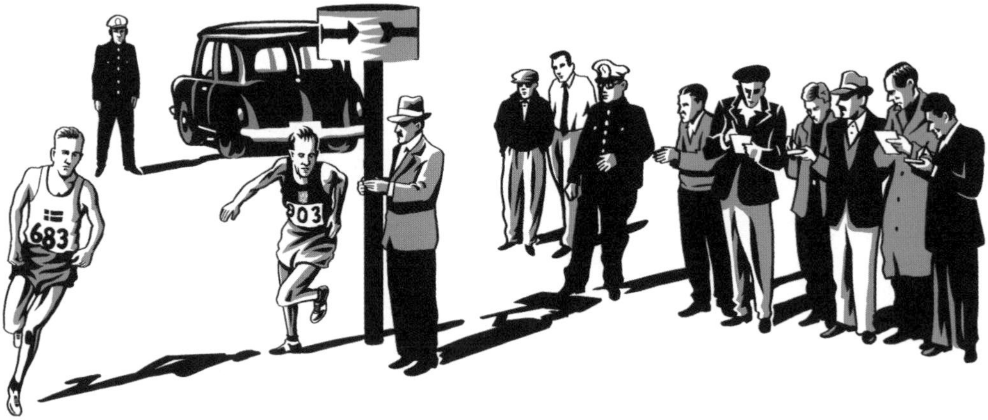
683
903

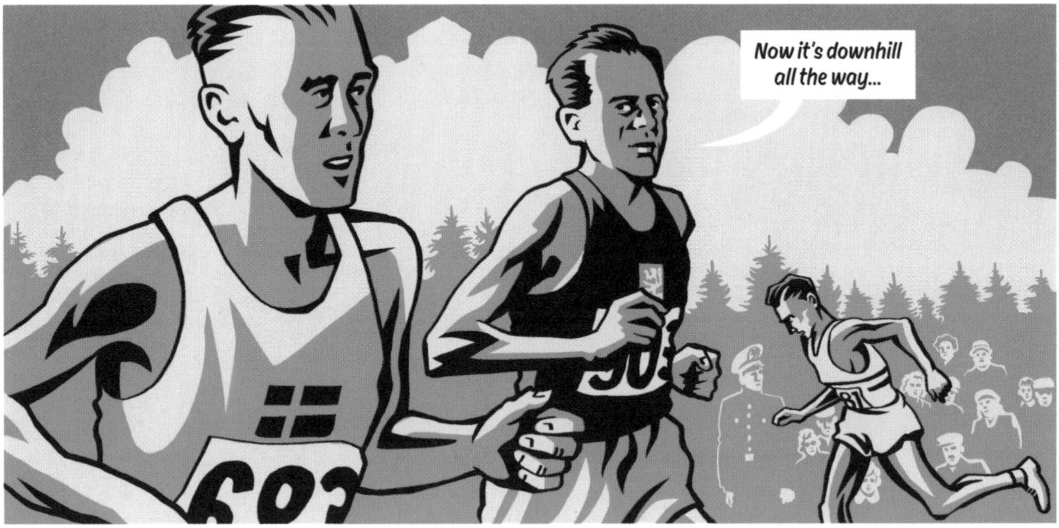
Now it's downhill all the way...

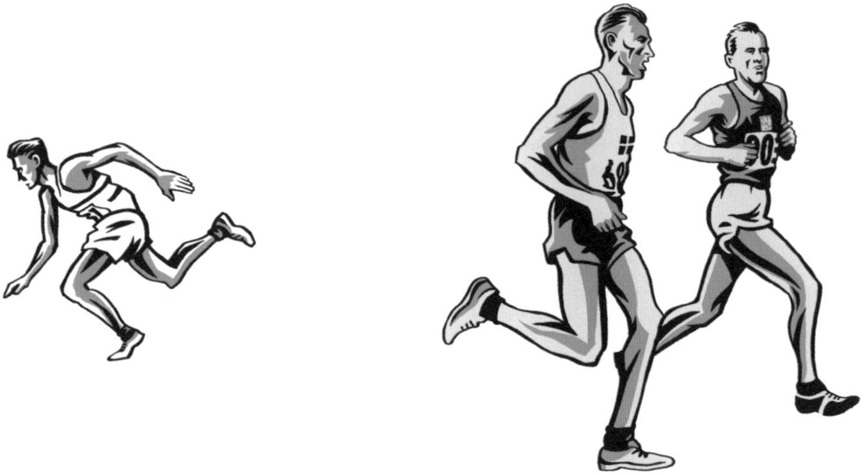

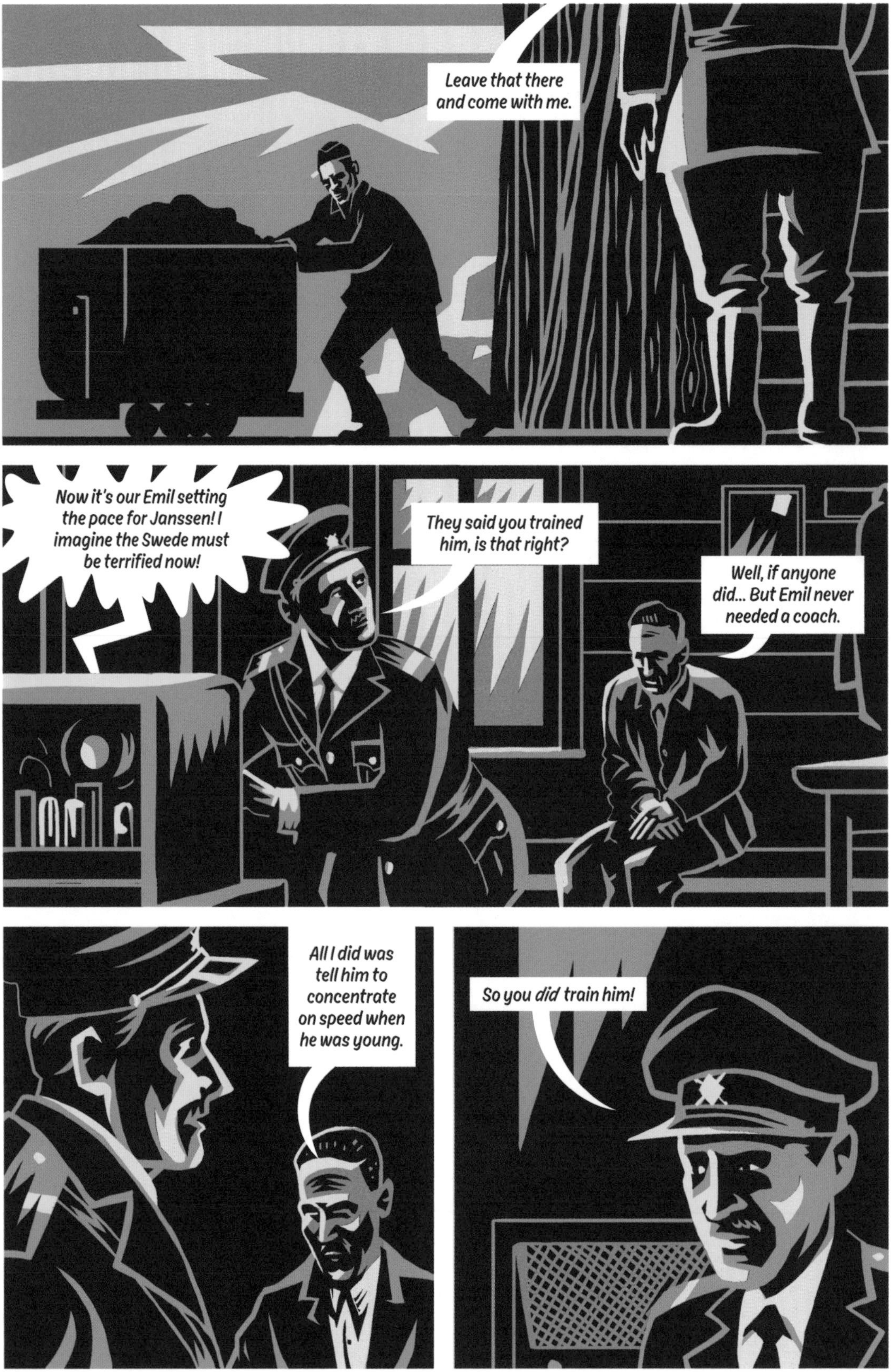
Leave that there and come with me.
Now it's our Emil setting the pace for Janssen! I imagine the Swede must be terrified now!
They said you trained him, is that right?
Well, if anyone did... But Emil never needed a coach.
All I did was tell him to concentrate on speed when he was young.
So you *did* train him!

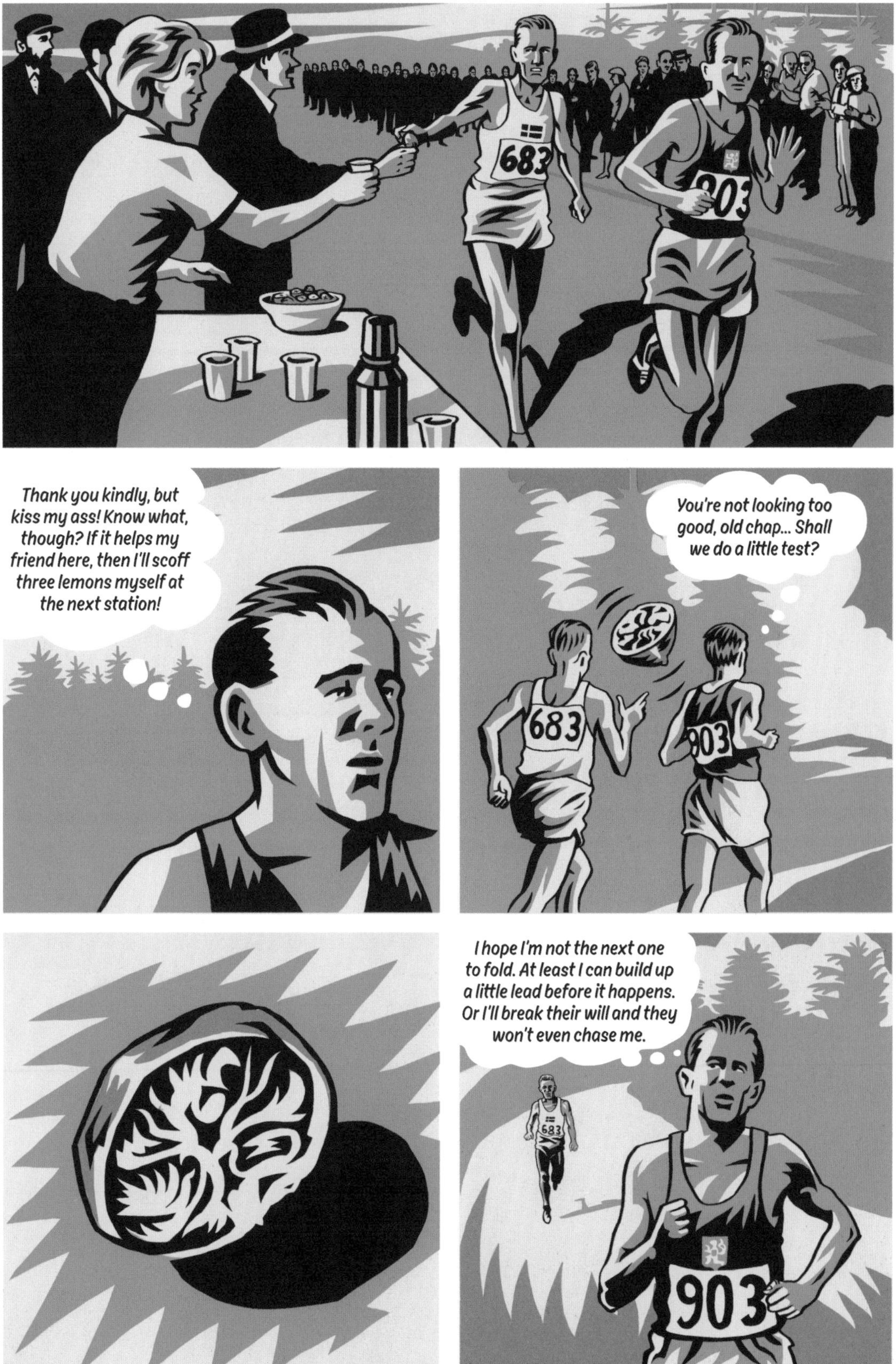
683
903
Thank you kindly, but kiss my ass! Know what, though? If it helps my friend here, then I'll scoff three lemons myself at the next station!
You're not looking too good, old chap... Shall we do a little test?
683
903
I hope I'm not the next one to fold. At least I can build up a little lead before it happens. Or I'll break their will and they won't even chase me.
683
903

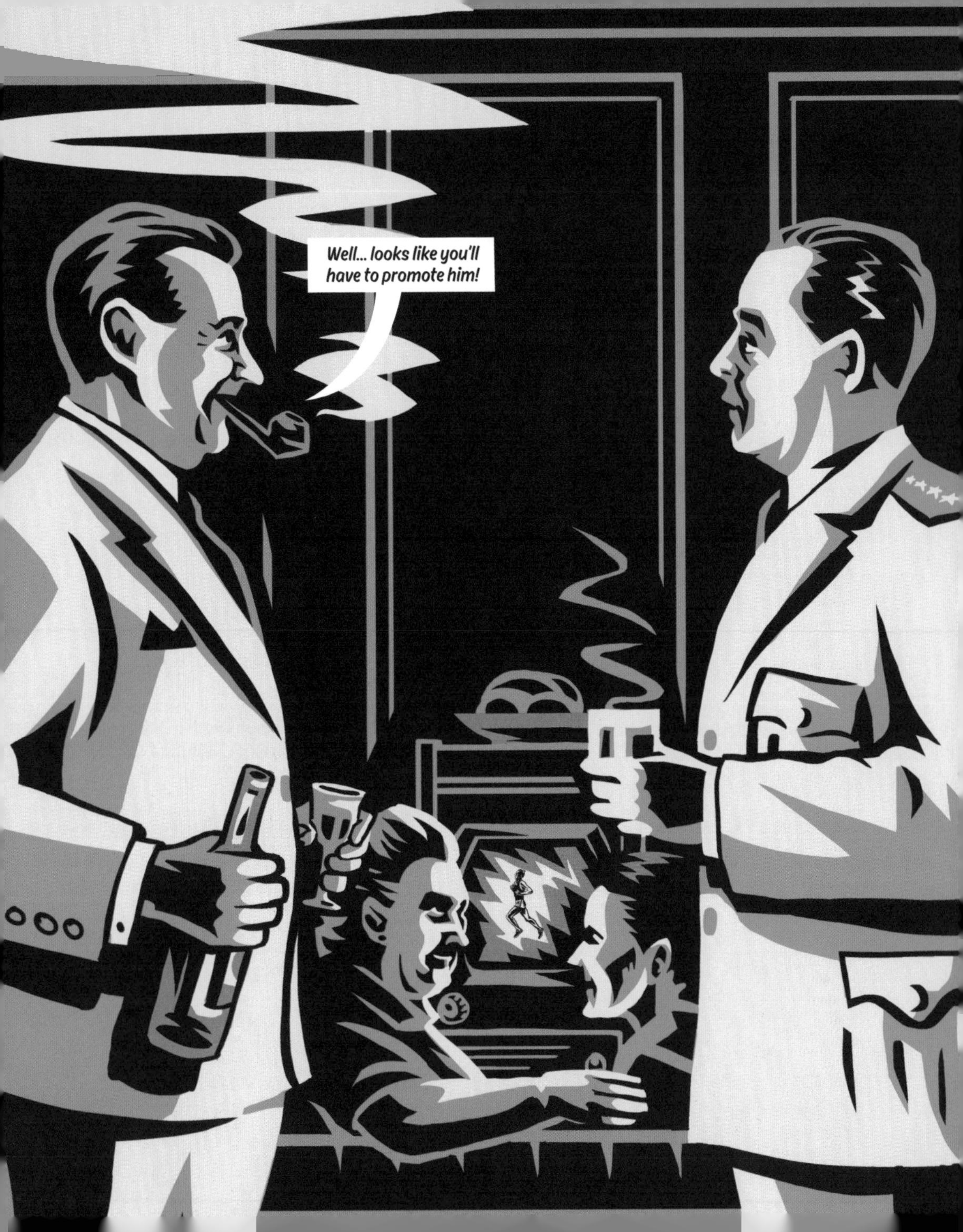
Well... looks like you'll have to promote him!

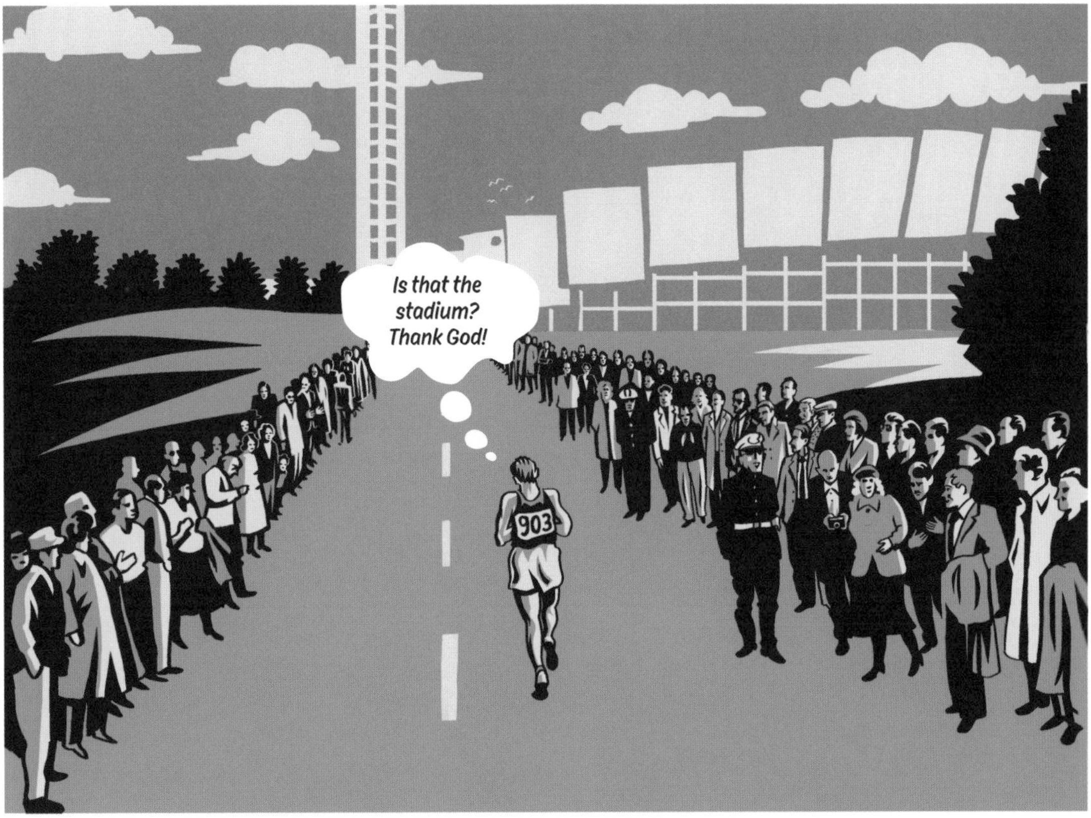
Is that the stadium? Thank God!

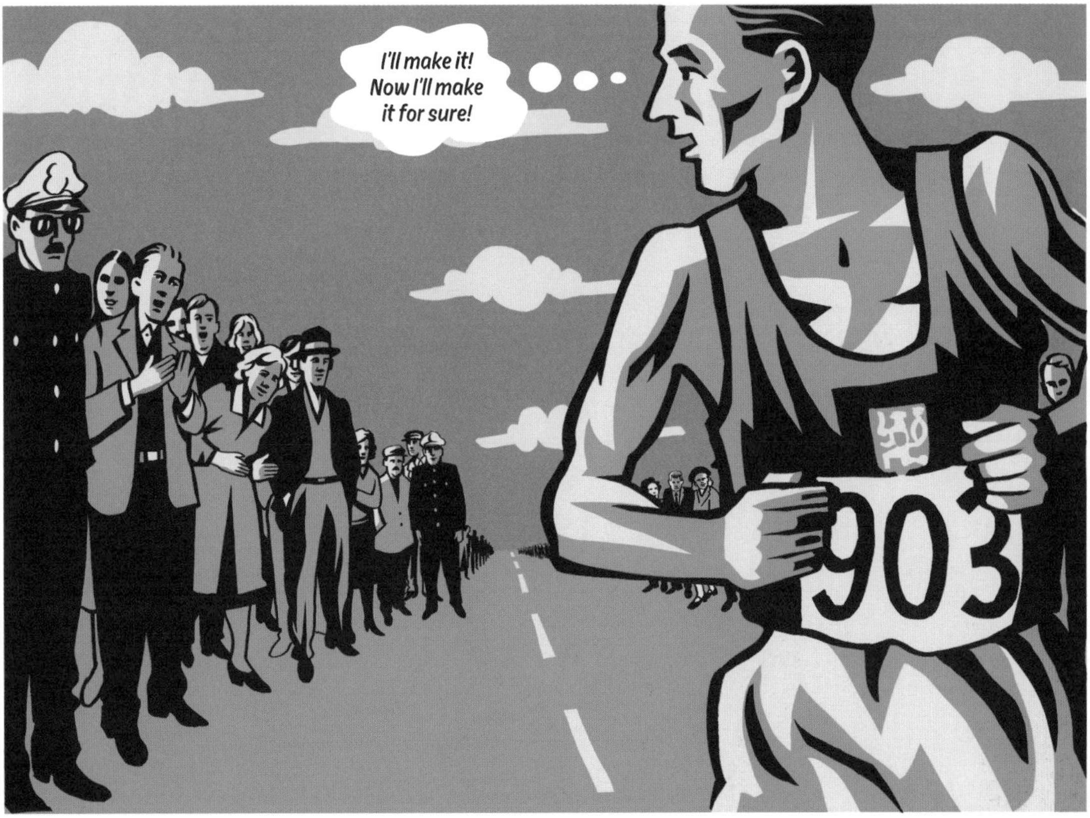
I'll make it! Now I'll make it for sure!
903

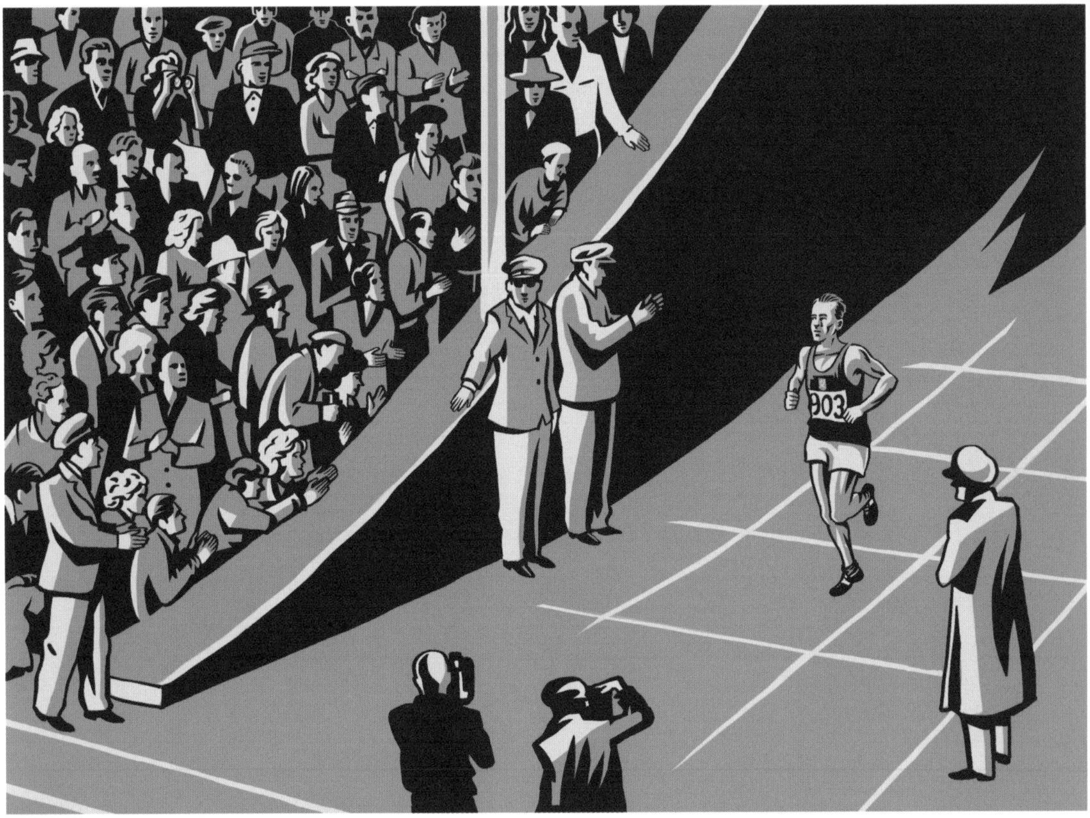
903

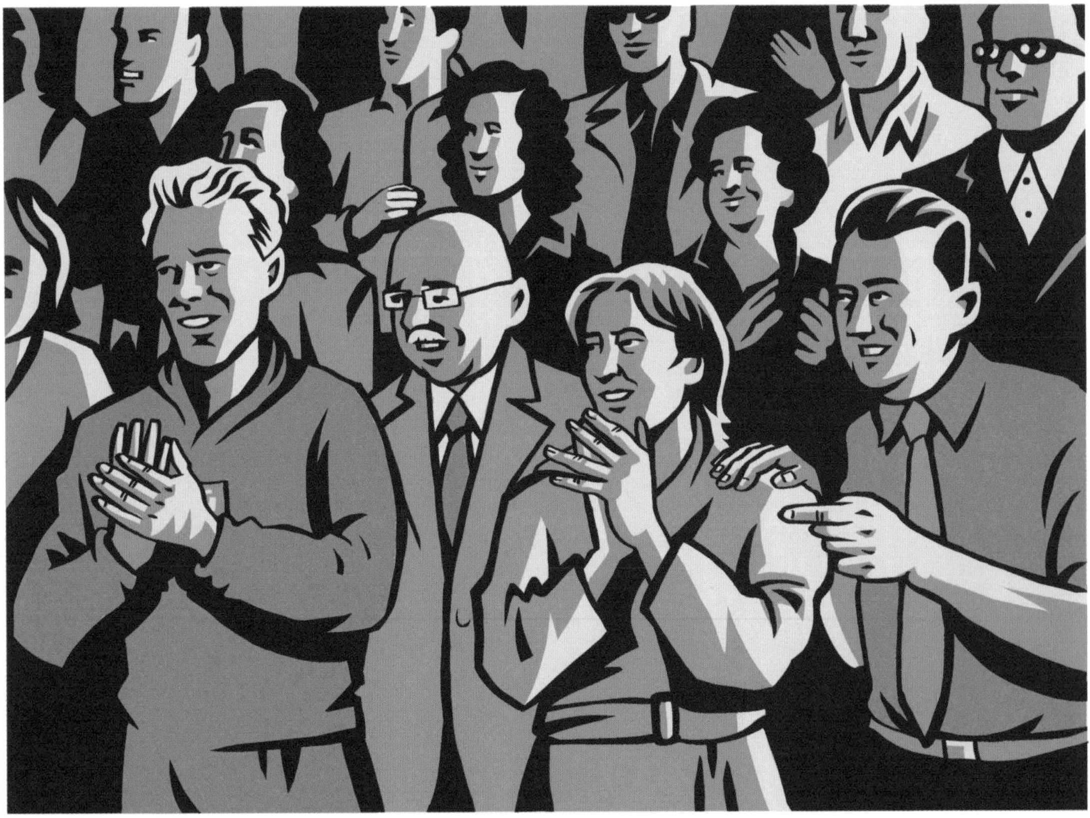

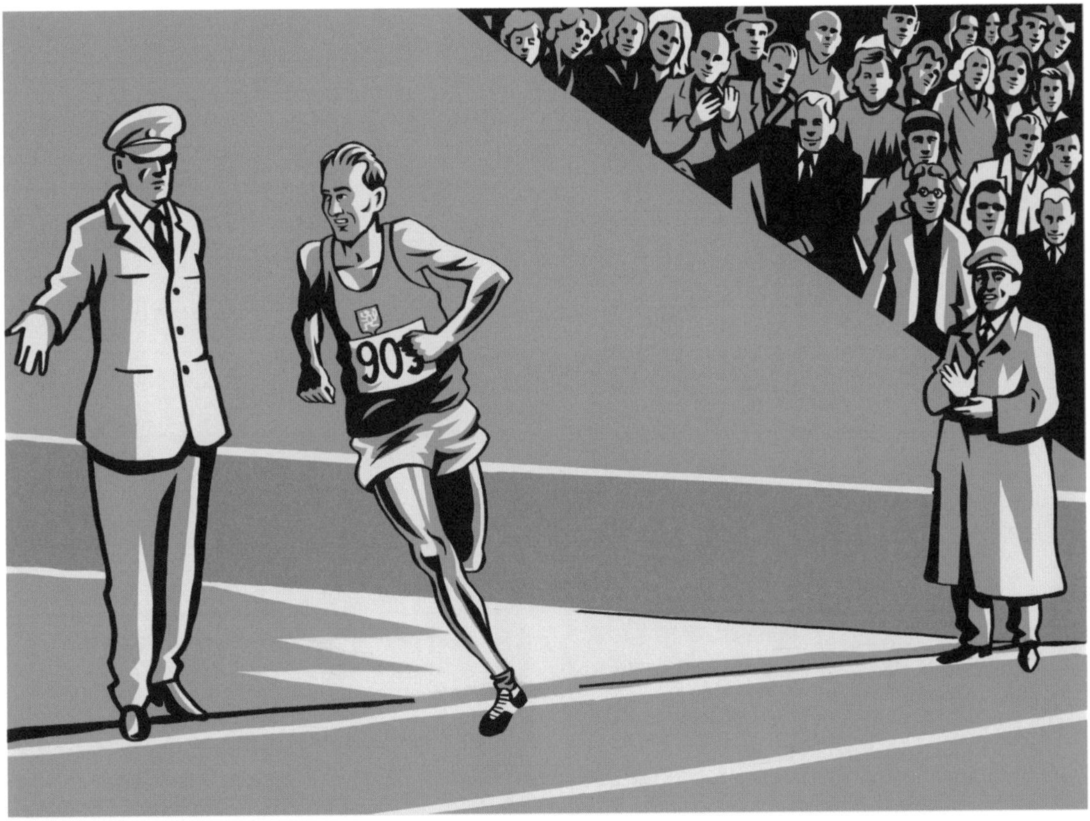
903

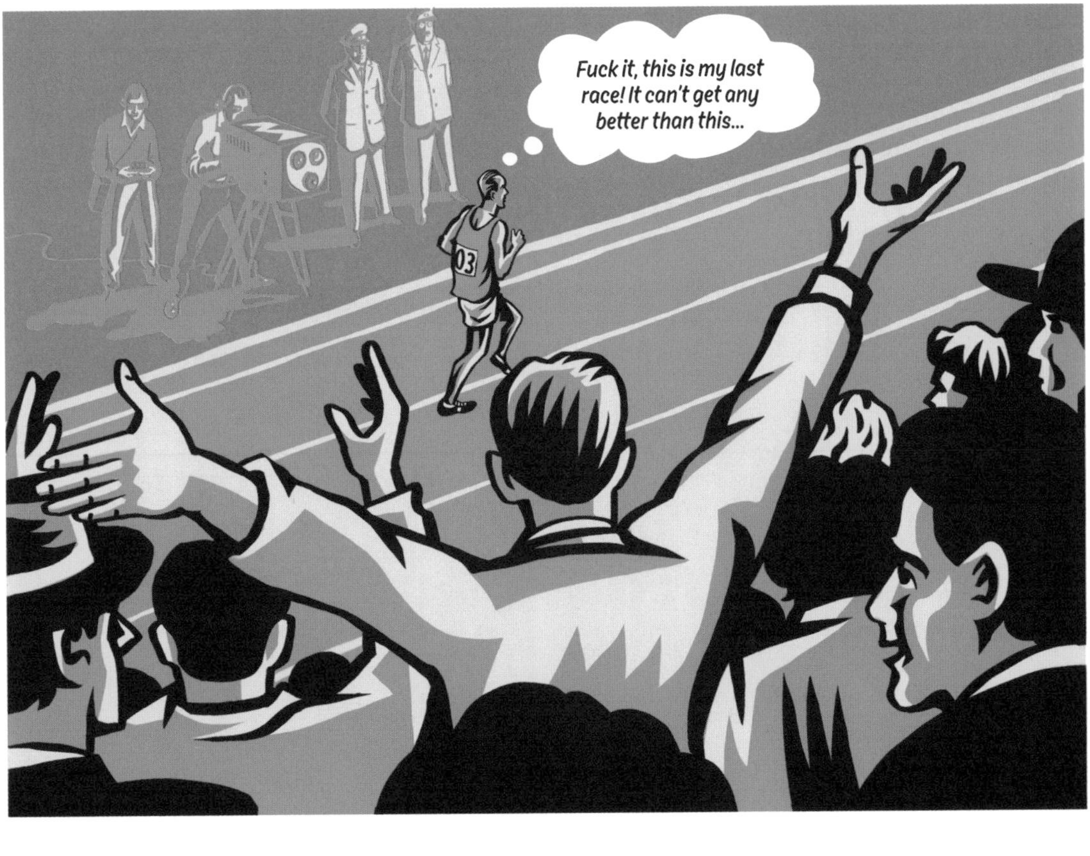
Fuck it, this is my last race! It can't get any better than this...
03

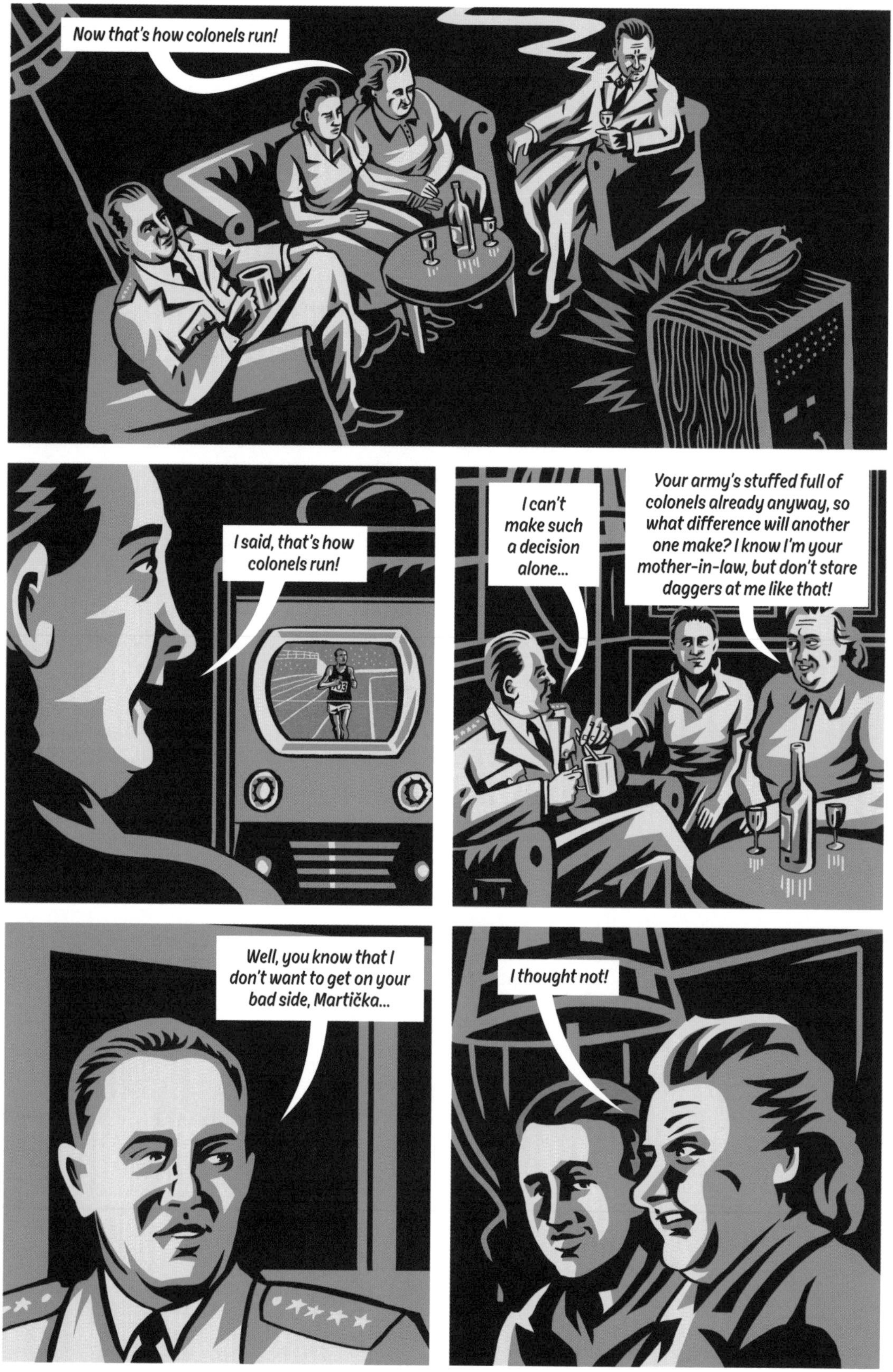
Now that's how colonels run!
I said, that's how colonels run!
I can't make such a decision alone...
Your army's stuffed full of colonels already anyway, so what difference will another one make? I know I'm your mother-in-law, but don't stare daggers at me like that!
Well, you know that I don't want to get on your bad side, Martička...
I thought not!

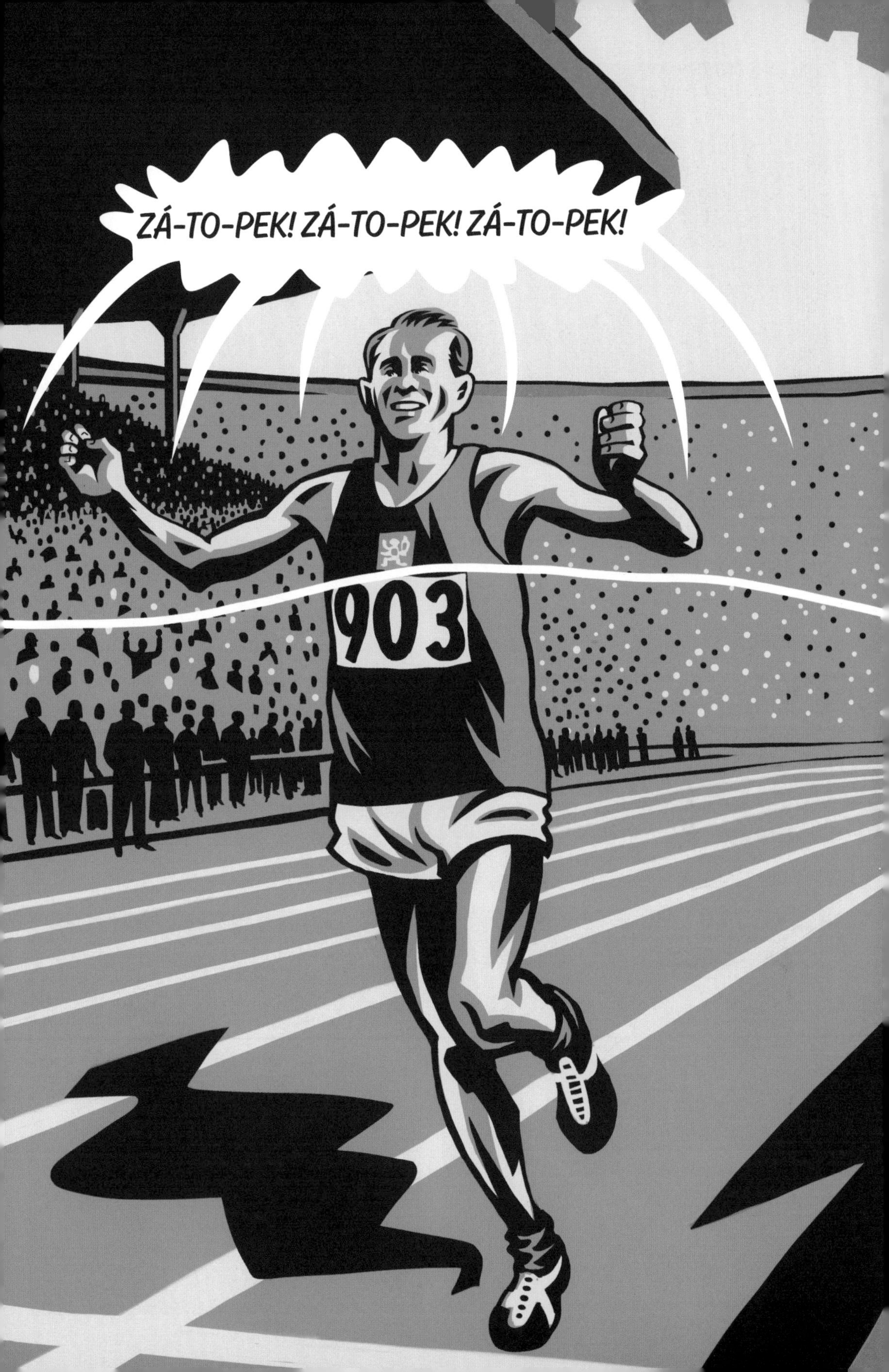
ZÁ-TO-PEK! ZÁ-TO-PEK! ZÁ-TO-PEK!
903

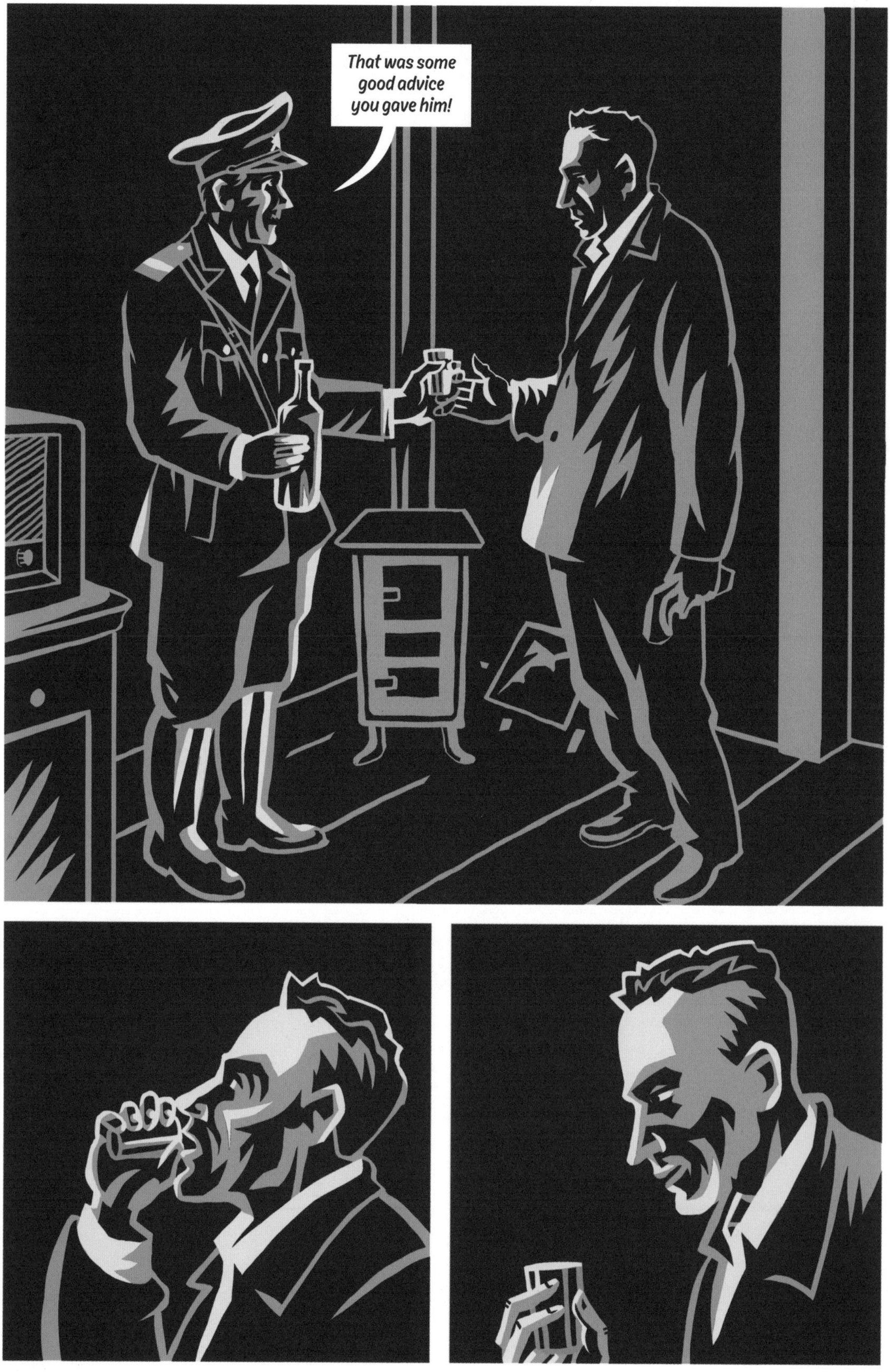
That was some good advice you gave him!

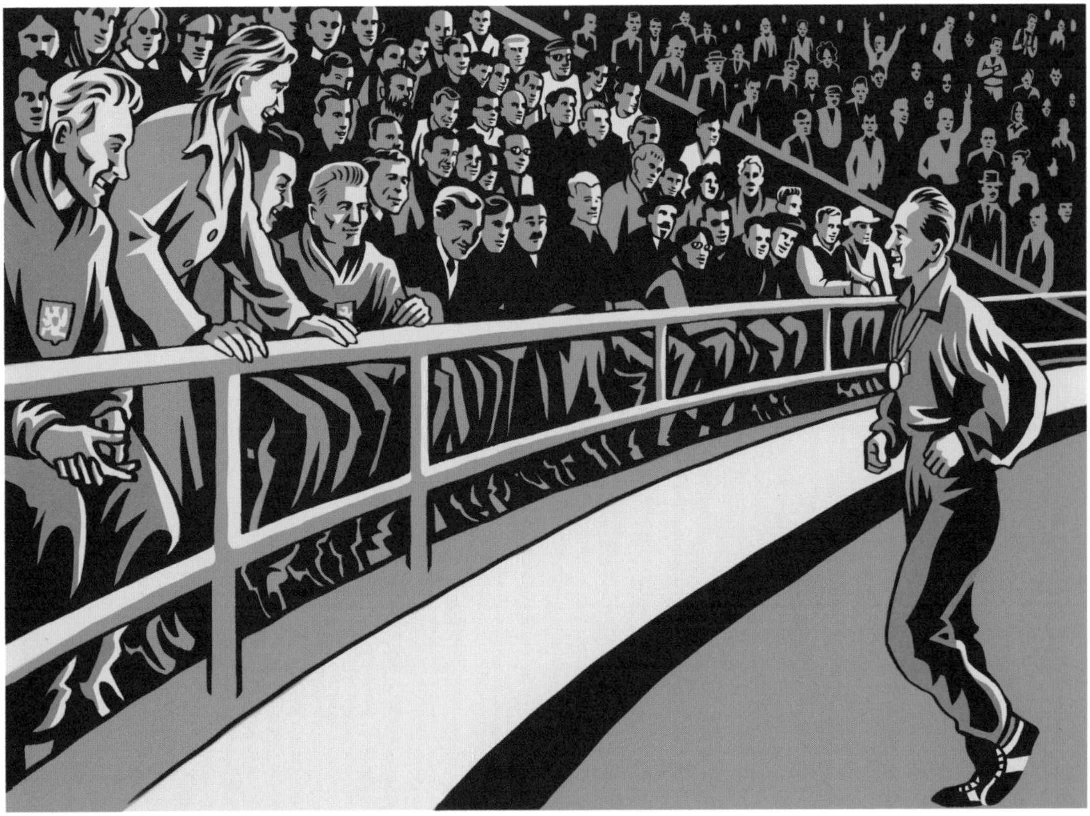

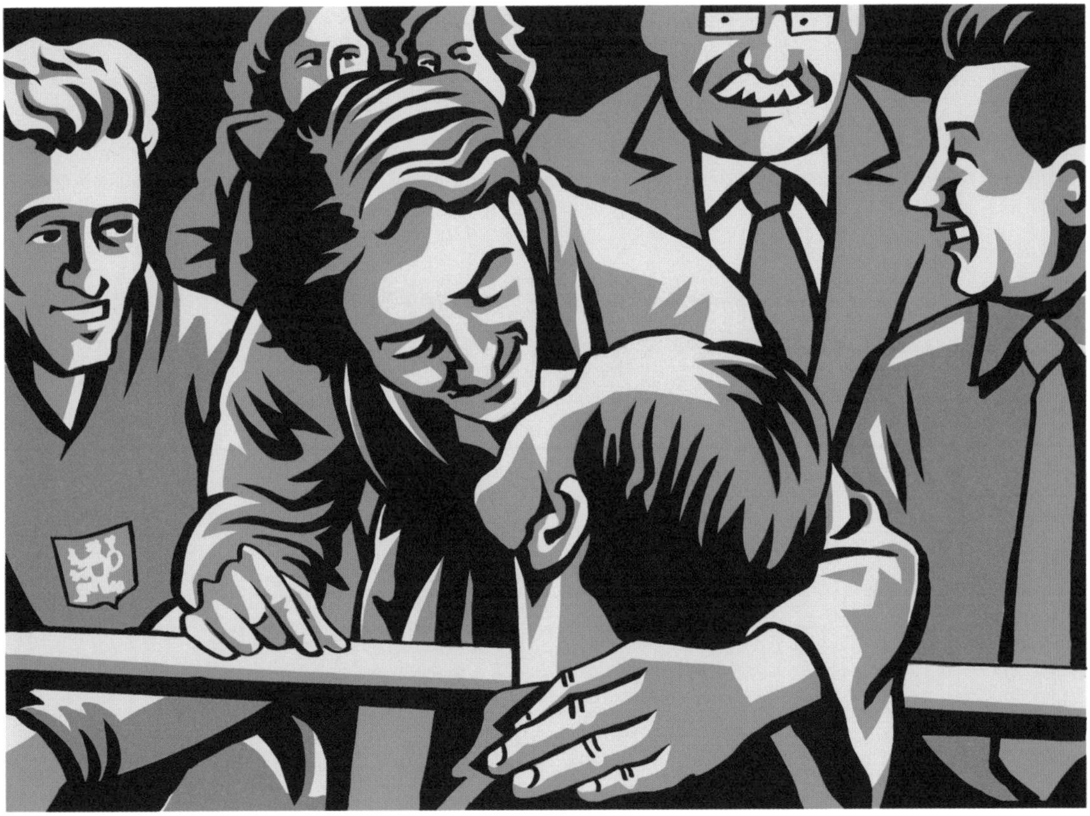

AFTER THE OLYMPICS, **EMIL ZÁTOPEK** WAS PROMOTED TO COLONEL. HE WENT UNDEFEATED FOR THE NEXT TWO YEARS. IN AUTUMN 1954, HE BECAME THE FIRST MAN TO RUN 5 KILOMETRES IN UNDER 14 MINUTES. AT THAT TIME, HE HELD ALL THE WORLD RECORDS IN DISTANCES FROM 5 TO 30 KILOMETRES.

DANA ZÁTOPKOVÁ BECAME THE WORLD RECORD-HOLDER IN 1958 WHEN SHE THREW THE JAVELIN 55.73 METRES. IN 1960, IN ROME, SHE WENT ON TO WIN ANOTHER OLYMPIC MEDAL, TAKING SILVER THERE.

STANISLAV JUNGWIRTH BROKE THE WORLD RECORD FOR THE 1,500 METRES IN 1957. HE WAS THE FIRST MAN TO COVER THE DISTANCE IN LESS THAN 3:40 MINUTES. HIS FATHER WAS SUBSEQUENTLY RELEASED FROM PRISON.

THE ONLY COACH THAT ZÁTOPEK EVER HAD, **DR. JAN HALUZA**, SERVED OUT HIS SENTENCE IN FULL. WHEN HE WAS RELEASED FROM THE URANIUM MINES IN 1955, EMIL ZÁTOPEK HELPED HIM TO FIND A JOB.

THE END

Jan Novák is a leading Czech writer and documentary maker. In the years 1970-2008, he lived in Chicago, where he attended the University of Chicago and where his books *The Willys Dream Kit* (1985) and *Commies, Crooks, Gypsies, Spooks & Poets* (1995) won the Carl Sandburg Prize for Chicago's book of the year. He also co-authored *The Turnaround* (1994), Miloš Forman's autobiography. Novák is now resident once more in the Czech Republic. His novel *So Far, So Good* was the Magnesia Litera Awards Book of the Year 2005, and in 2020 he published a controversial literary biography, entitled *Kundera, His Czech Life and Times. Zátopek* is his debut work in the field of graphic novels.

Jaromír 99, whose real name is Jaromír Švejdík, divides his time between the worlds of music and comics. He is well-known as a member of the groups Priessnitz and Umakart, and as the artist behind the *Alois Nebel* (2003) trilogy. He also worked as a co-screenwriter and artist on its film adaptation (2011), which was awarded Best Animated Film by the European Film Academy. He won a Muriel Award for his comic strip *Bomber* (2007) and he adapted Kafka's *The Castle* (2013) as a graphic novel for SelfMadeHero, which was nominated for the prestigious Eisner Award. Jaromír 99 lives and works in Prague.

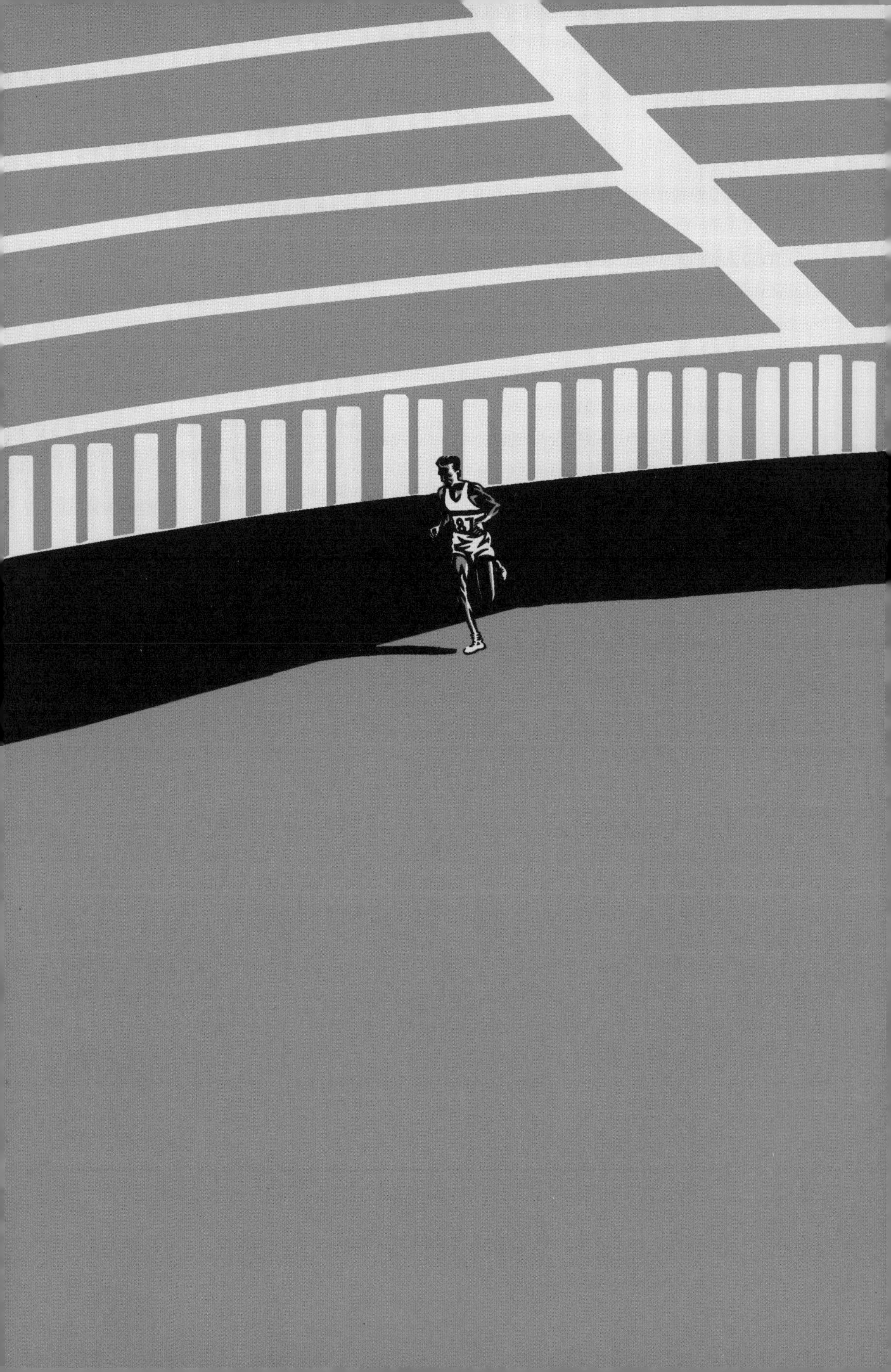